Introducing L...ඉ

Grammar

Introducing English Grammar introduces readers to the methodology and terminology needed to analyse English sentences. The approach taken is in line with current research in grammar, a particular advantage for students who may go on to study syntax in more depth. All the examples and exercises use real language taken from both standard and non-standard geographical areas and dialects, and include excerpts from Australian and British newspaper articles. Students are encouraged to think about the terminology as a tool kit for studying language and to test what can and cannot be described using these tools.

This new edition has been fully updated and features:

- ❏ an expanded introduction;
- ❏ new texts and exercises that include data from social media;
- ❏ revised material on 'Grammar at work' and 'English worldwide';
- ❏ more suggestions for further reading at the end of the book;
- ❏ a brand new companion website with extensive further reading and answers to the exercises, which can be found at www.routledge.com/cw/borjars.

Written for readers with no previous experience of grammatical analysis, *Introducing English Grammar* is suited to anyone beginning a study of linguistics, English language or speech pathology, as well as to students whose interests are primarily literary but who need a better understanding of the structure of English.

Kersti Börjars is Professor of Linguistics at the University of Manchester, UK.

Kate Burridge is Professor of Linguistics at Monash University, Australia.

Kersti Börjars
and Kate Burridge

Introducing
English
Grammar

third edition

Routledge
Taylor & Francis Group

LONDON AND NEW YORK

Third edition published 2019
by Routledge
2 Park Square, Milton Park, Abingdon, Oxon, OX14 4RN

and by Routledge
52 Vanderbilt Avenue, New York, NY 10017

Routledge is an imprint of the Taylor & Francis Group, an informa business

First edition published by Hodder 2010
Second edition published by Routledge 2012

British Library Cataloguing-in-Publication Data
A catalogue record for this book is available from the British Library

Library of Congress Cataloging-in-Publication Data
A catalog record for this book has been requested

ISBN: 978-1-138-63529-6 (hbk)
ISBN: 978-1-138-63531-9 (pbk)
ISBN: 978-0-429-02329-3 (ebk)

Typeset in ITC Stone Serif
by Apex CoVantage, LLC

Visit the companion website: www.routledge.com/cw/borjars

Printed and bound in Great Britain by
TJ International Ltd, Padstow, Cornwall

In memory of
Joan Burridge and Elof Börjars

Contents

Preface to the third edition

For this third edition, we have revised the text and modified terminology where we thought explanations could be made clearer; we have updated examples, added some exercises and modified the discussion of the exercises on the supporting website. One aim has been to further broaden the data to illustrate the sheer variety that exists. Changes have been made throughout the book, but Chapter 9 has been particularly extensively revised. We have of course also updated the reading list.

In order to illustrate how much speakers engage with language issues, we have added examples of how people have played with language, been annoyed by language or used language in arguments. These are separated from the text in boxes since they are additional rather than part of the core material.

Our own use of the book in teaching has influenced the revisions and we are grateful for comments from students at Monash University and The University of Manchester. Nick Reid and his students at the University of New England (Australia) have provided useful suggestions and corrections. We are grateful to Doug Arnold for recommending areas that could be expanded and to three anonymous referees for their comments.

Preface to the second edition

Both of us have used this book in teaching at our respective universities and we have benefited from our students' views on how the book could be improved. Colleagues who have used the book with students have also made many helpful suggestions for changes. We are particularly grateful to Professor Jean-Jacques Weber, University of Luxembourg, for his valuable comments. The feedback we have received from all these different sources has helped to shape the new edition. In addition to adding snippets of new information here and there and changing the text in places where explanations were not clear, we have thoroughly revised the exercises and further reading. Solutions to and discussion of the exercises, as well as additional exercises and readings, can be found at www.routledge.com/cw/bor jars. We have also added a global perspective with the provision of a new chapter that explores some of the strikingly different grammatical features of newer varieties around the English-speaking world.

We are very grateful to our editor, Bianca Knights. Without her gentle chivvying we would not have got round to producing a second edition – well, for a little while at least! We are also grateful to our desk editor, Deborah Edwards Noble. It has been a pleasure working with her and the rest of the Hodder team.

Preface to the first edition

This book is meant as an introduction to the sentence structure of English. As such, it can be used by many different kinds of students: those who are going to teach English grammar at some level (and given the kind of knowledge that is required to teach even at primary schools under new government directions in many English-speaking countries, it contains the kind of things that teachers of English need to know); those who want to teach or even learn a foreign language; those who will carry on to do different kinds of language analysis for the purpose of speech therapy; those who will use it for literary studies; but also those who will carry on to do more formal grammar.

Of course, one thing we need to do in this book is impart to students a body of terminology that they need in order to discuss language conveniently. Taking all this in is sometimes hard work, but it is unavoidable. However, another very important aim is to make the reader realise that the kinds of things we study in English grammar are all around us all the time. This holds not just for English-speaking countries; most countries now have access to a lot of English through music, television and other mass media. So, even though there are many good grammars of English around, you don't actually need a grammar book to study English grammar. You just need to listen and look around you. We cannot emphasise this too much. English grammar is happening all around you; language change is going on in front of your very eyes. In order to emphasise this point, we have decided to use real-life examples taken, for example, from a magazine called *The Big Issue*. This is an initiative set up in 1991 aimed at giving homeless or vulnerably housed people a chance to make a living and gradually move towards more permanent housing. Most of our examples come from the English North and the Australian editions, but we also have some from *The Big Issue in Scotland*. We believe that this is a cause that deserves as much public exposure as it can get, even though we realise that our grammar book is not likely to reach the masses (one can dream, though). Still, we have to admit that our reasons for using *The Big Issue* for language examples are not philanthropic, but linguistic. Invented sentences like the ones so often used in textbooks are just sterile fragments of that wonderfully rich language they are supposed to be identifying. By contrast, the language in *The Big Issue* is close to the language that is actually spoken by the majority of people. It is less influenced by rules about 'proper English.' We hope that by using these examples we can make readers realise that

English grammar is not about learning what you are allowed to say and what you are not allowed to say (though if you are a learner of English as a foreign language this is, of course, important too). Instead, it is about a way of looking at the English around you and at language in general. Once you have acquired this way of looking at language, then you can use the tools to study other languages.

Before we continue, we should just mention a bit about the annotation of the data. We refer to the Australian *Big Issue* as AUS, the Northern English one as N, and the Scottish one as SCO. This label is followed by a number which indicates the issue in which the example can be found, and the page number. Some of the examples are marked 'adapted.' This doesn't mean that we have changed the whole example around; it just means that we have omitted some adverbials which made the example less clear, or removed a sub-clause that made things more complex than necessary. We have not 'cheated' by creating a type of example that wasn't really there. Sometimes adapted examples are not marked explicitly, but it should be clear from the context that they are adapted; for instance, when we have turned original sentences into questions. Finally, in some cases we have used our own invented examples, but again we have either marked these or it should be clear from the context.

What do we do with all this marvellously rich data? Well, we try to find patterns in it. The discovery of such patterns leads to the formulation of analyses. Of course, many analyses have already been provided for English and by and large we do not come up with anything revolutionary or frightfully controversial, as far as analyses go. In some cases, proposed analyses of one particular phenomenon disagree. Sometimes we feel that the arguments are actually stronger one way than the other. In these cases we will tell you what we think. At other times we feel that there are advantages and disadvantages with both ways of looking at something. You may find this annoying – why write a textbook if you don't know the answer? Well, probably the truth is that in many of these cases, there is no right answer, just different ways of looking at things. We hope readers will get used to this idea, and maybe be able to decide for themselves.

One thing that we keep coming back to throughout this book is the structure of language. Sentences and phrases are not just flat strings; they have structure. We then need some reasonably formal way of representing this structure. The standard way of doing this is with tree diagrams, or phrase markers. Now, some people who find English grammar quite exciting find trees bothersome and off-putting. We feel it would be a shame to put such people off the topic by littering the text with tree structures. Instead, we have kept the trees in the running text to a minimum, and at the end of each chapter we have a section that provides the tree structures relevant for that chapter. We hope that those of you who are already familiar with phrase markers will find this arrangement acceptable too.

A terminological issue is that language can be either spoken or written, and hence every sentence could have been either written or spoken. However, in order to simplify, we have referred to the producer as 'the speaker' (rather than 'the writer') and the person at the other end of the stream of sounds as 'the hearer' (rather than 'the reader'). This is just a matter of simplicity; for speaker you can always read 'speaker or writer' and for hearer 'hearer or reader.' Also, we have followed reasonably common practice and used the pronoun he to refer to the speaker and she for the hearer. Using he/she every time becomes too cumbersome and using either he or she in every instance doesn't seem right. Occasionally we have also used singular they as a gender-neutral pronoun. Shakespeare used it this way, so we feel we are in good company. In fact, we include a discussion of exactly this point on p. 58.

Finally, we both have people we would like to thank, both individually and jointly. Kersti would like to thank the Department of Linguistics at the University of Manchester, which has provided an ideal gradual introduction to how to teach English grammar. When it comes to teaching in general and teaching English grammar in particular, two people have been especially influential: Katharine Perera and John Payne. Many thanks to them and to all students of LI104. Anne Hesketh and Alison Crutchley in the Centre for Audiology, Education of the Deaf and Speech Therapy at Manchester University have both been helpful in providing data. Kersti would also like to thank Dolor MacCarron who has helped with this book in many ways, first by being a student of LI104, then later by providing comments on English grammar in general, and last but not least by being prepared to look after the Masters brood to aid the writing of this book. Kate is grateful to her colleagues, in particular Barry Blake, whose Movie Goers' Guide to Grammar showed it is possible to write a syntax book that makes good bedtime reading. Kate is also grateful to Susan Hendtlass (for helping transcribe The Titans versus The Hawks), to Pia Herbert, Andy Pawley, Julie Reid for their wonderful examples, to Allison Pritchard for bravely reading some early drafts and to those La Trobe students who were such willing guinea pigs. Both of us are grateful to our editors at Arnold. To our shame we must admit that we have gone through three of them (this is no reflection on what we do to our editors, but on how long we have been intending to write this book): Naomi Meredith, Christina Wipf-Perry and Lesley Riddle. Their patience has been impressive. Finally, there are Ross, Andrew, Robin, Ellen, Nils and Philip, some of whom have also showed patience with us and most of whom have provided us with examples of living English.

Introduction: the glamour of grammar

We've called this chapter 'The glamour of grammar' for a reason – *grammar* and *glamour* are historically one and the same word. *Grammar* happens to be the older form – it first entered English in the 1300s from French (although ultimately from Greek *grammata*, 'letters'). It came to mean 'learning,' but then acquired additional senses to do with magic and the inexplicable (this shift makes sense when you bear in mind that the majority of people at this time were illiterate). In Scottish English a form appeared whereby [r] had changed to [l]. *Glamour* retained this earlier mysterious and magical sense, later shifting to its current meaning, 'enchantment, allure.' Nowadays the study of grammar still holds a lot of mystery and perplexity for students – what we're hoping here is that it will also develop something of the newer sense of enchantment and allure that it holds for both of us.

1.1 Purpose and nature of grammatical description

There are many reasons why you might want to study the grammar of a language. You might, for instance, want to write a grammar of that language, say English, which can then be used by people to learn English. This is an extremely difficult task for many reasons. First, of course, you have to write it in such a way that the task of learning English is made easy for the language learner; in other words, it must be pedagogically sound. A problem more relevant to linguists is which constructions you will include as correct structures of English, and which you will exclude, or mark as ungrammatical. Consider the following sentences:

(1) Oscar is een lieve maar niet zo slimme poes.

(2) Maybe he's dead? Killed his self getting out of the bath. (AUS#36:16)

(3) Yeah, but speaking 'proper' means using all them posh f***ing words, innit? (online comment on the article 'Curse this outbreak of repetitive swearing,' *The Times* 31 May 2016)

(4) It's eerie that uncanny rusted Milo tin. (AUS#75:9)

(5) That it's eerie tin rusted Milo uncanny. (Adapted)

(6) There's several fridges packed full of bottles too. (comment on Tripadvisor in 2018)

(7) There are several fridges packed full of bottles too. (Adapted)

(8) Bloody hell, just whipped that up in his garage in between episodes of *Game of Thrones*. (AUS#563:13)

We are quite sure that all of you will agree that (1) and (5) should not be included in a grammar of English. If you are writing a grammar of English intended for language learners you might also want to exclude (2) and (3), perhaps some of the others too, even though many people who are native speakers of English would use and accept such sentences. How would you describe these sentences? Would you call them ungrammatical or dialectal? Do you think that some of them belong more to speech than writing? The sentences (6) and (7), for example, exemplify a notorious problem in English. Many grammars would describe (6) as 'wrong' (or 'bad English') and (7) as 'correct' (or 'good English'). Which of the two sentences do you think you would you use? Which would you consider acceptable English? People, even linguists, are not always good at knowing what they would and would not use: if you ask people about things like this, you will quickly find that what they say they do and what they actually do can be quite different.

1.2 Standard English and variation

Sentences like those in the previous section which people might take exception to as being 'bad English' are not really errors of English, but rather errors of STANDARD ENGLISH. The thing to always bear in mind is that all speakers of English are dialect speakers – they all speak at least one dialect of English. Standard English happens to be the most important dialect in terms of the way society operates. It might surprise you to hear this called a dialect, because people tend to talk about the STANDARD LANGUAGE, but this is a misleading label. Standard English is one of many different dialects of English – it just happens to be the dialect that currently has the greatest clout. How it got to this elevated position, however, is a series of geographical and historical coincidences. Standard English was originally a local (prestigious) dialect of the London–Central Midland region and it just ended up at the right place at the right time. When varieties come to dominate in this way, it is never on account of linguistic reasons. London English piggybacked on a series of geographical, cultural, economic and political episodes. They include, for example, the emergence of London as a political and commercial centre and its proximity to Oxford and Cambridge; Chaucer's literary genius; and William Caxton's first printing presses (1476) in Westminster. These had the effect of putting London English in such a position that standardisation was inevitable. If a city other than London had had the same non-linguistic advantages (let's say, Manchester), the socially prestigious dialect of that region would have been subject to the same spread. This is typically how 'standard languages' arise. It has nothing to do with a variety being perfect, but it has everything to do with economic, political and social context.

Standard English is a good dialect to know. For one thing, it's a variety without a home – all over the globe people are using it and there's very little variation. If you read newspapers around the English-speaking world or use email, bulletin boards on list-servers or electronic 'conversation' programs, you will have observed that there is already a fairly uniform world standard, at least in writing. In many ways Standard English now represents a kind of global *lingua franca*; it has been CODIFIED; in other words, recorded in grammars, dictionaries and style books. For example, if we think of the English used in Manchester or Melbourne (the two varieties that make up the bulk of the examples in this textbook), their distinctive character is to be found largely in phonology (i.e. differences of accent) and perhaps also some (colloquial) vocabulary items, but the two are not strikingly different from other standard varieties at the level of grammar. Speakers of non-standard varieties in these places, however, show not only differences of accent and vocabulary, but also significant grammatical differences. A distinctively Manchester or Melbourne English is much more apparent in these varieties, especially in colloquial or informal usage. You will be seeing some spectacular examples of non-standard grammatical diversity later in this book.

The fact that the standard variety has been codified must not be taken to mean that it is intrinsically better than other dialects. NON-STANDARD (or VERNACULAR) must never be equated with SUBSTANDARD. All dialects are equally good for the purposes they serve. They all have their own particular conventions; they just do things differently.

In this book we will not concern ourselves with questions of correctness. Statements like 'The sentence in (6) is ungrammatical in English' is an example of a PRESCRIPTIVE statement; in other words, it is stating what people should be saying. If you are doing grammar in order to teach people English, then you will have to make statements like these. Our task, however, is not to tell people what they should say, but to study what they do in fact say. Our aim is to make DESCRIPTIVE statements and to make you good at studying the English that exists around you. We will discover that native speakers of English will not use sentences like (1) and (5), unless they are speaking Dutch, in which case they might use (1), or have a serious speech impediment, in which case they might possibly use constructions similar to (5). With respect to the other sentences presented previously, however, we will find that some native speakers of English do in fact use them (even if they think they don't), and hence we must take them seriously. In fact with the exception of the two we adapted ourselves, all of these were naturally occurring fairly recent sentences. (Just as an aside here – you don't have to be a native speaker of a language in order to study it. You can make descriptive statements about English by studying native speakers of English.)

Frequently, constructions which are considered ungrammatical by prescriptionists are in fact examples of change in progress. In spite of the feelings of some people, you can never stop a living language from changing. For example, a sentence like *There's always been songs about sex and death* is now frequent in speech and writing of many educated speakers. Yet it still hovers on the border between standard and non-standard – and certainly none of the linguistic inspectors would recommend its usage! However, give it time and we suspect it will become fully accepted.

One of the problems is that linguistic labels like Standard and non-Standard English suggest that we're always dealing with clear-cut distinctions. In fact, behind these labels lies a reality of tremendous flux and variance. Some of the sentence examples earlier gave you a taste of this. Now look at those following to see how far this variation extends. Once again these are actual examples – we didn't invent them!

(9) Genim swines lungenne gebræd and on neaht nerstig genim fif snida simle

'Take a pig's lung, roast it, and at night fasting take five slices always' (10th c. cure for hangovers)

(10) Cast þe flessh þerto ihewed & messe it forth with þe swan irostede. It schal beon god vor to eten.

'Cast the flesh thereto hewn & mess it forth with the swan roasted. It shall be good for to eat' (= add the minced meat and serve it up with the roasted swan. It'll be good to eat). (14th c. recipe for Swan Chowder)

(11) If you not in business, like me, not lawyer, not those big shot, speak so good English for what? Let people laugh at you only. (Singapore English (or Singlish))

(12) He'll might could get you one. [Hawick Scots]

(13) She's **like**: <facial expression>. [Female Australian high school student]

(14) You don't, you don't wanna have sort of around 13 turnovers at, uh, three-quarter time, but it's saying that, uh, both teams have had . . . are being very active in their defence. (Basketball – between-action commentary)

(15) > Having a nice holiday?

Yep! Too much chocolate though :/ (Email message)

Just these few examples give you an idea of the extraordinary array of 'Englishes' encompassed under that one label 'English.' The diversity, as you can see, exists in many forms – there is exotic vocabulary and some structures that look very 'unEnglish' at times. The variation we see here falls along two dimensions. The first, illustrated by examples (9) and (10) as opposed to the rest, involves variation across time. Time influences language. Shifts in grammar, words and pronunciation occur even within one's own lifetime. And if the time span is long enough, the changes can be truly spectacular, as these examples show.

The second dimension is variation across space. There are two types of space involved – geographical and social. At any given point in time, English will differ both between countries and within the same country. In this respect, English is probably more diverse than ever before. As it trots around the globe (as it has been doing since its initial expansion 450 years ago towards Wales and Scotland), it comes into contact with many different environments and languages. This triggers a burgeoning of diversity in the form of hybrids, dialects, nativised varieties, pidgins and creoles. Some of these are illustrated in examples (11) and (12).

Any socially significant group of people will differ in their linguistic behaviour. For example, social parameters to do with age, sex, sexual preference, socio-economic class, education and occupational status of speakers will typically correlate with the way sounds, vocabulary and grammar vary – people wear different linguistic features like badges of identity. Example (13) is a piece of colloquial teenspeak not confined to Australia. Age is an important social division in all cultures, and not surprisingly it is something people demonstrate through their use of language. As example (15) also illustrates, we alter our language to suit the occasions in which we find ourselves. Our language varies constantly in response to different situational factors, including things like the relationship between speakers and their audience (and even others who might be within earshot), the setting, the subject matter, or whether a spoken or written medium is used.

In a sense 'English' is a bit of a fiction. There is no one English, no one monolithic entity with a fixed, unchanging set of linguistic features. Rather, the label 'the English language' is a convenient shorthand for what is a remarkable assortment of different varieties. What they have in common is a shared history. All have links of some sort with the group of continental Germanic dialects that ended up in the British Isles sometime in the fifth century AD. And most are, to a greater or lesser extent, mutually comprehensible.

Obviously, in order to make this introductory look at the structure of English work, given that it will inevitably attract a diverse reading audience, we need to settle on one kind of English. We will therefore be using Standard English. Nearly all of our sentence examples are of naturally occurring language use by native speakers and come mainly from *The Big Issue* (mostly the English North and the Australian editions) or other sources where people write more or less as they would speak. As we wrote in the Preface to the first edition, our reasons here are two-fold. First, we would like to advertise *The Big Issue*, a good cause that deserves as much public exposure as it can get. Second, we are interested in language that is close to what is actually spoken by the majority of people – something that can't always be said about the invented sentences that so often appear in textbooks.

We want to emphasise that choosing Standard English is not at all intended to be a judgement on which English is 'best.' We also want to emphasise the fact that as linguists our role is to study English as it is used, and so we include many examples from *The Big Issue* and other

5

sources which can be said to live in the borderlands of what is acceptable in Standard English. Given English is such a hybrid and rapidly changing language, we feel we need to showcase some of this variation. So in each chapter we have breakout boxes illustrating some of the variation out there in grammar, including variation from some of the non-mainstream 'traditional dialects' that can have strikingly different structures. There is also a great diversity in the form of contact varieties such as pidgins, creoles and mixed languages. There are also many new varieties of English as a second language (or even a second first language) and in Chapter 11, we examine some of their very different grammatical features.

1.3 English rules, ok?

Let's further explore the two different approaches we mentioned earlier – prescription versus description. Basically the prescriptive approach is one that tells you how you ought to speak. Prescriptive grammar books comprise a hodgepodge of 'do's' and 'don'ts' about sentence structure, word meaning and word usage. Much like etiquette books, which outline for us the rules of polite behaviour, rules like the following outline the 'best' sort of linguistic behaviour. This is language doing the right thing – language that wipes its feet before it enters a room and that leaves the room before it breaks wind!

Do not use *lay* as an intransitive verb.

Do not use an apostrophe for possessive *its*.

Do not use *who* as the object of a verb or preposition.

Do not use *data* as a singular noun.

Do not end a sentence with a preposition like *to*.

Case study – to lay *or* to lie?

Let's examine one of these prescriptive rules closely – the notorious *lay–lie* rule. Some of you might remember the lines of Bob Dylan's famous song *Lay, lady, lay. Lay across my big brass bed*. Or take the following *Big Issue* example:

If you lay down with dogs, you get up with fleas. (AUS#66:23)

The Oxford English Dictionary describes this use of *lay* as 'only dialectal or an illiterate substitute for *lie*.' The argument goes that it indicates an ignorance of a feature in English known as TRANSITIVITY. (Transitive verbs, as you'll soon learn, are those that must have something following them, to put it simply for the time being.) The verb *lay* is transitive; hence *hens lay eggs. Lie* is intransitive; you can't *lie something*. So according to the linguistic inspectors who write such grammar books – *to lay down with dogs* instead of *to lie down with dogs* is 'a mark of illiteracy.' Linguists have for some time been pointing out the problems of the *lay–lie* rule for modern-day speakers (see for example, Dwight Bolinger 1980: 167). For a start, these two verbs *lay* and *lie* share forms – the past of *lie* is *lay*. The verb *lie* also means 'to fib'; so we need to add *down* to avoid confusion. For example, you can't say, *I think I'll lie for a bit* – you have to say *I think I'll lie down for a bit*. The problem then is, if you put this in the past you get *I lay down for a bit*. In normal fast speech the [d] of *down* transfers to the end of *lay* and you get *laid* (the past tense of *lay*) – is it any wonder that speakers confuse the verbs and arrive at *to lay down*! It is time to switch off the life support system for the *lay–lie* distinction – as Dwight Bolinger argued, the price of maintaining it is just too high.

The problem is of course that language so often becomes the arena where social issues are played out. The use of a particular word or construction can be a social advantage or disadvantage. Linguistic bigotry is rife and language prejudices are often simply accepted, never challenged. People constantly judge others on the basis of superficial linguistic features (e.g. pronunciation *haitch* for *aitch*, second person plural *yous*, aberrant apostrophe use), and such is the importance placed on language that these judgements can even go on to affect a person's employment opportunities, their social mobility, even their personal relationships. In short, because of the way society operates, sentences like *If you lay down with dogs, you get up with fleas* can put people at a disadvantage. For this reason English teachers must give students access to these rules. This is why at the beginning of this chapter we mentioned that if you are writing a grammar in order to teach people English, then you will have to make prescriptive statements like 'The sentence in (6) is ungrammatical in English.' But do guard against putting the prescriptive cart before the usage horse! All sorts of things, including language change, means the line between 'right' and 'wrong' is often very murky.

Certainly a book like this one will always emphasise the need for linguists to retain an objectively descriptive stance and to avoid anything that smacks of moral and aesthetic judgement. Imagine a linguist who condemns a native speaker for saying *yous*, not *you*. It would be rather like a zoologist who condemns a dromedary for having one hump, not two! Linguistic science has to found its theories on observed behaviour. To construct a theory about Modern English grammar that refuses to acknowledge a construction like *If you lay down with dogs* would be about as sensible as a sociologist constructing a theory of human society based only on 'proper' behaviour and ignoring those aspects of our society that others consider 'improper' or 'deviant.'

Some linguists are ultimately interested in the way people's minds work, how our brains deal with language (in a sense, being a native speaker of something as complex as a human language is your most amazing intellectual achievement). For this purpose we need to study objectively the language that people do use, and the changes that actually take place. Other linguists are interested in the factors which motivate people to use one construction rather than another. Hence their attempts to replace absolute labels of prescriptive grammar like 'right' and 'wrong,' 'mistake' and 'error' with labels like 'appropriate' and 'suitable.' Take the example *Whom did you see?* versus *Who did you see?* Both alternatives are still being used – but in quite different contexts. Imagine saying *Whom did you see?* on the phone to a good friend. You'd be laughed at, or at least accused of putting on airs! But there are contexts, say a formal piece of prose, where you might well imagine writing something like that. Language is clearly not an absolute matter of putting a tick or an asterisk beside a sentence. It's much more interesting than that.

1.4 Why study English grammar?

Apart from believing the study of language should fall into general knowledge, why might linguists want to make descriptive statements about English? For those linguists who specialise in grammar, or syntax, there are in fact a number of different reasons.

Typology

For instance, we might be interested in comparing English with other languages, and in order to do so, we need a detailed description of English. Those linguists who are interested in comparing the world's languages, to find out how languages group together either genetically or according to what types of constructions they allow or disallow, are referred to as TYPOLOGISTS. When we classify languages typologically, we look for similarities between the languages, and group them accordingly. If we consider English in a typological perspective, we can say, for instance, that it belongs to the group of languages which require a subject. Compare the following four English sentences with the two Italian ones. Note, linguists use the asterisk * to indicate that a sentence is ungrammatical. Hence the English sentences (18) and (19) are ungrammatical, whereas (16) and (17) are perfectly okay:

English

(16) I am eating.
(17) It rains./It is raining.
(18) *Am eating
(19) *Rains./*Is raining.

Italian

(20) Mangio.
  'I eat' (first person singular)
(21) Piove.
  rains
  'It rains.'

These sentences show that, in English, a grammatical sentence requires that there is a subject like *I* and *it*. (We will return to the issue of what a subject is later.) Even in (17), where the subject *it* cannot really be said to carry any meaning, it is still obligatory, since (19) is ungrammatical. This contrasts with Italian, where a subject is not obligatory, as the grammatical sentences (20) and (21) show.

We've just said that a grammatical sentence of English requires a subject. What about examples like the following?

Here's my old tartan-colour thermos from Fosseys. Still got tea in it from last year. Might have a slug. (AUS#36:16)

This is written English, obviously, but it is deliberately imitating a casual spoken style; hence the lack of subjects. English can leave things out under special circumstances. Diary, or postcard, writing, for example, is distinguished by missing subject pronouns (*Felt sick. Spent day in bed* or *Arrived in Stockholm. Saw the palace*). Cookery-speak may also leave out otherwise obligatory elements when they can be understood from context: *Dice elephant; cook over kerosene fire. Serves 3,800 people.* However, we don't think of these as Standard English. These are known as different REGISTERS of the standard; in other words, varieties associated with particular contexts or purposes (see also Chapter 10).

This seems a good point to stop and consider possible definitions of 'an English sentence.' Look at the examples in the following little piece from *The Big Issue* (N#301:15):

> First Stockport then the world. Steven Warrington, king of the on-line ostrich-dealers, talks to Richard Ewart. Stockport is not a place usually associated with Australian exotica. But that didn't stop one of the sons of this unremarkable Cheshire town forging a remarkable reputation. From the other side of the Atlantic.

There are some factual errors here, like the fact that the ostrich is not actually Australian, that's the emu they are thinking of, and Stockport being an unremarkable town – whatever next! However, what we are more interested in here are the first and the last sentences. Or are they sentences? Well, they are clearly a tad unconventional, and your English teacher would probably have corrected them, but they are used. We have nothing to say about whether or not people should be using them, we just want to say that throughout this book, when we use the term *sentence*, we will mean the more conventional type like the other sentences of this example.

It is only through detailed studies of the grammars of many languages that we can make statements about differences and similarities between languages. Interesting questions arise as to why certain languages share properties while others do not. Sometimes shared typological features are the result of genetic inheritance, but not necessarily. Similarities can also arise because languages have undergone the same sort of changes, either independently motivated or perhaps brought about through contact. In order to pursue these questions, we need to know a little bit about the family history of English: English is a Germanic language, related to other Germanic languages, like Dutch or Swedish, and if you study the grammars of these languages, you will find that they have a number of features in common (even though English is in many ways an 'odd' Germanic language). Tree (1) shows you a simple illustration of how the Germanic languages are related. Note, Gothic is now extinct; all that remains are partial records of a Bible translation from the fourth century. There were other East Germanic languages for which we have no records.

(1)

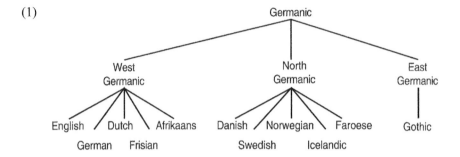

Language change may mean that genetically related languages end up being quite different. English and German are genetically related but they belong to different word order typologies, English being S(ubject) V(erb) O(bject) and German Verb-Second (i.e. at least one of the verbs occurs in second position, but not necessarily preceded by the subject). Old English, on the other hand, was typologically more like German in its word order. Conversely, English and Chinese are both SVO languages; yet they do not belong to the same genetic group.

Universal grammar

For a number of linguists, the ultimate goal of the study of the grammars of individual languages is not to compare languages, but to find out how the human brain deals with language. Of particular inspiration to these linguists is the mystery of CHILDREN'S LANGUAGE ACQUISITION. There are a number of reasons why children's language acquisition is such a fascinating phenomenon.

Children learn language surprisingly quickly and accurately considering the input they get. For instance, most of the language that a child hears does not actually consist of full grammatical sentences; people are always interrupting themselves or changing their minds halfway through a sentence. As you'll see in Chapter 10, when we examine a piece of spontaneous conversation, we find that speech contains utterances that simply do not correspond to what we would consider a well-formed sentence of English. Young children don't usually have the benefit of a written language. They get language almost entirely in the shape of long strings of sounds where there are no significant pauses between words. Children also get language input mainly in a positive form, and rarely in a negative form. What we mean by this is that they hear lots of language which they can assume to be correct, but they rarely get told what is incorrect. Parents do sometimes try to correct their children, but often they are not conscious enough of their own language to do it to any greater extent. Furthermore, children very early on become interestingly creative with language. It is quite clear that they cannot be learning language by straight imitation, since they understand and produce strings of words which they have never heard.

Facts like these have led some linguists and psychologists to assume that the human mind must be somehow pre-disposed towards learning a language; others link the development of language more closely to the general cognitive development of children. According to those who favour a predisposition explanation, there is a part of the brain which contains knowledge at birth of what is and what is not a possible language. We are, then, said to be born with an INNATE GRAMMAR, or a LANGUAGE ACQUISITION DEVICE (LAD), and a task for linguistics is to find out more about this innate grammar. If you have ever heard of the linguist Noam Chomsky (and if people have heard of one linguist, he is usually the one), this is the line of research that he proposes to follow.

A child will learn the language or languages spoken around him or her, even if this is not the language of the biological parents. Also, there is no clear evidence that children learn some languages faster than others. Children growing up in a monolingual Cantonese community will learn Cantonese at the same age that children growing up in a monolingual English environment learn English. A 'monolingual' community is one that uses only one language and children growing up in such a community will usually become native speakers of only one language. In a worldwide perspective such communities are in fact rare. Most children in the world grow up learning at least two languages. The fact that children will learn whatever language is used around them in roughly the same way, regardless of the language, has led those who believe in innate grammar to assume that it is the same for any language, hence we have an innate UNIVERSAL GRAMMAR. Remember that the innate grammar, which is assumed to be universal, is a mental phenomenon, an abstract structure in the brain. Even if we don't believe in an innate grammar, but assume that our linguistic ability is part of our general cognitive abilities, the similarities between genetically very different languages are still striking and of great interest.

One goal of linguistic research is to find out more about universal grammar, regardless of whether one assumes this is an abstract language-specific component of the brain or the result of general properties of human cognition. However, there is no obvious direct way of studying universal grammar since it is an abstract entity. There is (as yet) no brain scanner that can be used to study this innate grammar. What linguists who pursue this line of research do is study in great depth the grammars of individual languages. By comparing in-depth studies of many different languages, we can find out more about properties shared by languages and maybe also about properties that no language has. A detailed study of English grammar can reveal things about universal grammar. So, under this approach, we can say that the ultimate purpose of our study of English grammar is to understand

11

universal grammar and how children acquire language. (But there is a long way to go from one to the other!)

It should be pointed out here that a linguist need not be either a typologist or a person who believes in innate grammar. He or she can be both, or indeed neither. There are a number of proposed explanations for language acquisition. It is also important to remember that innate grammar is just one proposed hypothesis; it may turn out to be entirely the wrong way of thinking about things, but for the time being, a large number of linguists use it as their working hypothesis.

Speech therapy

The two motivations for doing English grammar which we have mentioned so far have important repercussions in other fields. For instance, SPEECH THERAPY, or the more general study of communication disorders, is concerned with people whose language faculty is somehow different from the expected. This can be due to developmental problems or to illness which damages a language faculty that had previously been fully developed. An important task for speech therapists is to develop techniques which can help these people improve their communicative abilities. In order to study and describe language which is 'not normal' it is important to know what the structure of 'normal' language is, and to master the terminology used to describe it. In this book, we aim to teach you this and provide the tools you need.

Foreign language learning

The teaching profession, above all foreign language learning, is another obvious practical application of the study of English grammar. A knowledge of English grammatical structures is helpful when you are learning the grammatical structures of another language, or having to teach them to others. In particular, if you are a native speaker of English, being trained to think about your language in a scientific way is very different from the sort of unconscious knowledge you have by simply being a speaker of the language. Formal linguistic training will make you a much more effective language learner and teacher.

Stylistics

Some of you may be more interested in literature than in linguistics. Let us assure you that the things you learn in this book can be of great use also to people who study literature. Literature in any form, be it prose, poetry or drama, is built up of language, and a detailed study of the language used in any piece of literature can be very revealing. There is one branch of linguistics called STYLISTICS which is devoted to the study of how language is used in literature. But also in non-literary texts you will find grammatical analysis a useful tool.

Under stylistics we can also include the field of effective communication, in particular effective writing. This is not to say that linguistic awareness will instantly make you a stellar communicator. You just have to read some examples of linguistic prose to know that this is not the case – there is a lot of turgid and very obscure writing around. Certainly an ignorance of linguistics won't prevent you from becoming an effective communicator either. If that were the case, William Shakespeare would have probably ended up a glove maker like his father John! Nonetheless, there is now no doubt that a knowledge of language structure does help you become more skilled in handling your own language, particularly when it comes to good writing. After all, writing is not a natural activity in the same way that speech is – writing has to be explicitly taught after basic grammar, sounds and vocabulary have been acquired as spoken language. While there are many societies whose languages remain unwritten, ours is one that places considerable emphasis on writing. With an awareness of grammar comes a feeling for sentence patterning, and this means we can better evaluate the different choices that confront us when we draft something written, such as a speech or a report.

1.5 English language in the workplace

We have just mentioned here a number of fields for which a detailed study of English grammar is required. In all these it is very important that the people working within the field use the same terminology. You cannot discuss your thoughts and conclusions with other people unless you can be reasonably certain that when you say 'subject' or 'auxiliary verb' you mean the same thing as your hearer. For this reason, an important aspect of this book will be to define a common terminology.

Since this is a book on English grammar, and not on typology, stylistics or communication disorders, we will not discuss these topics any further here, but we mention them in order to give you an idea of why one might want to embark on a study of English grammar. And if we still haven't persuaded you that knowing about English grammar is useful, we now offer some specific ideas of where in later life you might be able to apply this knowledge. The facts you learn to do with English grammar turn out to have all sorts of applications in the workplace and are useful in a variety of jobs. Here are some you might not have thought about.

❑ The film industry: who do you think it is that invents all those artificial languages in films? J. R. R. Tolkien's fantasy world contains a number of them. Tolkien himself was an Oxford professor of English language and literature and he spent a lot of his time on constructed languages (he also nearly became a codebreaker during World War II). One of our colleagues, Professor Francis Nolan at Cambridge University, created the fragment of Parseltongue that is used in the Harry Potter films. Conlangs (constructed languages) are becoming more usual, and the best ones are created by linguists; not just the two already mentioned, but also for instance Klingon, Na'vi, Dothraki and Valyrian are among them.

❑ Writing: at least three groups of people end up having careers in writing. There are, of course, the authors who produce material for print and

13

online media. There are the technical writers who specialise in producing materials such as instruction manuals and software documentation. And there are the editors who appraise and select content for publication. These are the people with a keen nose for ill-chosen words, grammatical errors, infelicities of style and punctuation.

☐ Information technology: with speech-based applications now used increasingly in human – computer interfaces, natural language processing and speech recognition technology have become two very significant areas of IT. Linguistic research is the key to progress in these areas and training in language structure is a necessity for these new career paths.

☐ Advertising and marketing: companies spend millions of dollars annually researching exactly the kind of wording that helps to implant desire in potential consumers – and this is where linguists come in. Increasingly companies consult people with linguistic awareness when they are creating slogans, product names and preparing sales campaigns. Such information becomes increasingly important for products being sold globally.

☐ Safety measures: there are many applications of a formal linguistic training to safety in the workplace. In the airline industry, for example, disasters have occurred because of misunderstandings between control towers and pilots. While faulty communication is a linguistic fact of life, there is much that can be done, particularly in the development of technology, to help avoid such communication tragedies.

☐ The law: more and more legal cases now involve linguists who are called upon for expert testimony. In fact, there is even a separate discipline called forensic linguistics that connects language, law and crime. Work here might involve, for instance, the handwriting and stylistic analyses of documents to develop writer profiles to determine authorship (perhaps resolving that it was the deceased who actually wrote the suicide note). Some linguists have also been working hard to expose the kinds of miscommunication that can arise when defendants speak a non-standard form of English.

☐ The Plain English movement: since the late 1970s, people with expertise in English language have been helping to translate all kinds of specialist language into a form that is more accessible to people. Language in legal settings, in particular, is characterised by a highly technical vocabulary and difficult structure and expert evidence in and outside the courtroom, police warnings, even jury instructions, have been shown to be notoriously difficult for non-lawyers to understand.

These are just a taste of the sorts of enterprising things you can do with the specific facts you learn in this book. But you know, there are also people who actually like doing English grammar for its own sake (and these are people who lead otherwise perfectly normal lives!). However, if you are not one of those, it might be nice to know that in all likelihood the things you learn here will prove useful to you in other areas.

1.6 The branches of linguistics

We have now narrowed down what we mean by English sentences, but there are still a number of ways in which we could study such sentences. For example, we could study the way they sound, or the way in which people interpret them. However, this is a book specifically about grammar, and we will study how words are put together to make up the sentences. Things like the sound or the meaning of English are studied in other sub-fields of linguistics. The core parts of linguistics can be seen as a spectrum:

Phonetics/Phonology – Morphology – Syntax – Semantics – Pragmatics

These sub-fields of linguistics can be defined (very) roughly as follows:

PHONETICS/PHONOLOGY: sounds, how they are made and how they are used in language;

MORPHOLOGY: the structure of words, about the smallest meaningful parts of a language;

SYNTAX: the structure of sentences and phrases;

SEMANTICS: the meaning of words and how these meanings combine when words are combined into phrases and sentences;

PRAGMATICS: how meaning interacts with our knowledge of the real world (whatever the real world may be).

So far, we have defined the main concern of this book as GRAMMAR. Apart from its appalling reputation as being dry and boring (quite undeserved!), grammar is not a very clear term, since some people use it to mean the same as 'syntax,' and others take it to refer both to syntax and to morphology. There are those who even use grammar to mean the whole system of language – namely, all the sounds, words and possible sentences. It is therefore more accurate to say that this is a book about the syntax of English. It is, however, virtually impossible to study syntax without also considering at least morphology and semantics; so these two fields will also play some part in the book. Very often, there are different grammatical constructions that can be used to represent the same basic information, as in *Harry Kane scored the crucial goals that took England beyond the group stage at the World Cup* versus *The crucial goals that took England beyond the group stage at the Wold Cup were scored by Harry Kane*. The choice between two constructions is frequently determined by how the speaker (or writer) wants to present the information to the hearer (or reader); in this case, this involves things like the amount of emphasis on *Harry Kane* for instance. Grammar is then influenced by what we may call DISCOURSE (or INFORMATION) STRUCTURE. In Chapter 9 we will be venturing beyond the sentence to see how chunks of text are organised and how this may influence the structure of sentences. This involves the field of DISCOURSE (or COMMUNICATIVE) STRUCTURE. Basically it deals with how we as speakers and writers go about packaging our messages;

how we distribute information in a text to help our audience interpret the text appropriately.

We also venture beyond the sentence in Chapter 10 where we introduce the notion of REGISTERS; in other words, varieties to do with physical mode (speech versus writing for example), as well as those peculiar to the activities of a trade, profession or some other group sharing an interest. Also important here are the effects of new and emerging media. We are seeing considerable linguistic fallout from the Internet and the global trend towards e-communication, as we did with other major shifts in the past (from pen and ink, printing to the telephone, radio and television broadcasting). E-communication is blurring even further the (already rather blurry) traditional distinction between speech and writing.

Exercises

1. Public opinions about English

The following statements illustrate some popular beliefs about language and the English language, in particular. You can hear them aired on talkback radio and you can read them in letters to the editor. Discuss these statements – think about whether you agree or disagree with them and try to support your answers with examples.

(a) English is the language of England.

(b) English is the hardest language to learn.

(c) Writing is a more perfect form of language than speech.

(d) The English language is going to the dogs.

(e) It would be simpler, and more sociable, if we all spoke the same.

(f) People who say *nobody saw nothing* can't think logically.

(g) Bringing up a child bilingually is damaging.

2. Language prescription

The following letter by A. P. Taskunas (Sandy Bay, Tasmania) appeared in *The Australian Magazine*, 9–10 October 1999:

> Shame on you! You've killed the accusative ('Deaths in the family: Who killed who?' – Sept 25–26), one of the most endangered species in our language. Whom can we enlist to protect it?

What arguments do you think A. P. Taskunas would use to defend the existence of *whom*? What do you think a descriptive grammarian would have to say on the matter?

3. Acceptability

Read each of the following sentences. Your task is to make a judgement on the relative acceptability of each sentence. Try to answer as honestly as you can and give reasons for your view! You can also do a small survey among other native speakers to see how similar your views are. Indicate your judgement by placing a number 1–4 by each of the sentences. The scale of acceptability is as follows:

(a) Totally unacceptable

(b) I would not use it but some people would

(c) I would use it, but only in some contexts

(d) Totally acceptable and natural

(1) See yous later!

(2) (Who ate the chocolate?) It was me.

(3) It is I who am responsible.

(4) The mission of the USS *Enterprise* is to boldly go where no man has gone before.

(5) There's fairies at the bottom of my garden.

(6) I aren't bothered.

(7) I ain't bothered.

(8) I'm right, aren't I?

(9) He's fatter than me.

(10) Everyone can come if they want to.

(11) Between you and I, he's a bit of an idiot.

(12) There's a man on the phone wants to talk to you.

(13) He objected to my arriving late.

(14) He objected to me arriving late.

(15) It was meant to be made a joke of, money was! (AUS#69:9)

(16) Then I got eaten by flies. (AUS#69:9)

(17) Maybe he's dead? Killed his self getting out of the bath. (AUS#36:16)

4. Non-standard versus standard English

Here is an example of a dialogue in non-standard English (from Tasmania). Make a list of the non-standard forms and give the standard equivalents.

Harv:
Old Kit . . . 'e 'ad the only chopping axe John Behan had,
Nobody 'd two them days y'know, in the bad old days,
And John 'ad a pretty good axe . . .
. . . they got Kit entered in this Chop y'know . . .
'e was off say three or five or whatever.
When they said 'Five!' 'e's no sooner [unclear] than 'e hit
'er [= the block], y'know,
and 'e chopped two or three six-inch nails clean off . . .
'e dug himself in too low, y'see,

and 'e fetches 'er [= the axe]
and 'e looks at 'er, y'see,
. . . and 'e holds 'er round to John,
And 'e's got a great big gap clean through the face of 'er,
and 'e said 'CRIPES!' Hahaha!
when 'e turned – when 'e showed it [the axe or the face?] to John.

5. Research question – grammar awareness and writing skills

In this chapter, we made the claim that there are beneficial links between language awareness and language skills, especially writing. But this is a controversial area. A number of early research projects (that matched the writing skills of children both with and without formal grammar instruction) found no positive correlation between grammar-knowledge and writing skills. In this essay, argue for one position or the other. A good place to start is Dick Hudson's website: http://dickhudson.com/papers/

The structure of sentences

2.1 Introduction

In this chapter and in the next we start to look at basic sentence structure or syntax. This involves, among other things, two important tasks: (a) determining what the structure of a sentence is; and (b) describing the elements which make up the structure.

In this chapter we concentrate on the first. The second of these tasks involves attaching some sort of category label to the parts of a sentence and we come to that in Chapter 3.

Before we begin, though, we need to look at some aspects to do with words and word-building, because it's not just sentences that have structure – words also have their own internal structure.

2.2 The structure of words

The sound structure of a word is, as we have said, studied in the sub-branches of linguistics called phonology and phonetics. There is, however, also a different kind of structure to words. For one, they can be divided into smaller units of meaning. There is good evidence that even quite young children are aware of this, and often children's misunderstanding of structure provides the clearest evidence of this. Nils, for instance, when he was about 2½ years old, was told off for having thrown his bowl of cereal on the floor. He defended himself by saying that there was only one 'Weetabick' left in the bowl. In this case, Nils analysed the final /s/ sound of the brand name *Weetabix* as the English plural marker, which you get in words like *trick*s. Ellen at the age of 3 fell over in the playground and through her tears informed the nursery staff that she had hurt her 'two-head.' Once she had calmed down a bit she said 'I mean my forehead.' Ellen seems to have been aware that words can consist of parts which both exist separately as words. She would appear to have thought of this word as 'four head,' but being upset from her fall she got the number wrong. Finally, when Paul was told by his father not to argue he replied 'Well, don't arg-me then.' The final sounds of *argue* are identical to the pronoun *you* and Paul had therefore assigned the structure 'arg-you' to the word. Nils, Ellen and Paul all seem to be aware of the fact that words have internal structure.

As already mentioned in Chapter 1, the area which deals with the structure of words is called morphology. The parts which make up words are MORPHEMES. The morpheme is best described as the smallest unit of meaning in the structure of the language. However, a potential unit of meaning is only a morpheme of a word if the meaning it contributes is part of that word. By this we mean that we cannot divide the unit any more without severely altering the meaning. For example, *cardigan, pumpkin* and *cook* are all words and they are also single morphemes. Take the word *cardigan*. As one complete unit by itself, it has meaning, and while we can apparently divide it into smaller units like *car, dig* and *an*, these have meanings which are not associated with the word *cardigan*. We wouldn't dissect *cardigan* in this way, any more than we would *pumpkin* into *pump* and *kin*; these segments have meanings totally unrelated to *pumpkin*. On the other hand, a word like *cardigans* has a meaning as a whole, but we can also divide it into two smaller meaningful units: *cardigan* + the plural ending *s*; in other words, it is made up of two morphemes.

Now, there are a number of different types of morphemes. Two of these are going to be important for our discussion of word classes and we will discuss them in Chapter 3. There are also a number of different ways in which you can combine morphemes, something which we go on to discuss under the heading 'Building words – inflection versus derivation.' Note that, unless specified, all our examples in this chapter are taken from a story which tells of the tribulations of one stressed slimmer at an exclusive Miami health spa (AUS#75:9).

Bound versus free morphemes

First we can make a division of morphemes, based on where they can appear. Consider, for example, the words in the following sentence:

The spa's regime disagreed with the gluttonous guest.

Morphemes such as *spa* and *regime* can exist in isolation; we describe such morphemes as FREE. Other morphemes, like the past tense ending *-ed*, cannot exist on their own, but are only ever found attached to other morphemes as part of words. These we describe as BOUND morphemes. Using slightly different terminology, free morphemes function as the STEMS (or ROOTS) to which bound morphemes can attach. Bound morphemes are normally AFFIXES. Affixes can be divided into sub-classes depending on whether they attach before the stem, in which case they are PREFIXES, or after the stem, in which case they are SUFFIXES. There is a third type; namely, INFIXES, which, as you might have guessed, must occur inside the stem. English does not really use infixes, though non-standard intensifiers like *bloody* in *fan-bloody-tastic* can be described as an infix (Homer Simpson provides another rare example for English with his *-ma-* infix in words such as *edu-ma-cation, sophisti-ma-cated* and *vio-ma-lin*).

The 's attached to *spa* in the previous example is different from the *-ed* of *disagreed*. If we add something after *disagree*, like *strongly*, the *-ed* still attaches to *disagree*:

The spa's regime disagreed strongly with the gluttonous guest.

* The spa's regime disagree strongly ed with the gluttonous guest.

However, if we add something after *spa*, the 's attaches to the end of that word instead:

The spa in the city's regime disagreed with the gluttonous guest.

*The spa's in the city regime disagreed with the gluttonous guest.

Whereas *-ed* attaches to the right edge of the **word** it combines with, 's attaches to the right edge of the **phrase** it combines with. The 's can be said to belong to morphology since it cannot stand on its own, but has to attach to another element. At the same time it goes beyond morphology when it comes to its position; it is placed with respect to a phrase rather than a word. Elements that show this mixture of morphological and syntactic properties are referred to as CLITICS.

In English, bound morphemes typically are what are called GRAMMATICAL (or FUNCTIONAL) morphemes. This has to do with the type of meaning they express. Grammatical morphemes express rather abstract information like person (first, second, third), plural, possession or case. Free morphemes, on the other hand, are normally LEXICAL morphemes and are more contentful, like *spa*, *regime* and *guest*. Grammatical morphemes don't have to be bound; many are free-standing. Consider *the* in the previous example sentence. This little word tells us that the writer is referring to something she assumes is already familiar to the reader. In this case she wouldn't have used *the* unless both 'the spa' and 'the gluttonous guest' were already somehow known to us and were readily identifiable, in this particular case because they have occurred earlier in the text.

Building words – inflection versus derivation

There are two main types of word-building involving bound morphemes. The first is called INFLECTION. Examples of inflection are the plural *-s* which is added to nouns (*dog-s*), the past tense *-ed* which is added to regular verbs (*bark-ed*) and the comparative *-er* which is added to adjectives (*louder*) (more about how to spot nouns, adjectives and verbs in Chapter 3). Inflection adds some functional information to the element to which it is added, but does not drastically change the meaning of the word or the word class it belongs to (again, more about word classes in Chapter 3). The second type of word-building is called DERIVATION and it changes the category or at least the meaning of the element to which it is added. An example is the difference between *run* and *runner*; by adding *-er* we change the meaning from an activity to a person involved in that activity, probably more precisely a person regularly involved in this activity. Another example of derivation is when *un-*, *in-* or *im-* is added to a word to make it negative: *unhappy*, *indiscreet* or *impossible*. Both types of word-building involve affixation; that is, the addition of bound morphemes (or affixes) to a word stem. Accordingly, we can identify two types of affixes by their function – INFLECTIONAL and DERIVATIONAL.

First, consider the inflections in English – or what's left of them. History has seen the unrelenting erosion of what was once a rich inflectional system to the modest little group of suffixes represented in Table 2.1. Despite its small membership, however, this class remains an important feature of English structure, and represents one of the criteria we use to identify our word classes. Have a look at Table 2.1, but for the moment don't worry too much about labels like 'third person singular present.' We go on to look at some of these more closely in this chapter and all of them will be important in Chapter 3. As we saw earlier, the possessive *'s* has some properties which are quite unusual for an English inflection, but we include it in Table 2.1 since this seems more appropriate than to call it derivational.

Table 2.1 English suffixes

Stem	Suffix	Function	Example
clean	-*s*	Third person singular present	He clean*s* every day.
clean	-*ed*	past tense	She clean*ed* yesterday.
clean	-*ing*	Progressive	He is clean*ing* right now.
beat	-*en*	past participle	She has beat*en* the dog.
dog	-*s*	Plural	The dog*s* are kelpies.
dog	*'s*	Possessive	The dog*'s* lead is broken.
fast (adj/adverb)	-*er*	Comparative	He's a fast*er* runner.
fast (adj/adverb)	-*est*	Superlative	She's the fast*est* runner.

First, inflectional morphemes (or inflections) are grammatical. They do not change the meaning of the stem or its category. For instance, *fast*, *faster* and *fastest* are all adjectives; they are all simply different forms of the one word *fast*. Second, inflections are changes made in the form of words to express their semantic and syntactic relationships to other words in a sentence. For instance, the agreement morpheme *s* on *He cleans* indicates that we are dealing with present tense and that the person doing the cleaning is third person and singular, in this case *he*. Finally, in Modern English, inflections occur only at the ends of words; they are now all suffixes.

Derivation differs from inflection in that it has a more dramatic effect on the category or meaning of the word. If we return to the words *clean* and *dog*, we see that adding the inflections -*ed* and -*s*, respectively, gives us words – *cleaned* and *dogs* – which basically refer to the same kind of thing, the activity of cleaning or the animal dog in general. If instead, a derivational affix is added to form *cleaner* or *dogged*, then the meaning and the category change. *Cleaner* does not refer to an activity, but to a person who performs that activity, and *dogged* as in *dogged resistance* does in fact no longer have anything to do with dogs. More formally, we can say that whereas inflection always leaves the word in the same word class, derivation may change the word class; *clean* is a verb and *dog* is a noun, the derived *cleaner* is a noun and *dogged* is an adjective. Don't worry if you are not familiar with the word classes, we will discuss them in greater detail in Chapter 3. Derivation does not, however, have to change the word class. Take a derivational prefix like *un-* or *im-*, for example; both *clean* and *unclean* are adjectives and so are both *possible* and *impossible*, but the meaning change within the two pairs is very drastic; in fact the meaning after derivation becomes the opposite of that of the original. The examples given in this paragraph also illustrate another difference between inflections and derivational affixes in English. Whereas inflections are always suffixes, we have both derivational prefixes (like *un-* and *im-*) and derivational suffixes (like -*er* in *runner* and -*ed* in *dogged*).

A thing to note is that English has a number of affixes which have the same form but can fill different functions, more or less accidentally (though in a historical perspective, it may not be entirely accidental). Take -*ed*, for instance. If added to *clean* as in *She cleaned yesterday* it is an inflectional affix. It doesn't change the meaning drastically; it has a grammatical effect (and therefore it wouldn't have its own dictionary entry). If added to *dog* on the other hand, to give *dogged*, then it changes the category and the meaning of the word (so it does get its own dictionary entry). Similarly with -*er*, it can be derivational as in *We employ a cleaner* or inflectional as in *That dog is cleaner than this one.*

As we have said, modern English is relatively poor when it comes to morphology and sometimes a word class can be changed without any addition of a morpheme, this is referred to a ZERO-DERIVATION or CONVERSION. A verb like *to run* can be converted into a noun: *a run*; a noun *a fool* can be converted to a verb: *to fool someone*; an adjective like *empty* can be converted to a verb: *to empty*; a preposition like *down* can be converted to a verb as in *to down a beer*. We expect you can come up with further examples.

The stress on a particular part of a word can also be used to change the category of the word (we use ′ to indicate stress on the following part of the word): *to im′port* versus *the ′import* or the verb *to pro′duce* versus the noun *′produce.*

Branding new conversions

This elasticity in our word classes is a handy offshoot of the loss of inflection. But curiously it is a convenience of English often not appreciated by its speakers. Here is a recent letter of complaint to the editor of *The Age* (2 July 2018), complaining about the nouns *podium* and *medal* and the adjective *hot* being used as verbs and the verb *reveal* as a noun:

> *Sports commentators talking of athletes 'podiuming' or 'medalling'; home renovation presenters promising 'reveals'; weather presenters talking of it 'hotting up'. We never heard these terms before the TV media started using them. When are the broadcasting companies going to pull into line the illiterati among their staff?*
>
> (Anthony Whitmarsh, Viewbank)

In fact, for some time now people have been condemning conversions. The verb *to contact* (from the noun *contact*) was once considered pretentious jargon and 80 years ago there was ferocious resistance, with an outraged public using descriptions like 'lubricious barbarism' for the new arrival. Samuel Johnson in his 1755 dictionary disapproved of the verb *to colour*, which he described as 'a low word, used only in conversation.' Nathan Bailey, in his *Universal Etymological English Dictionary* (1727), even branded some conversions with asterisks (*) and obelisks (†).

Sometimes we don't know what social meaning people attached to these early conversions, but any linguistic newcomer can provoke hostility simply because it's unfamiliar. As we noted in Chapter 1, there have always been urges to clean up the language – what changes with time though is the definition of *dirt*. Eventually *to podium* and *to medal* will sound as everyday as the golden oldies *to contact* and *to colour* (though we note people have been 'podiuming' since the 1940s and 'medalling' since the 1860s, so these are hardly new arrivals!).

Compounding

We mentioned at the start of this chapter that there are two main types of word-building: inflection and derivation. So far, we have only discussed combinations involving just one free morpheme. Words can, however, be built from more than one free morpheme. This is called COMPOUNDING. Compounding is never inflectional but always derivational; for example, *dog collar* or *spring clean*. In Germanic languages other than English this closeness is easy to spot because compounds would be written as one word. In English, however, they may still be written as two words (with or without a hyphen), but you can hear the difference in that in a compound, the main stress falls on the first element only. It is easier to illustrate this with an example that can occur both as a compound and as an ordinary string of two free morphemes. Take the two words *dark* and *room*. We can combine them and put the stress on the first element only as in *'dark room*. In this case, it has the quite specific meaning of a room which is used for developing and printing photographic film. If on the other hand we put stress on both parts as in *'dark 'room*, then it refers to any old room which happens to be dark. This example also illustrates a second property of compounds: the meaning is often more specific than just the sum of the two parts and it may often also become figurative. A *dog collar*, for instance is not just the kind of collar that a dog would wear; it can also refer to the white collar worn by some ordained clergy.

Typically you'll find that newer compounds like *dog collar* will appear as separate words or hyphenated, whereas well-aged compounds like *breakfast* and *cupboard* will lose their hyphens and appear as a single word. Not only will familiarity remove hyphenation in well-established compounds, it can bring about even further reduction as the morphemes become more and more closely associated to the point where we don't want to consider them compounds any more. As morpheme boundaries become blurred, so the meaning of the parts themselves may become obscure. This is to some extent true of *breakfast* and *cupboard*. For a more radical example take a word like *nostril*. Now, only a real word enthusiast will be aware that this little lexical item began life as a compound of two nouns: Old English *nos* 'nose' + *thirl* 'hole.' Even if *thirl* were not obsolete as an independent item, it has undergone such a transformation in the word *nostril* that it's no longer recognisable. In fact, it makes sense now to treat *nostril* as a single morpheme.

Although the majority of roots that make up compounds are freestanding morphemes, as in all the previous examples, there are some roots which can never occur independently. These are sometimes called CRANMORPHEMES because of the word *cranberry*, which looks like a compound, similar to items like *blueberry* and *blackberry*. The problem is – after we've identified *berry*, what do we do with *cran*, which in isolation has no meaning? These are special instances of bound root morphemes. It's only when they're in combination with other morphemes that they have meaning. In fact, *cran-* does exist independently, being the same word as *crane*, the large bird with long legs. These berries started life as *crane berries*, but we no longer think of them as such. The compounding process has obscured this relationship over time and although the history of these words might tell us to consider *cran-* and *crane* as the one morpheme, clearly, speakers never connect the two. Again we face the problem of the extent to which historical detail should be allowed to influence our analyses.

Before we turn to the structure of sentences rather than words, we should point out that for some words that look like they are the result of a productive derivational affix and a stem, the stem cannot actually occur as a word on its own. The smooth British jazz musician John Dankworth was once described with the words 'couth, kempt and shevelled,' all words that are words of English that only exist with a negative prefix: *uncouth*, *unkempt* and *dishevelled*.

2.3 How do we know sentences have structure?

Having looked briefly at how morphemes combine to build words, we now go on to look at the way words themselves combine to form sentences. When we see a sentence written or hear it spoken, we see or hear a string of words. (In fact this is a little misleading. We never really hear strings of words – what we actually hear is a constant stream of sound; word boundaries aren't usually obvious in normal speech.) For us the question is now whether these strings of words are indeed just that – a list of words without any internal structure – or whether we can find reasons to assume that words form groups within sentences. It is, in fact, quite clear that native speakers feel that in English, a sentence is not just a plain sequence of words. Native speakers can divide sentences into groups of words which seem to belong together more closely than others. To begin, consider the following sentence. We return to the tale of Timothy Toast and his ordeal at the Miami health spa:

The weight-loss program was unleashed upon 19-stone Timothy Toast at an exclusive Miami health spa.

Probably everyone reading this book will share the intuition that *weight-loss* somehow modifies *program* and together these words form a natural unit in this sentence – *weight-loss program*. Similarly, *19-stone Timothy Toast* forms a single unit, as does *an exclusive Miami health spa*. These groups of words which 'go together' form what is called a CONSTITUENT. In other words, we can say that *the weight-loss program*, *19-stone Timothy Toast* and *an exclusive Miami health spa* are constituents in this sentence. A constituent can then form a close group with another constituent; i.e. two constituents can together form a new constituent. If we look again at the previous example sentence, the constituent *an exclusive Miami health spa* combines with *at*, to form another constituent, *at an exclusive Miami health spa*. So, constituents exist at different levels – a constituent can form a close group with another constituent; i.e. two constituents can together form a new constituent. They are really like linguistic Lego pieces in the way they pattern together to form larger and larger constituent structures. As you will see more clearly in a little while, even the single words of a sentence are themselves constituents.

It is important to note here that a constituent is always a constituent of something. The question 'Is the string *19-stone Timothy Toast* a constituent?' doesn't make sense – it has to be 'Is the string *19-stone Timothy Toast* a constituent of the following sentence?' Look at the following sentences and think about the difference between the two ways of asking this question. (The first is original and the second we have adapted.)

The weight-loss program was unleashed upon 19-stone Timothy Toast.

Because he was 19-stone Timothy Toast had dabbled with a variety of slimming methods.

The string *19-stone Timothy Toast* occurs in both sentences. Intuitively, native speakers of English will judge *19-stone Timothy Toast* to be a constituent in the first sentence, but not in the second. If you don't see this difference, or if you share the intuition, but you want to check it, then we suggest that you come back to this example when you have read the whole chapter. Then you'll be able to apply all the constituency tests we'll be discussing to *19-stone Timothy Toast* in both these sentences.

Constituency tests can be useful to show up sentences that on account of their syntax have multiple meanings, i.e. that show STRUCTURAL AMBIGUITY. For example, a sentence like the following, which is based on the description of food-rejection therapy, is actually ambiguous in two ways because there are two different ways of grouping the italic words together to form a single phrase.

The seven days of extensive food-rejection therapy included *the staff beating the patients with barbecue chicken legs*.

As is often the case with ambiguity, there is one interpretation that's more natural, because of what we know about the world. In this case, it's where the phrase *with barbecue chicken legs* has an instrumental function and is what the staff use to beat the patients with. The second, probably less natural, interpretation is where the phrase *with barbecue chicken legs* modifies the noun *patients;* in other words, the only patients who were beaten were those with barbecue chicken legs. We can use brackets to show the two different ways the words can be grouped:

. . . the staff [[beating the patients] with barbecue chicken legs]
. . . the staff [beating [the patients with barbecue chicken legs]]

In both cases, the *staff beating the patients with barbecue chicken legs* forms a constituent of the sentence, but they differ in the structural position of *with barbecue chicken legs*; in one case it combines with *beating the patients* and in another it combines only with *the patients*.

2.4 Constituency tests

So far we have assigned constituency purely on the basis of intuition. But how can we be so sure that words pattern in this way – other than our gut feelings? In this book, one of our main tasks will be to translate these kinds of intuitions into more formal criteria. So what sort of arguments can we offer that sentences do have this sort of hierarchical structure? We next look at some of the formal arguments which justify these choices. In this case, we will use CONSTITUENCY TESTS, rather than just intuition, to decide whether a particular string is a constituent or not. A constituent is by definition a string of words which functions as a group at some level. All the constituency tests are therefore designed to check whether the string in question can function as a unit. We will start by using four tests:

❑ Substitution
❑ Unit of sense/Sentence fragment

❑ Movement
❑ Coordination

With all these tests, it is important that they are applied only to the string we are interested in, and not to any of the surrounding words. Often, especially if we're dealing with something which isn't a constituent, the result of applying a test will be an ungrammatical sentence. The standard way of indicating that a sentence is ungrammatical is to put an asterisk in front of it. Understandably, native speakers of a language often find it difficult to write down an ungrammatical sentence, and therefore it is very important that you understand exactly how each test works. You should also get used to thinking of grammaticality as different from 'makes sense.' A sentence like *The tall obscurity has drawn a dark green imagination* makes no sense, but formally it is grammatical. *The tall men has drawn a dark green cars*, on the other hand, makes sense, but is not grammatical.

Note, too, that none of these tests is sufficient alone to justify constituent structure. You will find that you have to apply all the tests and then weigh up the evidence to arrive at a decision. When the different tests give contradictory results, you also need to think about the reasons why a particular test has not worked. Some of the tests you may find work better than others – often it depends on the type of constituent, for instance.

Let's continue with Timothy Toast's ordeal at the Miami health spa. Consider the following sentence:

The seven days of extensive food-rejection therapy included *near-drowning in a soup-filled Jacuzzi.*

Assume now we want to know whether or not the string *near-drowning in a soup-filled Jacuzzi* forms a constituent of this sentence. We'll apply the tests one by one and then weigh up the evidence.

Substitution

One thing we can be sure of is that a string of only one word forms a constituent. A word certainly does act as a unit in terms of sentence structure; i.e. in terms of the syntax. This means that if the string we are investigating can be SUBSTITUTED by a single word, then this is an indication that the string is indeed a constituent. When using this test, the meaning of the new sentence is not so important, as long as the structure of the sentence is preserved. Any word that can fill a similar function to the string it replaces can be used here. For example, we can replace *near-drowning in a soup-filled Jacuzzi* with *manipulation* to get the following grammatical sentence:

The seven days of extensive food-rejection therapy included *manipulation.*

There are, however, some words which more naturally replace other constituents and are therefore easy to use. Such words include items like PRONOUNS; for example, *he, her, they* and so on, the word *one* as in *the old ones,* or *wh*-words. So back to our original sentence – we want to know whether the string of words *near-drowning in a soup-filled Jacuzzi* forms a constituent of this sentence or not. If we find we can replace it with a single word like a pronoun, then this string is likely to be a constituent. And indeed we can.

The seven days of extensive food-rejection therapy included *this*.

If you are having trouble finding a single word to substitute for the string in this way, you should try to form what's called an ECHO QUESTION. We talk more about echoes in Chapter 5, but basically they involve echoing a speaker's words in order to ask for a repetition of information – or it might be a case of simply expressing disbelief. We substitute that part of the sentence which we want repeated with a question word like *who, what, which, when, why, where* and so on. These *wh*-question words don't substitute for just any old string – as you will have guessed, the string must form a constituent:

The seven days of extensive food-rejection therapy included *what?!*

Consider a bigger constituent of the same sentence: *included near-drowning in a soup-filled Jacuzzi*. This phrase includes the verb. We will discover how to identify verb phrases in Chapter 3, but for now, let's consider how we can use the replacement test with this kind of constituent. We could, of course, replace it with a word with a different meaning, to give something like:

The seven days of extensive food-rejection therapy *failed*.

However, there is no straightforward pronoun-like test for these verb phrases; there are no clear 'pro-verbs' that can just be fitted into this structure. There is, however, a slightly more complicated substitution test for verbs, the *so do* test. You can think of *so* as a kind of complex proform that can refer back to verb phrases. We cannot just replace the constituent with a form of *so do*; we need to add something that contrasts with the original sentence. It is easier to explain by using an example. We take the original sentence and add *and so did* and then a suitable contrasting phrase, for example:

The seven days of extensive food-rejection therapy included near-drowning in a soup-filled Jacuzzi and *so did* the four-day therapy.

Consider this sentence and think especially about what *so did* refers to. That's right, to *included near-drowning in a soup-filled Jacuzzi*. So, we can say that *so did* substitutes for *included near-drowning in a soup-filled Jacuzzi* and hence we can see this as evidence of this being a constituent.

This test is a very firm one and if a word cannot be found to substitute for the string, then this will most likely genuinely mean that it is not a constituent. As we shall see, not all tests are this helpful.

Unit of sense/sentence fragment

The next test that we shall be using is to see whether the string forms a UNIT OF SENSE. This is not a test based on grammaticality judgements but on semantic judgements. Not only should the string form a unit of sense, its meaning should also be an identifiable part of the meaning of the whole sentence. The test is based on the assumption that something which forms a syntactic unit will also form a semantic unit. For the vast majority of syntactic constituents this is indeed the case. If we now take the string we are examining, we can say that the string of words *near-drowning in a soup-filled Jacuzzi* does indeed form a unit of sense. Furthermore, its meaning contributes straightforwardly to the meaning of the sentence as a whole; we can imagine (or at least try to!) what 'near-drowning in a soup-filled Jacuzzi' entails and we can identify the meaning of that string.

The test which we refer to as the SENTENCE FRAGMENT is similar in function, but more restricted than the unit of sense one. In English we can reply to questions with short sentence fragments as long as these fragments form constituents. What you do then is make a question – answer sequence based on the original sentence, again using one of those *wh*-question words. You can either leave the question word in its place and thus get an echo question, or move it to the front and get a normal *wh*-question (more about how to do a *wh*-question in Chapter 5). You might imagine an exchange something along the lines of the following:

Question: What did you say the food-rejection therapy included? (or The food-rejection therapy included what?!)

Answer: *Near-drowning in a soup-filled Jacuzzi!*

If the string itself forms the answer in this way, then you have confirmation that it is a constituent. It's important here to make sure that the question contains all the material except the string itself – the whole string should be removed, but nothing else should be left out. The answer which results is not so much judged on whether it is grammatical, since it's not a full sentence, but rather the whole question – answer sequence is judged on whether or not it makes sense – though of course the question itself must be grammatical. If a sensible question – answer sequence results, where the string is the answer, then we can be reasonably sure that the string is indeed a constituent of the sentence on which the question is based. However, if something ungrammatical or nonsensical results, then it could be either because the string is not a constituent of the sentence, or because it is too nested to be a reasonable answer to a question. We'll see an example of this a little later.

Movement

Constituents behave distributionally as single units of structure – and as single units they may have the ability to appear in a variety of sentence positions. In short, we can move constituents around in a sentence, but we can't move strings that do not form constituents. It follows then that if a string can be taken out of its place and moved to another part of the sentence, then the string clearly functions as a unit. Hence MOVEMENT makes up another of our constituency tests.

Word order in English isn't as flexible as it is in many other languages. Nonetheless, for a number of constituents, we still have at our disposal a variety of different word order arrangements which we can use for special expressive or communicational ends. In other words, speakers may 'move' items into other positions in order for instance to emphasise crucial parts of their message. We'll look at a variety of movement possibilities here because some of them you may find work better than others – it can depend, for example, on the type of constituent you're trying to move.

One important movement rule is FRONTING. Basically, this is a device whereby we shunt elements to the first position in the sentence for special emphasis or focus. Only constituents can be fronted in this way, but not all constituents, as we shall see. Sometimes when you apply this particular movement test you may produce a sequence that, out of context, sounds a little unnatural or contrived. For this reason, you may find it easier to create a context. Take once again the example of our suspect string. Move it to the front of the sentence, but also contrast it with another bit of information:

Near-drowning in a soup-filled Jacuzzi the seven days of extensive food-rejection therapy included – not daily beatings with barbecued chicken legs!

The result is an acceptable, although admittedly rather theatrical-sounding, sentence.

Sometimes strings can be moved in this way either to the front or to the end of a sentence without anything else changing. But more often than not, movement of one constituent will involve other changes in the sentence. For example, English has another focusing device which is known as CLEFTING. It does more than just shift elements around in a sentence; it actually builds a new structure. As the name suggests, clefting has the effect of 'cleaving' an original sentence into two clauses. Like fronting, it's another test which we can apply to enable us to discover what the constituents of a sentence are.

Here's a clefted version of our original sentence. As you can see, clefts are a way of getting our attention and focusing on what is of special significance (which in this case is the nasty business of drowning in a Jacuzzi filled with soup). As with fronting, the meaning of the sentence doesn't really change, just the emphasis:

It was *near-drowning in a soup-filled Jacuzzi* that the seven days of extensive food-rejection therapy included – not daily beatings with barbecued chicken legs.

The formula for forming a cleft is quite straightforward – *It is/was . . . that . . .* The first gap (indicated by . . .) is the place where the string which we suspect of being a constituent goes, and the second gap is for the rest of the sentence. This involves three basic steps:

(1) You take the suspect string of words (let's call this string X).
(2) You move it into the position where it follows the sequence *It was/is . . .*
(3) The rest of the clause is then introduced by *that/who* following X.

31

There's another kind of cleft we can apply here that focuses by using an introductory *wh*-word followed by either *be* or *do*. What follows the verb is then given extra prominence. For example, the *wh*-cleft version of the previous example sentence would read:

What the seven days of extensive food-rejection therapy included was *near-drowning in a soup-filled Jacuzzi* – not daily beatings with barbecued chicken legs.

We talk more about both these types of clefts in Chapter 9 when we look at what it is that motivates speakers and writers to use these sorts of constructions. It should be pointed out here also that most of the movement tests don't work terribly well if the constituent is deeply nested within the sentence. We will return to this in Section 2.6.

Coordination

English has a number of linking items like *and, but* and *or* which are used to COORDINATE (or to conjoin) sequences of words or phrases. Here are some examples based on our story. In each case *and* has been used to conjoin the pair of italicised expressions:

The weight-loss program was *extreme* and *unsuccessful*.

He was called an *obese* and *wobbly* hippo.

He was ordered *to strip naked* and *to do 100 press-ups*.

He was subjected to a barrage of *subliminal tape recordings* and *food-rejection therapies*.

There are two constraints on coordination, and one of these is of special interest to us here: only those strings that make up constituents can be conjoined; hence, coordination is another test that we can use to determine constituency. The second constraint on coordination is that in general only constituents of the same category can be conjoined in this way, and the resulting string is then also of that category, but this is something we will return to in Chapter 3.

So to apply this test, you try to link a string which you suspect is a constituent with one containing different words (but with what seems to be the same internal structure). For instance: we have suggested that the string *near-drowning in a soup-filled Jacuzzi* is a constituent – try to conjoin it with something similar like *daily beatings with barbecued chicken legs*. And the result is a perfectly grammatical sequence. This was in fact the sentence as it originally occurred in *The Big Issue* piece:

The seven days of extensive food-rejection therapy included *near-drowning in a soup-filled Jacuzzi* and *daily beatings with barbecued chicken legs*.

What we've done here is coordinate *near-drowning in a soup-filled Jacuzzi* with a string of the same category (these are both noun phrases – more about what noun phrases are in Chapters 3 and 7). The result is a larger constituent of the same category: *near-drowning in a soup-filled Jacuzzi and daily beatings with barbecued chicken legs.*

With this particular example we've been fortunate. Every one of our constituency tests so far has yielded the same result – our suspect string *near-drowning in a soup-filled Jacuzzi* looks straightforwardly like a constituent. But, as we'll see towards the end of this chapter, the tests are not always this obliging. It can happen that one or more tests give a different result from the other ones. When this happens, it is important to think why this may be the case.

As a final example, take another sentence from the exploits of our stressed slimmer, Timothy Toast (who at this stage is eating to forget his Miami spa experience). Is the italicised sequence of words a constituent of this sentence?

I've put *on 24 pounds.*

First, can we find a single word which can be used to replace this string? It seems not. This test at least suggests that our string is probably not a constituent of the sentence.

*I've put *there.*

*I've put *what?*

*I've put *where?*

Second, in a question – answer sequence, can our suspect string be used as a short reply; in other words, a sentence fragment? Again, it seems not – our string can't stand alone as a single expression.

Question: What have you put?

Answer: *On 24 pounds.*

Third, is it possible to move our string to any other position in the sentence, either by simple movement (to the front of the sentence, for example) or by building additional structure (as in the cleft test)? Once again our suspicions are confirmed – this string is not a constituent. It doesn't front nicely, nor does it appear in focus position in our cleft.

On 24 pounds I've put.

*It's *on 24 pounds* that I've put.

Last, can we coordinate this string with a similar type of string? As it turns out, when we coordinate a string of the same structure like *on several ounces* an ungrammatical sequence results.

*I've put *on 24 pounds* and *on several ounces.*

It's not looking good for this particular suspect string. All evidence points to it not being a constituent of this sentence. You've probably guessed that in this case *on* actually belongs to the verb *put* – together they form a kind of complex verb that has the meaning 'gain' (or in a different context 'clothe oneself'). Using bracket notation we can show the structure of the sentence in the following way – the brackets here identify the groups of words that make up the constituents of the sentence.

I've [put *on*] [*24 pounds*].

Compare this sentence with one that we've made up for comparison and which (at first blush at least) appears to have a very similar constituent structure. Certainly it contains the same types of words and in the same order – you might expect it to share the same structure:

I've sat *on 24 snails.*

But apply the four constituency tests and you'll find a very different structure. Unlike the previous string, this one passes all the tests: substitution with one word, sentence fragment, movement and coordination. Here are the results:

I've sat *where?!*

Question: Where have you sat?
Answer: *On 24 snails.*

On 24 snails I've sat.

It's *on 24 snails* that I've sat.

I've sat *on 24 snails* and *on 35 cockroaches.*

This string does not share the same grouping of words as the string *on 24 stone* in *I've put on 24 stone.* Here *on* clearly belongs to the phrase *24 snails* and together the sequence *on 24 snails* makes up a constituent of this sentence.

Let's return to a simplified version of our earlier ambiguous sentence and apply each of the tests to uncover more about the different constituent structures for the two interpretations.

The staff beat the patients with barbecue chicken legs.

The more natural interpretation is that the beatings were performed with barbecue chicken legs; we'll refer to this as meaning (a), and we assume its structure is:

(a) The staff [[beat the patients] [with barbecue chicken legs]].

In the second interpretation, which we will refer to as meaning (b), only a subset of the patients were beaten, namely those with barbecue chicken legs. We assume that *the patients with barbecue chicken legs* forms a constituent:

(b) The staff [beat [the patients with barbecue chicken legs]].

If the structures we have assumed for (a) and (b) are correct, the main differences lie in the fact that *beat the patients* is a constituent in meaning (a), but not in meaning (b); in (b) *the patients* combines with *with barbecue chicken legs* before it combines with *beat*. On the other hand, *the patients with barbecue chicken legs* is a constituent only with the (b) meaning; in (a) *the patients* combines with *beat* before it combines with *with barbecue chicken legs*. This means that if we apply the constituency tests to the two strings, we should get different meanings; if applied to *beat the patients*, only meaning (a) and if applied to *patients with barbecue chicken legs*, only meaning (b). Let's try.

Applying constituency tests to *beat the patients:*

Substitution

The staff played with chicken legs.

The staff beat the patients with barbecue chicken legs and the assistants did so with pork chops.

Unit of sense/sentence fragment

Question: What did the staff do with barbecue chicken legs?!

Answer: Beat the patients.

Movement

?It was beat the patients that the staff did with barbecue chicken legs.

What the staff did with chicken legs was beat the patients. (The *wh*-clefts sound far better when verb phrases are involved.)

Coordination

The staff beat the patients and whacked the visitors with barbecue chicken legs.

In all these sentences, the only meaning present in the sentences is meaning (a); the staff are using barbecue chicken legs to beat patients. We can conclude that our assumed structure for the (a) meaning was correct.

Applying constituency tests to *the patients with barbecue chicken legs:*

Substitution

The staff beat them.

The staff beat who?!

Unit of sense/sentence fragment

Question: Who did the staff beat?

Answer: The patients with barbecue chicken legs.

Movement

It was the patients with the barbecue chicken legs that the staff beat.

Coordination

The staff beat the patients with barbecue chicken wings and those with pork chops.

For these sentences, only the meaning in which the patients have the barbecue chicken legs is available; that is, meaning (b).

What we have done here, apart from put you off eating barbecue chicken legs, is to show that the ambiguity in the original sentence is structural in nature; the constituency differs between the two interpretations. Not all ambiguities are structural as we shall see in Chapter 4.

2.5 Three additional tests

We now introduce three more tests which can also be used to discover the constituent structure of sentences. As you'll see, however, these tests are not always reliable and need to be applied with caution.

Reduction

REDUCTION is similar to our earlier test of substitution in that we will try to replace the suspect string with one word. The difference is that here we will try to use one of the words of the string, i.e. we attempt to reduce the string to one of its own words. When this test yields a grammatical sentence, it is an indication that the string is indeed a constituent.

The seven days of extensive food-rejection therapy included *near-drowning*.

This is an indication that the string *near-drowning in a soup-filled Jacuzzi* forms a constituent of the sentence.

However, there is a danger with this test. When an ungrammatical sentence results, this could indeed be because the string isn't a constituent. But it could also be because more than one part of the sentence is obligatory. We'll see an example of this later. Furthermore, this test does not really add anything to the substitution test and we include it here only because many other textbooks use it. We wouldn't want you to think that we hadn't heard of it.

Omission

Under special circumstances, material can be OMITTED from a sentence – we'll be looking at this more closely in Chapters 9 and 10. But we can't just randomly omit any sequence of words; only sequences of words that make up a constituent can be omitted. Therefore, if we can delete the whole string from the sentence, leaving behind a complete grammatical sentence, this is evidence that the string does form a constituent.

Just as with reduction, however, we need to proceed with caution here; if the string cannot be omitted, this could be because one or more parts of the string is obligatory. In the case of our sample sentence, there is strong evidence to suggest that the suspect string is indeed a constituent; yet if we omit it, the result is an ungrammatical sentence.

*The seven days of extensive food-rejection therapy included.

The ungrammaticality here arises from the fact that the verb *include* is a verb which actually requires a following phrase for it to be grammatical; in other words, our suspect string here happens to be an obligatory constituent of this sentence.

So this is another test where a grammatical sentence is evidence for constituent status, but where an ungrammatical sentence does not necessarily mean that the string is not a constituent.

Intrusion

English has an abundance of phrases like *between you and me*, a sort of 'aside' which can be added to provide some kind of comment on the sentence. But it turns out they can't be inserted just anywhere in the sentence – only at the boundaries of constituents. Let's return to our sample sentence and see just where we can insert an expression like *between you and me*:

The seven days of extensive food-rejection therapy, *between you and me*, included near-drowning in a soup-filled Jacuzzi.

The seven days of extensive food-rejection therapy included, *between you and me*, near-drowning in a soup-filled Jacuzzi.

This is a useful test for identifying the major constituents of a sentence. But it's not helpful for identifying the smaller constituents that make up these larger ones. For example, the test cannot reveal the constituent structure inside the phrase *the seven days of extensive food-rejection therapy*. If you try to insert material anywhere inside this phrase an unacceptable sentence results. For example:

*The seven days, *between you and me*, of extensive food-rejection therapy included near-drowning in a soup-filled Jacuzzi.

2.6 Nested constituents

As we've been hinting all along, it is possible for constituents to be made up of smaller constituents. And we can use our constituency tests to check for this. Consider the following sentence example; in particular, the italicised string:

An ultimately unsuccessful weight-loss program was unleashed upon a shell-shocked Mr Toast.

There is no doubt that this string forms a constituent of this sentence. It passes with flying colours each of our main constituent tests:

Substitution

It was unleashed upon a shell-shocked Mr Toast.

What was unleashed upon a shell-shocked Mr Toast?

Unit of sense/sentence fragment

Question: What was unleashed upon a shell-shocked Mr Toast?

Answer: *An ultimately unsuccessful weight-loss program.*

Movement

Unleashed upon a shell-shocked Mr Toast was *an ultimately unsuccessful weight-loss program.*

It was *an ultimately unsuccessful weight-loss program* that was unleashed upon a shell-shocked Mr Toast.

Coordination

An ultimately unsuccessful weight-loss program and *an extremely unwelcome food-rejection therapy* were unleashed upon a shell-shocked Mr Toast.

But there is also the question of the internal structure of this phrase *an ultimately unsuccessful weight-loss program.* How should we divide this string up? Let's test, for example, whether or not *unsuccessful weight-loss program* is a natural grouping, without *ultimately*, and therefore a constituent within our string. Remember in all these tests we must apply it only to the string and nothing else.

Substitution

*An ultimately *what* was unleashed upon a shell-shocked Mr Toast?

*An ultimately *therapy* was unleashed upon a shell-shocked Mr Toast.

Sentence fragment

Question: An ultimately *what* was unleashed upon a shell-shocked Mr Toast?!

Answer: *Unsuccessful weight-loss program.*

Movement

*It was *unsuccessful weight-loss program* that an ultimately was unleashed upon a shell-shocked Mr Toast.

Coordination

An ultimately *unsuccessful weight-loss program* and *disastrous food-rejection therapy* was unleashed upon a shell-shocked Mr Toast.

In the last test, if the coordination here really is of only *unsuccessful weight-loss program*, then *ultimately* must apply also to *disastrous food-rejection therapy*. Whether or not this is the case is quite a subtle judgement. We may just interpret this as a coordination of *ultimately unsuccessful weight-loss program* and *disastrous food-rejection therapy*, in which case we have not said anything about the constituent structure of *unsuccessful weight-loss program* without *ultimately*.

As you can see, the tests won't always work as straightforwardly as they did for the structure of *an ultimately unsuccessful weight-loss program*. In this case the first three – substitution with a pronoun, sentence fragment and movement – yielded ungrammatical structures and suggested our grouping was incorrect. The fourth test suggested our string may be a natural unit of the sentence. Before we weigh up the evidence, let's apply the last three tests we looked at.

Reduction

*An ultimately *unsuccessful* was unleashed upon a shell-shocked Mr Toast.

*An ultimately *weight-loss* was unleashed upon a shell-shocked Mr Toast.

*An ultimately *program* was unleashed upon a shell-shocked Mr Toast.

Again, when the test gives only ungrammatical sentences we can't really tell whether this truly is because the string doesn't form a constituent or because more than one part is obligatory.

Omission

*An ultimately was unleashed upon a shell-shocked Mr Toast.

What we've got is another ungrammatical sentence. But remember, just as with reduction, we need to tread cautiously here; if the string can't be omitted, it could be because one or more parts of the string is obligatory. It doesn't necessarily signal that it's not a constituent.

Intrusion

*An ultimately, *between you and me*, unsuccessful weight-loss program was unleashed upon a shell-shocked Mr Toast.

Like movement, this test isn't terribly useful here since the ungrammaticality could be either because it isn't a constituent *or* because the constituent is too far down in the structure for this test to be useful.

If we now sum up our results for the constituent status of *unsuccessful weight-loss program*, we get the following. We use an asterisk * here to indicate that an ungrammatical sentence results and a √ to show that we got a grammatical sentence.

Substitution	An ultimately *what* was unleashed upon a shell-shocked Mr Toast	*
Sentence fragment	*Unsuccessful weight-loss program*	*
Movement	It was *unsuccessful weight-loss program* that an ultimately was unleashed upon a shell-shocked Mr Toast	*
Coordination	An ultimately *unsuccessful weight-loss program* and disastrous food-rejection therapy was unleashed upon a shell-shocked Mr Toast	√
Intrusion	An ultimately, almost certainly, *unsuccessful weight-loss program* was unleashed upon a shell-shocked Mr Toast	*
Reduction	An ultimately *unsuccessful* was unleashed upon a shell-shocked Mr Toast	*
Omission	An ultimately was unleashed upon a shell-shocked Mr Toast	*

Unsuccessful weight-loss program would then appear not to be a constituent of *An ultimately unsuccessful weight-loss program was unleashed upon a shell-shocked Mr Toast.* The only test to yield a positive result was coordination.

It is, in fact, quite common to find that one test (or more) gives a different result from the other ones. As we mentioned earlier, when this happens, it is important to think about why this may be the case. For both reduction and omission, we saw that problems could arise if obligatory parts were involved. We have also seen that there are certain constituents to which movement does not apply – for example, constituents which are deeply nested within the kind of phrase that is built around a noun. Intrusion is also unhelpful when we are testing for intermediate structure.

Another way of dealing with a string for which the tests give a mixed result is to try an alternative constituent structure. Let's again use *unsuccessful weight-loss program* as an example here; since it is clearly not a constituent, at least one of its parts must belong to a different constituent. The obvious alternative is that *unsuccessful* forms a constituent with *ultimately* at this level. We can then try the alternative, and we get the following result:

An *ultimately unsuccessful* weight-loss program was unleashed upon a shell-shocked Mr Toast.

Substitution	A *disastrous* weight-loss program was unleashed upon a shell-shocked Mr Toast	√
Sentence fragment	*Ultimately unsuccessful*	√
Movement	It was *ultimately unsuccessful* that a weight-loss program was unleashed upon a shell-shocked Mr Toast	*
Coordination	An *ultimately unsuccessful* and *extremely unwelcome* weight-loss program was unleashed upon a shell-shocked Mr Toast	√
Intrusion	An *ultimately unsuccessful*, between you and me, weight-loss program was unleashed upon a shell-shocked Mr Toast	?
Reduction	An *unsuccessful* weight-loss program was unleashed upon a shell-shocked Mr Toast	√
Omission	A weight-loss program was unleashed upon a shell-shocked Mr Toast	√

The judgements here make it quite clear that *ultimately unsuccessful* is a constituent of the sentence. The only tests here that didn't yield grammatical strings were movement and possibly intrusion; in other words, tests that we know do not always work for constituents nested deep within the sentence. This means that *unsuccessful weight-loss program* cannot be a constituent. This is because the string *ultimately unsuccessful* does form a constituent. On the other hand, *ultimately unsuccessful* can and does form a constituent with *weight-loss program*. We return to the internal structure of larger constituents in later chapters, in particular Chapters 3 and 6.

2.7 Representing structure

As long as we're dealing with small constituents like *an ultimately unsuccessful weight-loss program*, it's quite easy to describe the structure in words. If, however, we are wanting to discuss the constituent structure of the whole example sentence, then we need a neater way than ordinary language: *weight-loss* and *program* go together to form a constituent *weight-loss program*, *ultimately unsuccessful* go together and in turn form a constituent with *weight-loss program* which in turn . . . This way of describing the constituent structure of a whole sentence quickly becomes cumbersome and non-transparent. Instead, there are a number of more formal ways of expressing constituent structure. One that you may have come across at school is underlining. Since it becomes very cumbersome when more complex structures are involved, underlining is not really used in linguistics.

The two common ways of indicating constituent structures are BRACKETS, which we have used already, and TREES. One of the structures we have discussed earlier looks like this when brackets are used to indicate its structure:

[An [[ultimately unsuccessful] [weight-loss program]]] was unleashed upon a shell-shocked Mr Toast.

Brackets become pretty unwieldy when we deal with more complex structures and the main reason they are still used is that when you use a word processor it is more of an effort to draw a tree than to add brackets.

The trees used to show constituent structure are also known as PHRASE MARKERS. When you start out, trees may also look a bit unfamiliar and frightening. However, once you get used to them, they really do give a good overview of the structure. The trees for the sub-structures we have established here look like this:

(1)

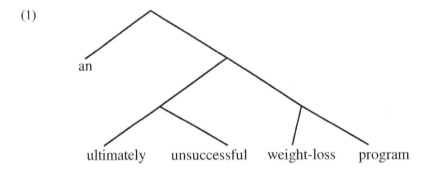

Since trees will be the normal way of indicating structure in this book, we will have a little more to say about them here. First of all some terminology: we use the term BRANCH in an obvious way to refer to the lines. The point at which two or more lines come together is called a NODE. In the following example, we have circled and numbered all the nodes:

(2)

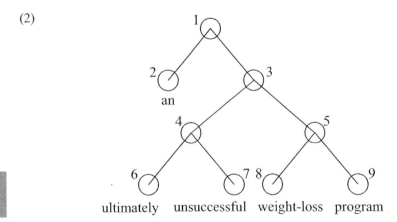

A node represents a constituent. In order for a string to be a constituent in a tree, there must be one node which is associated with that string and with no other words. In this example, the whole string *an ultimately unsuccessful weight-loss program* is a constituent because there is a node, node 1, which represents that string and nothing else. On the other hand, *unsuccessful weight-loss program* is not a constituent, since the only node that covers this whole string, i.e. node 3, also covers *ultimately*. *Ultimately unsuccessful* is a constituent since node 4 covers this string and nothing else.

Two nodes which are separated by just one branch are said to have a special relationship, where the higher node is the MOTHER and the lower one is the DAUGHTER. In this little tree, node 1 is the mother of nodes 2 and 3, nodes 4 and 5 are the daughters of node 3, etc. There are five nodes which do not have any daughters, namely 2, 6, 7, 8 and 9. These are called TERMINAL NODES. The node which is at the top of a tree with no mother above it, like 1, is usually called the ROOT NODE.

In the chapters to follow, when we will also want to assign each constituent to a particular category and indicate the category of each constituent in the representation, we will see further advantages of using tree structures. In Chapter 3, we will put a label on each node and in this way name the constituents represented by that node.

2.8 Points to remember

❑ Morphology can be defined as the study of how words are built up from morphemes. Morphemes are the smallest units of meaning in the structure of a language; together morphemes can build up bigger words.

❑ Some morphemes can function as words on their own. These are called free morphemes. Others can only occur with some other morpheme. These are called bound morphemes.

❑ Bound morphemes are generally affixes; when they precede the stem they are called prefixes, and when they follow the stem, suffixes.

❑ A bound morpheme that is positioned with respect to a phrase is called a clitic.

❑ There are two types of word-building, namely, inflection and derivation.

❑ Inflection involves combining a free form with an inflectional affix, chosen from a small set of affixes (all suffixes in English). These don't form new words but have a purely grammatical meaning.

❑ Derivation involves creating new meanings, for example by adding a derivational affix. The set of derivational affixes is much larger than that of inflectional affixes and they can be either prefixes or suffixes.

❑ New words can also be formed by conversion (by changing one word class to another without anything being added) and compounding (involving the combination of two (occasionally more) free-standing forms).

❑ Syntax can be defined as the study of the structure of sentences.

❑ There is a definite hierarchy of structural units in an English sentence, ranging from the largest unit (which is the sentence) down to the level of the word. These structural units are called constituents.

- Constituents, then, are strings of words which function as a group at some level; they work like linguistic building blocks that combine to make larger and larger constituents.
- As speakers of a language we intuitively know that some words in a sentence are linked more closely than others. The arguments we use to translate these intuitions into more formal criteria are known as constituency tests. The most important constituency tests are substitution, unit of sense/sentence fragment, movement and coordination.
- It is not uncommon to get contradictory results when applying the constituency tests and in these cases it is important first of all to think about why a particular test gives a different result. Also, one can test for an alternative arrangement to see if that gives a more unambiguous result.
- We can represent constituent structure using brackets to show the groupings of words. However, the more usual way is by using tree diagrams.

Exercises

1. Identifying morphemes

The following piece is taken from 'Here Comes the Son,' a review of the 2009 film about John Lennon (N#803:48). Divide each word that has internal structure into morphemes and indicate whether each morpheme is free or bound. If bound, state whether derivational or inflectional. Are there any grammatical free morphemes? Discuss any problems which you encountered in your analysis.

> But here we have **Nowhere Boy**, a new biopic of John Lennon, and the surprise is that it's rather fresh and watchable. Director Sam Taylor Wood avoids the Beatles clichés by focusing on John's early years, before he left for Hamburg with Paul and George, and long before he became more famous than Jesus.

2. Determining constituents

If, by using the tests for constituency, we can establish that *extremely silly* is a constituent in the sentence *He always tells extremely silly jokes*, does this mean that *extremely silly jokes* cannot be a constituent of the same sentence? How about *silly jokes* in the same sentence, can that be a constituent of that sentence if *extremely silly* is?

3. Determining constituents

Decide whether or not the bracketed sequence of words in each of the following sentences is a constituent of that sentence. Remember that some tests will work better than others depending on the nature of the string. If the result is ambiguous, test an alternative constituent to see if that gives a clearer result.

(a) The Telegraph called [David Beckham's new beard] the most memorable part of England's 3–0 win over Belarus.

(b) Giggs scored a truly [sublime goal].

(c) Alf Ramsey gave [Colin Bell his England debut] against Sweden at Wembley in May 1968.

(d) The objective is to hit [the goal keeper with the ball].

4. Constituency

The following pairs of sentences are superficially similar in structure. In fact they have quite different constituent structures. Use two constituency tests to uncover the differences. (In each case the (1) versions are the original.)

(a) (1) Mrs Birpitz accidentally bit off her husband's nose. (AUS#51:39)

    (2) Mrs Birpitz accidentally fell off her husband's ladder.

(b) (1) She brings in the garbage cans every week. (AUS#65:29)

    (2) She sits in the garbage cans every week.

(c) (1) You've met someone gorgeous. (AUS#51:38–39)

    (2) You've made someone gorgeous.

Now draw a tree for each of the sentences.

5. Constituency and morphological category

Apply the constituency tests to the sentence in (a), and use any method to indicate the structure.

(a) The cat will eat the tuna.

How does your analysis carry over to the example in (b)?

(b) The cat'll eat the tuna.

The words of English

3.1 Introduction

In any language, words can be divided into WORD CLASSES, or SYNTACTIC CATEGO-
RIES. This division only makes sense if there are sets of words which behave
similarly in some ways – for instance, they can take the same inflections
(look back at 'Building words – inflection versus derivation' in Section 2.2
if you need to remind yourself) and they can occur in the same positions
in phrases. So, again, the division and the terminology which it inevitably
involves are not there for their own sake; they are there because they reflect
the way in which the language organises itself, or maybe more correctly, how
speakers organise the language. As a consequence, if a language is organised
in such a way that, for instance, words which mean the same as the adjectives of English and words that mean the same as the verbs of English do not
behave differently in any way, then for that language, there is no reason to
distinguish between two syntactic categories 'verbs' and 'adjectives.'

In this chapter we look more closely at the way in which words are
grouped into their various categories in English and we provide an overview of each of these categories and how they form phrases. Most of the
examples in this chapter are taken or adapted from Simon Stuart's 'Uncensored Cardboard' (*The Big Issue* AUS#51:23), which discusses the TV hit
South Park (this animated sitcom was a fairly recent hit when we first published this book and has since grown into something of an institution).

3.2 The meaning of lexical categories

We distinguish eight categories for English: VERBS (including AUXILIARIES),
NOUNS (including PRONOUNS), ADJECTIVES, ADVERBS, PREPOSITIONS, DETERMINERS, CON-
JUNCTIONS and INTERJECTIONS. There is a fair amount of agreement on which
word classes (or parts of speech) should be recognised for English, but there
is some disagreement as to the exact relation between classes. Interjections
include items like *phwoar!*, *yuck!* and *shhh!*, and are quite peripheral to the
language. We won't pay much attention to them here.

At some stage in your life you probably have come across definitions like
the following:

❏ a noun is the name of a person, place or thing;
❏ a verb is a doing word;
❏ an adjective is a describing word.

These traditional semantic definitions are based on meaning, and simple examples will illustrate just how inadequate these sorts of notional descriptions are. Compare the strings *my love of linguistics* and *I love linguistics*. Both instances of *love* express the same emotion of 'fondness, deep attachment'; yet one is a noun (although not a person, place or physical thing) and one is a verb (although not an action). Clearly, semantics is not a lot of help here. In fact, what makes a noun a noun and a verb a verb is not their meaning – other aspects of their behaviour are more telling. Therefore in this chapter, we will use criteria based on structural properties rather than meaning to distinguish categories.

To illustrate this point, consider the following piece and then try to answer the questions:

They gulched and guttled. Mephitically alliaceous ventripotent fop-doodles and gotchy slubberdegullions, she mussitated. She fibulated, piddling moliminously at the jejune and unsaporous grots tofore her. Fackins! Pabulous comessations were an ephialtes for the deipnetic. It was a niminy gulosity, she wiste it, but they begat swilk an increment in her recrement, a cupidity that was ineluctable – it was the flurch of postjentacular flampoints and licious lozens. Thilke trogalions she yissed avidulously. She could but gorm esuriently at the ashet. She fimbled her falbala aganacticiously.

1 What type of fopdoodles are they?
2 How did she yiss?
3 What did she fimble?

As you can see, this piece is full of inordinately long and unusual words, most of which will be unfamiliar to you, but all of which are words of the English language. Yet you could probably make quite a lot of sense of the structure of the story. (You probably reacted much like Alice did to the poem 'Jabberwocky' – 'Somehow it seems to fill my head with ideas – only I don't exactly know what they are!') What we've done here is make up a story where all the lexical words are obsolete or archaic. All the grammatical morphemes, except three, are perfectly good Modern English. The result: syntactically well-formed sentences which you can break down into their various categories. This is why you could make sense of the structure of the text, even though you didn't have a clue what these words meant. Obviously, then, it wasn't meaning that was guiding you. When you answered the previous questions, you were relying on grammatical cues, not semantic ones.

3.3 Structural criteria

We can classify all these items on the basis of their grammatical behaviour – in particular, two aspects of their grammatical behaviour: their shape (i.e. their morphology) and their position in the sentence (i.e. their syntax). Let's start with MORPHOLOGICAL BEHAVIOUR. Words of the same class will typically show the same morphological possibilities; in other words, they'll take the same sort of affixes. You may not know what *gulched* means, but the -*ed* ending here suggests we're dealing with a verb. As a verb, *gulch* (meaning 'to swallow greedily') takes a characteristic range of grammatical endings (or inflections): *gulch*; *gulches*; *gulched*; *gulching*. Other categories don't take these endings. As we've seen, English doesn't have much in the way of inflections, but English is rich in a range of the other types of affixes – derivational affixes. For example, by adding -*er* to *gulch* we can turn it into a noun, i.e. *gulcher* 'someone who gulches.' Or take the word *gotchy* (meaning 'full, bloated'). It looks like an adjective; the -*y* ending typically derives adjectives from nouns: *gotch* → *gotchy* (*gotch* being defined in the *Oxford English Dictionary* as 'a big-bellied earthenware pot or jug'). Like many other adjectives, it will take two inflections: *gotchier* and *gotchiest*. We can also turn it into an adverb with the derivational -*ly* ending and a noun with -*ness*: *gotchily*, 'in a gotchy fashion,' and *gotchiness*, 'the condition of being gotchy.'

Equally important is a second criterion, namely, the SYNTACTIC BEHAVIOUR of words. By this we mean where words position themselves in a sentence and the sorts of things they can combine with. Words of the same class (like *food, dinner, pastries, flampoint, slubberdegullions* and *flurch*) will fill the same basic slots in the recurrent patterns of a language. Consider the distribution of words in the following sentences:

1	2	3	4	5	6	7	8	9	10	11
a	tall	waiter	served	the	portly	man	at	a	nearby	table
the	nearby	table	devoured	those	delicious	pastries	in	that	famous	restaurant
the	gotchy	gulcher	guttled	those	gustful	grots	near	the	licious	lozens

Words that share inflectional possibilities in English also appear to be able to fill the same slots in sentences and other phrases. We can, then, say with some confidence that categories such as nouns or verbs have not been invented by linguists. It is in fact the language itself which organises words into categories. The speakers of the language can be said to recognise these categories, albeit subconsciously. Linguists are then responsible only for naming these categories, not for having 'invented' them.

In the preceding chapter we established that words form structural units or constituents with each other. These are PHRASES, groups of words which have some sort of grammatical relationship with one another. For example, if you look at the previous table again, the strings of words in columns 1, 2, 3, in 5, 6, 7 and in 9, 10, 11 all seem to form natural units that also show the same distributional possibilities. These phrases are always named after the word which is the most important in the string. This word is called the HEAD. It's really the core of the phrase. All of the five major word classes of nouns, verbs, adjectives, adverbs and prepositions have corresponding PHRASAL CATEGORIES, namely, noun phrases, verb phrases, adjective phrases, adverb phrases and preposition phrases. To contrast with the phrasal categories, we describe the one-word categories as LEXICAL CATEGORIES. ('Lexical,' then, is used in two ways. As we saw in Chapter 2, it is contrasted with functional or grammatical. Here, on the other hand, it is contrasted with phrasal. In both uses 'lexical' is the most common term, and we shall stick with this. There is usually little potential for confusion.) So we can say, for example, that there is a lexical category 'noun' and a corresponding phrasal category 'noun phrase'; a lexical category 'verb' and a corresponding phrasal category 'verb phrase,' and so on. For convenience, these phrasal categories are usually abbreviated in the following way:

noun phrase	NP
verb phrase	VP
adjective phrase	AP
adverb phrase	AdvP
preposition phrase	PP

In summary, we will be using MORPHOLOGICAL (relating to the form of words) and SYNTACTIC (relating to distribution) criteria to help us establish category membership. For each category, we also give a very brief semantic characterisation, but do keep in mind that this can never be used to uniquely distinguish the members of that category.

Just before we tackle each of the lexical categories, we need to make two final points. The first is that not all the members of a class will necessarily have all the identifying properties. Membership of a particular class is really a matter of degree. In this regard, grammar is not so different from the real world. There are prototypical sports like 'football' and not so sporty sports like 'darts.' There are exemplary mammals like 'dogs' and freakish ones like the 'platypus.' Similarly, there are good examples of verbs like *watch* and lousy examples like *beware*; exemplary nouns like *chair* that display all the features of a typical noun and some not so good ones like *Kenny*. Many linguistic categories you will find have fuzzy edges. We will, however, be giving some useful strategies for coping with this sort of fuzziness.

The second point is that some words belong to more than one class. Have a look at the word in italics in the following two sentences:

Now 35 dedicated artists *work* on the program. (verb)

The whole thing's the *work* of two self-confessed drug-addled loons. (noun)

In the first sentence, *work* can be substituted by *sing* or *perform*. In the second sentence, on the other hand, if you substituted *work* with these words you would get ungrammaticalities like *the whole thing is the sing/perform of two self-confessed drug-addled loons*. In this case we would do better by substituting the words *idea* or *creation*. Here the two words are closely related semantically, but there are also accidental ambiguities, e.g. *saw*, either a tool or past tense of *see*. In these two example sentences, the linguistic context made clear which *work* was a verb and which was a noun. As the following headline shows though, if you remove the grammatical cues it is not always easy to decide on the category of a word:

Fur Flies on the Catwalk (SCO#113:3)

Crash blossoms

In their effort for conciseness (also at times as a deliberate attention seeking device), journalists often leave out the grammatical words from their headlines and the result can be ambiguity. These ambiguous headlines now have a linguistic label – 'crash blossoms.' This rather curious name first appeared in the Testy Copy Editors discussion group (August 2009), and was the brainchild of Danny Bloom. He based it on the headline *Violinist Linked to JAL Crash Blossoms.*

For a treasure trove of crash blossoms, we recommend you visit the various posts on 'Language Log'; http://languagelog.ldc.upenn.edu/nll/, where you'll find gems of ambiguity such as:

Truck leads police to molest suspect.

Giant Waves Down Queen Mary's Funnel

MacArthur Flies Back to Front

Eighth Army Push Bottles Up Germans

Squad Helps Dog Bite Victim

And many more . . .

When you have finished this chapter, you might want to go back and try to determine which words are causing the ambiguity here, and which lexical categories are involved.

3.4 Major categories

English lexical categories fall into two main groups: MAJOR and MINOR. Major classes comprise nouns, verbs, adjectives and adverbs. These classes are very large and most importantly they are open, meaning that they have an ever-changing membership. As the vocabulary needs of the society change, so new members can be incorporated. Members of the major classes are lexical in the sense that they are more contentful than the functional categories. Minor classes, on the other hand, consist of words with grammatical rather than lexical meaning and we will return to these in Section 3.5.

Nouns

Semantic characterisation

Typically nouns refer to objects (both physical objects and abstractions) and people.

Morphological features

Some properties which are associated with nouns are NUMBER, GENDER and CASE. For English these are not marked to the same extent that they used to be. Old English was highly inflecting with a very elaborate system of suffixes, but only traces of this system survive today. English has now completely lost the earlier system of grammatical gender – it seems curious to us now that we once had such things as masculine *feet*, feminine *hands* and neuter *eyes*, but the fact that English no longer classifies nouns in this way actually makes it very different from its Germanic relatives (more on this feature in Section 3.4). It's really only number and, to a very limited extent, case that continue to be marked by morphological means on nouns other than pronouns.

It is very common for language to distinguish nouns by number, and most English nouns express number obligatorily in their morphology. The singular is unmarked (i.e. coincides with the noun stem), while the plural is expressed by a suffix *-(e)s*. There are some irregularities in number marking, however; some nouns change their stem vowel (*man–men, louse–lice*), others add the suffix *-en* (*ox–oxen*), one even does both (*brother – brethren*, as in 'member of a religious society') and still others have identical singular and plural forms (*sheep, fish*). Plural variations like these are in fact an inherited feature from Germanic. The history of English has seen the spread of one particular suffix at the expense of all others – and that is of course *-(e)s*.

Occasionally you find nouns whose grammatical number is at odds with their meaning. For example, there are nouns like *trousers* and *knickers* that are grammatically plural but they refer to singular objects. We know that these nouns are plural grammatically, because they must be used with a plural verb, so it is *the trousers are too long* rather than **the trousers is too long* even when it refers to just one piece of clothing. Nouns of this particular group (and they include tools like *scissors* and *pliers* as well) are made up of two parts and can perhaps be thought of as notionally plural. Then again, nouns like *bikini* denote two separate objects, but they are singular nouns; *the bikini is yellow* rather than **the bikini are yellow*. Another group of nouns includes words like *news* and *linguistics* – these end with the *-s* typical of plural marking but are in fact singular. Conversely, others like *cattle* and *people* look singular but behave grammatically as if they were plural. A handful of nouns do not inflect for number at all, e.g. *rice* has no plural partner. Others are plural but have no singular partner. You find *dregs* in the teacup, or *greens* on the plate, but you won't find a single *dreg* or a *green* (although you might perhaps refer to an individual as *a bit of a dreg!*). Some of these irregularities we can account for by assuming different subtypes of nouns and we discuss these later. Others are simply exceptional.

Case involves grammatical markers (or inflections) which signal the relationship of nouns to each other and to the verb; in other words, they signal who is doing what and to whom. English doesn't really have much in the way of case any more, although relics are preserved in the pronoun system (see later). We now mark this sort of information via word order or with prepositions. There is one kind of morphological marking which is sometimes referred to as case, namely the possessive 's. We really don't think it makes sense to refer to this as case, but the fact remains that this is quite a convenient way of spotting a noun, because all nouns in English can occur on their own with the possessive 's (though for some, an alternative with an *of*-phrase is preferred). It codes quite a grab-bag of different relations between two nouns, including of course possession. For example, *the boy's photo* can be interpreted in a number of different ways: 'the photo of the boy,' 'the photo the boy owns,' 'the photo the boy took,' and so on. We don't think of it as a case marker, though, because, as we saw in Chapter 2, rather than attach to the main noun only, 's can now actually attach to the right edge of the noun phrase, which may be much larger than just the noun, e.g. we say *the boy's photo* but also *the boy in the corner's photo*, and not **the boy's in the corner photo*. In spoken English you can occasionally encounter extraordinary examples like the following: *this guy who I used to know at school and who went to Cambridge and got a first in engineering's brother* (and many thanks to J.C. Smith for this gem!).

As far as derivational morphology goes, the most frequent noun-forming suffixes are the *-ness* and *-ity* (adjective → noun) and *-er, -ee, -ation, -ment* (verb → noun).

Syntactic behaviour

The most striking syntactic property of a noun is that it can combine with *the* to form a complete phrase. For example, we know that *leaflet* and *unemployment* are nouns because *the leaflet* and *the unemployment* are complete phrases. Later in this chapter we will return to the issue of how words form bigger phrases. For the time being we can just say that we know *the leaflet* and *the unemployment* are full phrases because they can combine with a verb to form a full sentence. Full phrases built up around nouns will be referred to as noun phrases and Chapter 7 deals with these.

The leaflet arrived.

The unemployment rose.

In Chapter 4 we will learn to put this more succinctly: *the leaflet* and *the unemployment* are full phrases because they can occur as subjects. We should also point out that some nouns can function as subjects on their own, but we will return to this matter.

Sub-classes of nouns

One of the distinctions relevant to the grammatical behaviour of nouns is that between COMMON and PROPER NOUNS. As the name implies, common nouns are the most typical nouns, like *word, school, fascination* or *magic*. A common noun can always form a phrase with *the*. Proper nouns are names of things like persons, places and organisations. English is nice in that proper nouns are the only nouns that are always spelled with a capital. Many proper nouns would not be listed in a dictionary, e.g. *Kenny* and *South Park*, but some would, e.g. *Monday, Christmas* and *Scotland*. In normal use, proper nouns lack the possibility of modification. Generally speaking, they can't be made plural either. It is possible, though, for proper nouns to lose their capital letter and come into the language as ordinary words. This process gives rise to a surprising number of new words. For example, trade names have given us *biro, playdough, velcro* and *gunk*, to name just a few. Place names can also become common nouns. For example, the word *jeans* has its origin in the town of Genoa, where a type of heavy cotton fabric (resembling denim) was once made; *denim* itself derives from Nîmes, the name of a city in southern France (originally *serge de Nîmes* 'serge (cloth) of Nîmes'). When personal names convert to ordinary nouns, their behaviour is no different from that of other common nouns (e.g. *cardigans* and *sandwiches* from the Earls of Cardigan and Sandwich). It is also possible to do a more spontaneous reanalysis of proper nouns as common nouns, as in *all the Andrews that I know like chess*. This shouldn't really be taken as a sign that proper nouns admit the same modification as common nouns. Instead it shows that proper nouns can be used as common nouns under specific circumstances.

Common nouns can be further subdivided into COUNT or NON-COUNT (or MASS). Count nouns like *word* and *school* can be interpreted as individuated entities and therefore can be counted. They can occur with the indefinite article *a/an* and cardinal numbers; they can also be pluralised. Non-count nouns, on the other hand, like *rice* and *bread*, are interpreted as indivisible masses of material. If we want to talk about one or more individual units we have to resort to expressions like *a grain of rice/a loaf of bread*. Non-count nouns are therefore usually treated as singular and are therefore incompatible with expressions like *a, many, those, three*, e.g. **a bread; *two breads*. You might be wondering about special uses like *This shop has a wide range of breads*. In this case someone would be referring to the type or class of bread. It is quite common that non-count nouns can be used as count nouns, but that they then acquire a narrower meaning; *beer* is any old beer, but *a beer* is either a glass of beer or a kind of beer.

Languages do not necessarily see eye to eye as to whether nouns are individuated entities or groups of unindividuated entities. What is a count noun in one language may be a mass noun in another and vice versa (e.g. the English noun *furniture* is mass, but the Swedish equivalent *möbler* is a plural form of the count noun *möbel*). There can be significant differences between English dialects too. For example, in Australian English, *lettuce* is both a count and mass noun (e.g. *I'd like two lettuces, please* versus *I like lettuce*). For some speakers of American and British English, *lettuce* is only a mass noun (e.g. *I'd like two heads of lettuce, please* versus *I like lettuce*). As we'll see in Chapter 11, the Englishes around the world can differ strikingly in this feature.

Further evidence that number is a question not just of form, but that semantics also plays a role is provided by a class of nouns which have both a plural and a singular form, but where the singular form can also occur with plural agreement. Examples of such words are *government* and *team*. Both have clear morphological plural forms which always take plural agreement: *these committees are/*is a waste of time* and *the two teams have/*has met twice*. However, even their singular forms can occur with plural verbs. These nouns are usually referred to as COLLECTIVE NOUNS. They represent groups; a committee consists of a number of members and a team consists of a number of players, so that there are two ways of thinking of the entities referred to by the nouns: either as one single group or as a number of individuals. Depending on how they are viewed, the agreement can vary, as in the following examples, taken from the web, which both comment on Birmingham City's performance:

Other than Aston Villa, Birmingham has been the team I've been most impressed with this season.

The team are now 13th in the Barclays Premier League and aiming higher.

We can then sum up the major division of nouns as the flowchart in Figure 3.1. This looks neat and we think it is quite useful, but remember that when you see a division of language that looks this neat you should also be suspicious – it may sometimes be an over-simplification. So use this flow chart as a guideline, but remember that there are exceptions and special cases that slightly cloud the picture.

Pronouns

We now come to a tricky class of words: pronouns. It is tricky in that it is sometimes considered a separate word class, in which case it is a minor (closed) class, or it is seen as a sub-class of noun. In fact, as we shall see in this section, for a number of pronouns there are also good arguments for assuming that they are determiners. We will deal with pronouns at this point since a number of the features relevant to nouns are also relevant to pronouns. Pronouns differ from nouns in that they generally don't like being modified by elements which precede them and examples like *silly me* and *poor you* are exceptional. On the other hand, examples like *she in the corner* and *he who enters this room* are fine and very similar to *the girl in the corner* or *the man who enters this room*. Basically pronouns substitute not for nouns, but for full noun phrases. 'Pro-NP' would be a more accurate term. Consider the following short extract. We have italicised the pronouns:

The genius of 'South Park' lies in the fact that *it* just doesn't know when to stop. Cartman is the local fat kid, so everyone teases *him* cruelly and mercilessly. Mr Garrison is the gang's mentally unstable teacher. *They* make *his* life hell, too. In one episode *he* decides *he's* tired of being a loser and has plastic surgery so *he* looks like David Hasselhoff.

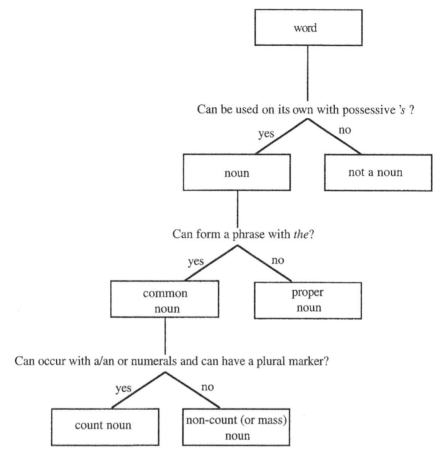

Figure 3.1 Major subdivisions of nouns

In each instance, these little words stand in place of a full NP. It would sound curious indeed if the writer here were to repeat the full noun phrase instead – *The genius of 'South Park' lies in the fact that* 'South Park' *just doesn't know when to stop. Cartman is the local fat kid, so everyone teases* Cartman *cruelly and mercilessly*. And so on!

We can identify several different sub-classes of pronoun:

- ❑ personal pronouns
- ❑ indefinite pronouns
- ❑ reflexive pronouns
- ❑ reciprocal pronouns
- ❑ possessive pronouns
- ❑ demonstrative pronouns
- ❑ interrogative pronouns
- ❑ relative pronouns.

Personal pronouns

These make up the central class of pronouns. All of the italicised pronouns in the previous extract are of this type. Table 3.1 gives the full inventory of the personal pronouns of Modern English.

Table 3.1 Personal pronouns

Person	Number		Subject case	Object case
First	Singular		I	me
	Plural		we	us
Second	Singular		you	you
	Plural		you	you
Third	Singular	masculine	he	him
		feminine	she	her
		non-personal	it	it
	Plural		they	them

A quick comparison with the pronouns from earlier stages of English would show that we have lost many of the original contrasts. Nonetheless, the properties of PERSON, NUMBER and CASE are better preserved in the morphology of these pronouns than in that of nouns.

Let's look at person first; English has three persons:

First person (i.e. speaker(s))
Singular: *I* remember when *I* met Matt.
Plural: *We* mimicked Terry Gilliam's style of animation.

Second person (i.e. person(s) spoken to)
Singular or plural: If *you* want subtlety, *you*'re in the wrong place.

Third person (i.e. neither speaker nor person spoken to)
Singular: *He* decides *he*'s tired of being a loser.
Plural: *They* say whatever bad word *they* can think of.

The label third person is a little curious. For one thing, it can include semantically empty items like *it*, as in these two examples:

It seems that everyone wants a piece of the clunky action.
It's not hard to see why.

Or it can refer to inanimates:
I was making *a film* [. . .] *It* was sort of a Godzilla thing – but with a huge beaver instead.
The resulting escapade [. . .] *It* was puerile, silly and immature.

As you can see in Table 3.1, third person singular distinguishes between 'male,' 'female' and 'neither male nor female.'

Unlike nouns, some pronouns have distinct forms for cases. Remember that we don't count the possessive *'s* as a case. All the pronouns except *you* and *it* preserve separate case forms for (roughly) subject and object functions. We will be examining in detail these different functions in the next chapter. For the moment, just compare the forms in the following examples:

He (Subject) commissioned them (Object).

They (Subject) make his life hell.

Everyone teases *him* (Object) cruelly.

In Standard English, the second person form *you* no longer has any contrasting forms for singular and plural, although this is not the case for all dialects. Some varieties of rural British English, for example, have retained a *thou* series (*thou, thee, thine, thyself*) for second person singular and many varieties of English as spoken in Ireland, Australia, New Zealand and parts of the United States have a plural form *yous* (although in Australia *yous* is often singular with *youses, all yous* or *yous guys* used as the plural); compare also *you'uns, you'all, you together, you guys* found in varieties elsewhere.

Looking at the earlier table for Standard English, you might be tempted to think our pronouns *he/she/it* reveal a fourth property, namely, the property of GENDER. Gender is a rather confusing term, however. If you forget the associations with biological sex and focus on its original meaning of 'class' or 'kind' (from Latin *genus*), you will better understand its grammatical application. In this context, gender refers to the classification of nouns into groups for the purposes of agreement (as in the earlier example of masculine *feet*, feminine *hands* and neuter *eyes*). It is a grammatical feature of nouns which also affects the form of other words in the sentence, namely, its dependents. In Old English all nouns fell into one of three genders or classes: masculine, feminine and neuter. True, the classes might have occasionally corresponded to the sex or sexlessness of entities, but not necessarily (Old English *wifmann* 'woman' was masculine, *wif* 'woman' was neuter and *mædencild* 'girl' was neuter). This system of grammatical gender has now completely disappeared in English. The fact that the third person singular pronoun occurs in three different forms, *he/she/it*, has traditionally been related to biological sex and is not a sign that English really does have a gender system for its nouns.

Note that although it is true to say that first person refers to speaker/writer, second person to hearer/reader and third person to third parties, English shows some untypical uses. Plural *we* can refer to the hearer, e.g. *Let's eat up our mashed potatoes now, shall* we? (a sort of condescending 'hospitalese' – you could imagine a nurse speaking to an elderly patient here); *you* can be used to refer to people in general (preferable in some varieties of English to the indefinite *one*), e.g. *Chocolate is actually good for you;* in special cases of extreme politeness third person forms can be used to refer to the hearer (a kind of distancing technique), e.g. *If Madam so desires*, she *could have the waist taken in a little; they* often appears as a gender-neutral

57

third person singular pronoun, e.g. *If anyone wants it*, they *can have pavlova with extra whipped cream*. And those who identify as neither male or female, or both, often choose to be referred to by other pronouns such as gender neutral *they* and *them*. Occasionally we still hear the argument that this 'singular *they*' is grammatically incorrect because a plural pronoun shouldn't refer back to a singular word and that *he* should be used instead, but clearly this is linguistically quite unfounded. As we've just discussed, English has many examples where for special purposes pronouns depart from their central meaning – as so often is the case, there is no perfect match between form and meaning here. Besides, surely so-called generic *he* would also be incorrect, if the same formal criterion were to apply across the board!

'They is illiterate'

In her book *Between you and me. Confessions of a comma queen*, Mary Norris writes about the use of forms of *they* with singular reference: 'the use of "their" when you mean "his" or "her" is just wrong,' and she asks, 'Why should a lowly common-gender plural pronoun trump our singular feminine and masculine pronouns, our kings and queens and jacks?' (p 68–69). Even though the idea of a gender-neutral pronoun has caused strong emotions also in Sweden, Swedish appears to have successfully introduced a gender-neutral singular pronoun. Swedish, like English, has had three singular pronouns: *hon* 'she,' *han* 'he' and *den* 'it.' Recently a gender-neutral pronoun to refer to people has been introduced: *hen*. The use of *hen* was first proposed in 1966, but it really took off around 2010; in March 2017 an article on the website of *SVT*, the Swedish national public TV broadcaster, reported that *hen* was used 636 times in the media in 2006, whereas for 2016, the same number was 27,076. Since 2015, it has been included in the standard dictionary of Swedish, *Svenska Akademiens Ordlista*.

Indefinite pronouns

These express notions involving definiteness or quantity and comprise the largest group of pronouns. They fall into two types. One includes compounds consisting of two elements: *some-*, *any-*, *every-* and *no-* with *-thing*, *-one* and *-body*; e.g. *everything*, *someone* and *nobody*. Note that, unlike the personal pronouns, these do not stand in the place of previously occurring noun phrases; in other words, they do not have what is called an ANTECEDENT.

If you do *something* that's got a little heart then it's 10 times worse.

That's why 'South Park' couldn't work as *anything* other than a cartoon.

Everyone who saw it thought it was a work of side-splitting wonder.

Note that not included in this group is *anyway*. Even though it looks as though it does belong here, it is a kind of adverb (often marking attitude), as in the following:

And *anyway*, it might be hard to make live-action little kids dying funny.

The other group of indefinite pronouns may appear alone, or followed by *of*. They include items like *many, more, both, most, some, neither*, and so on.

Many/most/several/some who saw it thought it was a work of side-splitting wonder. [adapted]

Yet there's *more* to 'South Park' than jokes about sex and swearing.

These items can be quite controversial and people do analyse them differently. In the context we have given them here, they belong to the class of pronouns. However, in Chapter 7 we will see that they can also function within a noun phrase and in that case they will often fit naturally into the class of determiners or adjectives. It should also be pointed out here that personal pronouns can also double as determiners, as in *We Swedes celebrate Christmas a day earlier* or *People think that us Australians are too laid-back*. In the section on determiners we talk more about why these elements can be considered determiners.

Reflexive pronouns

Reflexive pronouns all end in *-self* or *-selves*. Theses pronouns are used instead of personal pronouns when the noun phrase to which the pronoun refers can be found elsewhere in the same sentence (or more accurately in the same clause; more about this distinction in Chapter 8). Another way of saying this is that reflexive pronouns must have an antecedent somewhere in the same clause (think of these pronouns as reflecting (or being 'reflexes' of) noun phrases that occur elsewhere in the same clause). In the following example the reflexive *himself* refers to the same person as the underlined noun phrase; the underlined phrase is its antecedent:

The 47-year-old American kept asking *himself* . . . (N#151:8)

Even though this is the core use of reflexive pronouns, there is also something which can be described as emphatic, where the reflexive immediately follows the noun phrase as in:

Simon Stuart *himself* talks to the masterminds. [adapted]

There are lots of corny jokes out there that play on this double function of reflexive pronouns: *Tired of cleaning* **yourself** *– let our trained staff do it for you!* Here the ambiguity occurs because *yourself* could be understood reflexively (**you** *clean* **yourself**) or emphatically (**you** **yourself** *clean*).

Finally, there is a rapidly spreading use of the reflexive, where it does not appear to need an antecedent at all. A financial advisor explained the details of an insurance policy to one of us as follows:

If, heaven forbid, *yourselves* were to die before the children, the money would be put in a trust fund.

Contemptible in the ears of persons of any taste

These non-reflexive reflexives have been in the language for some time; many examples can be found in early literature, including the works of writers such Thomas Malory, William Shakespeare and Jane Austen:

Hit is yourself I loue so wel. (Malory 1475)

My illness had been entirely brought on by myself. (Austen 1811)

The question then is – if people have been using these -*self* pronouns in this way for so long, then why didn't the feature end up enshrined in the standard language?

It seems it fell from grace, and rather badly. In one of the first usage guides for Early Modern English, *Reflections on the English Language* (1770), the author Robert Baker provides quite a blacklist. And on page 117 he cites an example of a non-reflexive reflexive from the London periodical the *Monthly Review*.

They are so far from promoting real Trade, that the Support of themselves and Families are a dead Weight on its Profits.

Baker points out the incorrect use of the plural verb here (effectively *the support are a dead weight*) and then goes on to write:

But there is another Fault in these Lines. – *Of themselves and Families*, for *of themselves and their Families*, is a very bad Expression, though very common. It is mere Shopkeepers Cant (*Harris and Son, Clarke and Son, Brown and Son*) and will always be found contemptible in the Ears of Persons of any Taste.

So Baker dismisses the construction as 'mere Shopkeepers Cant' [= jargon] and 'contemptible in the Ears of Persons of any Taste.' From this time on, usage guides followed his practice and poor old non-reflexive -*self* pronouns were snubbed.

Reciprocal pronouns

Reciprocal pronouns are used to express a two-way relationship and include pronouns like *each other* and *one another*. Like reflexives, reciprocals need an antecedent in the same clause.

'The Spirit of Christmas' featured *four foul-mouthed kids, Jesus and Santa Claus* beating seven bells out of *each other*.

Possessive pronouns

Possessive pronouns come in two kinds: those that occur independently as full noun phrases and those that form part of a noun phrase. The latter can be categorised as determiners:

Determiner possessive pronoun	Independent possessive pronoun
my	mine
your	yours
his	his
her	hers
its	(its)
our	ours
your	yours
their	theirs

As we shall see, full noun phrases with the possessive 's can also function in a way similar to determiners. This means that in both functions, these pronouns replace possessive noun phrases. As we have said before about possessives, the notion of ownership is their central sense, but the possessive can encode a variety of different associations. Some adapted examples, where we also give the parallel example with a full noun phrase, are given here:

Their crusade to capture our attention.

The advertisers' crusade to capture our attention.

The gay dog Sparky is *his*.

The gay dog Sparky is *Stan's*.

Demonstrative pronouns

English has four demonstrative pronouns: singular *this* and *that* versus plural *these* and *those*. As their name suggests, they typically have to do with the orientational features of language. You could imagine, for example, that a sentence like *This is better than that* might be accompanied by a pointing gesture. Here the two pronouns *this* and *that* contrast with respect to location, i.e. near to speaker (*this*) and relatively distant (*that*). This is their most basic, DEICTIC (= 'pointing') use.

Examples like those in the following piece, however, show a slightly different use. The interpretation of each of these demonstratives derives from something that has preceded in the text rather than from the immediate non-linguistic context. These pronouns are ANAPHORIC (= 'referring to or replacing earlier word(s)').

That's why 'South Park' couldn't work as anything other than a cartoon, he says. '*This* is the only way we can make the characters act the way real kids act. A kid actor would try to be all sweet, and who needs *that*?'

Interrogative pronouns

Interrogative pronouns are used to ask questions. If one expects the answer to be a person, then there are three different forms: *who* (subject case), *whom* (object case) and *whose* (possessive). In ordinary speech, however, most of us would probably not be tempted to say *Whom did you see 'South Park' with?* but rather *Who did you see 'South Park' with?* (although some may still prefer to write the former). In most colloquial spoken varieties, *whom* would be classed as an endangered species.

The pronouns *which* and *what* have only one form. *What* is non-personal (e.g. *What did you cook?*) and *which* can be either personal or non-personal (e.g. *Which is your brother? Which is your favourite recipe?*)

. . . and *who* needs that?

The question is *what* it's all been spent on. (SCO#113:9)

Which are his Glaswegian favourites? (SCO#113:24)

Relative pronouns

Relative pronouns are used in relative clauses. We will explain what they are in Chapter 8; at this stage it is enough to give some examples. The relative pronouns include *who, whom, whose, what, which* and *that* (the status of the last item as a relative pronoun is controversial, but the term will do for our purposes here). In all the examples, the relative pronouns are part of the underlined relative clause (and stand for an understood NP).

'South Park' has . . . become the wildest, funniest, most disrespectful thing <u>*that's ever hit the screen*</u>.

Everyone <u>*who saw it*</u> thought it was a work of side-splitting wonder.

Verbs

Semantic features

In very general terms, verbs are those words denoting actions, processes, states or events.

Morphological features

Verbs can be readily identified in terms of their inflectional morphology; in fact, most inflectional complexity in English is associated with the verb. English verbs have up to five different forms and this makes them quite easy to distinguish. The different forms are illustrated with LEXICAL – or MAIN – verbs in the Table 3.2. For the time being you can think of lexical verbs as the most contentful verbs. They are contrasted with AUXILIARY verbs. In Chapter 6, we give formal criteria for distinguishing between these two types of verbs and discuss the way in which the forms of auxiliary verbs differ from those of the lexical verbs. In Table 3.2, we use some terminology that we have not defined yet. For the time being we are only interested in the forms as such, but in Chapter 6, we will talk more about how the forms are used.

The base form is the form under which the verb would be entered in a dictionary, and it is the form which follows the so-called INFINITIVAL MARKER *to*. The base form is also identical to the form used in the present tense with subjects that are not third person singular. The present tense form used with third person singular is often referred to as the *-s* form because, regardless of what lexical verb it is, the present tense form which agrees with a third person singular subject ends in *-s*. The third column contains the past tense form which occurs in contexts like: *Yesterday, the authors . . . it.* The form ends in *-ed* for all regular verbs, but as Table 3.2 shows, there are different forms for irregular verbs. The irregular forms can be sorted into classes of verbs which behave in a similar way, so that they are not quite as irregular as it may appear. The form which we have referred to as 'past participle' in Table 3.2 is always identical to the passive participle, so that the best abbreviation for it is actually 'PPART.' Because it also ends in *-ed* for all regular verbs, it is sometimes referred to as the '-*ed* participle.' This is the form which co-occurs with 'have' as in: *The authors have . . . it.* Finally, there is the *-ing* form, which is easy to spot because it always ends in *-ing*. This is the form which co-occurs with 'be' as in: *The authors are . . . it.*

Table 3.2 Verb forms

Base form	3rd sing present	Past tense	Past participle	-ing form
want	wants	wanted	wanted	wanting
eat	eats	ate	eaten	eating
hit	hits	hit	hit	hitting
make	makes	made	made	making
drink	drinks	drank	drunk	drinking

An important distinction for verb forms is between FINITE and NON-FINITE forms. Verbs that are 'finite' are so described because they are limited (or made finite) with respect to the categories person, number and tense; non-finite forms are not limited by inflection in this way. The *-ing* form and the PPART are always non-finite, but since PPART and the past tense form are sometimes identical, it is not always easy to tell whether a form ending in *-ed* is finite or not. The base form can be used both as a finite (present tense) form and as non-finite form. The finite forms are those that can show a difference between present and past tense (we will go into more detail about tenses in Section 6.2) and which take the third person singular *-s* when occurring in present tense. If there is just the one verb in a sentence it is finite, as in the following sentences, where the verb can be present or past tense.

Sir Alex *sends* his apologies. (N#642:9)

Sir Alex *sent* his apologies.

Bobby Charlton *embodied* to me what being great really is. (N#642:9)

Bobby Charlton *embodies* to me what being great really is.

If there are a number of verbs in one string, then only the first one can be finite. This happens when we have one or more auxiliary verbs (more about them in Section 6.3). As you can see, only the first of these verbs can change between present and past.

In that time, Chelsea *have* had nine managers and local rivals Manchester City 11. (N#642:9)

In that time, Chelsea *had* had nine managers and local rivals Manchester City 11.

*In that time, Chelsea have *have* nine managers and local rivals Manchester City 11.

They *don't* expect to win an England cap. (N#642:9)

They *didn't* expect to win an England cap.

*They *don't/didn't* expected to win an England cap.

Then you *would* go and watch Rangers or Celtic or Partick Thistle. (N#642:9)

Then you *will* go and watch Rangers or Celtic or Partick Thistle.

*Then you *will/would* went and watched Rangers or Celtic or Partick Thistle.

The first verb of a string does not have to be finite. A sentence can contain more than one verb string; this happens when a sentence contains more than one clause. We'll discuss this further in Chapter 8. When there is more than one verb string, they don't both have to contain a finite verb (but they can do). Some verbs take a complement which is built around a verb, but this verb has to be non-finite, that is to say, it has to be in a form that does not allow a change between present and past form. Here are some comments from the Internet on the general topic that our example sentences have been dealing with.

United *made* them pay by opening the scoring.

United *makes* them pay by opening the scoring.

*United made them *paid* by opening the scoring.

In these examples, the first verb string, *made*, contains just one finite verb, we know it is finite since it can be changed to *makes*. The second verb string, which also just contains one verb, *pay* cannot be changed in any way and hence it is non-finite.

In addition to these inflectional characteristics, there are also some derivational affixes which are characteristic of verbs, like *-ee, -er* and *-ment* (verb → noun) and *-able, -ing* and *-ive* (verb → adjective).

Syntactic behaviour

The syntax of verbs is complex enough to warrant separate treatment and we explore this in detail in Chapter 6. At this point we will just make some general comments. There is a sense in which the verb and its inflection form the central part of a sentence. To a certain extent, the verb decides what other parts can occur in the sentence. Consider the following example:

He wears her knickers. (N#240:8)

In this sentence, the verb is *wears* (just check for yourself, it has all the forms described in Table 3.2) and because it is this verb, we need a phrase to follow it, as the ungrammaticality of **He wears* shows. Similarly, *wears* also rules out the use of two phrases following it. If the verb had been for instance *give*, this would have been acceptable:

*He wears her her knickers.

He gives her her knickers.

In Chapter 6, we will show that lexical verbs can be divided into groups, depending on what elements they select.

The verb also decides what kinds of phrases are possible; *he* could not have been replaced by something like *the idea* in the previous examples. Similarly, not any old phrase could modify this sentence, so that *he wears her knickers often* sounds fine, but *he wears her knickers slowly* sounds strange, whereas *He washes her knickers often/slowly* are both fine. These are some simple arguments for why the verb should be considered the central part of a clause; in other words, the HEAD. In the linguistic literature you can find more subtle arguments, and in all the major theories of syntax, the verb, or at least the properties associated with it, is considered the head of the sentence.

Adjectives

Semantic features

The core members of the class of adjectives typically refer to qualities or states (relating to things like shape, taste, size, colour, or judgements like good/bad, pretty/ugly, and so on).

Morphological features

Typical adjectives are gradable or scalar, which means that they refer to properties or states that can be possessed in varying degrees. In this capacity, most adjectives inflect for degree in a three-term system:

ABSOLUTE	funny	bad	old
COMPARATIVE	funnier	worse	elder/older
SUPERLATIVE	funniest	worst	eldest/oldest

Normally, the endings *-er* and *-est* are added to the adjective stem. But as you can see, English also has some eccentric forms like *bad, worse, worst* (known as SUPPLETIVE forms). In some cases you also get a modification of the stem, e.g. *old/elder/eldest*. The sort of vowel mutation you find in *old* was once upon a time quite widespread and forms like *strong–strenger–strengest* were common. But now even *elder/eldest* has given way to *older/oldest* and is confined to specialised contexts, e.g. *elder statesman* or *elder brother*.

Not all adjectives are able to carry these inflections, however. For one thing, they are going the way of the rest of our inflections, being replaced by free-standing forms, in this case the quantifying expressions *more* and *most*. Rather than a neat clean takeover, however, what we find is the usual messiness associated with language change. For example:

'South Park' has . . . become the *wildest, funniest, most disrespectful* thing that's ever hit the screen.

Typically, it is adjectives of one syllable (but even not all of these) which are hanging onto the endings, e.g. *wilder/wildest*. Adjectives of three or more syllables have lost them and require *more* and *most*; e.g. **disrespectfuller/ disrespectfullest*. Adjectives of two syllables have a kind of split personality: some do, some don't, some go both ways and not all speakers will agree, e.g. *funnier/funniest* versus *more/most funny* but *?wickeder/?wickedest* versus *more/most wicked*.

The other difficulty here is that not all adjectives denote properties which are naturally gradable and therefore won't take degree modification – for example, *pregnant, dead, married*, and so on. Sometimes you find speakers will play with this property for special effect. For instance, the adjective *Australian* is non-gradable – you either are or you're not. But in an extended sense it is possible to say something like *he's more Australian than Paul Hogan*, in which case you are invoking the caricature of the rough uncultivated Australian male (the stereotype of a beer gut in shorts, singlet and thongs – cheerful, unpretentious but probably not a lot between the ears).

As far as derivational morphology goes, there are quite a lot of suffixes which derive adjectives from nouns (e.g. *-ful, -less, -ly, -y, -ish, -al, -ic, -ese*) and a number from verbs (e.g. *-able, -ible*). Many adjectives are in fact derived in some ways, and these derivational endings can then be used to spot adjectives.

Syntactic behaviour

There is, in fact, no syntactic behaviour which is unique to adjectives, for everything we say here holds that not only adjectives can occur in these positions and that not all adjectives can. We will return to some of the difficulties with spotting adjectives a little later when we look at the tests for determining the category of words (see also Section 7.4).

Adjectives, either on their own or with some modifiers, can occur in two positions: ATTRIBUTIVELY or PREDICATIVELY. When an adjective occurs inside the noun phrase it is said to function attributively, usually it precedes the noun, but as we shall see attributive adjectives can also follow the noun. For example:

the *rampant* chef

the *unstable* teacher

Adjectives or the phrases formed around them may also follow a verb. Some verbs that allow this are *be* and *become*, but we will see examples of other verbs in Chapter 4. This is referred to as the predicative use of the adjective.

Kids are *malicious*.

Kids became *malicious*.

Almost all members within the adjective class have both these functions; in other words, can function attributively and predicatively.

Kids are *malicious* versus *Malicious* kids

However, English has plenty of examples of fringe dwellers too. Adjectives like *awake, asleep, main* and *utter* are exceptional. The first two are not attributive – *the awake dog; *the asleep student*. The other two are not predicative – *the point was main; *the chaos was utter*.

One property which adjectives share with adverbs (see later) is that they can be modified. Some of these modifiers are adverbs like *thoroughly*; in some cases a modifier before the adjective is itself modified by something that follows the adjective, as in the cracking song title from B. A. Johnston in the second example below.

thoroughly unpleasant

too messed up *to be in this canoe*

As is often the case with elements that function as intensifiers, they are subject to some turnover and new ones appear. *Dead* is an example of a recent invention, and *dirty* is used as an intensifier in the line from Marc Bolan and T-Rex's *Get it on*.

dead scared of Saigon or Dallas (N#258:13)

You're *dirty* sweet and you're my girl

All gradable adjectives will be able to take these kinds of intensifying expressions. And as described earlier, even adjectives that are non-gradable in their central sense can be used as gradable adjectives in some circumstances and hence take intensifiers – for example, describing someone as *very pregnant*.

An interesting change that is taking place at the moment can be seen in the following examples:

very here-and-now (N#269:22)

so Graham Norton (British television show)

so last year (said by Graham Norton in his show)

She considers it *too* showbiz. (AUS#65:24)

Here we have typical modifiers of adjectives like *very, so* and *too* modifying elements which certainly do not look like adjectives. In fact, most of them can be converted into adjectives, albeit slightly odd adjectives, by the derivational affixes *-y* or *-ish*: *Graham-Nortony* or *last-year-ish*. So, what is happening in these examples? Have *here-and-now, Graham Norton* and *last year* been converted to adjectives? Or has the distribution of *very* and *so* changed from modifying adjectives to modifying more widely things that can be seen as denoting properties the way many adjectives do? We don't really have an answer; just another example of language changing all around us.

We said earlier that attributive adjectives generally precede the noun, however, there are a few cases when adjectives follow the noun within the noun phrase. This happens, for instance, when the noun the adjective modifies is an indefinite pronoun like *something, anyone, someone* or *anything*. For example:

Ever done something *stupid* in the name of love? . . . You've met someone *gorgeous* and s/he's returning your interest in kind. (AUS#43:38)

There are also a few adjectives which always follow the noun. Linguistic curiosities in the legal world like *the heir presumptive, court martial, heir apparent* also show this less usual ordering, but so do some everyday adjectives like *the information available* and *the money due*.

Adjectives which themselves have post-modifiers normally also follow the noun they modify (more about this in Section 7.6).

a man *lustful towards women*

*a *lustful towards women* man

There seem to be some exceptions to this rule, so that a big supermarket in Britain sells all its biscuits in packets with *now in easy to open pack* written on them. (What's wrong with these people? We can travel in space, we can build vacuum cleaners and we boast about being able to make a packet of biscuits that is easy to open!?) Here an adjective *easy* is followed by *to open*, but still the whole phrase precedes the noun. This type of construction seems to be a general feature of advertising, often combined with a whole stack of other modifiers. Consider other examples like: butter that's available in *a convenient, easy to spread dairy blend* or bread mixes obtainable in *value-for-money 6 kg boxes*. This must sound snappier to advertising agencies than 'this dairy blend is convenient and easy to spread' or 'these 6kg boxes are value-for-money.' But very complex mixed pre-modifiers are also found elsewhere as the following three *Big Issue* examples illustrate (for those of you unfamiliar with Australian English, a *chook* is a 'chicken'):

a faintly burned-out advertising creative turned tree-change chook obsessive (AUS#547:13)

a transformational yet achingly simply paradigm shifting piece of technology (AUS#563:13)

Adverbs

Semantic features

The class of adverbs is a real mixed bag and therefore a notoriously difficult class to define, both semantically and grammatically. Adverbs can range from the purely lexical to the grammatical and show diversity not only in meaning, but also in their grammatical behaviour. Perhaps what we might think of as prototypical adverbs fall closer to the more lexical end. These express information like time, manner, place, frequency, and so on.

Morphological features

As far as inflectional endings go, adverbs fare rather badly. Many fall along some sort of scale and are therefore gradable, but they generally take *more* and *most*; e.g. *more/most quickly*. Only a handful like *well–better–best; soon–sooner–soonest* will inflect for grade.

As far as derivational morphology goes, a large proportion of adverbs are derived from adjectives via the *-ly* suffix (*fresh-ly; slow-ly*). This is a highly productive suffix and speakers can be quite inventive when it comes to forming adverbs from adjectives:

toe-curlingly sluggish (N#258:12)

pant-wettingly hilarious

But don't rely on *-ly* to tell you when you have an adverb. For one thing, many adverbs don't have the ending (*soon, fast, often, nevertheless*), while there are adjectives that do, e.g. *friendly, deadly, beastly*. Other adverb-making suffixes include *-wards* (*eastwards, upwards*) and *-wise* (*timewise, healthwise*).

Syntactic behaviour

Adverbs are the head of adverb phrases (AdvPs), which function as modifiers of verbs, adjectives, other adverbs and even entire clauses. For example, they are regularly used to modify verbs, adding information, for instance, about the way something happens or the time it happens:

Everyone teases him *cruelly* and *mercilessly*.

They . . . *immediately* hit it off.

Already they're one of the comic success stories of the decade.

Other adverbs express the attitude of the speaker or writer:

Fortunately we can't hear because of his anorak hood.

OK, it's not exactly educational – but at least its heart's in the right place.

They may also be emphatic:

That's *entirely* the point.

Finally there are those adverbs which, as we saw earlier, are used to modify the meaning of adjectives. Some, like the following ones, are full of meaning:

eminently memorable

horribly maimed

Others simply serve to intensify the interpretation of whatever they are modifying:

all sweet

so innocent and pure

As heads of AdvPs, they themselves can be modified. Gradable adverbs, for example, will take the same sort of intensifiers as adjectives (e.g. the usual suspects like *too, rather, very*), but otherwise they are quite limited in the modifiers they can take. For example, in the following sentence, the manner adverb *mentally* can modify the adjective *unstable*. However, as the adapted versions illustrate, the adverb *unstably* can be comfortably modified by the intensifier *very*, but not with *mentally*:

Mr Garrison is the gang's mentally unstable teacher.

He behaves unstably [adapted]

?*He behaves mentally unstably [adapted]

He behaves very unstably [adapted]

Occasionally, adverbs appear with a following prepositional phrase. For example:

Fortunately for us we can't hear because of his anorak hood. [adapted]

Note that adverbs with a connective role like *however, then, nevertheless* and *therefore* cannot take any modifiers at all:

Matt Stone, *however*, thinks the distinctly low-fi animation . . . only adds to the 'South Park' charm.

Then there's the Thanksgiving episode, where Cartman travels to Africa to learn about starvation.

General tests for determining category membership

At the beginning of this chapter we warned you that not every member of a class will necessarily have all the identifying properties. We're dealing here with fuzzy categories. Some words, for example, simply do not behave like good category members. So how do we determine what category they belong to? There are two tests you can apply.

One is the SUBSTITUTION TEST. As we discussed earlier, we can identify members of the same category on the basis of the fact that they occur in the same slots. Let's say you're trying to establish the category of a certain word. Find a prototypical member of the category you suspect it of being and see if it can fill the same positions in a sentence as the word in question. Take the example of *real* in the following sentence:

We can make the characters act the way a *real* kid acts.

Now, *real* is a modifier, but it doesn't show the usual attributes of an adjective – it's not clearly any other category either. It doesn't have comparative or superlative forms – *a realler kid/*the reallest kid;* nor does it sit happily with the usual range of intensifiers like *very* or *rather* – *a very real kid* (unless you extend its central meaning). We still suspect it's an adjective. To confirm our suspicions we can take a typical adjective like *happy* (which has all the characteristics of an adjective; *very happy, happier–happiest*) and try putting it in the same sentence slot. If the result is a grammatical sentence, then this strongly suggests that *real* is an adjective.

We can make the characters act the way a *happy* kid acts.

Note, there is one danger with this test: slots aren't always confined to one lexical category. As we shall see in Chapter 7, the sentence slot Determiner _____ Noun is also hospitable to nouns and verbs; nouns, verbs as well as adjectives can pre-modify nouns.

We saw earlier that typical adjectives can also occur predicatively, following the verb *be*. This is a useful indicator for adjective status and nicely shows up the difference between different modifying words like *real* (adjective) and *kid* (noun) – *The kid was real* versus **The actor was kid*. If these two words belonged to the same class, we would expect them to fill the same position in the sentence, though of course we said earlier that not all adjectives can occur both attributively and predicatively.

There is another test we can apply here, namely, the COORDINATION TEST. As we saw when we discussed constituency tests in Chapter 2, normally, only words of the same category can be linked using typical coordinators like *and* or *but*. Nouns coordinate with nouns, verbs with verbs, adjectives with adjectives, and so on. Using a similar procedure to the previously mentioned one, find a prototypical category member and try coordinating it with the problematical word. Take the first example again and see if you can coordinate *happy* with *real*. If a grammatical sentence results, this is evidence that *real* is an adjective.

We can make the characters act the way a *real* and *happy* kid acts.

This test nicely shows up the 'unadjective-like' character of noun modifiers too. We cannot find any adjective to coordinate with *kid* that will result in a grammatical sentence.

*A *kid* and *immature* actor would try to be all sweet, and who needs that?

Because the substitution and coordination tests can show different results, you need to apply both and weigh up the evidence, together with what you know about the morphological character of the word in question. For example, if you suspect something of being an adjective, then you would expect it to show at least some of the following attributes:

❏ can take comparative *-er* and superlative *-est* endings (as opposed to plural or possessive *-s*);

- can occur with intensifiers like *very*;
- can occur attributively within the noun phrase;
- can occur predicatively;
- can be coordinated with another adjective;
- can be substituted by another adjective.

If after applying all these tests you are still not sure whether it is an adjective or not, then try to show that it belongs to another category; if it is not an adjective, then it must belong to another category, probably noun or verb.

As a final illustration, compare the following sentences (the second one is adapted):

The resulting escapade was *silly*.

The resulting escapade was *rubbish*.

At first blush, the two words that we have italicised look as if they should belong to the same category. Both words *silly* and *rubbish* have a modifying function. They describe here a property of *the resulting escapade* and share a similar meaning, something like 'trivial, stupid.' They are looking very much like adjectives. So let's see how they behave with respect to the other adjective attributes.

- Can they take comparative and superlative endings?

  The resulting escapade was *sillier*.
  *The resulting escapade was *rubbisher*.

- Can they take intensifying expressions (= degree adverbs)?

  The resulting escapade was very *silly*.
  *The resulting escapade was very *rubbish*.

- Do they occur in the same slots?

  Clearly, both words can occur predicatively. In both instances they appear at the end of the sentence after the verb *be*. Let's see if the noun phrase slot accepts them both – typical adjectives also occur between a determiner and noun.
  The resulting *silly* escapade . . .
  ?The resulting *rubbish* escapade . . .

- Can they be coordinated with another adjective?

  The resulting escapade was *silly and puerile*.
  *The resulting escapade was *rubbish and puerile*.

As you might have guessed by now, on these grammaticality judgements, only *silly* is an adjective. *Rubbish* is actually a noun and it conjoins beautifully with other nouns and noun phrases.

The resulting escapade was *rubbish but a ratings gold mine*.

However, if you can say things like *the rubbish actor* or *very rubbish*, the word may have undergone a change in your English and actually now be an example of a zero derivation (see Chapter 2).

3.5 Minor categories

Minor categories, like PREPOSITIONS, DETERMINERS and CONJUNCTIONS, involve grammatical words; i.e. those words which help to build the grammatical structure of the language but have less meaning content than the lexical categories. These classes have far fewer members than major classes and they are closed; in other words, they are not easily receptive to new members. There are two classes which are sometimes included under a section on minor classes, but which we have decided to put as sub-classes of a major class, namely pronouns (under nouns) and auxiliaries (under verbs). There are arguments both for and against this decision. It seems to us that auxiliaries share so many properties with other verbs that they are best considered as a specific type of verb. In the case of pronouns, there are maybe stronger arguments for keeping them as a separate class, but we felt it was easier in this kind of textbook to deal in one place with the properties nouns and pronouns share.

Prepositions

Semantic features

Prepositions are the most difficult elements to spot by structural criteria, and hence we will say a bit more about their semantics. The majority of prepositions express relationships between things and events; their basic sense is spatial. Imagine a tennis ball and a brick wall – you can throw the ball over/under/at/through/by the wall. These little location markers are all prepositions.

Unfortunately, it's not as straightforward as brick walls and tennis balls. Some of these location markers have been recruited for a more grammatical function, taking over the roles of our disappearing inflections. For example, *to* indicates 'direction towards' but over time has also come to mean more abstract distance, as with the italic instances in the following examples:

> Their warped sense of humour came *to* the attention of Fox Television executive Brian Graden. Impressed by what he saw, he commissioned them to make a Christmas video-card he could send *to* his friends.

You may have noticed that there is a third *to* in this piece which is not in italics. This is an instance of the infinitival marker *to*, which has developed out of the more abstract uses of the preposition *to*. However, as we shall see in Section 6.7, the infinitival *to* no longer shares any structural properties with the preposition *to*.

The preposition *of* once indicated 'away from' but now encodes quite a hotchpotch of different relations between two nouns, principally possession:

We mimicked Terry Gilliam's style *of* animation.

The genius *of* 'South Park' lies in the fact that it just doesn't know when to stop.

The preposition *by* can mean 'near, to the side of' but can also be used in a more abstract role as in the following example; this is the passive construction which is something we examine in Chapter 6:

Stan's gay dog Sparky is played *by* no less a luminary than *ER* star George Clooney.

Morphological features

Prepositions can be simple (*to, from, of, with, by*) or complex (*in front of, on top of*). Prepositions do not allow any inflectional morphology and there is no derivational morphology to speak of. Some grammar books claim that *near* is a preposition that has two inflectional forms: *nearer, nearest*. However, there are better arguments for classifying near as an adjective rather than a preposition. Run all the tests from previous sections on *near* and see what conclusion you arrive at.

Syntactic behaviour

Syntactic criteria aren't terribly useful either for spotting prepositions; prepositions generally combine with noun phrases to form prepositional phrases (PPs), which in turn can have almost any function within the sentence. In Chapters 4, 6 and 7, we will give examples of PPs in various functions.

Unlike the classes we have just been looking at, prepositions do not allow very much in the way of modification; examples usually involve prepositions of time or place which can be graded, as in *deep/far/almost into the jungle*; *way/just/straight before the lecture*. The following example shows *right* modifying the following PP *onto America's televisions*:

It's less than a year since Stan, Kyle, Cartman and Kenny . . . burst *right* onto America's televisions.

Very occasionally you find degree modification with intensifying expressions like *very much*. This is more usual when the preposition has a metaphorical sense rather than its literal sense. For example, compare the following two sentences. In the adapted version, we have changed the sense totally by adding the intensifier.

Meet the Dudes behind 'South Park.'

Meet the Dudes *very much* behind 'South Park.'

Conjunctions

Conjunctions are items which link phrases together. We will only briefly describe the two different types of conjunctions without going into any detail.

COORDINATORS link units of the same category like two noun phrases, two clauses and so on. The resulting phrase is then also of the same category; two coordinated clauses form a new clause, etc. (Remember the coordination test we gave earlier for checking category membership.) The central coordinators are *and*, *but* and *or*, but they can also be reinforced with additional words, e.g. *either . . . or; not only . . . but also; both . . . and*.

Kyle: Works hard *and* gets good grades *but* still finds himself in trouble.
Cartman: Spends most of his time sitting on the sofa eating cheesy puffs *or* being insulted by the rest of 'South Park.'

There are some examples of phrases that can be coordinated even though they are not of the same category. The example standardly used to illustrate this is *happy and in the pink*, where *happy* is an adjective and *in the pink* is a preposition phrase. *In the pink* is used figuratively here to mean roughly 'healthy' and that is probably the reason why it works. It is also the case that the coordinated elements (even those that don't belong to the same category) must be alike in their function (in other words, they must have the same grammatical relationship with surrounding material). Functions are something we take up in the next chapter.

SUBORDINATORS, now often referred to as COMPLEMENTISERS (this is the term we will use in Chapter 8), link a clause to some other element. Hence a clause introduced by a complementiser forms part of some other phrase. There are more subordinators than coordinators; common ones include *after, although, as, because, if, that, until* and *while*.

And *if that wasn't weird enough*, the subplot has Stan and his pals trying to be lesbians.
The genius of 'South Park' lies in the fact *that it just doesn't know when to stop.*
It's 10 times worse *because it sucks you in.*

Determiners

Determiners are function words within noun phrases, like *a(n)*, *the* or *this*. The job of a determiner is related to the details of how a noun phrase is used to refer to something in some world (real or imagined). We will return to the properties of determiners in Chapter 7.

3.6 Phrasal categories and their structure

In Section 2.7, we discussed different ways of representing linguistic structure and concluded that a tree, or phrase marker, was the best way of doing so. For people who concern themselves with the structure of language, trees are an invaluable help in representing it. Many of you will really take to this idea and find that it gives the feel of a pleasant mixture of the exciting messiness of language and the comfort of the formality of subjects like mathematics. That is certainly how at least one of us feels about syntactic trees. Most people, we suspect, end up having quite a lukewarm relationship with syntactic trees. However, there is a third group of people who might otherwise enjoy language, but find that trees and other formal representations scare the living daylights out of them. This is a serious drawback with formal representations for a book such as this. It is with this in mind that we have decided to keep formal representations out of the main part of the chapters as far as possible. Instead, each chapter will end with a section on tree representations. If you really find that they just confuse things for you and you don't have to use trees for the course you are doing, then you can just skip each of these sections. If you do have to learn how to draw trees, but find them a bit scary, then we hope that being able to go through each chapter in peace without having to look at trees will still be helpful. Finally, if you belong to the people who really love syntactic trees, well, then you have something to look forward to at the end of each chapter!

For all the major categories, we have said that they can form larger phrases which are named after the central categories; nouns form noun phrases, verbs form verb phrases, etc. We abbreviate these phrasal categories NP, VP, AP (for adjective), AdvP (for adverb) and PP. In all these cases, we will say that the lexical category is the HEAD of the phrasal category; the head of a noun phrase is a noun and so on. It turns out that there are similarities between the way in which heads combine with different elements. For instance, each kind of element can combine with elements which are very closely related to the head. Consider the following phrases, adapted from one of the earlier examples:

their *disrespect* of good taste

They *disrespect* good taste.

They are *disrespectful* of good taste.

The noun *disrespect* in the first example, the identical verb in the second and the adjective *disrespectful* in the third all combine with a phrase which is strongly linked to the head; if you show disrespect, you must show it for something, and that something must be something that one can show disrespect for. These elements which have a close relationship with the head are referred to generally as COMPLEMENTS and they are assumed to combine only with single lexical elements, with heads; the lexical elements *disrespect* (which is a noun) and *disrespectful* combine with a complement *of good taste*, the lexical element *disrespect* (the verb) combines with a complement *good taste*. Note that it is important not to confuse this term with the function PREDICATIVE COMPLEMENT (Section 4.5). Complement is a general term; it refers to any element that is selected by a head, be that head a verb, a noun, an adjective or a preposition. This ability of a head to select its complement(s) is referred to as SUB-CATEGORISATION; in the previous examples, the verb *disrespect* sub-categorises for an NP complement whereas the noun *disrespect* and the adjective *disrespectful* both sub-categorise for a PP complement.

The exact shape of the complement, i.e. *of good taste* versus *good taste*, depends on the category of the head: generally verbs take noun phrases like *good taste* and nouns and adjectives take preposition phrases like *of good taste*. These number of complements is determined by the head; we cannot add another one without getting ungrammatical phrases:

*their disrespect of good taste of all things sacred

*They disrespect good taste all things sacred.

*They are disrespectful of good taste of all things sacred.

The reason for this is that the words *disrespect* and *disrespectful* only permit one complement. You can make these phrases grammatical by inserting an *and* but then they end up forming one phrase together and therefore do not disprove our point.

If we expand these phrases further, we see that the similarities continue:

their *constant* disrespect of good taste

They *constantly* disrespect good taste.

They are *constantly* disrespectful of good taste.

The words we have added here are not complements. For one thing, they can be much more freely chosen by the speaker than the complements; they are not unique and their order can be varied.

their *unpleasant constant persistent* disrespect of good taste

They *constantly unpleasantly persistently* disrespect good taste.

They are *constantly persistently unpleasantly* disrespectful of good taste.

These freer elements clearly belong within the same phrases as the head and the complement, but they are not as closely linked to the head. They are usually referred to as MODIFIERS. Whereas complements follow their heads in English, modifiers may precede or follow the head.

the disrespect of good taste [*by the authors*] [*which offended many watchers*]

They disrespect good taste [*constantly*] [*with great enthusiasm*].

In these examples, we have two different modifiers, as indicated by the parentheses. Whereas there is some freedom as to the order between modifiers, sentences usually become either ungrammatical or at least very awkward when complements are separated from their heads (we have marked the first one with a question mark rather than an asterisk, since there are circumstances under which it could be used):

?the disrespect by the authors of good taste

*They disrespect constantly good taste.

The first of these examples can be considered completely grammatical, albeit slightly strange, if the *of good taste* modifies *authors*, but that is a different matter.

To account for similarities like these between phrases, a system for representing constituent structure has been developed which is called x-BAR SYNTAX. It uses trees just like we did in Chapter 2, but the trees are labelled this time. We said there that a node represents a constituent, so that means that a label for a certain constituent can be put at the node associated with that constituent. In these trees, we want to make sure that the differences between complements and modifiers are represented. If we consider *disrespect of good taste* and *disrespect good taste* first, we know that *disrespect* is a noun and a verb, respectively. We can then draw the following trees, where for the time being we need not discuss the category status of the complement:

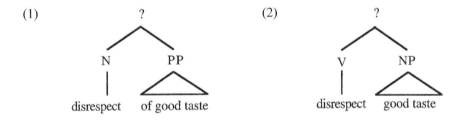

The question then is what to call the mother node of this little tree. Now, it does not seem right to call it a full noun or verb phrase, i.e. we do not want to label the nodes NP and VP, because the phrases are not really complete yet. On the other hand, the phrases represented by the mother node, *disrespect of good taste* and *disrespect good taste*, are clearly not nouns or verbs either – they are far too complex for that. Instead, a label is used which means 'neither lexical nor fully phrasal,' and that label is N' and V', pronounced N-bar and V-bar, or N-single-bar and V-single-bar. We then get:

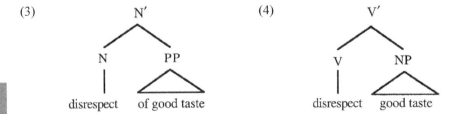

This kind of structure would hold also for *disrespectful of good taste*, where the head is an adjective; we could draw the same tree for that category. In fact, in phrases like *of good taste*, which are headed by prepositions, the head combines with its complement in much the same way. The complement of a category then combines with the lexical category, N, V or A and forms a different category, N', V' or A'. Since this structure is so general, we can replace the category with a variable, say X, and state that a category X may combine with a complement to form a phrase of category X', and hence the name X-bar syntax. From this definition it follows that you cannot add complements at will. We have just said that a complement combines with X and since the result is an X', another complement could not combine with it. This is then the reason why, say *disrespect good taste*, which is a V', cannot combine with another complement, such as *all things sacred*, which would want to combine with a V, not a V'. Hence *They disrespect good taste all things sacred* is ungrammatical. A complement needs to combine with a category X and hence you could not add a complement on top of these trees; a second complement would have to combine with a phrase of category X'.

As we saw, the story for modifiers is very different: they need not be closest to the head and they can be repeated. It seems reasonable, then, to assume that modifiers combine with an X' phrase. The question is what the resulting category is, i.e. what should be in place of the question marks in the following trees?

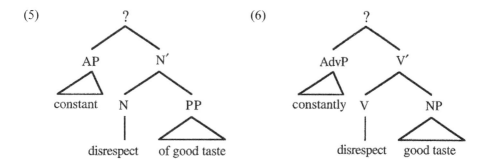

Again, one possibility would be to say that we now have complete phrases, so that they should be labelled NP and VP, respectively. This is not a good idea, however, for two reasons. First, there is a sense in which these phrases are not complete yet. This is particularly obvious with the phrase headed by the noun, where we still have a determiner to add. The second argument against XP at this point is that if the phrase as a whole is an XP and modifiers combine with X', then we would not expect it to be possible to add another modifier to the trees in (5). This is not what we want since we can add further modifiers, as in *unpleasant constant disrespect*

of good taste. If, on the other hand, we assume that the question mark in (5) should be replaced with N', and V', then we would expect another modifier to be possible. A technical way of putting this is that modifiers may occur RECURSIVELY, and that for this reason, the resulting category must be identical to the category with which they combine. We then get the following trees, with a recursive X' node:

(7)   (8)

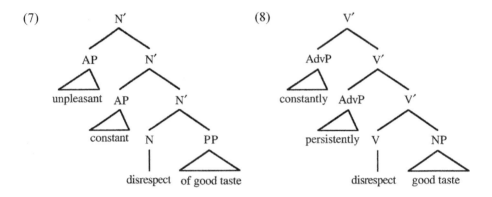

By using the constituency tests introduced in Chapter 2, you can check for yourself that this is the right constituent structure and that *unpleasant constant* and *constantly persistently* do not form constituents.

Now, we can complete the noun phrase by adding a determiner, which certainly does make it a full phrase, an NP. We then get the final tree:

(9)

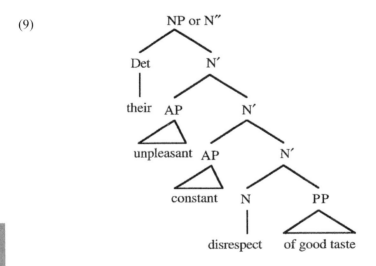

We have now taken a phrase right from a noun, N, via N' to the phrasal level, which we can refer to as either N" (N-double-bar) or NP. Whenever you see a category X" it means exactly the same as XP. All the properties we want are neatly represented in this tree. The determiner combines with a phrase of the category N' and it must be unique, since once you have added a determiner, the mother node is of the category NP, not the right category for a determiner to combine with. The kind of element which combines with an X' to form an X" is referred to as a SPECIFIER. The tree predicts that modifiers can stack up since they combine with an N' to give another N'. The complement, finally, must also be unique, since it combines with an N to form an N'.

Given what we have said so far about generality and X-bar theory, you would expect that we could draw equally neat trees for all the other categories. The general X-bar tree would look like this, where modifiers can be stacked on top of each other and can occur on both sides of the phrase with which they combine:

(10)

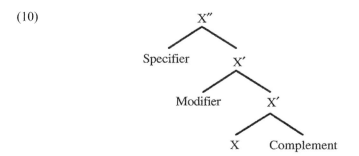

Let's turn to VPs first. The specifier of V' would have to be something that was unique and that somehow 'completed' the phrase. The only thing that seems to do this is the subject, so that we would get the following tree for the sentence *They constantly disrespect good taste*:

(11)

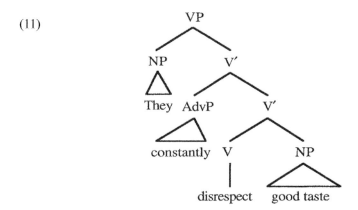

This actually seems to fit all the criteria to do with unique and recursively occurring constituents. It forms a full, complete XP just like the NP, and we said in the section about verbs that there is some sense in which the verb is the head of the sentence. This is indeed exactly the structure many theories of syntax assign to a sentence and we actually rather like the approach represented by this tree. But in order to make things simpler when we come to talk about clauses in Chapter 8, we will follow a long tradition and say that a sentence is of category S and it consists of an NP and a VP, where the NP is a subject.

So, as far as N and V go, this notion of a category-neutral X-bar system seems to be holding up reasonably well. However, when we turn to APs, AdvPs and PPs the outlook is gloomier. For all these categories, it is quite easy to see that we can identify some complements, and for APs and AdvPs, we can also find recursive modifiers. As we said in the section about prepositions, they don't have much in the line of modifiers, so that there are very few elements which can combine with a P' to form another P'. It gets even trickier when we try to think of specifiers for these categories. What can we add to APs, AdvPs or PPs which is unique and which somehow completes the phrase in the way that a determiner or a subject does? The elements mentioned in some textbooks on syntactic theory strike us as typical modifiers, and we can't really think of any good examples. Our conclusion is, then, that X-bar syntax is a really valuable way of looking at constituent structure as long as one doesn't go to town completely with the idea of parallelism between categories.

3.7 Points to remember

- ❏ Words fall into various categories or classes. These classes include nouns, verbs, adjectives and adverbs (major classes) and prepositions, conjunctions and determiners (minor classes).
- ❏ In order to define these categories, we use structural tests, based on the syntactic and morphological behaviour of the words. For words whose category membership is more difficult to establish, we can use coordination with and substitution by a prototypical member of that category to indicate its category membership.
- ❏ From each category, phrases can be built up by adding other elements. The elements which are added are the dependents; the element around which we build the phrase is the head. The result is a phrasal category which is named after the category of its head.
- ❏ A characteristic of all nouns is that they can combine on their own with the possessive 's. All nouns except proper nouns can form a noun phrase with *the*. Count nouns can also occur in plural form, combine with *a(n)* to form a noun phrase and with numerals; non-count nouns cannot.
- ❏ Verbs are characterised by having five different inflectional forms: base, *-s* form, past tense form, past participle form and the *-ing* form. An important distinction for verbs is between the finite forms, that is, those

which can show present and past tense, and non-finite forms, those that occur in an environment where they cannot change their form. Any string of verbs can have at most one finite verb, the first one.

❑ The ability to occur in comparative and superlative forms is character-istic of adjectives and adverbs. However, not all of them are gradable in this way, and particularly for adjectives we need to use coordination and substitution to establish category membership. Adjectives can often be turned into adverbs by the addition of the derivational affix -ly.

❑ Pronouns substitute for NPs and include personal, reflexive, possessive, demonstrative, and relative pronouns. With only a few exceptions, they take no modifiers.

❑ The majority of prepositions express spatial relations, but are also used for more abstract relations; they do not allow any inflection and they combine with NPs to form PPs.

❑ Determiners combine with nouns to form noun phrases. There are five categories: articles, demonstratives, wh-determiners, quantificational determiners and possessive determiners.

❑ Conjunctions are items which link elements. They include coordinators and subordinators.

Exercises

1. Spot the word class

Return to our piece made up of archaic and obsolete words in Section 3.2. State the word class of each of the unusual words. Explain how you decided on the word class in each instance – since the words are probably unfamil-iar to you, you should be using grammatical cues to make your decision.

2. Word classes in non-normal speech

The following is part of a picture description task by an aphasic patient (- indicates a pause). For each word, decide to which category it belongs. Now comment on the categories used; for instance, are there any categories that occur more or less frequently than usual?

> Well the - - boy is - - slipped - going - over - but he's getting the - - - - what d'you call em - - oh - - cakes any anyway - he's getting but slowly coming bang and he's over - and second one she's just watching and - oh terrible - she's just running the hot water or something just - all over the place - everywhere - washing - that's all right but she still sees the - - turns it off - but no she doesn't it's everything's terrible

3. Classes and forms of nouns and verbs

Part 1: In the following text, from *The Big Issue in the North* (#801:12), iden-tify all the nouns and all the verbs. In each case state what form the word occurs in (for instance singular/plural, present/past, ppart etc); for nouns, also give the sub-class (common/proper, count/non-count). Comment on any difficulties you encounter.

> From the very first, this was an artist who made us look at the familiar with new eyes and ears. While some critics tie themselves in knots analysing Dylan's motives, it has usually turned out that he means exactly what he says.

Part 2: For the nouns and verbs you've just found, identify the full phrases they head. Do these phrases contain complements, modifiers and specifiers? Remember that phrases can contain other phrases. When you find it difficult to choose between different ways of analysing things, describe why.

4. An analysis of crash blossoms

Early in this chapter we described how journalists leave out the grammatical words from their headlines – the resulting compact headline, dubbed the crash blossom, is often ambiguous. This exercise requires you to collect your own crash blossoms to analyse (if you have trouble finding these, there are plenty of ambiguous headlines on the Internet). First use paraphrases to establish the different interpretations; in other words, write complete sentences to show all possible meanings. Then decide whether the ambiguity in these headlines is structural, lexical (i.e. based on an ambiguous word) or both. You might then want to try your hand at writing your own crash blossoms.

5. Trees

If you read Section 3.6, here are some phrases to analyse and draw labelled trees for:

(a) a truly magical moment

(b) incredibly proud of his dog

(c) The dog performed impressive tricks.

In each case you need to determine which words form constituents, what is the head of each constituent and what the category is of each word before you can draw the tree.

4

Functions within the clause

4.1 Introduction

So far we have been talking about syntactic structure purely in terms of constituency, using terms like *subject* and *object* without going into exactly what we mean by these notions. We've been concerned with isolating constituents and with labelling these constituents in terms of the categories to which they belong, but we haven't as yet considered their FUNCTION, or, as it is sometimes called, their GRAMMATICAL RELATION; in other words, the role they play within the sentence. In short, phrasal categories like noun phrases and verb phrases are what constituents **are**. Functions like SUBJECT and OBJECT are what constituents **do**. You can usually tell what category an element belongs to by just looking at the word or phrase, its morphology, etc. In order to establish the function of a phrase, on the other hand, you need to know the sentence in which it occurs.

We need to maintain a consistent distinction between what phrases are and what they do because most phrasal categories have a variety of different functions. For example, while it's true that subjects are usually noun phrases, not all noun phrases function as subjects:

The bride's mother threw *a large pickled gherkin*. (AUS#47: 9)

Here both *the bride's mother* and *a large pickled gherkin* are noun phrases. The first functions as a subject and the second functions as an object. So although both *the bride's mother* and *a large pickled gherkin* belong to the same phrasal category, their functions do differ. In English, it's their position in the sentence that tells us who is doing what and to whom (also of course the knowledge that large pickled gherkins don't usually throw people!).

As we shall see later, the converse is also true: a particular function can be filled by different phrasal categories; indeed, even the subject position can be filled by categories other than noun phrases. It is, then, very important to remember to make a distinction between category and function.

There is a sense in which we paint with a broader brush when we talk about functions, rather than categories: as we have seen, phrases like NPs have internal structure which can be represented. However, when we discuss functions, we only refer to clause-level functions and hence we do not need to know anything about the internal structure of, say, the NP, as long as we know it functions as, say, a subject.

We will be focusing here on what can be thought of as the basic clause of English. This is a clause which involves a statement (we will say more about different kinds of sentences in Chapter 5). It is also a clause which is structurally complete in itself; in other words, it doesn't form part of any other clause. The following extract on virtual pet ownership gives you an idea of some of the different types of basic clause patterns that are available. (Until otherwise stated, all examples which follow are taken (or adapted) from David Nichols' 'The pet hate'; *The Big Issue* (AUS#36:17).) (Okay, so the Tamagotchi does date us a little – but, as the Wiki entry reminds us, this virtual pet was one of the biggest fads of the 1990s and early 2000s, and apparently the re-released versions are now hot fashion accessories.)

Although all these share the same initial division between noun phrase and verb phrase, they differ radically at the lower, more detailed level within the hierarchical structure of the verb phrase.

NP	VP
I	have pulled out the plastic tab.
A checkered shape	bursts unconvincingly into a small, intelligent-eyed blob.
It	sits above me, pacing from side to side inside its tiny white egg.
Its small square eyes	stare meaningfully.
The Tamagotchi	goes to sleep.
It	wakes up.
This cycle	continues.
It	's much like your life, really.

These sentences are quite typical of English statements in that the initial division is between a noun phrase and a verb phrase. In these examples, that initial noun phrase functions as the subject. The fact that the subject comes first in the sentence is also typical of English. Furthermore, it is almost obligatory for English sentences to have a subject. In Chapter 5 we will discuss some sentence types which either do not have subjects or in which the subjects do not precede the verb phrase. The verb phrase always contains a verbal element but will vary considerably according to the nature and function of the phrases accompanying it.

In this book, we will look at the following functions: predicate, subject, object (direct and indirect), predicative complement (subject complement or object complement) and adverbial. We should point out at this stage that other terms are sometimes used for some of these functions. We will tell you about some of these in the relevant subsections later. Also, you should know that this is not the only way of looking at the major parts of a sentence. In Chapter 10, when we consider how sentences combine to constitute a discourse in speech and writing, we see that, in addition to functions within the sentence, phrases also have functions within the larger discourse unit and these include things such as focus, topic/comment, and old versus new information.

4.2 The predicate

The PREDICATE is quite easy to spot, since it is what is left of the sentence when you have removed the subject. In the example sentences in the previous section, the parts of the sentences in the VP column all function as predicates. In fact, the function of predicate is always filled by a verb phrase. There is one obligatory part to the predicate and that is the verb. In fact, it is more accurate to say that the central part is the string of verbs, since there can be more than one. In the following two examples, the core part of the predicate is in italics and the whole predicate is underlined. In Chapter 6, we will look at how to analyse these strings of verbs in terms of constituents.

Tamagotchis <u>*are rank*</u>.

Most schools <u>*have banned* Tamagotchis</u>.

4.3 The subject

You will find that many textbooks use notional (or semantic) criteria rather than grammatical criteria to define SUBJECT. For example, they will point out that subjects often involve the semantic role of agent (sometimes called actor). This means that the subject is the 'doer.' Certainly it is the case that subjects are often the instigators of an action expressed in the verb string, as in the following:

I have pulled out the plastic tab.

But there are many cases where subjects are not clear agents in that they do not volitionally instigate an action. What do we do in the case of 'calls of nature,' for example (especially those of a virtual pet!)? The Tamagotchi, or the pronoun *it* referring to the Tamagotchi, is the subject of each of the following clauses, but can we really describe it as an agent, a doer?

At around 6.00 p.m. *the Tamagotchi* goes to sleep. At around 8 a.m. *it* wakes up. Then *it* eats and shits. *A Tamagotchi* treated badly will go 'back to its planet' (i.e. die).

It turns out that defining an agent becomes as tricky as defining a subject. What's more, there are many clauses where there is simply no action involved – therefore no agent. In fact, it would be problematic to define subjects with any semantic notion since subjects can have so many different semantic relationships with the predicate. For example, try to assign a semantic role to each of the subjects in the following:

The following Tamagotchi facts were gleaned in a conversation.

A checkered shape is pulsating.

It sits above me.

One button at the bottom of the Tamagotchi's egg selects certain icons (food, medicine, discipline) and *others* administer the discipline or the cake or whatever.

My Tamagotchi has carked it.

At first *I* felt a degree of unease.

It is well known *that Tamagotchi is a lovable cyberspace virtual reality creature.*

The participants expressed by the subjects here involve an array of different roles, none of them that of agent. They include: patient (is affected by another participant), instrument (is involved in an action but controlled by another participant), location (is situated in space), experiencer (undergoes a physical effect from some stimulus) and recipient (receives something). In the very last example the subject doesn't appear to have a semantic role at all. The pronoun *it* here is acting as a kind of empty placeholder, fulfilling the grammatical requirement in English that sentences have a subject, but contributes nothing semantically to the clause. It's what is sometimes called a DUMMY SUBJECT. Even putting aside the problems of coming up with a satisfactory definition of an agent role (or actor), it is clear that agent will never provide us with much more than a rough characterisation of subject.

Other textbooks identify the subject with the topic of the sentence; in other words, what the sentence is basically about. Certainly there are many instances where the subject nicely correlates with the topic. A construction which we call the PASSIVE offers a good illustration. Compare the following two sentences – the first is the ACTIVE and the second the PASSIVE. Don't worry about the details for the moment; we will return to the distinction between active and passive sentences in Section 4.4.

Active: *Most schools* have banned Tamagotchis. (AUS#36:17)

Passive: *Tamagotchis* have been banned by most schools.

Both the active and passive versions describe the same situation and have the same basic meaning, but they differ in their choice of subject. This immediately raises further problems for the characterisation of subject as agent (or actor). The subject *most schools* may be agent-like in the first sentence, but it has precisely the same role in the second sentence; yet it is not the subject. When there is a choice of what to have in the subject position, as when a passive counterpart is available (not all sentences can occur in the passive, as we shall see in Chapter 6), the choice is often determined by discourse considerations, one of which is determining what is the TOPIC, essentially 'what the sentence is about.' One could argue that the active sentence 'is about' schools and what they do, whereas the second is about Tamagotchis and what happens to them. There are a number of problems with defining subjects in terms of topic status, however. In the sentence like *It is snowing*, we would hardly want to say that the sentence 'is about' *it*. Furthermore, as we shall see in Chapter 9, establishing what is a topic is even more complicated than establishing what is the subject. As with categories, then, we find that it is really only structural criteria that will do the job.

We will now give five structural characteristics of subjects. Of these, the first two are pretty much unique to subjects and can therefore be used as tests for subjecthood, whereas the last three are general characteristics which are not unique to subjects.

Subject–operator inversion in questions

The clearest way of spotting the subject of a sentence is to turn the sentence into a *yes–no* question (by this we mean a question which can be answered with either 'yes' or 'no'; more about them in Chapter 5). In English, questions are formed by reversing the order between the subject and the first verb which follows it. Look at the following example:

He *can* keep a Tamagotchi alive for more than a week?

The appropriate question here if we want a 'yes' or a 'no' as an answer is:

Can *he* keep a Tamagotchi alive for more than a week?

Here 'he' and 'can' have changed places and that means that 'he' must be the subject in the first sentence.

English differs from its Germanic relatives in question formation in that it only permits this inversion with a small subset of the verbs, the so-called auxiliary verbs (more about them in Chapter 6; in fact when we discuss auxiliaries there we will conclude that only the finite auxiliary, the OPERATOR, can invert, and hence the term SUBJECT–OPERATOR inversion). Consider the adapted sentence:

He keeps a Tamagotchi alive for more than a week.

If *keeps* allowed inversion with the subject, then we would have a question like:

*Keeps he a Tamagotchi alive for more than a week?

However, *keep* is not an auxiliary verb, so that in order to form a question we need to introduce a dummy auxiliary *do*, which does invert with the subject to give the correct question:

He *does* keep a Tamagotchi alive for more than a week.

Does he keep a Tamagotchi alive for more than a week?

So in order to establish whether a constituent is the subject of a sentence, turn the sentence into a *yes–no* question; the element which has inverted with an auxiliary is the subject. If there is no suitable verb in the original sentence, then use dummy *do* and the subject is the constituent which occurs between *do* and the original verb. You can now go back to the collection of sentences at the start of this chapter and check that all the phrases in the NP column are indeed subjects.

Verb agreement

In Chapter 3 we talked about how the noun phrases have 'person' and 'number' properties. We saw that pronouns vary in form according to these properties. Traditionally, these properties are often also ascribed to verbs. As we saw, the reason for this is that verbs agree with the properties of noun phrases in English. Verbs agree only with subjects in this way, and hence we can say that the subject is that element with which the verb agrees. Since verbs have different forms only in the present tense, this criterion is limited. (Look back at Table 3.2 for more details about the different verb forms. We will say more about tense in Chapter 6.)

Consider now the following two sentences:

My Tamagotchi *has* carked it.

Tamagotchis *are* rank.

Here we suspect that *my Tamagotchi* and *Tamagotchis* are the respective subjects. To test this hypothesis, we change the number of the two noun phrases and see whether the form of the verb then has to change:

My Tamagotchis *has/have carked it.

Tamagotchi *are/is rank.

Indeed, the form of the verb has to change when we change the number of that particular noun phrase and this shows that the noun phrase in question is the subject.

Case

As we discussed in Chapter 3, English doesn't really have case anymore, although relics are preserved in the pronoun system. A handful of pronouns remain that continue to distinguish subject and object on the basis of form. We are pre-empting our discussion of objects here, but have a look at the form of the third person pronouns in the following example. Here the subject and object appear in the SUBJECT CASE and the OBJECT CASE, respectively.

They're banned, because you have to keep on feeding *them*.

subject   object

We need to be a bit careful with using this criterion, however, not just because it only applies to pronouns and only some of them at that, but also because there are some things which are subjects but which actually do occur in the objective form. This happens only under very special circumstances and we will discuss them in more detail in Chapter 8.

Phrasal category

The subject of a clause is almost always a noun phrase (i.e. including single nouns and pronouns) as in:

Tamagotchi is a gift to this world.

It sits above me.

This cannot be used as a criterion to identify subjects, though, because noun phrases can occur in almost any function within the sentence, and there are also occasional subjects which are not noun phrases (we give examples later).

Clauses (more about this category in Chapter 8) may also function as subjects, as in:

That Tamagotchi is a lovable cyberspace virtual reality creature is well known.

When clauses function as subjects, the main criteria for subject status don't work; we cannot make a corresponding *yes–no* question, because English doesn't like moving such big heavy chunks as clauses around the verb, and we cannot check agreement, because a clause always takes singular third person agreement. Since English is generally quite keen to avoid whole clauses in subject position, it will instead move them to the end of the sentence. This is known as EXTRAPOSING and we will come back to it in Chapter 9. Since English sentences need a subject, we then get *it* in the subject position:

It is well known *that Tamagotchi is a lovable cyberspace virtual reality creature.*

It's great *how a perception held to be true can be overturned by simply crossing a border.* (N#274:29)

In these sentences we refer to *it* as the subject and to the constituent beginning with *that* as the EXTRAPOSED SUBJECT. Once we have done this, we can apply the subject–operator criterion to *it* and we find that it does behave like a good subject:

Is it well known that Tamagotchi is a lovable cyberspace virtual reality creature?

We should point out here that some textbook writers use the following line of reasoning with respect to clausal subjects like *that Tamagotchi is a lovable cyberspace virtual reality creature* in *That Tamagotchi is a lovable cyberspace virtual reality creature is well known*: this phrase can function as a subject, a subject is always a noun phrase, hence *that Tamagotchi is a lovable cyberspace virtual reality creature* must be a noun phrase. To be honest, we find this a misguided approach to the whole issue. The fault lies in the assumption that a subject must be a noun phrase. If you return to this section when you have gone into the structure of noun phrases in some detail in Chapter 7, you will hopefully agree with us that *that Tamagotchi is a lovable cyberspace virtual reality creature* is not a noun phrase.

Finally, under very special circumstances, a preposition phrase can function as the subject. The standard kinds of examples given in textbooks are:

Under the bed is a good place to hide.

Down the street is much posher than here.

The argument for saying that *under the bed* and *down the street* are subjects here is that they can invert with the verb to form a *yes–no* question:

Is under the bed a good place to hide?

Is down the street posher than here?

It is in fact not that easy to think of other examples of PP subjects. We mention these here mainly for their curiosity value.

Basic position

The basic position of the subject is sentence-initially (or more correctly clause-initially, but more about that in Chapter 8), before the predicate, as in all the examples just given. Occasionally an adverbial can either precede it or intervene between it and the predicate.

Yesterday I reset the bugger.

I *just* reset the bugger.

Although other positions for subjects are possible, these are marked (i.e. non-basic) constructions and we will deal with these in later chapters. The first example shows the subject moved from its usual position to follow the finite verb. This the normal way of forming a question in English. But as the second example shows, it can also happen in other limited contexts:

Is football fascist? *Is life* meaningless? *Did Al* ever love anybody? (AUS#45:19)

Had he been really brave, rather than derivative of his own formula, he might have created something . . . (N#269:26)

There are also a small number of adverbials that force the verb and the subject to invert when they occur initially, as when Piglet says to himself that

Never had he seen so much rain.

The special case of *there*

We've identified some characteristics of the typical English subject. Now let's put these to the test and turn to the controversial case of dummy *there*. Consider the following examples:

There are exceptions.

There is a disagreement among experts.

There's nothing exactly quirky about my Tamagotchi.

Traditional grammars would assume *there* to be an adverbial in each of these examples. The subject they would claim is the noun phrase following the verb *be* in each case. Certainly in an example like the following *there* is an adverb indicating location:

There's Gorgeous, still sitting on the couch, patiently awaiting your return and looking even better now than 10 minutes ago. (AUS#43:38)

We can for instance change this to *Gorgeous is there, still sitting* . . . and we can stress *there*. But we are not dealing with location in our first three examples. We cannot sensibly say *Exceptions are there* for instance. In fact, in these examples *there* seems to contribute nothing at all semantically to the clause. It is also impossible to put stress on *there* in the first three examples.

We shall now see whether *there* may function as a subject in the three first examples. Let's try the most reliable criterion first: subject–operator inversion:

There are exceptions.

Are *there* exceptions?

There is a disagreement among experts.

Is *there* a disagreement among experts?

So far then, *there* looks like a subject.

Case is initially not all that revealing since *there* does not show a contrast – but then remember neither do the pronouns *you* and *it*. More interesting, however, is the case of the constituent that follows the verb; if *there* is not the subject, then we would have to assume that the constituent following the verb is the subject (since every English sentence appears to need a subject). However, as the next invented example shows, this pronoun appears in the objective case and is therefore an unlikely subject.

[Who's coming to the party?] Well, there's *me* and my Tamagotchi.

Verb agreement is slightly problematic. As you can see from the first three examples, the verb form can be either singular or plural. It would seem that in each case the verb is agreeing with the person and number properties not from *there* but rather from the meaningful constituents which follow, namely, *exceptions*, *disagreement* and *nothing*. But even though the first example shows the plural verb *are* (to agree with *exceptions*), in spoken and more colloquial written varieties you might also encounter *There's exceptions* with a singular, usually contracted, verb. It's a construction widely condemned, but also widely produced as the following examples confirm. (Note, although some of these examples are drawn from the same magazine, they do involve different writers.)

There's so many beautiful dancers. (AUS#66:14)

And then there's the paparazzi. (N#274:12)
(The fact that *paparazzi* is a plural noun is indicated in the next sentence where we find plural agreement: *I think the paparazzi are . . .*)

Bloody oath there's reasons people sleep on the streets. (AUS#66:23)

There *is* invisible thanks involved. (AUS#66:9)

There's always been songs about sex and death. (N#301:24)

There's people who don't want you sleeping near their spot. (AUS#66:24)

Coordinated subjects normally require plural verbs (*wine and cheese are in the fridge*). Yet when they are part of a *there* clause, even Standard English requires a singular verb (*there is wine and cheese in the fridge*). In the following example, notice the mismatch in verb agreement between the first sentence (*is*) with *there* and the bracketed version (*are*):

There's a long-legged dominatrix, a nun in vinyl, a gum-chewing school-girl, an inflatable doll, a double D fat-o-gram wench and Edwina scissor hands . . . (AUS#45:33)

[A long-legged dominatrix, a nun in vinyl, a gum-chewing schoolgirl, an inflatable doll, a double D fat-o-gram wench and Edwina scissor hands *are* . . .]

In cases like this one, the form of the verb does not depend on the plural elements that follow, but is taken from *there*. Clearly, *there* in these sentences is involved in the assignment of person and number properties to the verb – not only in non-standard varieties of English.

A grammatical feature of Modern English is the now obligatory expression of the subject. Whereas in earlier times subjectless sentences were perfectly acceptable, the history of English has seen the evolution of structural (or dummy) subjects like *it* and *there* that have now become a basic requirement of the language for a number of different constructions (see Chapter 9). Although *there* is not a typical subject, it does clearly have one of the fundamental subject properties, namely, it participates in subject auxiliary inversion; and with respect to agreement, we are seeing a development towards *there* participating more in that. The matter of its category is still quite tricky, but we will (nonetheless) assume that like dummy *it, there* is also a member of the class of pronouns (in pronunciation there is a clear contrast with the pronoun *there* showing a reduced pronunciation [ðə/ðər] compared to adverb *there* [ðɛə/ðɛər]).

4.4 The object

There are two types of objects: DIRECT OBJECT and INDIRECT OBJECT. A lot of what we shall have to say here holds for both types of object. They do differ semantically, however. The indirect object is one function where a semantic definition actually works quite well. As in the following two examples, it typically involves the semantic role of either recipient or benefactor (or malefactor in situations where the entity is adversely affected), meaning that it is the participant that receives something or benefits from the action. Accordingly, verbs that can take indirect objects are verbs of giving, wishing, communicating, causing, and so on. You've probably had enough of virtual reality creatures, so here are some sentence examples gleaned from other *The Big Issue* articles. The indirect object is the one italicised:

You should never have fed *that fish* steroids. (AUS#56:7)

I lit *him* one of my last smokes. (AUS#65:9)

My placid humour gives *the virtual yoga teacher* a run for her virtual money. (AUS#343:13)

The semantic role of direct objects is more complex; they have traditionally been linked to the noun phrase which is most affected by the action of the verb. The direct object is frequently described as the participant that has the role of patient, the participant that is affected by the action. In actual usage, though, objects cover a much wider range of semantic roles than simply the 'patient' or 'target' of the action. Have a look at the wide range of roles that objects can assume:

None of these criticisms significantly diminish *the triumph of this movie.* (AUS#60:32)

I hate *housework.* (AUS#65:8)

The figure surprised *me.* (N#791:32)

It definitely creates *tension.* (N#801:15)

I've cried *a river.* (AUS#558:11)

While some of these objects are directly affected by the actions expressed by the verb, in most cases it is not clear how the objects are affected when they are *diminished, hated, surprised* and so on. Once again, meaning will take us only so far. And once again we must look to structural properties to help us identify a particular function, namely object, in English clauses. As with subjects, some of these properties are pretty much unique to objects (particularly passive), whereas others are not unique to objects.

Passive

An important property of mainstream objects is their ability to be shifted to initial position to become the new grammatical subject of a passive sentence. (We discuss passive sentences in detail in Chapter 9, but because it is such a significant test for objecthood, we will very briefly outline the process for forming passives here.)

Take the following active sentence with *The Big Issue* as its direct object:

I purchased *The Big Issue.* (AUS#60:36)

        object

In forming the passive counterpart to this sentence we 'promote' the old object to become a new subject; we insert the appropriate form of the auxiliary verb *be* and the original verb becomes a passive participle (PPART); we demote the original subject to the end of the sentence to form a new prepositional phrase with *by.* The prepositional phrase is optional; hence the brackets in the following example:

The Big Issue was purchased (by me).

  subject

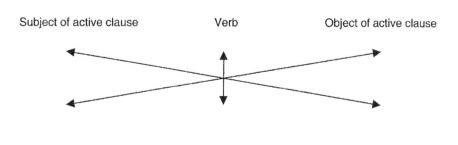

Subject of active clause   Verb   Object of active clause

Subject of passive   *be*+PPART of verb   (*by* object)

Only a sentence with an object can undergo passivisation in this way and therefore the ability to passivise can be used as a criterion for object status. For the time being, we needn't worry too much about exactly what a passive verb is; we will deal with that in detail in Chapter 6. In Chapters 9 and 10, we will talk about some possible reasons why a passive sentence is used rather than an active one.

We need to point out here that not all verbs will be able to form passives to the same extent. Take the following two examples (the objects are in italics):

Being late to bed inclines me to die *an early death.* (AUS#563:13)

My Tamagotchi has carked *it.* (AUS#36:17)

The first example illustrates something called a COGNATE OBJECT. Ordinarily the verb *to die* cannot take an object – unless it is a noun based on *die* (in this case *death*). These are unusual objects, and they have a more modifying function (*an early death* here says more about how the person might die). In the second example, the pronoun *it* following *cark* doesn't appear to contribute anything semantically to the clause and is a kind of dummy object (it can't be replaced by an expanded NP; compare constructions like *leg it, hoof it, fang it*). These unusual objects cannot undergo passive in the same way.

Case

Some pronouns have a distinctive case when functioning as an object. Recall the earlier examples we gave under subject. Here's another example, using the passive to illustrate the contrasting pronouns:

You should never have fed *him* steroids.

                     Object

He should never have been fed steroids.

subject

However, the object forms of pronouns occur not only as objects, but also as objects of prepositions, and as already mentioned under very special circumstances also as subject. It is therefore not a solid test for object status.

Phrasal category

The object of a clause is usually a noun phrase as in all the examples given so far in this section. We will consider verbs that take clauses as their complements in Section 6.6.

Basic position

The object usually immediately follows the verb(s) in basic clauses:

Sharon Osborne, . . ., is in London to *promote* [*the yard sale to end all yard sales*]. (N#697:9)

She *eats* [*fruits and whole grains*]. (N#697:9)

Ozzy would *love* [*her*] if she was the size of a shed. (N#697:10)

If there is both a direct object and an indirect object, then the indirect object precedes the direct one:

You should never have fed   that fish   steroids. (AUS#56:7)
                               indirect   direct

I lit   him   one of my last smokes. (AUS#65:9)
                               indirect   direct

    If there is only one object in the clause, then this is usually the direct one, as in the following examples:

She can't possibly have bought [*all of the stuff in here*]. (N#697:9)

I lit *one of my last smokes*.

There are some verbs which allow either the direct or the indirect object to be left out as in the following example:

They just tell each other lies. (AUS#54:9)

They just tell each other.

They just tell lies.

There are, in fact, one or two verbs in English which take two objects, but which can also occur with the indirect object only; here, this is *feed*:

You should never have fed *that fish*.

In English, for every sentence with two objects, there is normally a corresponding one in which the indirect object is expressed instead as a preposition phrase headed by either of the prepositions *to* or *for*. Unlike the ordinary indirect object these preposition phrases follow the direct object. We can modify the previous examples in this way:

You should never have fed steroids *to that fish*.

I lit one of my last smokes *for him*.

Both versions have the same basic meaning, and which version you choose can depend on the information status of the constituents. As in the case of the passive construction, this has to do with how we as speakers and writers go about packing our messages and is something we deal with in more detail in Chapter 9. Take note that when the recipient or benefactor appears in a prepositional phrase it is no longer an indirect object, but is something called an ADVERBIAL COMPLEMENT. These adverbial complements behave quite differently syntactically from indirect objects. For one thing, they show greater flexibility of word order. In the next example we have moved the adverbial complements to initial position for special emphasis. The indirect objects cannot be fronted in this way; hence the asterisk on two of the examples:

To that fish you should never have fed steroids.

For him I lit one of my last smokes.

*That fish you should never have fed steroids.

*Him I lit one of my last smokes.

Second, adverbial complements respond differently when it comes to forming the passive. Take the example *You should never have fed that fish steroids*. Since we have said that it has two objects, in principle it has two passive counterparts:

Active: You should never have fed *that fish steroids.*

Passive: *That fish* should never have been fed steroids.

Passive: ??*Steroids* should never have been fed that fish.

The last of these examples, where the direct object has become the subject of the corresponding passive, and the indirect object remains in its place following the verb, is considered ungrammatical by most people. For these speakers only the indirect object can occur as the subject of the corresponding passive sentence here. Some dialects, however, accept sentences like *Steroids should never have been fed that fish* and we have therefore given it question marks rather than an asterisk.

With the prepositional phrase construction only one passive construction is possible. Adverbial complements cannot become the subject of a passive sentence; hence the asterisk in the second passive version. As these examples show, the passive sentence in which the direct object is the subject sounds perfectly acceptable in all dialects, so that we can make the generalisation for most dialects of English that only the object nearest the verb can become the subject of a corresponding passive.

Active: You should never have fed steroids *to that fish.*

Passive: *Steroids* should never have been fed to that fish.

Passive: **To that fish* should never have been fed steroids.

It is not always possible to have both indirect object and adverbial complement versions. Much will depend on the nature of the verb. For example, the recipient of the verb *donate* cannot appear as an indirect object for most speakers, but only in a prepositional construction.

He's donating the album's proceeds to homelessness groups. (N#801:12)

[?He's donating homelessness groups the album's proceeds.]

Other verbs like *deny, allow, charge, bet, fine* will only take indirect objects with no corresponding prepositional phrase construction.

They denied Simone the chance. (AUS#66:26)

[*They denied the chance to Simone.]

Idioms will also resist paraphrase by a prepositional construction:

Mirrors also give me the heebie-jeebies. (AUS#331:12a)

[*Mirrors also give the heebie-jeebies to me.]

Idioms generally behave syntactically not like phrases but more like intact chunks. They cannot be interrupted and their word order cannot be rearranged. If it is, they immediately lose their idiomatic sense and the literal sense is restored. In the following, we have asterisked the sentence in brackets because it is unacceptable in the sense of 'phoning Dad,' the sense in the original text. Of course, you can say this if you intend the non-idiomatic meaning; in other words, if you were physically presenting Dad with a bell.

I'll give *Dad* a bell from this stinking public phone box. (AUS#36:16)

[*I'll give a bell to Dad from this stinking public phone box.]

I wanted me some sandwiches

Vernacular varieties of southern American English have a construction involving what look to be rather unusual indirect objects. Christian (2017) describes this for Appalachian English and dubs it 'the personal dative.' Consider the following example:

I got **me** some sandwiches.

As we described in Chapter 3, Standard English would require a reflexive pronoun here – when the same referent is mentioned twice in a clause the second must be reflexive, as in:

I got **myself** some sandwiches.

But the interesting feature of the non-standard personal dative is that it can appear with verbs that that don't happily take the reflexive:

I'm gonna write **me** a letter to my brother.

*I'm gonna write myself a letter to my brother.

I wanted **me** some sandwiches.

*I wanted myself some sandwiches.

You can now see the extent to which this is a different grammatical beast from the usual indirect object. We've just seen for example that indirect objects can be expressed as a prepositional phrase headed by either the preposition *to* or *for*, and these prepositional phrases then follow the direct object:

(a) I gave **him** some sandwiches. → (b) I gave some sandwiches **to him**.

But look what happens when you apply this to the personal dative:

(a) I got **me** some sandwiches. → (b) ?I got some sandwiches **for me**.

Though *I got some sandwiches for me* is grammatical, it doesn't capture the basic meaning of the personal dative, which isn't a beneficiary (this is the interpretation of b). These pronouns aren't recipients or benefactors in the same way that indirect objects are. They are more like interested parties; what they do is bring to prominence the idea of a person (or personified entity) that is in some way involved in an activity, or affected by an event.

4.5 The predicative complement

A note of caution is in order here. The function we refer to as PREDICATIVE COMPLEMENT is often called simply complement. However, unfortunately, the term complement is used for another thing in grammar. The other use of the term is more general and refers to any phrasal category which is selected by a lexical element. In this latter use, it is particularly common when the discussion involves lexical categories other than verb. We discussed this use of the term in Section 3.6. In order to avoid any confusion between these two, we will use predicative complement for the function and reserve the term complement for the more general use of any subcategorised element.

At first blush, predicative complements appear very much like objects. However, there are a number of characteristics which can be used to distinguish between them.

Co-reference

Compare the following sentences:

Zelda is *a pug*. (AUS#47:38)

Zelda bought *a pug*.

Why is the first italicised constituent a predicative complement and the second an object? It's really quite simple – in the first example the noun phrase has the same referent as the subject; it is co-referential with the subject. *Zelda* and *the pug* refer to one and the same entity. Subjects and objects, on the other hand, normally have distinct references (if they don't, you expect the object to take the form of a reflexive or reciprocal pronoun as we saw in Chapter 3; e.g. *Zelda washed herself*). This is the case in the second example where *Zelda* and *the pug* refer to two quite different entities.

From our discussion of objects, we also know that an object can become the subject of a corresponding passive sentence. We can show that the previous examples behave differently in this respect:

*A pug is been (by Zelda).

A pug was bought by Zelda.

This confirms our suspicion that *a pug* is an object in *Zelda bought a pug* but not in *Zelda is a pug*.

We can distinguish two types of predicative complement – a SUBJECT COMPLEMENT and an OBJECT COMPLEMENT, depending on which element in the clause the predicative complement is co-referential with. The contrast between the two types of predicative complements is illustrated by the following.

Zelda	is	*a pug*. (AUS#47:38)	
subject		subject complement	

I	called	*my pug*	*Fufu*. (AUS#47:38)
subject		object	object complement

As already discussed, the first example has a predicative complement *a pug* which refers to the subject *Zelda* and is thus a subject complement. In the second example the predicative complement *Fufu* refers to the object *my pug* and is thus an object complement.

In the two examples we have looked at so far the predicative complement has referred to the same thing as the subject or the object: 'Zelda *is* a pug' and 'my pug *is* Fufu.' However, the predicate complement can also describe the subject or the object, as in the following examples:

Zelda	is	cute.	
subject		subject complement	

I	consider	my pug	impressive.
subject		object	object complement

Of course we can still use the construction with a form of 'be' here: 'Zelda *is* cute' and 'my pug *is* impressive' (at least in the view of the speaker).

Predicate complements can also describe the location of the subject or the object:

We were recently *in America*. (N#697:20)

Phil Spector put the wall of sound *around the Christmas tree*. (N#801:12)

In Section 4.6, we will say that a characteristic of adverbials is that they answer questions like *where?*, which is of course also what *in America* and *around the Christmas tree* do in these two sentences. However, both phrases are obligatory in these sentences as shown by the ungrammaticality of the following examples:

*We were recently.

*Phil Spector put the wall of sound.

Just like with other predicate complements, we can also put a form of the verb 'be' between the two parts: 'we *were* in America' and 'the wall of sound *is* around the Christmas tree.'

Number agreement

Since a predicative complement refers to or describes the same entity as something else in the sentence, it will normally agree with that phrase in things like number and gender. In the following examples, we see how the subject and its predicative complement agree in number:

He is *a one-man juggernaut*. (N#269:9)

[*They are a one-man juggernaut.]

Australians are *great givers to charity*. (AUS#65:4)

[*Australians* are *a great giver to charity*.]

Nonetheless, examples are easy to find where the two co-referential constituents do not agree in number. In both the following examples, we have singular complements predicated of plural subjects; yet there is no anomaly in any case.

Vendors of 'The Big Issue' in the UK have been *a big hit.* (AUS#65:4)

The paparazzi are *a nightmare.* (N#274:12)

In these examples we could argue that the subjects form collective entities (i.e. involving a single collection of individuals). This might explain the singular predicative complement. However, the verb in all sentences occurs in its plural form, which would indicate a plural interpretation of the subject. So it's probably the meaning of the predicative complements in these instances that allows for a plural co-referential subject.

Just as all predicative complements must agree with their subject or object in number, there must also be gender agreement; we illustrate this with an object complement:

Mrs Blackman considers herself a dishonourable lady. (N#274:30)

#Mrs Blackman considers herself a dishonourable man.

We put a # rather than an asterisk, since the sentence would be infelicitous here rather than ungrammatical (of course given there are those whose gender identity or gender expression differs from their assigned sex, it is also conceivable that Mrs Blackman might consider herself a dishonourable man).

Phrasal category

Predicative complements can be filled by a noun phrase, an adjective phrase or a preposition phrase, as in all the examples given so far in this section.

Basic position

A subject complement (italic) usually immediately follows the verb (underlined) and an object complement (italic) follows the object (underlined).

I'<u>m</u> *stronger than a silly computer game.* (N#269:22)

He <u>appeared</u> *a no-bullshit kind of person.* (AUS#54:10)

I just find <u>men in overalls</u> *attractive.* (AUS#66:21)

Younger cinema-goers will doubtless find <u>it all</u> *enormously entertaining.* (N#269:26)

4.6 The adverbial

We have already seen that constituents which may accompany the verbal element in the predicate can include objects and predicative complements. Adverbials can also form part of the predicate and we can distinguish them from the other two predicate elements by the following properties. Note, we will first talk in general terms about these adverbials and then move on to distinguish a number of sub-types of adverbials.

Optional status

Adverbials are the peripheral elements of the clause. Typically they are optional and can be freely added or removed without disturbing the grammaticality of the clause. By comparison, either a clause becomes unacceptable or its meaning changes significantly if an object or predicative complement is omitted.

The bride's mother threw a large pickled gherkin *at the tormented lover*. (AUS#47:9)

The bride's mother threw a large pickled gherkin.

*The bride's mother threw at the tormented lover.

Flexible word order

Modern English is generally characterised by fairly rigid ordering rules with respect to most constituents. Adverbials are, however, quite flexible in their positioning. Unlike objects and predicative complements, they move with ease about the sentence.

It's a small world *after all*. (AUS#51:7)

After all it's a small world.

It's *after all* a small world.

Meaning of adverbials

In everything we have said so far about how to spot the functions of phrases, we have emphasised how important it is not to rely on semantic, or notional, definitions of functions, or indeed of categories. We do, however, think that they can be quite useful for identifying the members of the rather heterogeneous function of adverbial. Adverbials typically say something about when, where or how something happened; so we can then have a criterion that an adverbial is the answer to a question beginning with something like *when?*, *where?*, *why?*, *how?*, *how long?*, *how often?*, *with whom?* But they never answer questions like *what?* or *who?* Consider the following sentence, where the two bracketed phrases are adverbials and answer the questions *when?* and *how?*, respectively. The only elements in the sentence which can form the answer to a simple *who?* or *what?* question are *he* and *his career*, and those are indeed not adverbials, but subject and object, respectively.

He began his career [at the tender age of 13] [with the Latin boy-band Menudo]. (N#269:10)

As we shall see later, this characteristic holds most obviously for adjuncts and adverbial complements.

Stacking

While clauses permit at most one subject, one finite verb, one predicative complement, one direct object and one indirect object, there are no such restrictions with respect to the number of adverbials. Indeed, there is no theoretical limit to the number of adverbials we can include – we can in principle keep adding them indefinitely. We can say, then, that adverbials can OCCUR RECURSIVELY, or that they can be STACKED. There is of course a practical limit and in the following example with four adverbials the addition of too many more would make it cumbersome.

[*One Christmas*], I went [*with my boyfriend*] [*to his parents' home*] [*for a few days*]. (AUS#43:39)

Phrasal category

In what we have said already about adverbials, they are more unwieldy than the other functions. This holds also for the type of categories that can fill the function; almost anything can function as an adverbial: adverb phrases, prepositional phrases, clauses and even some noun phrases can function as adverbials.

He *eventually* collapsed. (AUS#47:9)

    adverb phrase

With an entourage the size of the Miami Dolphins, a mini-industry has sprung up

prepositional phrase

around the doe-eyed adonis. (N#269:10)

prepositional phrase

I need it *because it's the control, the power that you feel.* (N#269:10)

      clause

The ticket inspectors got on *three times.* (AUS#66:10)

        noun phrase

Adverbial sub-types

Having identified some of the properties of basic adverbials, we are now in a position to make further distinctions. On the basis of both semantic and syntactic criteria it is possible to distinguish three different sub-types of adverbials: ADJUNCTS, DISJUNCTS and CONJUNCTS.

Adjuncts

Adjuncts are your typical adverbials. They are optional and they provide circumstantial information to do with location, manner, attitude, time, instrument, degree, frequency and so on. The sorts of questions adjuncts answer are *how?, where?, why?, when?, what for?, how long?* and so on. The following – all from *The Big Issue* (AUS#47:9) – offer just a taste of the wide range of meanings that adjuncts can cover.

The bride's mother threw a large pickled gherkin *at the tormented lover.*

Place [= where?]

The other guests pelted the weeping Lothario *with an assortment of crustless sandwiches and condiments.*

instrument [= what with?]

He *eventually* collapsed *under a welter of pastries and stewed fruit.*

    time [= when?]   place [= where?]

I gave her my heart but she threw it *back*   *in a mushroom vol-au-vent*

                  place [= where?]   manner [= how?]

When you end up being pelted *with pretzels and smoked salmon sandwiches,*

                  instrument [= what with?]

you know Destiny's *really* got it in for you.

        degree [= how much?]

In all these examples the adjuncts have in some way modified the meaning of the rest of the predicate verb phrase. Adjuncts will always tell us something about what is happening within the clause and they properly belong within the clause as constituents of the predicate verb phrase.

It is usual to further divide adjuncts into groups on the basis of their meaning. We can distinguish, for example, time adjuncts, manner adjuncts, place adjuncts, reason adjuncts and so on. This semantic sub-division can have consequences for the syntax, in particular with respect to placement, but we will not go into that level of detail here.

Disjuncts

Now compare what you know about adjuncts with the italicised adverbials in the following sentences:

Of course I'm a bit disappointed. (N#629:26)

This book is crap, *alright.* (AUS#54:31)

It's a mirage, *surely.* (AUS#55:4)

Frankly, I feel Lucas has missed an opportunity. (N#269:26)

As you can see, disjuncts are like attitude markers. They tell us something about the speaker's attitude towards what is being said. Unlike adjuncts, they don't actually modify anything within the sentence, but rather provide comment on the whole sentence itself. Because they are only loosely associated with the sentence in this way they are separated from the rest of the sentence by an intonation break, often indicated by a comma. Typically, disjuncts occur at the beginning of the sentence, but they also show great flexibility in movement.

To illustrate more clearly the difference between adjuncts and disjuncts compare the following invented sentences. As you can see, this particular adverbial *naturally* can be both an adjunct and a disjunct.

The Tamagotchi died naturally.

The Tamagotchi died, naturally.

In the first example the adjunct *naturally* is a modifier within the verb phrase. It tells us how the Tamagotchi died. In the second, the disjunct *naturally* reflects the speaker's attitude towards the sentence as a whole; the speaker thinks it is obvious that the Tamagotchi died.

Conjuncts

Conjuncts do not modify anything within the verb phrase, but nor do they have anything to say about the speaker. Their function is connective. They therefore resemble disjuncts in only being very loosely associated with the rest of the sentence and like disjuncts also belong outside the predicate.

This film . . . is faster, glitzier and perhaps a tad overdone. *Nevertheless* it gives us occasional reminders of the kind of quiet humour and Aussie understatement so obvious in the first movie. (AUS#62:35)

So anyway, that's that. (N#269:22)

Conjuncts like *nevertheless, nonetheless, therefore, furthermore, thus* and *however* express the relationship between the sentence and its discourse context. In the following extract, have a look at how the (italic) conjuncts relate each sentence to what has preceded in the discourse.

I'm sorry to interrupt this reverie but sadly my Tamagotchi has carked it. *At first*, I felt a degree of unease, imagining its little screen flashing the 'illness' sign. *Then*, I started to feel a kind of relief, as it dawned on me that I had become a slave to Tamagotchi. *So* I felt good it was dead, I mean, 'back on its planet.' *Then* something else took over. What did I do? I didn't think – I just reset the bugger. (AUS#36:17)

As with adjuncts and disjuncts, conjuncts can move quite freely within the clause. They may appear at the beginning, the end, or somewhere in the middle (although given their connective function, early in the clause is preferred).

The special case of phrasal verbs

One very distinctive feature of English syntax is the very obvious presence of a (rapidly growing) class of verbs called PHRASAL VERBS. Phrasal verbs require particular adverbial-like elements to follow them in order to form a complete sentence.

A phrasal verb consists of a verb and an adverb particle which function together as a unit. We call the second parts of these verbs particles because they differ from mainstream adverbs in having very little semantic content. Often you'll find the phrasal verb unit assumes a quite idiomatic sense; that is, a unique meaning which in no way derives from the sum of the parts. These verbs can be both transitive and intransitive.

Mrs Birpitz accidentally *bit off* her husband's nose. (AUS#51:39)

I *wrote* the fare *off*. (AUS#59:25)

They *backed off*. (AUS#59:25)

Being a selfish prick will eventually *pay off*. (AUS#66:8)

As the second of these examples reveals, when phrasal verbs are transitive, the particle can also appear after the direct object (but this arrangement has special conditions, as we will see in Chapter 6).

Constituency tests like those for movement and conjoinability confirm that these adverb particles form a syntactic unit with the verb phrase and not with the object noun phrase.

*It was off her husband's nose that Mrs Birpitz accidentally bit.

*Off her husband's nose Mrs Birpitz accidentally bit.

*Mrs Birpitz accidentally bit off her husband's nose and off one of his ears.

The unit status of these phrasal verbs also prevents the introduction of adverbial material between the verb and its particle:

*Mrs Birpitz bit accidentally off her husband's nose.

4.7 Basic categories of lexical verbs

As we've just seen basic clauses are built around a subject and predicate, and what appears in the predicate varies depending on which grammatical functions are required by the lexical verb. On the basis of these functions we can identify five basic patterns which are used to divide lexical verbs into classes: INTRANSITIVE, MONO-TRANSITIVE, DI-TRANSITIVE, COMPLEX INTRANSITIVE and COMPLEX TRANSITIVE. These categories will be discussed fully in Chapter 6 when we focus on the verbs, but it's appropriate to give you a taste of them here.

Most of the following examples are based on Fiona Scott-Norman's tale of woe – finding shoes for her 'size 12 flippers' (AUS#558:11). The predicate is in square brackets in each case.

Intransitive: no complements

> *The illusion of sexiness*   [*evaporates*]
>   V

Mono-transitive: direct object

> *My Mum*   [*loved*   *those shoes*]
>   V   object

Di-transitive: indirect object + direct object

They	[bought	me	some kick arse shoes]
	V	object$_{indir}$	object$_{dir}$

Complex intransitive: subject complement

My feet [*were   size 12 flippers*]
         V   complement$_{subj}$

Complex transitive: direct object + object complement

They	[made	us	weak].
	V	object$_{dir}$	complement$_{obj}$

You can see that the subject function does not have a role to play in this classification, since all verbs in English need a subject. Optional adverbials don't either, since any number of them can be freely added to any sentence; as we discussed earlier, adverbials are generally more peripheral than the other phrasal elements, supplying additional circumstantial information such as location, manner, attitude and so on and they can appear with all verbs.

4.8 Trees

We will turn now to the issue of how to represent the functional structure of a sentence in terms of a tree diagram. As we have said before, when you look at a sentence in terms of functions, you don't look into as much detailed structure as you would if you considered the structure of a sentence in terms of categories. You don't look inside the functions; once you have found, say, a subject, you stop. Hence the trees here will be relatively simple. First of all, the sentence divides up into subject and predicate (unless there are any disjuncts or conjuncts, but we shall come to those later):

(1)

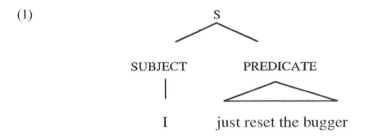

The predicate can have further internal structure; it obligatorily consists of one string of verbs and can consist of one or two other grammatical functions in addition. We illustrate here with trees for a sentence with one object and a sentence with one complement. The two trees are structurally identical. The difference lies in the function of the constituent following the verb.

(2)

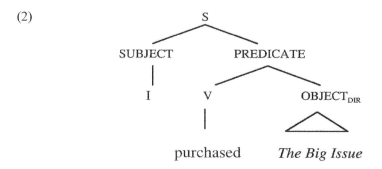

(3)

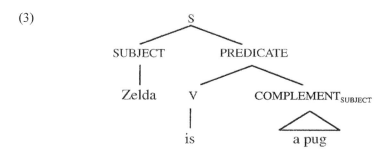

In terms of tree structure we also get a very similar structure for a sentence with two objects and one with an object and a predicative complement.

(4)

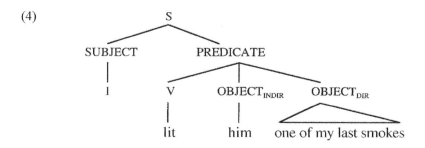

(5)

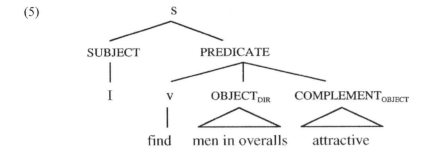

Adverbial complements are found in the tree in exactly the same positions as predicative complements and little more needs to be said about them here. We provide an example here of a sentence with a subject and an adverbial complement. An adverbial object complement would occur in the same position in the tree as the object complement in (5).

(6)

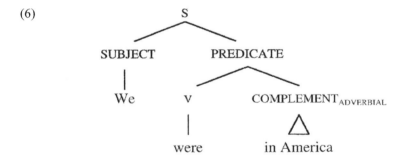

Optional adverbials, on the other hand, are different in terms of their structural position. Clearly, we do not want them in the same position as objects or predicative complements as sisters of the verb, since this is a position reserved for elements very closely connected to the verb. Hence all optional adverbials need to be added a level higher than that of the obligatory elements. If we start with adjuncts, we have said that they modify the content of the predicate. This means that they should be a sister of a predicate node. The resulting node must also be a predicate node since another adverbial could attach at that level; as we said, optional adverbials occur recursively. Hence we get trees like the following:

(7)

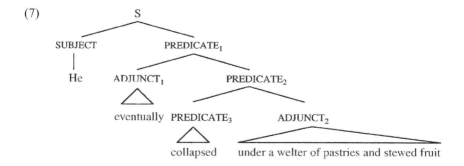

Note that the adjunct belongs 'on top of' the predicate it modifies. The mother node of an adjunct and a predicate is also a predicate since it has exactly the same distribution as any other predicate constituent. As is clear from the tree, an adjunct can appear either before or after the predicate. This freedom of position is common to the optional adverbials.

Since disjuncts and conjuncts do not modify anything within the sentence itself, we attach them structurally on top of the sentence, as in the following trees:

(8)

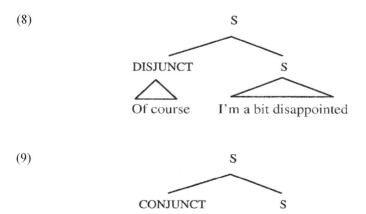

(9)

The resulting constituent is, of course, also a sentence (S). Given the usual flexibility of the position of adverbials, the two daughters of the higher S occur in the opposite order.

We can illustrate the difference between adjuncts and disjuncts, that we saw in the two sentences on p. 106, as in (10) and (11).

(10)

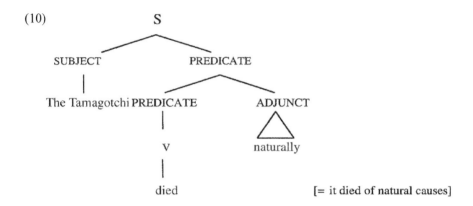

[= it died of natural causes]

(11)

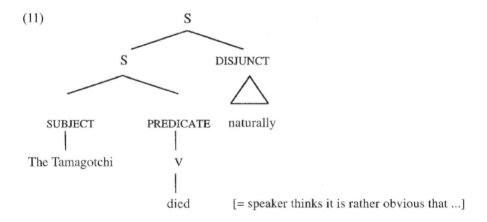

[= speaker thinks it is rather obvious that ...]

4.9 Points to remember

- ❏ The main clause functions relevant to English and the phrasal categories that can fill them can be summed up as in Table 4.1.
- ❏ The subject is the element which inverts with a finite auxiliary to form an interrogative.
- ❏ There are two kinds of objects: direct object and indirect object. The most certain test for object status is the passive.
- ❏ There are two main kinds of predicative complements, subject complements and object complements. They are characterised by being co-referential with some other element within the sentence.

Table 4.1 English functions and phrasal category

Function	Phrasal category
subject	noun phrase/clause
predicate	verb phrase
direct object	noun phrase/clause
indirect object	noun phrase
subject complement	noun phrase/adjective phrase
object complement	noun phrase/adjective phrase
adverbial	adverb phrase/prepositional phrase/clause/ noun phrase

❑ Adverbials are normally optional and supply information about things like the time, manner, duration or place of an event. There are three kinds of optional adverbials: adjunct, disjunct and conjunct.
❑ The subject-predicate frame falls into five basic patterns: intransitive, mono-transitive, di-transitive, complex intransitive and complex transitive.

Exercises

1. Phrasal Category and Function

The following basic clauses have already been analysed into constituents. Identify the phrasal category (noun phrase, adjective phrase, prepositional phrase, adverb phrase) and function (subject, object, predicative complement, adverbial) of each bracketed phrase. Identify the type of object (direct versus indirect), the type of predicative complement (subject versus object) and the type of adverbial (adjunct, conjunct, disjunct, adverbial complement).

(a) [It] was [a light brown dog with the biggest brown eyes I have ever seen].

(b) [This dog] looked [quite old].

(c) [You] can tell [by its teeth].

(d) [At first] [it] was not [so friendly]

(e) [so] [I] stroked [its fur]

(f) and [I] gave [it] [a piece of ham which I had on me at the time].

(g) [It] [suddenly] dawned [on me]

(h) [the dog] might have been [a stray].

(j) [I] rang [the nearest animal shelter].

(k) [I] was throwing [the dog] [a stick].

(l) [Most dogs] bark [at people].

(m) [It] picked [the dog] up.

(Adapted from Larry De La Garde's 'The Shaggy Dog', *The Big Issue* (AUS#56:10))

2. Clause analysis

For each pair of sentences, discuss the difference between the two sentences referring to notions such as phrasal categories and functions. (In each example, the first version is original and the second has been adapted.)

(a) He appeared a no-bullshit kind of person. (AUS#54:10)

He appeared a week later.

(b) Our work with them finishes this autumn. (AUS#51:7)

Our work with them finishes this project.

(c) Keating calls a press conference. (AUS#60:38)

Keating calls it a press conference.

(d) I linger a bit. (AUS#66:10)

I eat a bit.

(e) The book makes a seasoned reviewer physically sick. (AUS#65:27)

The book makes a seasoned reviewer a lot of money.

3. Grammatical variation and functions

The following sentences are from different parts of the English-speaking world. They illustrate variation in the grammar of English using traditional non-standard regional dialects, New and Other Englishes. Describe each of the sentences (identifying phrases and their categories). State how the clause types illustrated here differ from their mainstream Standard English counterparts. (Some of these will hover somewhere on the border between standard and non-standard; many are common to more than one dialect.)

(a) Give it to he, not they – her don't need it. [South-West England]

(b) We like us town. [Northern England]

(c) I'm gonna write me a letter to my cousin. [Appalachia, United States]

(d) John gave it me. [Northern England]

(e) There was a new law but teachers did not follow. [Papua New Guinea]

(f) Here is not allowed to stop the car. [Hong Kong]

4. Phrasal verbs

Each of the following sentences contains a phrasal verb (i.e. consisting of a verb plus its adverb particle). When phrasal verbs are transitive the particle has the option of appearing later in the clause. Examine the following sentences and briefly explain the rules in English whereby the particle can be separated from its verb.

(a) Mrs Birpitz accidentally bit her husband's nose off. (AUS#51:39)

(b) Mrs Birpitz accidentally bit off her husband's nose.

(c) Mrs Birpitz accidentally bit it off.

(d) *Mrs Birpitz accidentally bit off it.

(e) I picked up a strange young passenger the other day outside Myers in Lonsdale Street. (AUS#59:25)

(f) ?I picked a strange young passenger the other day outside Myers in Lonsdale Street up.

(g) I picked him up.

(h) *I picked up him.

5. Clause analysis (more challenging)

Analyse the following sentences in terms of their phrases, and give the function and category of each, as well as the clause pattern. As part of your answer pay particular attention to the italicised constituent. Give one **grammatical** argument to show why its behaviour is unusual; e.g. in the sentence *More worrying is his poor attitude*, *his poor attitude* is the NP:SUBJ but it appears out of its usual position.

(a) She ran *nude* across the grass.

(b) The bag of oranges weighs *2 kilos*.

(c) *Forty kilometres* isn't all that far!

(d) *Under the bed* is full of dust.

(e) John will make her *a good husband*.

Different sentence types

5.1 Introduction

In Chapter 4, we looked at the functions that phrases can have within sentences. We will now turn to structure again and consider the different structures that sentences can have and how they correspond to different meanings. There are four main types of sentences which can be distinguished structurally for English. They are:

(a) DECLARATIVES

Esther Luer discovered a giant arachnid in her weekly groceries. (AUS#73:9)

(b) IMPERATIVES

Discover arachnids in your weekly groceries!

(c) INTERROGATIVES

Did Esther Luer discover a giant arachnid in her weekly groceries? What did Esther Luer discover? Where did she discover this arachnid?

(d) EXCLAMATIVES

And what an arachnid it was!

The important thing about all these sentence types is that they can be defined simply in terms of structure; in other words, we can tell by the form of a sentence which type it belongs to, and we shall show in the following subsections exactly how this is done. We refer to 'sentences' here; once you have worked through Chapter 8, you might want to refer to these as 'clauses' instead, and in the particular examples we will look at, specifically as 'main clauses.'

We can also distinguish four different **uses** of sentences, often referred to as MEANING TYPE or ILLOCUTIONARY FORCE. Of course we can make much finer-grained divisions of the ways in which we use sentences, but these are the ones that are standardly assumed:

❏ Statement: roughly to tell the hearer or reader about something.
❏ Question: asking the hearer or reader for information about something; either this can be about whether something is or isn't true or it can be a request for more specific information.

❑ Directive: a cover term for issuing commands, requests, instructions, prohibitions, permission and even providing advice.
❑ Exclamation: to express surprise, disgust, annoyance at something.

In short, for each of the structural sentence types, there is a typical function. Declaratives are usually used to make a statement, interrogatives normally pose questions, imperatives issue directives and exclamatives make exclamations. However, this is just the typical correspondence between form and function; in fact, interrogatives can be used for purposes other than posing a question and questions can be asked without using an interrogative structure. *Why don't you mind your own business!* looks like a question, for instance, in that it starts with *why*, but the intonation indicated by the exclamation mark here means that it was most likely intended as a directive to stay out of the speaker's hair. It's for this reason we need to distinguish form and function. In the following sections we will discuss the typical use of that structure, but also provide examples of atypical uses.

5.2 Declaratives

In a declarative sentence the subject NP precedes the predicate VP:

Declarative: Subject   Predicate

The declarative structure is probably what you would think of as the most normal way of arranging a sentence. Two examples are:

I have the circadian rhythms of a vampire. (AUS#563:13)

Bob Dylan has at various times revolutionised folk, rock, country and gospel music. (N#801:12)

The normal interpretation of these sentences would be that the speaker is making a statement. However, as we shall see in later sections, there are other ways of making statements. It is also possible to pose a *yes–no* question using a declarative sentence but with a rising intonation (indicated in writing by a question mark). The following examples have the structure of ordinary declaratives, with the subject preceding the entire predicate, but the question mark to indicate that the intended meaning is a question:

She must have been desperately unhappy? (N#697:9)

So then it is possible that the patient was alive when you began the autopsy? (AUS#60:9)

5.3 Interrogatives

The basic structural characteristic of English interrogatives is the fact that one part of the predicate precedes the subject, namely, the first verb.

Interrogative: Operator (finite auxiliary)   Subject   rest of predicate

As we saw in Section 4.3, there are severe restrictions on which verbs can occur in front of the subject. Only finite auxiliaries, or OPERATORS, can invert with the subject. This process, which we refer to as SUBJECT–OPERATOR INVERSION, will be discussed in Section 6.3.

The most common function for interrogatives is as a question; in other words, a request for information. But, as we shall see later in this section, interrogatives can be used for other functions.

Yes–no interrogatives

The basic interrogative structure with just subject–operator inversion gives us what is known as a YES–NO INTERROGATIVE (or POLAR INTERROGATIVE).

Does darkness turn the whole city belly-up? Do these people only crawl out under cover of darkness? (AUS#43:19)

Do her and Ozzy still have their angry moments? (N#697:10)

Is there any point to Bruce Willis at all? (AUS#54:36)

Forming a *yes–no* question is quite straightforward: you invert the subject with a finite auxiliary verb (which we call an operator). Indeed, in Chapter 4, we used *yes–no* questions as a test for subject status. As usual, if there is no finite auxiliary in the original sentence, we insert a suitable form of dummy *do*.

The obvious function of YES–NO INTERROGATIVES is as a question expecting the answer *Yes* or *No* (hence their name). However, we have already seen that interrogative structures aren't the only ones which can be used to pose questions. Furthermore, as with declaratives, there are alternative functions for interrogatives, though these may require a particular context. In fact, it is possible for speaker and hearer not to have the same understanding as to the function of certain utterances. For instance, let's imagine a room with an open window, a frail old woman and her young nephew who has reluctantly come to visit. We can then imagine the woman using an interrogative structure like

Do you find it chilly in here?

and be surprised if all that happened was that her nephew answered *No*. Her intention may have been that this interrogative would be enough to make her nephew close the window; that is to say, she may have used an interrogative with the intended function of a directive.

In other cases, the intended function of a particular structure is clearer, even when it is not the most obvious one for the structure type. For example:

Can everybody leave by the emergency exit please.

This is clearly an interrogative structure; the operator *can* precedes the subject *everybody*. Still, the most natural interpretation is that it is intended as a directive rather than a request for information (with a *yes* or *no* response).

'The ideology of literalism'

Clearly interrogatives are frequently used for purposes other than posing a question. *Do you have the time?* is a *yes–no* interrogative but it doesn't normally require an answer of *yes* or *no*. So when a suspect in a crime asks *Could I have a lawyer?* this would normally be interpreted as a wish for access to a lawyer (but it's more polite than something like *I want a lawyer* or *Give me a lawyer*). However, police officers and courts sometimes disregard the pragmatic meaning of this sort of interrogative, understanding it to be a theoretical query about the availability of counsel. In her book on language and the law, Diana Eades dubs this 'the ideology of literalism.' In an ordinary interaction, the implication of *Could I get a lawyer?* would be a request for counsel. By appealing to the literal meaning here, these law enforcement professionals are violating the pragmatic principles that govern everyday exchanges of information between people – as sensible as interpreting an utterance phrased *Could you pass the salt?* (made at the dinner table) as an inquiry about a person's theoretical ability to pass the salt.

Alternative questions

A special kind of *yes–no* interrogative is something called the ALTERNATIVE QUESTION. It has the structure of a *yes–no* interrogative – the subject follows the auxiliary and the auxiliary *do* is added if no auxiliary is present. It differs only in that it has two coordinated elements:

Are you a Mod or a Rocker? (AUS#54:14)

Am I in, or am I out? Is it a slap on my back, or a raised middle finger? (AUS#536:13)

In the first example two NPs are coordinated with *or*; the answer could be either one of the alternatives given in the question; in other words, we assume the person asked is either a Mod or a Rocker. (In fact, in this case the response given was actually 'a Mocker'!) The second example shows a series of coordinated interrogatives clauses (though each expresses a single alternative question).

Intonation is significant here. Alternative questions show a rising intonation on the first of the alternatives and a falling intonation on the final one; so in example 1, the speaker's tone would rise on *Mod* and fall on *Rocker*:

Are you a Mod ↗ or a Rocker ↘?

If the intonation rose on *Rocker*, however, the interpretation would be quite different. It would express a *yes–no* question and the hearer would be expected to answer either *yes* or *no*:

Are you a Mod or a Rocker ↗ ?

You might well have had the experience of people playing on these alternatives, choosing to interpret, for example, *Would you like tea or coffee?* As a *yes–no* interrogative and answering *Yes please* rather than as an alternative interrogative with a more helpful response such as *Tea please.*

Tag questions

TAGS are little reduced questions which speakers tack onto declaratives generally in order to express their belief that a particular answer is likely to be correct, or at least they are seeking to confirm that the answer might be correct and want the hearer to agree or disagree. The following are examples of neutral tags (sometimes called REVERSE POLARITY TAGS).

You will take all the swear words out, *won't you?* (AUS#47:28)

That sort of thing doesn't really happen, *does it?* (AUS#66:21)

Here are steps in forming a reverse polarity tag:

- ❑ You take the finite verb of the sentence, in these examples *will* and *doesn't*, and reverse the polarity, which means that if it is positive, as with *will*, you make it negative, *won't*, and if it is negative, as with *doesn't*, you make it positive, *does*. As always with interrogatives, if there is no finite auxiliary in the sentence, you use a form of *do*.
- ❑ You then add a pronoun that can replace the original subject. In the first example, the subject is already a pronoun, so you use that. In the second sentence, you replace *that sort of thing* with *it*. So, *you will* becomes *won't you* and *that sort of thing doesn't really happen* becomes *does it*.

In speech, we can change the meaning of tags quite a lot by varying the pitch. The following is an example of a question posed by a lawyer during an actual trial. Imagine here a rising tone on the tag; in other words, a question intonation. This would indicate doubt. But if the lawyer's tone were to fall on the tag, it doesn't indicate doubt, but could sound quite menacing. In writing, we can indicate this difference using punctuation.

Mr Slattery, you went on a rather elaborate honeymoon, didn't you ↗ ? (AUS#60:9)

[here the tag turns the statement into a question]

Mr Slattery, you went on a rather elaborate honeymoon, didn't you ↘ !

[here the tag underlines the statement]

Another way of modifying the meaning of tags is to not reverse the polarity. Compare the following two examples. The first version, with the neutral tag, is the original question posed by the lawyer. In the second version we haven't reversed the polarity and as a result the tone of this one is more threatening.

Mr Slattery, you went on a rather elaborate honeymoon, didn't you? (AUS#60:9)

Mr Slattery, you went on a rather elaborate honeymoon, did you?

In this second example the statement is positive and the tag is too; it's what's called a CONSTANT POLARITY TAG. While the neutral tags typically seek simple agreement or disagreement, this time there doesn't seem to be much doubt in the lawyer's mind at all. What's more, these constant polarity tags are much more loaded, often expressing disapproval.

Curiously, if the statement is negative and the tag is kept negative, the result is usually unacceptable. For most speakers, constant polarity tags only seem to work if they are positive. For example, most of you will probably find this next version ungrammatical.

?*Mr Slattery, you didn't go on a rather elaborate honeymoon, didn't you?

The hidden bias of clause types

Human memories are rickety and untrustworthy things – just the simple phrasing of a question can substantially alter how a person recalls an event, perhaps even planting details that were never there in the first place. This was shown very early on in the 1970s by experiments carried out by Elizabeth Loftus. One well-known piece of her research, for example, involved subjects being shown different versions of a film (one containing a bicycle and one not). Loftus showed that the type of question used to interrogate subjects could influence their answers. If a person was asked, 'You did see a bicycle, didn't you?' this tag question was much more likely to produce a 'yes' response than the straightforward *yes–no* interrogative framed, 'Did you see a bicycle?' – even when there wasn't a bicycle. So 'new information' introduced through this kind of questioning then becomes indistinguishable from the facts acquired when the person actually did witness something – suddenly a false detail such as a bicycle is incorporated into the person's memory of the events.

Not all varieties of English show the complexity of the Standard English tag. Simplified versions of these tag questions are found in many colloquial and non-standard varieties around the world. Some of these are streamlined invariable forms of the standard tags, like *init*, *ini*, *ana* and *na*, but there are also other tag-like particles that can serve the same function, as in the following examples:

Yeah, he's not bad, *huh*? (AUS#51:9)

It's hard to get good materials, *y'know*. (AUS#51:30)

Let it be our little secret, *OK*? (AUS#54:38)

121

It is probably clear from just the few examples we have given so far that tags have a variety of functions. Sometimes they have to do with regulating conversational interaction and politeness. For example, tags can signal sensitivity towards a listener, actively inviting participation and emphasising common ground between speaker and listener. A speaker might use a tag, for example, to check that the listener has understood, to ask for the listener's reaction to what has been said, or to seek empathy from the listener. Such tags have been described as solidarity markers to maintain the engagement of conversational partners.

At the other end of the politeness spectrum, tags can be very hostile with considerable overtones of sarcasm. Jenny Cheshire (1981: 375) gives the following example from her taped interviews. She describes aggressive tags like these as a feature of urban working-class dialects:

Jacky: We're going to Southsea on the 17th of next month. And on Sunday they . . .
Cathy: Yeah, and I can't bloody go.
Jenny: Why not?
Cathy: 'Cos I'm going on fucking holiday, in I?

No answer is expected here! In fact the whole purpose of this tag seems to be to highlight the stupidity (in the speaker's mind) of the interviewer's question.

Wh-interrogatives

WH-INTERROGATIVES (or CONSTITUENT INTERROGATIVES) are a sub-class of interrogatives and share with other interrogatives the characteristic subject–operator inversion. However, as the following examples illustrate, they always begin with a constituent containing one of the interrogative words: *what, who(m), which, whose, where, when, why* and *how*. These are the so-called *wh*-words we mentioned in Chapter 2. (Something curious happened to *how* along the way and it's now the odd one out in that it does not begin with *wh*.) They are words that focus on that part of the proposition that we want information about.

What is the difference between a push and a shove? (AUS#306:12)

Which came first? The chicken or the chicken nuggets? (AUS#59:38)

Whose side will the police be on? (AUS#61:10)

Where are we meant to get that from? (N#801:4)

Just *why* do these trailers have to be so loud? (AUS#47:9)

How could she wear those earrings? (N#697:20)

The basic structure of a *wh*-interrogative is then as follows:

Wh-interrogative: *wh*-constituent   Operator   Subject   Predicate

As we shall see in Section 5.6, the case where the subject is the constituent which contains the *wh*-element is rather a special one; but for the general discussion here this need not concern us.

A characteristic feature of these sentences is that the interrogative word is always a constituent of the clause. The following outlines the basic correspondences between word classes (or parts of speech) and English *wh*-words.

who/whom	pronouns
which, whose, what	pronouns and determiners
when, where, how, why	adverbs

If we think about creating a *wh*-interrogative from its declarative counter-part, then there are four steps to follow. Take the example of the declarative sentence given at the start of this chapter: *Esther Luer discovered a giant arachnid in her weekly groceries.* Let's say we want to find out what it was that Esther Luer found in her weekly groceries.

❏ Convert the part of the proposition you are questioning to an appropriate *wh*-word.

Esther Luer discovered what in her weekly groceries?

❏ Move the *wh*-word to initial position.

What Esther Luer discovered in her weekly groceries

❏ Invert the subject and the operator. If there is no auxiliary, insert the dummy auxiliary *do* to fill the function of operator.

What did Esther Luer discover in her weekly groceries?

Obviously if the *wh*-constituent is the subject (and therefore already in initial position), there is no subject–operator inversion.

Which one of you has the smelly breath? (AUS#54:9)

Who would have thought I would become a disc jockey at my age? (says Dorothy Gartell, 75, N#801:5)

In fact, if you're a quiz master or a police interrogator (or if you simply find this piece of news astonishing), you might well stop earlier – after the first stage.

Esther Luer discovered what in her weekly groceries!?

If you remember, this is an ECHO QUESTION. They form one of the constituency tests we discussed in Chapter 2. We talk more about the formation of echo questions in Section 5.6.

If the *wh*-word forms part of a noun phrase, then it is not just the *wh*-word, but the whole NP (of which it's a part) that moves to the front:

Which singers do you associate with Christmas? (N#801:15)

*Which do you associate singers with Christmas?

Which side were the pigs on? (AUS#54:7)

*Which were the pigs on side?

At least in some varieties of English, *what* can be used in the same way, as in *What book did you buy?*

If the *wh*-constituent is associated with a preposition – in other words, if it is part of a PP – the preposition can be left stranded at the end of the sentence or it can be fronted with the interrogative word. From the point of view of prescriptive grammarians, prepositions shouldn't be left at the end of sentences. Since so many native speakers of English are happy to leave a preposition at the end of a clause, we assume that if there ever was a rule forbidding prepositions left at the end of clauses, then that rule is now rapidly losing ground. It was in fact irritation with this kind of prescriptiveness that made Winston Churchill exclaim (at least so the story goes – he probably never did say this; http://itre.cis.upenn.edu/~myl/languagelog/archives/001715.html): *This is the sort of nonsense up with which I will not put.* This sentence shows that there are cases where English does indeed have to leave prepositions stranded at the end of clauses. To get back to our example here, we can see that the example with the preposition fronted puts the sentence in a different style:

Which side were the pigs on? (AUS#54:7)

On which side were the pigs?

One striking property of *wh*-interrogatives is that you can move the *wh*-phrase quite a way; formally it is known as a LONG-DISTANCE DEPENDENCY. This is because we can describe the relation between the fronted element and the place in the sentence it would normally have occurred as a dependency and the distance between the two points can be several clauses (more about how to define and analyse clauses will follow in Chapter 8).

What do you think they'll make of this record? (question to Bob Dylan about his grandchildren, N#801:15)

What does she think her reputation is in the music business? (question to Sharon Osbourne, N#697:10)

In both cases, the *wh*-constituent 'belongs to' a verb that is below another word in the sentence; in the terms we will use later in this book, the gap is in a lower clause:

You <u>think</u> they'll <u>make</u> *what* of this record?!

She <u>thinks</u> her reputation <u>is</u> *what* in the music business?!

In principle the distance between the fronted *wh*-constituent and the gap can be any number of clauses. Needless to say, the following sentence is invented:

What did Oscar think that Sarah had said that Fred claimed Olivia had done?

What is a rhetorical question?

Before we leave interrogatives, it is appropriate to look at something called a RHETORICAL QUESTION. Rhetorical questions are formally identical to ordinary interrogatives in English. The following, for example, has the structure of a *yes–no* interrogative:

'Doesn't everyone wannabe a rock star?' I quipped rhetorically. (AUS#60:21)

Interrogatives like this one are used when the speaker is sure of the answer – they have the function of emphatic statements. The speaker in this case was not expecting an answer, certainly not a negative one. In the following examples, the writers are all using these questions to centre on a point. The answers to all of these are assumed to be obvious.

Have the critics forgotten that the first film revolved wholly around Babe's quest to avoid his destiny as Sunday roast? (AUS#62:35)

Isn't it funny how people aren't content to just be themselves these days? (AUS#51:16)

We can imagine the speaker having the following answers in mind; *no they clearly don't remember, but they should*; and *yes that is odd*. To use a rhetorical question successfully, the speaker must rely on the hearer to find the answer obvious too. Here's an example from *The Simpsons*:

Grandma Simpson:	How many roads must a man walk down before you can call him a man?
Homer:	Seven!
Lisa:	No, Dad, it's a rhetorical question.
Homer:	Rhetorical, eh? Eight!
Lisa:	Dad, do you even know what 'rhetorical' means?
Homer:	[*incredulous*] Do I know what 'rhetorical' means?! [From www.snpp.com/]

English has also a vast array of formulaic rhetoricals where the answer again is quite obvious, and this is then used to make some other point of view obvious. So if on coming back from a long hot walk your friend asks you whether you would like a pint of cold, crisp lager, you could give any of the following answers if you so choose: *Is the Pope a Catholic?*, *Does the Pope wear a funny hat?*, *Is a frog's arse watertight?*.

5.4 Imperatives

The most striking structural characteristic of an imperative is that it need not have an overt subject. (Some of the Australian examples we use contain *bloody*. We hope readers will not find this offensive. In Australian English, it is much milder than in British English; the Australian government even had a campaign which involved stickers with the official slogan *If you drink then drive, you're a bloody idiot*.) Some examples of imperatives are:

Stop your bloody whingeing! (AUS#56:19)

Hate the bastards, but vote carefully, early, and once! (AUS#54:37)

Even though there is no subject here, the intended subject in each case is clearly the hearer; in other words, second person *you* (singular or plural) – I am keen that *you* should stop whingeing, I advise you to hate the

125

bastards and so on. If you add a tag question, this becomes obvious – *Stop your bloody whingeing, will you!* We can say that imperatives normally have no overt subject, but the understood subject is second person. However, it is possible to insert the subject. *You stop your bloody whingeing* sounds fine, here is an actual example:

You eat that spinach boy! . . . You listen to your mother! (AUS#43:39)

Of course, if there is an explicit subject, then the structure is potentially ambiguous between a declarative and an imperative. In many languages this ambiguity does not arise because there is a separate verb form for imperatives. This is true for English too, though you usually cannot see it – a non-finite form is used rather than the finite form we get in declarative sentences (more about the distinction between finite and non-finite in Chapter 6). It's just that for virtually all verbs the form used in imperatives, the base form of the verb, is not distinguished from the form of the verb used with second person subjects.

Only the verb *be* has retained distinct base and person forms in Modern English. Compare the following two examples:

You *are* careful what you wish for.

You *be* careful what you wish for.

In the first example, we have the form *are* which is the expected form for a declarative, whereas in the second we have *be*. Only the second of these could be an imperative, since only in this could the subject be deleted: **Are careful what you wish for* is not an acceptable sentence, whereas *Be careful what you wish for* is. Here is how it appeared in the original:

Be careful what you wish for, girls – you just might get it! (AUS#60:8)

Similarly, verbs like *must, will* or *should* (the modal verbs) cannot occur in imperatives because they do not have any non-finite form: **Will go to Amsterdam tomorrow, will you!* Or **Must wash yourself!* Hence we can assume that sentences like *You will go to Amersterdam tomorrow* and *You must wash yourself* are ordinary declaratives rather than imperatives with inserted subjects. In fact, most dialects of English are very restrictive with the use of auxiliaries generally in imperatives. (See Section 6.4 for a discussion of auxiliary verbs.) The *do* imperative works well (for emphasis), but how do you find the examples with the question mark?

Read *the 'Issue'*! (AUS#51:11)

Do read *the 'Issue'*!

?Be reading *the 'Issue'* (by the time I come home)!

?Have read *the 'Issue'* (by the time I come home)!

An interesting structural feature of imperatives is that they always form the negative with the dummy auxiliary *do*.

Do not bother wrestling with all the symptoms of age. (AUS#305:13)

Don't have a cow man! (N#279:9)

This goes even with a verb like *be* which otherwise doesn't require *do* to form its negative. Take the earlier example with *be* and make it negative. Compare the result with the basic declarative and its negative counterpart.

Imperative	Declarative
Don't be careful what you wish for	You are not careful what you wish for
[*Be not careful what you wish for]	[*You don't be careful what you wish for]

Also note that where there is an overt subject *you*, it always follows *don't*, as in the following:

Don't you cross the line! (AUS#54:6)

Curiously, the auxiliary of the passive can occur quite freely in imperatives when it is accompanied by the negation:

Don't be intimidated by grammar books!

Don't be made to feel inferior by those loud-mouthed friends of yours!

Some imperatives appear to have a third person subject as in the following:

Somebody, strike a light! (AUS#47:24)

Even in a sentence like this one, though, there is an understood second person subject; in other words, the implied subject is somebody among you all out there. Again, this becomes clearer when we tack on a question tag – suddenly the second person subject pronoun surfaces:

Somebody, strike a light, will you?

In an example like this, it is quite clear that we are not dealing with a declarative, since the verb form would then be different: *somebody strikes a light*.

We can, then, describe the structure of an imperative as follows. (The brackets indicate that the subject can be omitted.)

Imperative: (Subject second person)   Predicate with verb in base form

The most common function of imperatives is to issue directives; so they aren't like statements, which can be true or false. In this case, speakers are directing someone to do something, and this can include a range of things like commands (to be quiet), requests (to open the window), instructions (to cream the butter and sugar), prohibitions (not to walk on the grass), permission (to help themselves to the cake) and even advice, as in the following recommendations (for those past their 'youthful sell-by-date'):

By all means, strive to adhere to a diet rich in wholefoods, purchase anti-wrinkle creams and jog. And/or realise whatever the verb form of Pilates might be. [. . .] But for HEAVEN'S sake, do not elect to undergo a Botox of the soul. (AUS#305:13)

Imperative clauses can even have a conditional interpretation (similar to an *if*-clause). For instance, Dr Frederic Brandt, who is apparently 'one of the world's most famous cosmetic dermatologists' says:

'Give me ten minutes a day, and I'll give you back your youthful skin.'

The interpretation here is that if you give Dr Brandt 10 minutes then you will get youthful skin. So the clause that is joined by *and* here contains the consequence of the condition expressed in the imperative (we look at complex sentence like this one in Chapter 8).

We have said that it is important to separate form and function when it comes to sentence structure since there isn't a one-to-one correspondence between them. Even though the typical way of issuing a directive is by means of an imperative, we saw in the sections on declarative and interrogatives that both these sentence types can also be used to issue directives. An imperative structure can also ask a question, given the right context. If someone uses the imperative *Stop tapping your feet to the music!* You might repeat the same structure with rising intonation *Stop tapping your feet to the music?* Meaning something like, 'Are you telling me to stop tapping my feet?! That seems a bit strong given that you have been sitting here humming out of tune for the last half hour or so.'

The imperative particle

English has something which we can describe as an IMPERATIVE PARTICLE (sometimes called a FIRST PERSON IMPERATIVE).

Let's go eh? (AUS#54:10)

But let's not get carried away with fear and loathing. (AUS#47:8)

As you can see from these examples, this imperative is formed with a contracted form of *let us* in which *us* functions as the object of the verb *let*. But in these examples, *you* is not the understood subject as we saw earlier for the ordinary imperative. Compare the earlier examples with the ordinary imperative example:

Let me back on the computer – PLEASE!!? (AUS#56:38) [= 'You let me back on the computer, please']

Where the imperative particle is involved, the understood subject is *us*; in other words, the first person plural. Try substituting *let us* for *let's* in the first example and the difference between these two imperatives becomes clearer.

Let us go eh?

Out of context, there is potential ambiguity between the first person imperative reading 'I suggest that we go' and the ordinary second person imperative reading 'You let us [i.e. allow us to] go, will you?' But there is no ambiguity with the contracted form *let's* – it must be the imperative particle.

Interesting things are currently happening to this form, which confirms that *let's* should no longer be analysed as a contracted form of *let us* but as one word – indeed a kind of grammatical particle. Have a look at the following sentences which Hopper and Closs Traugott (2003: 11) have recorded from Midwestern American English speech. As they point out, the construction has expanded beyond first person subjects – well, at least for Midwestern American English speakers. In these examples, we could not replace *lets* with *let us*. We suspect other dialect speakers might find them rather peculiar.

Lets you go first, then if we have any money left I'll go.

Lets you and him fight.

But there are Standard English examples too that suggest that *let's* is no longer a simple contraction of *let us*, and is more appropriately written as the single word *lets*.

Lets you and I go then/Lets you and me go then.

What is significant about our example is that *you and I/me* appear to function as the object of *lets*. (Compare the first line of T.S. Eliot's 'The Love Song of J. Alfred Prufrock' – *Let us go then, you and I*.) What this suggests is that the first person plural pronoun *us* has lost its status as a separate morpheme and is simply part of a single morpheme *lets*. This word can then take its own object, which in these examples is *you and me*. In fact, in colloquial speech you will find that *let us* is usually even more reduced and is better represented as some sort of affix on the remaining verb.

'Sgo guys!

Imprecatives

The following examples illustrate another curious sub-type of imperatives, the so-called IMPRECATIVES:

Damn them and everyone who feeds the myth of these gangsters, villains, thieves and hustlers. (British actor Lennie James quoted in AUS#306:9)

Bugger it! (AUS#56:19)

Curse this damn faulty umbrella – waterproof my arse! (AUS#55:38)

These are of course used for making insults, curses and abusive comments. The reason we don't simply include them as straightforward imperatives is that they show an interesting difference. Like imperatives they clearly lack an overt subject. But remember, imperatives have an implicit *you* subject and this becomes evident when you form imperative tags. But try forming tag questions here – **Bugger it, will you*. What is the understood subject here? It clearly can't be *you*. The models for these are probably earlier English expressions like *God damn X*. These invoke God (or the Devil) as agent of malfeasance, but have been abbreviated to *Damn X* (to avoid explicit blasphemy or profanity). Expressions like *Damn X* are probably providing the model for these more potent modern expressions and account for their curious structure.

5.5 Exclamatives

EXCLAMATIVES have a very distinctive structure:

Exclamatives: *what* or *how*-phrase   Subject   Predicate

Note that *what* and *how* in examples like the following are not information-seeking, however, and exclamatives differ from their interrogative counterparts in that that they lack the subject–operator inversion characteristic of English interrogatives. Some examples are ('scuse the language):

What a bunch of wankers you lot are! (AUS#47:38)

How well I remember the old days when malted milks had real ice cream in them, and the milk bar bloke gave you a free straw to get into it! (AUS#56:19)

How we laughed! (AUS#527:12)

The exclamative function is also often filled by just the initial *what*/*how*-phrase:

What a spiteful, vindictive bloody sheep! (AUS#47:7)

If the *what*/*how*-phrase is the subject of the clause, then ambiguity can arise. This is because even though *wh*-interrogatives normally have subject–operator inversion, they don't when the *wh*-constituent is the subject. For example:

Boy, *how many people* can do this of a day! (AUS#56:17)

[Exclamative = 'what a lot of people can do this']

[Interrogative = 'what's the number of people that can do this']

The function of an exclamative sentence is much more restricted than that of any of the other sentence types we have discussed here. Exclamatives are used to make an exclamation (not surprisingly!). It therefore has a very expressive or emotive component. As you would expect from what we have said previously in this chapter, other sentence types can also be used with an exclamative meaning. Compare the following with the earlier version (with the structure of an exclamative).

How well do I remember the old days when malted milks had real ice cream in them, and the milk bar bloke gave you a free straw to get into it!

This is clearly a *wh*-interrogative in structure – it has the characteristic subject–operator inversion. However, given the meaning of the sentence it is most likely to be used as an exclamation here (after all, we do not normally ask others how well we remember things). This sort of exclamation has a rather archaic and literary flavour. In fact, it is possible to form exclamatory messages by simply using appropriate intonation on all sorts of sentence types. For example, the message can be expressed with a declarative structure as in the following sentences:

It's lovely here! (AUS#47:21)

You're alive, you stupid bastard! (AUS#51:16)

The following has the structure of a *wh*-interrogative, but is clearly intended here as an exclamation. (Note that this is not a rhetorical question, since the answer is not assumed to be obvious; on the contrary, it is a bit of a mystery.)

Why can't he get his dirty-bloody socks into the laundry basket – just once! (AUS#54:9)

Exclamatory meaning can also be expressed by using intensifying words like *wow, the hell, surely, so, such*, and so on. The first example has the structure of a declarative and the second is a *wh*-interrogative structurally.

But you surely never plotted for months to dance with Michael Jackson! (AUS#62:33)

What the hell was I thinking doing that last job? (AUS#56:16)

Since the exclamative structure is so narrow, for some of these examples there is no corresponding true exclamative structure to express the same exclamatory meaning.

5.6 Echoes

Earlier we described the structure of *wh*-interrogatives. Two of the key characteristics of this sentence type were the substitution of a *wh*-constituent and the fronting of this constituent. We will now show that there is another important use of *wh*-constituents, namely, in structures where they are not fronted, but left in their original place. This leads to an echo construction. An example is the one found in the following mini-discourse.

Have I ever *what*, Brandy? Heard 263 R & B ballads that sound exactly like this brown-coloured puree of cliches and spineless studio backing music? Oh yes, my dear, most certainly. (AUS#65:26)

Here we see that the *wh*-word replaces a VP which is the complement of *have*. We can imagine a corresponding non-*wh*-construction *Have I ever heard 263 R & B ballads that sound . . .* In this case, there is subject–operator inversion, but we can also use echo constructions without inversion, in which case we can describe it as a declarative echo construction. In fact, it is possible to leave a *wh*-constituent in its place in all construction types:

DECLARATIVE:	CORRESPONDING ECHO:
This cartoon has been cancelled. (AUS#43:4)	This cartoon has been what?
YES–NO INTERROGATIVE:	
Is there any point to Bruce Willis at all? (AUS#54:36)	Is there any point to who(m)?
WH-INTERROGATIVE:	
What did it cost them? (AUS#54:3)	What did it cost who?
IMPERATIVE:	
Pay no taxes! (AUS#45:20)	Pay no what?
EXCLAMATIVE:	
How well I remember the old days!	How well you remember what?

The meaning of echoes is normally exclamatory. This was particularly clear in the first example we gave in this section, since the speaker then went on to fill in the constituent: *Heard 263 R & B ballads that sound . . .* It is, then, clear in this example that the speaker is not asking for information. However, echoes can also be used as questions. Imagine a conversation in the pub, where the noise drowns out the second part of somebody's sentence. The hearer can then reply

Sorry, you did what yesterday?

Echoes are also an integral part of ridiculous 'knock-knock' jokes, and we can't resist the temptation to give an example here:

Knock knock.
Who's there?
Cash.
Cash who?
No thanks, I'll have some peanuts.

5.7 Trees

The structure of a declarative should be familiar by now since we have dealt with declaratives and functions. We will use categorical labels from now on, since these are more commonly used unless functions are specifically of interest. The advantage of category labels is also that we can go into more details when this is appropriate. Remember that trees with function labels can provide only a broader picture of constituent structure. The outline of a simple declarative structure would be as follows:

(1)

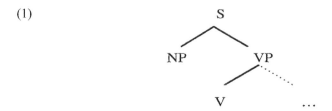

The interrogative structures pose a special problem, since we have moved out an element from the predicate, namely, the operator. At this stage, we will assume that this inverted auxiliary is still part of the same sentence, so that we get a tree like the following for a *yes–no* interrogative:

(2)

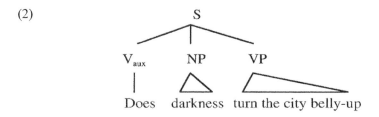

We should warn those of you who intend to carry on with syntactic theory that this particular type of sentence has been the subject of a lot of discussion in the literature and you are likely to encounter other ways of looking at it.

Turning now to *wh*-interrogatives, we have the same structure as in this tree, since we have subject–operator inversion, but we also have the added complexity of the fronted *wh*-constituent. We return to a sentence we used earlier in this chapter:

Why do these trailers have to be so loud?

Here we have subject–operator inversion since *do* precedes the subject *these trailers*. Before this we have the *wh*-constituent, which can be phrasal. This needs to go above the whole sentence in the tree. We then get a tree like the following:

(3)

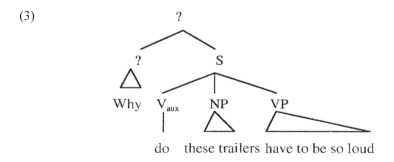

We haven't labelled either the root node or the node above the *wh*-constituent yet. Let's look at the root node first. When we added disjuncts and conjuncts to an S in Section 4.7, we called the resulting mother an S too, but that was different since several disjuncts or conjuncts could be added recursively to one S. In this case we can only have one *wh*-constituent and hence the position should be unique. Anticipating the discussion in Chapter 8, we will call this category S' (S-bar), so that the question mark for the root node in this tree can be replaced by S'. As for the label for the *wh*-constituent, again we anticipate the discussion in Section 8.5 and refer to it as COMP for complementiser. As we have seen, the *wh*-constituent can be a whole phrase, so you might think that it should have a phrasal name, rather than just COMP. This is a fair point, but we will still stick to COMP here. There are more detailed analyses of these constructions, but for the time being, we just want you to have an idea of where in the sentence tree to put the *wh*-constituent.

When we described how a *wh*-interrogative is formed, we said that some part of the clause has been substituted by a *wh*-constituent and this constituent has been fronted (if it wasn't already at the front by virtue of being the subject). This means that there is a gap somewhere in the clause. In this case it is an adverbial (adjunct) which has been substituted. Especially when the fronted phrase is an obligatory constituent of the sentence, some people prefer to mark this position with a zero in order to make clear where the *wh*-constituent came from. Later, when we look at an example in which the *wh*-constituent comes from a position which is obligatory, we will show you how this is done.

In this example, the *wh*-constituent consists of one word only, but in the examples we saw earlier, we find complex *wh*-constituents: *whose side, which one of you* and *on whose side*. Hence the COMP position must be able to host a phrasal element.

We turn now to a *wh*-interrogative in which the subject has been replaced by a *wh*-constituent, like *Which came first?* At first blush, this does not look very different from the previous example. However, there is clearly no subject–operator inversion; this is obvious since we can have a question without having an auxiliary. Since there is no inversion, the subject is initial as always. How could we then tell whether or not the subject has been fronted to comp or whether it is still in its old subject position? Depending on which view is taken, we could get either of the following two trees:

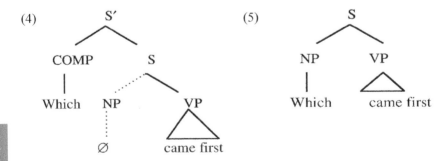

In order to decide on this one, we need to go back one step: why is there no subject–operator inversion? Well, if we assume that the subject has moved into the COMP position, then we could say that there is no subject–operator inversion, because there is no subject in that S for the operator to invert with. Hence we feel that the first of the two trees best represents the structure of *wh*-interrogatives in which the *wh*-constituent functions as subject. Whether or not you feel it makes sense to indicate the position of the subject we leave for the moment as a matter of taste. In this tree, we have indicated the missing subject with a dotted line. We prefer to avoid Ø (a zero symbol, as explained in Section 7.3) in our trees, but have inserted it here since it is quite common to do so, and it also helps indicate that the *wh*-constituent still functions as the subject of the sentence.

Finally, the tree for a *wh*-interrogative in which the *wh*-constituent functions as the object of a preposition is:

(6)

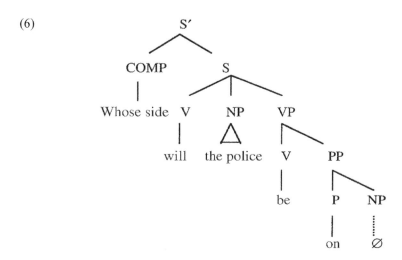

5.8 Points to remember

❑ There are four main sentence types: declaratives, imperatives, interrogatives and exclamatives. These four types can be defined in structural terms:

Declarative:	subject	Predicate	
Interrogative:	operator	subject	rest of predicate
Imperative:	(subject second person)	Predicate	
Exclamative:	*what*/*how* phrase	subject	Predicate

❏ There are two major types of interrogatives: *yes–no* interrogatives (where only subject–operator inversion has applied) and *wh*-interrogatives (in which subject–operator inversion has taken place and in which a *wh*-constituent has been fronted).

❏ There are also four major meaning types (or illocutionary force): statement, question, directive and exclamation.

❏ For each sentence type there is a corresponding meaning type which is typically expressed by that sentence type:

Declarative: making a statement
Interrogative: posing a question
Imperative: issuing a directive
Exclamative: making an exclamation

❏ There are many instances of how a particular sentence type is used to express a meaning type other than that typically associated with that sentence type. By the same token, each meaning type can be expressed by more than one sentence type.

Exercises

1. Sentence types

Are the sentences declarative, interrogative, imperative or exclamative?

(a) Why is anyone interested? (AUS#43:8)

(b) Is that love in your eyes, or just obsession? (AUS#45:23)

(c) C'mon, tax me out of here! (AUS#45:3)

(d) Try to get a look on your face that hints you might whip out a wad of cash at any moment, for the right price. (AUS#61:39)

(e) Oh Lord, won't you buy me a Mercedes Benz. (AUS#55:10)

(f) God damn it kid – just put the kayak under my arm and roll me off the grandstand! (AUS#61:38)

(g) Let's keep these people permanently where they belong! (AUS#47:8)

(h) You've seen that? (AUS#55:34)

(i) Who needs movies when Arsenal is enjoying such a wicked season? (AUS#60:29)

(j) Rollins *does* hate women far more than he hates everyone else. (AUS#45:30)

2. Sentence types and meaning

For any five of the sentences in exercise 1, discuss at least two plausible interpretations, that is, give at least two possible meaning types.

3. Types of interrogatives

The following extracts contain questions posed by an attorney during an actual trial (as reported by the *Massachusetts Bar Association Lawyers Journal* and reproduced in *The Big Issue* AUS#60:9). Examine these and then answer the two questions which follow.

Extract 1

Doctor, before you performed the autopsy, did you check for a pulse?
[No.]
Did you check for blood pressure?
[No.]
Did you check for breathing?
[No.]
So then it is possible that the patient was alive when you began the autopsy?
[No.]
How can you be so sure, doctor?
[Because his brain was sitting on my desk in a jar.]
But could the patient have still been alive nevertheless?
[It is possible that he could have been alive and practicing law somewhere.]

Extract 2

Mr Slattery, you went on a rather elaborate honeymoon, didn't you?
[I went to Europe, sir.]
And you took your new wife?
[Ummm, yeah . . .]
How was your first marriage terminated?
[By death.]
And by whose death was it terminated?
[Ahhh, my wife's.]
That would be your first wife?
[You got it.]
Right. So the date of conception [of the baby] was August 8th?
[Yes.]
And what were you doing at that time?
[Ummm, can I have a glass of water please? . . .]

In each of his lines, the lawyer asks a question; identify the type of structure he uses to do so each time.

4. Colloquial and regional English?

The following sentences are forms found in different parts of the English-speaking world. Some illustrate variations in the grammar of English which we would place together as dialectal non-standard, and some, from our stash of *Big Issues*, are colloquial and for some speakers will hover somewhere on the border between standard and non-standard. Identify and describe each of the constructions and say why they differ from mainstream Standard English sentence types.

(a) She ain't got to bother, have she?

(b) Who you have come to see?

(c) You are going home soon, isn't it?

(d) What you got? Where you live?

(e) I'm going out with my sheila now, ain't I.

(f) He'll might could do it for you. [= 'he might be able to do it for you in the future']

(g) Be you quiet! Come you on!

(h) You're going to struggle with no money, in't ya? (AUS#40:9)

(i) How about you play one for us? (AUS#60:22)

(j) How come I'm here? (AUS#56:13)

(k) Children, on the other hand . . . well, they don't have the blinkers on yet. (AUS#54:9)

5. Advertising English and clause types

The following are actual examples of advertising English. Classify each with respect to sentence type, and suggest what meaning each would typically have. Why do you think there are so many imperatives here?

(a) Relax with pure flowers of camomile.

(b) A Mars a day helps you work, rest and play.

(c) How you can eat sunshine! (Kellogg's cereal)

(d) Heineken refreshes the parts other beers cannot reach.

(e) When it comes to the crunch, who can you turn to? (Brownberry croutons)

(f) Have a break, have a KitKat.

(g) Get strong. (Scrumpy Strong Cider)

(h) [Boing, boing, boing, blleeaarrgghhhh!] Who ever heard of a kangaroo with travel sickness? (travel sickness tablets)

(i) Just add water. (Echinacea cold relief tablets)

(j) Get 200% fatter lashes now, with 2000 calorie. (mascara)

Identify what is unusual about the following examples of Adspeak.

(k) Summer lunch with crunch! (Brownberry croutons)

(l) New Sugar Free Soothers. A taste worth shouting about. Treat your throat to Allan's Soothers.

(m) Fosters the Australian for lager.

(n) Tastes like summer! (ice cream)

(o) Win a trip to New York. So exciting, de la Renta. (fragrance offer)

The verb phrase

6.1 The constituency of verb strings

In previous chapters, we've generally just talked about the verb of a clause, but it turns out to be more useful to talk about the VERB STRING of the clause. In the following examples from an article on *Futurama* (N#279:8–9), each sentence (clause) contains a string of verbs. In each example, the verb string is in italics.

Their inventor *has created* a new bunch of cartoon losers with 'Futurama.'

The Y3K bug *is threatening* to bring down society.

Parents *can't accuse* me of providing a bad role model for kids, because he is only a robot.

They *have been eaten* by owls.

The show *might meander*.

If a verb string consists of just one verb, then that is the LEXICAL VERB. Any other verbs in the verb string belong to the class of AUXILIARY VERBS. Verbs can be finite or non-finite; we dealt with this when we talked about verb forms in Chapter 3, but we will come back to it here. We can then also refer to verb strings as finite or non-finite depending on whether **the first verb** of the verb string is finite or not. In the previous examples, all the verb strings are finite, because the first verb in each case is finite: *has, is, can't, have* and *might*, respectively. They can all change form to *had, was, couldn't* etc. In a finite verb string **only** the first verb is finite. As we shall see later, the kind of verbs which can occur before other verbs in a verb string require that the verb which follows it occurs in one of its non-finite forms. A verb string does not have to contain a finite verb, however. There are non-finite verb strings, where all the verbs are non-finite, and we shall have more to say about this when we discuss clauses in Chapter 8.

In terms of meaning, the verb string could be said to form a unit; there is some sense in which the meanings of the auxiliaries modify the meaning of the lexical verb; just as we get *create* (present) versus *created* (past), we get *has created* (present perfect – we'll come back to what it means to be perfect, at least for a verb, very soon). This has led most traditional grammars to assume that the verb string forms a syntactic constituent as well as a semantic unit. However, given these examples, one could equally well say that the auxiliary of the perfect modifies the whole of the rest of the verb phrase: *has* modifies *created a new bunch of cartoon losers with 'Futurama.'* So, instead of relying on vague intuitions about meaning, we shall do what we aim to do throughout this book and use structural criteria to decide on the syntactic structure. We shall apply some of the constituency tests to the sentences containing verb strings in order to decide whether *has* forms a constituent just with the verb *created* or with the whole verb phrase *created a new bunch of cartoon losers with 'Futurama.'* The difference can be represented as follows (and this is one of those places where we feel we can't avoid trees in the general sections):

(1)

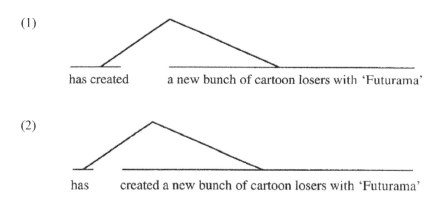

    has created   a new bunch of cartoon losers with 'Futurama'

(2)

    has   created a new bunch of cartoon losers with 'Futurama'

If *has created* forms a constituent, as in the first tree, then *created a new bunch of cartoon losers with 'Futurama'* does not – *created* cannot belong to both these constituents. On the other hand, if *created a new bunch of cartoon losers with 'Futurama'* does form a constituent, as in the second tree, then *has created* does not form a structural unit.

If you need to remind yourself of how constituency tests work, look back at Section 2.4. Here we shall just apply a selection of the tests to the string *created a new bunch of cartoon losers with 'Futurama'* in the sentence *Their inventor has created a new bunch of cartoon losers with 'Futurama,'* with the aim of discovering whether it forms a constituent or not. If it does, then the verb string does not form a constituent.

❑ Omission

(They haven't created a new bunch of cartoon losers with Futurama, but) their inventor has ~~created a new bunch of cartoon losers with Futurama~~.

❑ Substitution

Their inventor has *performed*.

❑ Coordination

Their inventor has *created a new bunch of cartoon losers with 'Futurama'* and *given us a new weird role model.*

❑ Movement

> What their inventor has done is *created a new bunch of cartoon losers with 'Futurama.'*

These tests show that *created a new bunch of cartoon losers with 'Futurama'* is a constituent of *Their inventor has created a new bunch of cartoon losers with 'Futurama'*; the string can be omitted, it can be replaced by one word, it can be coordinated with another string of a similar kind and it can be moved in a cleft sentence. When we have a verb string, we then 'peel off' one verb, and the rest of the verb phrase forms a constituent. If there are more verbs left, we 'peel off' the next one. The notion of verb string is then just a convenient way of referring to a string of one, two, three or even four auxiliaries and the lexical verb which follows, but the verb string does not have any status structurally. To illustrate this, we will indicate the structure for *They have been eaten by owls*. We have analysed *by owls* as an adjunct here, as evidenced by the fact that it combines with a VP to form another VP, but remember that the status of the *by*-phrase is not obvious.

(3)

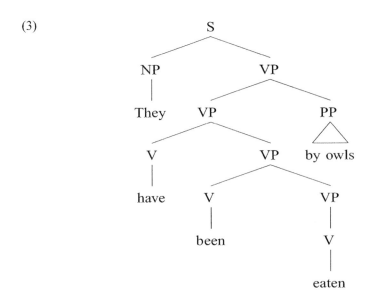

Verbs like *has, is, can't have* and *might* in the sentences we have discussed in this subsection are then examples of a special kind of verb that takes a VP as its complement. More about these verbs very soon.

One final thing is to point out that there are certain one-word modifiers that can occur in between the verbs in a verb string. We have already seen that the negator *not* usually occurs between the verbs of a verb string, immediately following the first verb:

142

Parents *can not accuse* me of providing a bad role model for kids, because he is only a robot.

As the following examples show, there are other one-word modifiers which can occur in the same position. (These examples come from an article on the 'bed-in' for peace which John Lennon and Yoko Ono held in Amsterdam reported in *The Big Issue* (N#258:12–13).)

People *should first take* their pants down before they start fighting. (Yoko Ono on how to achieve world peace.)

I *will probably dream up* a few songs.

I *might just break* the rules to go to the loo.

In these sentences, *not, first, probably* and *just* appear between the verbs of a verb string. These are one-word adverbials (i.e. adverbs forming AdvPs on their own, which function as adverbials) which modify the VP they precede. In fact, this can be seen as further evidence that the verb string as such does not form a constituent.

6.2 Time and tense

Let's return now to the notion of finite and non-finite forms. The characteristic of a finite verb form is that it carries TENSE, i.e. it is morphologically marked as either PRESENT or PAST. Tense is, then, a matter of morphological marking. This may sound strange to you, but the tense is not necessarily straightforwardly related to what time the event represented by the verb takes place. Of course, present tense will often be used to refer to present time, and past tense is common in sentences referring to events which happened in the past. However, the relation is not straightforward and we therefore need to distinguish between tense – a matter of morphological marking – and time – a matter of when events take place.

There are a number of reasons to make this distinction. For one thing, the SIMPLE PRESENT tense, i.e. one which involves only one verb in its present tense and no other verbs, is quite restricted in English. If one wants to talk about an event which is happening now, one can't always use the simple present tense. An example of this is the previous sentence, where it wouldn't have sounded as natural if we had said *to talk about an event which happens now*.

The simple present tense is used for events which happen regularly or form a habit, so that the robot Bender of the cartoon 'Futurama' is described as follows:

He *smokes, drinks, betrays* people and *has* no guilt whatsoever. (N#279:9)

The use of the simple present tense here means that we can assume that Bender has a very unhealthy life style. If, on the other hand we just wanted to show that the robot was having a temporary lapse so that his drinking and smoking were not likely to last for long, then we would have to use a form of the verb *be* together with the main one. This is what we will refer to as the PROGRESSIVE ASPECT:

He is *smoking* and *drinking* (at the moment).

It should be pointed out that this progressive sentence is still in the present tense, *is* is a present tense form, but it is in the present progressive rather than the simple present.

The simple present is also used for timeless truths: *Buying a house is a miserable business*; for stage directions: *In walks the ghost*; commentaries: *Kane scores a goal and England goes through to the knock-out stage*; in performatives (verbs with which you perform the action of the verb by saying the verb): *I promise to do it*; and some other specialised environments. For example, suddenly switching to the present tense in a narrative when talking about past events can make the action more lively and dramatic. Take the following extract where Simon the handyman is starting to tell a story:

A mate of mine was called out for a job in St Kilda to fix a sink at these two girls' place. He *gets* in there and they're checking him out as he's working away . . . (AUS#66:21)

A further reason to distinguish between time and tense is that we can use the present tense to refer to events that are expected to happen in the future.

When Fry *returns* to Manhattan 1000 years later, it has been destroyed and rebuilt three times. (N#279:8)

They actually *attack* and *destroy* earth at least twice over the next thousand years. (N#279:9)

In both these sentences, the events of returning, attacking and destroying are taking place not at the present time, but in the future – sometime during the next thousand years – and still the morphological form of the verb is present tense. Adverbials of time are often more useful than the verb form when it comes to giving us an idea of when events take place.

Since present tense seems to be able to refer to present time, future time and timeless statements, it might seem most appropriate to refer to this verb form as the NON-PAST, rather than the present, tense. However, for the sake of simplicity, we will go on referring to it as present tense, but keeping in mind that tense and time need not correspond.

So far, we have only talked about the present and the past tenses. How about the future? Well, English clearly does not have a separate verb form for the future, the way some other languages do. Hence there is no future tense in English, even though there are of course many different ways in which we can talk about the future. Let's return now to John Lennon and Yoko Ono's famous 'bed-in' at the Amsterdam Hilton, reported in *The Big Issue* (N#258:12–13):

I *won't* (will not) leave this bed.

I *might* just break the rules to go to the loo.

Everybody *should* do it. (refers to 'grow your hair')

I*'ll* probably dream up a few songs.

We*'re not going to* break up. (referring to fellow Beatle Paul McCartney, apparently)

People who have not studied linguistics, to the extent that they would have any view on the future tense of English, would probably think of *will*, or its abbreviated form *'ll*, as the marker of future. However, these examples show that there are many other ways of referring to future events: *might*, *should* and *be going to* for instance. We could say that the verbs used here are really used to make a prediction about how likely it is that something will happen in the future (but as the last example shows, it is easy to be wrong). The choice of verb then depends on how confident the speaker is. Some other forms that can be used for future events are the following:

A media frenzy greeted the news that 'Baywatch' *would film* an up-coming episode 'Down Under.' (AUS#63:17)

Mike *is about to* discover that the years have not been kind to Wayne Swain. (AUS#63:17)

A common way of referring to future events in many varieties of English is *be + gonna* (from *be going to*) plus the base form of the verb. Although still judged colloquial, it sometimes appears in writing:

Once I'm done with kindergarten I'm *gonna find* me a wife!

There are, then, so many ways of referring to the future in English that it does not make sense to refer to any one element as the future tense. A further complication is that *will*, which is probably the best candidate for a neutral future marker, can be used without any future interpretation:

They will be in Amsterdam now.

Here the speaker is making a prediction by using *will*, but this time not about the future, but about the present.

To sum up, a distinction should be made between time and tense. Tense is a matter of verb form and there are two tenses in English: present and past. There are many different ways of referring to future events in English, but nothing that we can describe as the future tense. With many verbs (like *will* and *would*) and even the present tense of lexical verbs, we must look at the time adverbials or the context to tell whether they are used to refer to future events.

6.3 Lexical verbs and auxiliary verbs

The lexical verbs (also referred to as 'full' or 'main' verbs) run the show in a sentence in the sense that the lexical verb decides what other elements the sentence may, must or must not contain. Nonetheless, there are other verbs that contribute in other ways to the sentence meaning. These are the verbs that we refer to as AUXILIARY VERBS. As the term implies, these verbs 'help' other verbs and they will always occur with another verb – or, in more technical terms, the complement of an auxiliary will always be verbal. (Remember that lexical categories may select phrases as their complements. Complement is a general term that covers for instance the object of a verb like *tickle* (*tickle his tummy*), the object of a preposition like *at* (*at home*) or the PP following *proud* (*proud of her children*). In a tree representation, the complement is always the sister of the head that selects it. Have a look again at Section 3.6 if you have forgotten.) There are some elliptical sentences where the verbal part is understood, but the crucial thing is that an auxiliary cannot take as its complement, say, a noun phrase or an adjective phrase.

A category of auxiliary verb can be distinguished in most languages on semantic criteria – auxiliary verbs provide information about the modality, aspect or voice of the sentence. MODALITY is quite a complex notion, and we will not go into any detail here. Suffice it to say that it is often related to how plausible the speaker thinks it is that what the sentence expresses will actually happen. The difference between the following sentences is then one of modality (and here we move from *Futurama* to another cartoon, *South Park*):

It *might* be hard to make live-action little kids dying funny. (AUS#51:23)

It *may* be hard to make live-action little kids dying funny.

Traditionally, the difference here is described in terms of likelihood, or tentativeness; *might* is assumed to be more tentative than *may*. Those of you who are native speakers may want to think about what you perceive to be the difference between the meaning of these two sentences. If you used *can* or *should* instead of *might* in this sentence, the modality would be even more different.

ASPECT relates to information about, for instance, whether an event is going on, has been completed or is being repeated. VOICE refers to the difference between ACTIVE and PASSIVE, and unlike modality and aspect, a change in voice has consequences for the whole structure of the sentence. This is something we mentioned in Chapter 4 and we'll return to it later.

Apart from the semantic characteristics, in English the auxiliary verbs also have some striking morpho-syntactic properties (i.e. properties related to their form and distribution) which lexical verbs do not have. This means that we can distinguish quite neatly a syntactic category of auxiliary verbs. The main reason for this is that due to a historical quirk, there are some jobs that English does not allow a lexical verb to do (with one or two exceptions). Returning to the terminology used in Chapter 4, we can say that there is a FUNCTION – which we will refer to as OPERATOR – which (almost) only the SUB-CATEGORY of auxiliary verb can fill. This distinction between category and function is important here for two reasons. First, auxiliaries do not always function as operators, and second, there are one or two non-auxiliaries which can be operators. We shall return to this point later. Let's first consider what the characteristics of an operator are. We will focus here on two of them.

Subject–operator inversion

This is often referred to as subject–auxiliary inversion, but there are really two functions involved here, namely, subject and operator, rather than a function and a category. At the end of this section, it should be clear why we want to make this distinction. As we saw in Chapter 5, questions are signalled in English by the subject occurring after a verb and not in its customary position before all the verbs. There is one important condition, though, and that is that the verb preceding the subject must be of a special kind – it must be one of the verbs capable of being an operator. Compare the following sentences:

Could you reinvent yourself as someone new? (N#279:9)

Does Blackman consider herself a dishonourable lady? (N#274:30)

Did they intend to become parents during their stay? (N#258:13) (back to John and Yoko)

with these:

*Reinvented you yourself as someone new?

*Considers Blackman herself a dishonourable lady?

*Intended they to become parents during their stay?

These examples show that *could*, *does* and *did* function as operators, and that the verbs in the starred sentences – *reinvent*, *consider* and *intend* – cannot. Indeed, in the last two sentences, *does* and *did* have been inserted just in order to make a question. Here 'do' does not have any other meaning than present or past tense, it is just there to fill the function of operator. This is what we refer to as the dummy *do*, about which we will hear more later.

We need to point out here that apart from interrogatives, there are a few other environments where you get subject–operator inversion; for instance, in so-called conditionals (as in the first example) and when certain negative adverbials have been moved to the front (as in the other two examples). As we would expect, unless there is an operator in the sentence naturally, dummy *do* must be inserted:

Had he been really brave, rather than derivative of his own formula, he might have created something truly . . . (N#269:26)

Nor *did I* imagine that I was in a picture that appeared within the sleeve of a Lennon LP . . . (N#258:12)

Never in the error-strewn history of English cricket, never in the rich 195-year history of Lord's, *has there* been a day as dark. (The *Daily Mail* lamenting the English cricket team's loss, AUS#331:11)

Negation

Consider the following negative sentences:

We*'re* (we *are*) *not* trying to have a baby . . . (N#258:13)

Why *can't* you do it in your vacation? (N#258:13) (this is John Lennon on everybody staging a 'bed-in' for peace)

I wish I *had not* gone that day. (N#258:12) [adapted]

Here we see that the clause negator *not*, or its contracted form *n't*, can occur with verbs like *can*, *be* and *have*. Compare this with the following ungrammatical sentences:

*I swear I *dreamt not/dreamtn't* it.

*I *wantn't* to make a habit out of it.

Just as in some of the interrogatives presented earlier, we have to insert the seemingly meaningless verb *do*:

I swear I *didn't* dream it. (N#258:12)

I *don't* want to make a habit out of it. (N#258:13) (John Lennon on how nice it is to get married)

There is a little quirk here – *I want not to make a habit out of it* is actually grammatical. However, the negator *not* doesn't negate the whole sentence. It only modifies *make a habit out of it*, not *want*. In the original example, Lennon says he has no particular desire to make a habit out it, whereas in the example with *not* following *want*, it means the speaker is actively trying to not make a habit out of it. Note also that you cannot use the contracted *n't* in this example: **I wantn't to make a habit out of it*.

We can conclude, then, that in English, sentence negation requires the presence of a special kind of verb. Verbs like *dream* and *want* cannot have negation attached to them. Instead we need an operator, just as with interrogatives.

If an operator is needed to make an interrogative and to add clausal negation, then there is one environment in which these two criteria are often combined: the TAG QUESTION. As we saw in Chapter 5, a tag question is often added at the end of a sentence, not always as a real question, but more to invite some sign from hearers that they are still with you. Being interrogatives, tag questions have subject–operator inversion and hence only finite auxiliaries can occur in tag questions.

We have insisted here on making the distinction between the function operator and the sub-category auxiliary. Not all elements that can function as operators are auxiliaries; there are one or two lexical verbs that can do it, too. We will return to the following exceptions in Section 6.5. This means that to define the sub-category of auxiliary verb, we need more than just its ability to function as an operator. We have seen that auxiliaries differ from all lexical verbs in that they take a verbal complement. We can say, then, that an auxiliary is a verb which can function as an operator and which takes a verbal complement.

We still want to distinguish between the function operator and the sub-category auxiliary, because auxiliaries do not always function as operators. Consider the following description of room 702 of the Amsterdam Hilton.

This hallowed venue *has been turned* into something of a stylised, all white shrine. (N#258:13)

In this sentence, there are three verbs: *has*, *been* and *turned* (*into*). Of these, only the first one can function as an operator, in that it can invert with the subject to form an interrogative and it can carry the negation:

Has this hallowed venue been turned into something of a stylised, all white shrine?

This hallowed venue *hasn't* been turned into something of a stylised, all white shrine.

Has clearly functions as an operator here. How about *been* in the same sentence? Well, it has the VP complement typical of an auxiliary: *turned into something of a stylised, all white shrine*; so it looks like an auxiliary. However, when we try to use *been* for subject–operator inversion and for negation the result is ungrammatical. In this sentence *been* doesn't function as an operator.

*Been this hallowed venue has turned into something of a stylised, all white shrine?

*This hallowed venue has *been't* turned into something of a stylised, all white shrine.

However, this shouldn't lead us to the conclusion that *be* isn't an auxiliary; if *has* wasn't there, then *be* (in the form of *was*) can do the operator jobs:

Was this hallowed venue turned into something of a stylised, all white shrine?

This hallowed venue *wasn't* turned into something of a stylised, all white shrine.

If we go back to the original sentence:

This hallowed venue *has been* turned into something of a stylised, all white shrine.

We can conclude that both *has* and *been* are auxiliary verbs – they both take VP complements and they can both, in principle, fill the function of operator. However, in this particular sentence, only *has* is an operator, because to be an operator, an auxiliary has to be finite, and only the first auxiliary of a verb string can be finite. This is similar to the fact that, say, *the peace-loving couple* is always a noun phrase and as such it can fill the subject function. However, just because it is a noun phrase, it doesn't always have to fill the subject function.

Hashtags #would and #wouldnt – stupidn't?

In July 2018, the inflection *n't* became the subject of a media frenzy when President Trump appeared to back-flip on his position regarding Russian involvement in the US election. As reported in the *Washington Post*, his defence was, 'It should have been obvious [. . .] I said the word *would* instead of *wouldn't*.'

In fact forensic linguists are sometimes required in legal cases precisely to verify the presence (or not) of a barely vocalised *n't* (Roger Shuy once famously determined that a Nevada brothel commissioner had actually said *I wouldn't take the bribe* rather than *I would take the bribe*, as was being alleged). Negation is an important feature of language, and it is one of the meaning items that tend to change quite regularly in language.

But now something unexpected has happened. The little *n't* has broken free and stepped into the limelight of an Internet-in-joke, or rather, innovative speakers have liberated it from the finite auxiliaries and allowed it to hang out with all kinds of categories. We find a meme headed 'Such a stupidn't dude' declaring '"The earth is not flat, it is roundn't" states gravity inventor Isaac Newton.' But *n't* hasn't just moved on to adjectives; in memes and tweets we can find it on lexical verbs as in *includen't* and on a noun in the unlikely combination *protuberancen't*. *Yesn't* is included in the *Urban Dictionary* and in July 2018 there was a rather optimistic change.org petition aiming to have this bit of creative morphology replace *no* in English.

It is a very rare thing to happen, for bound elements like *n't* to break free and attach themselves to other categories, so it seems unlikely that this is actually the beginning of real language change. But who knows . . .

6.4 Auxiliary verbs

Now that we know how to spot auxiliaries, let's take a closer look at what verbs are auxiliaries and what kind of meaning they may contribute to the sentence. A distinction is usually made between MODAL AUXILIARIES and PRIMARY AUXILIARIES. The core modal verbs are *can–could, may–might, shall–should, will–would* and *must*, and the primary auxiliaries are *be, have* and *do*.

Modal auxiliaries

In many ways, the modals form a very messy category in English. We shall have very little to say about their meaning since this is a very complex matter. There are also some irregularities to do with their form. The one thing you can say for core modals is that it is quite easy to distinguish them as a group on the basis of structural criteria. The modal auxiliaries have the properties all auxiliaries have, so that they can function as operators and as such can invert with the subject in interrogatives and occur with clausal negation. However, they also have some properties which are unique to modals. Let's look at these properties in the light of the following examples:

The show *might* meander. (N#279:9)

Why *can't* you do it in your vacation? (N#258:13)

People *should* first take their pants down before they start fighting. (N#258:13)

First, the first verb that follows a modal must appear in the bare infinitive form. In these examples we have *meander, do* and *take*. Second, in Standard English and most dialects, the modal itself only has a finite form; in other words, it can only occur in positions where you can have a finite verb, i.e. as the first verb of a verb string. It is not possible to say something like *has willed, to may* or *may will* (although some varieties of Scottish and American English allow double, even triple modals; see Chapter 11). Finally, the modals don't have a separate form for third person present tense. So whereas all other verbs have two present tense forms – an *-s* form for third person singular (*she/he/it*) and one without the *-s* for all other person – number combinations – modals have just one form. In these examples, the first one already has a third person singular subject (*the show*), but there is no *-s* on the verb. If we change the subject of the other sentences to third person singular, the form of the verb doesn't change:

Why *can't* she do it in her vacation?

She *should* first take her pants down before they start fighting.

The modals *will* and *would* can appear in a contracted form that is written as attached to the subject with an apostrophe: *I'll* for *I will* and *he'd* for *he would*. The contracted forms are most common with pronouns, but you can also find them with other subjects.

To judge by the form, the modals we have looked at so far occur in present and past tense. And there are indeed some environments in which the distinction between *will* and *would* or *can* and *could* is similar to that between the present and past forms of lexical verbs. Consider the following examples:

I *think* I'll go to work like normal. (AUS#33:16)

I *thought* I *would* go to work like normal.

When we have changed the tense of the first verb from present *think* to past *thought*, the natural thing is to change the modal in the lower clause from *will* to *would*. In this sense, then, *would* can be said to be the past tense form of *will*.

There are, however, many environments in which what we would call the past tense form of the modal is used with future meaning.

I *might* just break the rules to go to the loo. (N#258:13)

Could you reinvent yourself as someone new? (N#279:9)

'Baywatch' *would* film an up-coming episode 'Down Under.' (AUS#63:17)

As we have already said, it is extremely difficult to say what the relationship is between these and the following sentences:

I *may* just break the rules to go to the loo.

Can you reinvent yourself as someone new?

'Baywatch' *will* film an up-coming episode 'Down Under.'

These are environments in which the difference between what looks like the present tense of the modal and what looks like the past tense of the same modal has absolutely nothing to do with time. Instead the difference is associated with notions such as plausibility – *I may do it* is a bit more certain than *I might do it* – or sometimes politeness – *Could I have a word?* sounds more polite than *Can I have a word?* It is, then, not at all clear that we want to call *might* the past tense of *may*, at least not in all environments. The problem here is again one of language change. Although historically modal pairs like *may/might* and *can/could* were related by tense (i.e. *may* was to *might* as *kiss* is to *kissed*), over the years these forms have gradually been going their own separate ways and the original past tense forms have been establishing their identity as modal verbs in their own right with their own meanings.

In the introduction to this section, we gave modals in pairs, with the exception of *must*, which seems to be on its own. Let's consider, then, what happens when we have *must* in a lower clause and change the tense of the higher verb:

He says it *must* be worth getting married just for the paperwork. (adapted AUS#305:12)

He said it *had to* be worth getting married just for the paperwork.

It would seem that the most natural choice as a corresponding past tense form of *must* in this environment is *had to*. This is just another example of how complex the whole business of modal verbs are.

Another point to make about modals is that they interact with negation in peculiar ways, with respect to both form and meaning. We saw in Section 6.3 that the negation *not* has a contracted form *n't* which attaches to auxiliaries. Since modals are auxiliaries, we would expect that *n't* could attach to them, and it does, but there are some irregularities. Consider the following adapted sentences:

I *may* just break the rules to go to the loo.

I *will* probably dream up a few songs.

I *shall* probably dream up a few songs.

In all these cases, we cannot (or *can't*) just add *n't* to the auxiliary. Instead we have to change the forms: *will+n't* → *won't* and *shall+n't* →

shan't. For *may*, there seems not to be any corresponding abbreviated form, so that we have to use *may not* (although some speakers accept *mayn't*).

Finally, we want to point out that funny things may happen with the meaning when you add negation to a modal verb. Consider the following example, and in order to keep things simple here we have had to invent an example:

Oscar *may* eat the vegetables.

This means either that Oscar is allowed to eat the vegetables or that the speaker thinks it is likely that he will. Consider now the negative counterpart:

Oscar *may not* eat the vegetables.

This could mean either that Oscar is not allowed to eat the vegetables, or that he is allowed to not eat the vegetables, or that the speaker thinks it is plausible that he will not eat them. Can you follow that?

To add to the complexities, with *can*, negation may also work differently depending on whether or not the contracted form is used. The example often given is this:

You *can not* do your homework and still pass the exam.

There is a reasonable way of interpreting this, namely, that it is possible for you not to do your homework and still pass the exam. It may not be the best way to make sure that you pass, but it is possible. Consider now the contracted form:

You *can't* do your homework and still pass the exam.

Something seems to have changed here, since under normal assumptions about the relation between homework and exams, this is a weird statement to make – it implies that doing homework would get in the way of passing your exam. This is also a possible interpretation of the sentence with the full form of *not*, but since it is an unlikely thing to say, it would not normally occur to someone who heard or read that sentence. If the sentence was spoken, you would probably hear the difference, and even when written it is quite likely to be *cannot*, rather than *can not*. This is, then, an illustration that the scope of the negation varies depending on whether it occurs in its full form.

Marginal modals

Now consider the italic verbs in the following sentence in the light of what we have said about modal verbs:

The world *needs* to laugh more. (N#258:13)

Need in this sentence doesn't look like much like a modal verb; it has the third person singular present tense *-s* which modals cannot have, and the verb which follows it has the *to* infinitive, rather than the bare infinitive that modals normally take. Consider now also the following sentences with *need*. Which ones do you find acceptable?

Need we laugh more?

You needn't laugh.

The world needs to laugh more, needn't it?

The world needs to laugh more, doesn't it?

Do we need to laugh more?

You don't need to laugh, do you?

If you find the first three sentences grammatical, then you treat *need* as a modal verb – *need* is allowed to function as the operator both in the interrogative and in the negated sentence, and its complement can occur in the bare infinitive form, though in the third sentence, even though *need* functions as an operator in the tag, it takes a *to* infinitive complement in the main clause. In the last three sentences on the other hand, *need* is treated as a lexical verb, requiring dummy *do* as an operator. Verbs that are ambiguous in this way between modal status and lexical verb status are referred to as MARGINAL MODALS (or QUASI-MODALS); other examples are *dare, ought (to)* and *used to*. We will return to the behaviour of the other marginal modals in the exercises.

Losing verbs

Consider the following example from *The Big Issue*:

I better pull over at Bourke Street rank. (AUS#33:16)

We can assume that this has developed from:

I had better pull over at Bourke Street rank.

The speakers who started to use this must have felt that *had* didn't add much, so that here the element that we know as an adjective, *better*, is actually functioning as a verb. It may in fact for some speakers be an auxiliary verb, since the Australian among us can say:

I better pull over at Bourke Street rank, bettern't I?

It may sound odd to you that we talk about one speaker having left the verb out because they didn't think it added much. However, this is how language change happens; as one of our colleagues put it 'languages don't change, people change languages' (thanks to Bill Croft).

A different example in the semantic area is the line from a John Denver song (yes, that is how old we are!):

If I had my druthers, I'd go fishing

This is an American expression, which we can assume comes from *would rather* (or possibly *had rather*) but that phrase has been turned into a noun, *druthers*. Isn't it amazing what speakers do with language?

Primary auxiliaries

There are four different functions for primary auxiliaries: PERFECT ASPECT, PRO-
GRESSIVE ASPECT, PASSIVE VOICE and DUMMY AUXILIARY, and there are three verbs
that can be used to fill the different primary auxiliary functions: *have, be*
and *do*. This means that in a sense we can answer the question of how
many primary auxiliaries there are with either four or three; the verb *be*
does double duty as the auxiliary of the progressive and the auxiliary of
the passive. Since these are quite distinct functions, it is best to view them
as two different primary auxiliaries which have the same form. It is easy to
distinguish the two uses. First of all, the progressive *be* and the passive *be*
are followed by different forms of the verb, ING form (*be eating*) and PPART (*be
eaten*), respectively. Second, passive sentences have some particular characteristics: for instance, in a passive sentence you can usually have a *by*-phrase
(*be eaten by a shark*). We'll now take a look at each primary auxiliary in turn.

The auxiliary of the perfect *have*

The auxiliary of the perfect *have* introduces the perfect aspect into a sentence and is followed by the PPART form of the verb. If it co-occurs with
other auxiliaries, it follows the modal but precedes the progressive and
passive auxiliaries.

Have has three different contracted forms: in present tense *'s* (for *has*)
and *'ve* (for *have*) and in the past *'d* (for *had*). As with the contracted forms
of the modals, these are attached to the subject, mainly when the subject is
a pronoun. However, since the bare infinitive form of *have* is also *have*, *'ve*
can also attach to modals which can precede *have*, as in *You could've done
it*. It is even possible to get more than one of the auxiliaries contracted in
a string: *I'll've done it*.

Let us now look at some examples of the use of the auxiliary of the
perfect:

'The Simpsons' *has delivered* hip irreverence and clever satire for more than
ten years now. (N#279:8)

It was puerile, silly and immature – and everyone who saw it thought it
was a work of side-splitting wonder. The cult of 'South Park' *had been* born.
(AUS#51:23)

By this time next year they *will have become* a ratings goldmine.

In all three sentences, we have the auxiliary of the perfect, *have*, followed
by a verb in its PPART form, *delivered, been* and *become*, respectively. In the
first one, *have* occurs in the present tense, in the second in past tense and
in the third it is preceded by the modal *will*, and the adverbial *by this time
next year* indicates that the modal refers to future here. (Note that in the
last sentences, *have* itself occurs in its bare infinitive form since it is part of
the complement of *will*, and as we know, the modals take a bare infinitive
as their complement.) So, there are definite differences in tense here, but
given that the perfect auxiliary occurs in all of them, we would also expect
the three sentences to have something in common.

Often people confuse perfect aspect with past tense because the perfect aspect tends to be used to refer to events that took place in the past, but as we now know, we need to distinguish between time and tense. We find that the easiest way to disentangle this is to use a rather clever system introduced by a philosopher called Reichenbach in 1948. We can think of three points of time that are relevant to a normal statement (or question for that matter): the time the statement was spoken or written, S for 'speech time'; the time on which we focus, R (Reichenbach called this reference time, hence the R); and the time at which the event took place, E for 'event time.' These points are then put on a timeline, where time is seen as stretching from the past into the future. Which tense and aspect are used depends on the relation between S, R and E. Let's consider these three examples in the light of this. In *'The Simpsons'* has delivered *hip irreverence and clever satire for more than ten years now*, the adverbial *now* indicates that we are focusing on the present; hence speech time, S, and the time on which we focus, R, coincide. The event of delivering hip irreverence and clever satire started 10 years ago and continues until now. We can draw the following diagram for the first sentence:

Since the article in which this sentence occurs was written in 1998, the 'speech' time is 1998, and *now* indicating the focus time, is then also 1998. The event started 10 years earlier, and the dotted line indicates that it carries on into the present of the statement. The years are actually not important; what matters is the relation between S, R and E.

Turning now to *The cult of 'South Park' had been born*, the time of focus is in the past; there was a time in the past at which the birth of the cult had taken place. We know it is past, because the sentence preceding it sets the scene: *It was puerile, silly and immature – and everyone who saw it thought it was a work of side-splitting wonder* indicates that we are focusing on the past. At the time when people saw it, the cult had already been born, otherwise the simple past would have been used: *The cult of 'South Park' was born*. We can then draw the following diagram:

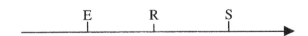

Here we haven't given any indication of the years, since that information is not known. What we do know is that there is a 'now,' S, the time at which the statement is made, and that at some time prior to that there were some people who saw *South Park* and liked it, that's the time on which the statement focuses, R, and that some time prior to that the cult of *South Park* was born, that is the event the statement talks about, E.

Turning now to the final sentence, *By this time next year they* will have become *a ratings goldmine*, here we are focusing on some time in the future, this time next year in fact. At that time, they will have become a ratings gold mine. Presumably, one would say this only if 'they' had not already become a ratings gold mine, so that this will take place sometime between now and this time next year. We can then draw another diagram:

Between S (now) and R, there is a year, and at some time between those two points the event of becoming a ratings gold mine happens.

In these examples, we can see that what the sentences have in common is the fact that E precedes R, i.e. that the event happened (or started happening) before the time we are focusing on. This is why the use of the auxiliary of the perfect is easily confused with past tense; past tense usually refers to an event that happened in the past, i.e. before now. The confusion is then between 'before the time we are focusing on' and 'before now.' However, as we see in the last example, the event itself can be in the future as long as it is before the focus point. Perfect aspect is then a way of indicating the relation between the focus point and the time at which the event took place. Tense, on the other hand, is a way of indicating the relation between focus time and speech time; in the first sentence, focus time and speech time coincide (hence the use of *now*) and we get present tense. In the second one, focus time precedes the speech time and hence we get past tense (since the event time also precedes the focus time, we also get perfect aspect). When the focus time is in the future, i.e. after S, we get some indication of future; in the third sentence this is *will* (though remember that there are reasons not to refer to this as the future tense).

Just for comparison, let's look now in the same way at some sentences without the perfect aspect. We can use the following adapted sentences:

Now 'South Park' *makes* a lot of money for the company.

Back in 1998 'South Park' *made* a lot of money for the company.

For the first of these sentences, the focus time is now, and the event time is also now, hence we get the following diagram:

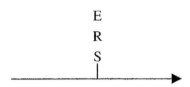

In the second sentence, we are focusing on a time in the past (that is, past from the time of the utterance), a time at which the event took place.

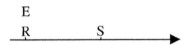

We can sum up the relation between tense and perfect aspect, then, as follows: when the event time precedes the focus time, perfect aspect is used; when the two coincide we do not get perfect aspect. When the event time precedes the speech time we get past tense, and when they coincide we get present tense (often with progressive aspect in English – more on that in the next section). When the event time follows the point of speech in time, then we get some future indication.

For an event that happened in the past, if we use perfect aspect, we are focusing not on the time of the event, but on some later time, for instance 'now.' Hence perfect aspect can be used when we want to indicate the importance of an event for what is going on now. This is often referred to as the 'current relevance' use of the perfect. It can also be used to express 'hot news,' for instance in headlines or advertisements (and police and news media reports). The following example is the headline announcing the *South Park* article that appears later in the magazine.

UNCENSORED CARDBOARD. A show that stars foul-mouthed cardboard cut-outs *has become* a cult hit for SBS. (AUS#51:23)

The 'hot news' perfective

In many varieties around the English-speaking world the perfect aspect is found in a much broader range of contexts than we have described here. Research by Engel and Ritz (2000), for example, shows that in Australian English the perfect is far more widespread than in either British English or American English, and they give examples such as the following – here you can see the perfect combining with past adverbials (*this morning* and *in March 1999*), something normally unacceptable for Standard English:

He has now met with Ayres this morning. (96 FM radio Perth: news)

Pernice, a legend of the 'alternative country' scene has toured the US and has also played in Australia in March 1999 to great response. (Advertising flyer)

It is actually a common change for perfects (past events with current relevance) to evolve into pasts (past events precede the speech time), and this has already occurred in a number of relatives of English (e.g. Yiddish and Pennsylvania German, for example, have lost their past tense). This may well be what we're seeing here, with the spearhead for the change being the use of the perfect as a stylistic feature for lively reporting of events.

The auxiliary of the progressive *be*

The progressive *be* is followed by a verb in its *-ing* form. It follows modals and perfect *have* if they co-occur, but precedes the auxiliary of the passive. Of course, if it follows a modal it occurs in its bare infinitive form, and if it follows the auxiliary of the perfect it occurs in its PPART form.

The progressive aspect is used to indicate that something is in progress, that it hasn't been completed or that it is temporary. It has a slightly different effect in present and past tense. In the present tense, as we have already pointed out in Section 6.2, the progressive is used when an activity is temporary rather than a more or less permanent characteristic of the subject. The examples we compared then were:

He *smokes, drinks, betrays* people and has no guilt whatsoever. (N#279:9)

He *is smoking* and *drinking*.

The interpretation of limited duration also means that the progressive goes better with some adverbials than the simple present. An example is the following, where *at the moment* would not combine well with the simple present:

Terry *is sleeping* rough at the moment. (N#235:34)

In the past, the progressive is often used to emphasise the fact that something is in progress. The simple past, by contrast, has more a sense of completion about it. This means, for instance, that if something is interrupted, the past progressive sounds more natural:

Just as Parker and Stone *were running* out of cash . . . (AUS#51:23)

Here the progressive is used, since the situation was interrupted, by Parker and Stone getting their big break with *South Park*. Also, the use of the progressive in this sentence implies that they never totally ran out of cash. Compare this with the simple past, where the 'running out of cash' has been completed (here we have deleted *just as* since this adverbial emphasises the in-progress aspect and therefore doesn't sound too good when the verb is not in progressive).

Parker and Stone *ran* out of cash . . .

Because of this interpretation of 'ongoingness,' the progressive form may have a special effect on some verbs, or it may just be ungrammatical. For instance, an event that is so brief that it cannot really be ongoing is *sneeze*; if this is used in the progressive, as in *Oscar was sneezing*, then rather than create an image of a long-drawn-out sneeze, it conveys repetition. Verbs like *have*, *know*, and *hate* don't happily combine with progressive aspect either. These are STATIVE verbs. They refer to a state of affairs rather than to an action or event. Unchanging states can't be 'in progress,' since they are static; hence sentences like *He is having a large nose* sound quite bizarre (though as we'll see in Chapter 11, there are dialects that do extend the progressive beyond the standard contexts of use).

Sometimes it can be very difficult to decide why the progressive is used. Compare the following two sentences.

One episode, 'Big Gay Al's Big Gay Boat Ride,' *makes* a strong and touching stand against homophobia. (AUS#51:23)

One episode, 'Big Gay Al's Big Gay Boat Ride,' *is making* a strong and touching stand against homophobia.

Both sentences sound perfectly natural, but what is the difference? It cannot really be that the second is more temporary, since an episode is rather a temporary thing anyway. Does the second one sound more active? We'll leave you to ponder this.

The progressive interacts with tense and perfect aspect, so that we can get the following:

Parker and Stone *are running* out of cash   PRESENT PROGRESSIVE
Parker and Stone *were running* out of cash   PAST PROGRESSIVE
Parker and Stone *have been running* out of cash   PRESENT PERFECT PROGRESSIVE

Parker and Stone *had been running* out of cash   PAST PERFECT PROGRESSIVE
Parker and Stone *will have been running* out of cash   MODAL PERFECT PROGRESSIVE

As always when auxiliary verbs interact, it is important to keep separate the form that the auxiliary of the progressive itself takes and the form that the verb following it takes. The verb following the progressive *be* will always occur in its *-ing* form, whereas the form of *be* itself depends on the verb which precedes it, if any. In the first two sentences, *be* is finite, present and past tense, respectively. In the third and fourth examples it follows the auxiliary of the perfect and hence takes its PPART form *been*. In the final example, it follows a modal and is therefore in its bare infinitival form.

As in many other languages, *be* has more forms than any other verb, regardless of whether it functions as the progressive or the passive auxiliary. Not only does it have three distinct present tense forms: *am*, *are* and *is*, it also has two separate past tense forms: *was* and *were*. Each of the present tense forms has a contracted form which can be attached to a pronoun subject: *'m* (for *am*), *'s* (for *is*) and *'re* (for *are*). Like the modals, the auxiliary *be* in both its uses interacts with the contracted negation form and inversion in peculiar ways. There is no contracted form *amn't* in Standard English; instead *aren't* is used in inverted contexts like *I am old-fashioned, aren't I?* However, native speakers do not seem to like the contracted negative form when there is no inversion; instead the non-contracted negative is used. Compare *I amn't/aren't old-fashioned* and *I am not old-fashioned* (or *I'm not old-fashioned*). Some non-standard varieties have a solution to this dilemma, they use *ain't*.

The auxiliary of the passive *be*

The passive *be* takes a complement headed by a verb in its PPART form. If the passive *be* co-occurs with other auxiliary verbs it follows them. As mentioned in Chapter 4, a passive sentence is formed by promoting an object to a subject and simultaneously demoting the subject to a *by*-phrase or leaving it out altogether. This can only be done if the auxiliary of the passive is inserted and the verb following it is changed into its PPART form. This was schematically shown in Section 4.4, repeated here.

Because of the simultaneous demotion of the subject and the promotion of the object, passives can be used both when one wants to highlight the

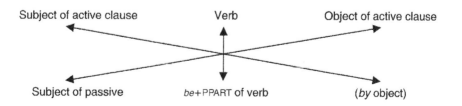

161

object, and when one wants to put less emphasis on the subject – or omit it altogether. In the following sentence about New New York in *Futurama*, we do not actually find out who did the destroying and the rebuilding.

Manhattan has been destroyed and rebuilt. (N#279:8)

The use of passive is then a matter of information packaging, something which we will return to in Chapter 9. However, before we move on, we should just point out that not all passive clauses have the *be* auxiliary; some contain *get* instead. Here's an example using *get* provided by Australian politician Nick Minchin after he was called a 'complete fruit loop' because of his views on climate change:

I get called lots of things as a politician, so being named after a breakfast cereal is pretty mild, really. (AUS#343:8)

These passives are more colloquial and tend to be avoided in formal language. They also give the interpretation that the subject is somehow more involved in the event; in other words, they provide a more agent-like reading of the subject (hence *get* is the expected auxiliary in something like *He deliberately got caught*).

The dummy auxiliary *do*

In Section 6.3, we saw that in interrogatives and sentences with clause negation, there had to be an operator, and we also said that (almost) only auxiliary verbs can function as operators. So, what happens when we want to turn a declarative that doesn't contain an auxiliary verb into an interrogative or a negated declarative? We don't want to insert one of the auxiliaries we have already dealt with, since this would change the meaning of the sentence. Instead, there is one auxiliary which doesn't seem to have much in the line of semantics – all it seems to do is to carry tense and function as the operator when there is no other auxiliary present. This is the DUMMY AUXILIARY *do*. Consider the following declaratives:

The Simpsons revolutionised cartoons. (N#279:8)

The sloth-like Homer Simpson and his knuckle-headed mishaps became essential viewing. (N#279:8)

In order to turn these into interrogatives or in order to negate them we need to insert a form of *do*:

Did the Simpsons revolutionise cartoons?

The sloth-like Homer Simpson and his knuckle-headed mishaps *did* not become essential viewing.

Given that it only occurs when there is no other auxiliary, dummy *do* cannot follow any other auxiliary, but occurs first in a verb string, followed by a lexical verb. Since dummy *do* always functions as an operator, it is always finite. Verbs like *revolutionise* and *become* that immediately follow it occur as the bare infinitive. Dummy *do* then resembles modals in two respects – it is always finite and it requires the following verb to take its bare infinitive form. This has led some grammars to consider dummy *do* as a modal verb. We think this is misguided. Modal verbs are used because they have meaning (even though it is difficult to define precisely what their meaning is), whereas dummy *do* is introduced purely for formal reasons: English does not allow (most) lexical verbs to function as operators.

Summing up auxiliaries

Table 6.1 summarises the auxiliary verbs.

Table 6.1 Auxiliary verbs

Auxiliary	Form of complement	Contracted form	Contracted negated form
Core modals: *can, could, may, might, shall, should, will, would, must*	V[BARE]	*'ll* for *will* *'d* for *would*	*can't, couldn't, mightn't, shan't, shouldn't, won't, wouldn't, mustn't*
Perfect aspect: *have*	V[PPART]	Pres *'ve, 's* Past *'d*	*haven't, hasn't, hadn't*
Progressive aspect: *be*	V[ING]	Pres *'m, 're, 's*	*aren't, isn't, wasn't, weren't*
Passive voice: *be*	V[PPART]	*'m, 're, 's*	*aren't, isn't, wasn't, weren't*
Dummy auxiliary: *do*	V[BARE]		*don't, doesn't, didn't*

In summary, it is possible to have as many as four auxiliaries in a single sentence, although this is unusual. Table 6.2 summarises the various possible combinations.

Table 6.2 Combinations of auxiliary verbs

	Auxiliary verbs				Main verb	
	Modal	Perfect	Progressive	Passive		
We	must				watch	'South Park'
We	must	have			watched	'South Park'
We	must	have	been		watching	'South Park'
'South Park'	must	have	been	being	watched	

6.5 Lexical *have, be* and *do*

We have just seen that *have, be* and *do* are auxiliary verbs; they can function as operators and they are followed by a verbal complement. Now let's look at the following sentences, particularly the verbs in italics:

Hey Spock, *do* <u>the thing</u>! (N#279:9)

Scented bras *are* <u>on their way</u>. (SCO#245:22)

Rupert Murdoch *has* <u>a lot to thank Bart Simpson for</u>. (N#279:8)

So, what's the big deal, you may wonder; more sentences with auxiliary *do, be* and *have*. However, we have said that auxiliaries take verbal complements – they are after all only 'help verbs' and need a lexical verb to add some real verb meaning to the sentence. However, look at the complements of *do, be* and *have* in these sentences. To make it clearer, we have underlined the complement in each case. These complements are not verbal, and hence the italicised verbs cannot be auxiliary verbs. It is then a fact of English that *do, be* and *have* also exist as lexical verbs. However, there are some twists here, and it is now that we finally come to this issue of lexical verbs that can function as operators. In several places so far, we have said that (almost) only auxiliaries can be operators. Well, now we come to the exceptions.

Let's take lexical *do* first; can it function as an operator? The answer is that it cannot. In fact, the reply from Spock to the question posed earlier is:

I *don't do* that anymore. (N#279:9)

We couldn't say **I don't that anymore*. We need to introduce dummy *do* to negate the sentence or to make an interrogative.

Do I *do* that anymore?

We can conclude, then, that lexical *do* is just like any other lexical verb.

How about lexical *be*? Let's turn the original sentence into its corresponding negative and interrogative:

Scented bras *aren't* on their way.

Are scented bras on their way?

Here we see that lexical *be* doesn't need dummy *do* in order to negate or to make an interrogative. Just as we concluded beyond any doubt that lexical *do* is a proper lexical verb, which cannot function as an operator, we can say with equal certainty that lexical *be* can function as an operator. We have, then, found our first lexical verb to function as an operator.

We turn now finally to lexical *have*; can it function as an operator? Well, John Lennon assured the interviewers:

I *don't have* as much money as you think. (N#258:13)

So, John Lennon clearly thought of lexical *have* as a proper lexical verb (though in all likelihood, he wasn't aware that he did); the operator required to use negation is dummy *do* in this example. So, is lexical *have* just like lexical *do* in this respect? Well, what do you think about the following adapted sentences in which the lexical *have* functions as an operator?

Have you as much money as I think?

I *haven't* as much money as you think.

Has Rupert Murdoch a lot to thank Bart Simpson for?

Rupert Murdoch *hasn't* a lot to thank Bart Simpson for.

Maybe most of you would use dummy *do* in these sentences, but we expect you wouldn't find them as bad as sentences with lexical *do* as an operator. It seems, then, that lexical *have*, has a funny sort of status. It can function as an operator sometimes for some people, but in other contexts and for other speakers it cannot. It is even more confusing, since sometimes when dummy *do* is used in the sentence, the tag question still may have lexical *have* as an operator:

I *don't have* as much money as you think, *have I?* (or *do* I?)

To conclude, we can say that *do*, *be* and *have* can all function as lexical verbs. *Do* as a lexical verb behaves exactly as you would expect a lexical verb to behave. Lexical *be*, on the other hand, can function as an operator and does not permit dummy *do*. Lexical *have*, finally, is messy – it can function as an operator in some environments, but not in others, and there is also variation between speakers.

6.6 Classes of lexical verbs

Potentially the unit we informally called the verb string in Section 6.1 can contain five verbs: four auxiliary verbs and one lexical verb. This happens only in quite contrived sentences such as *He must have been being eaten by sharks at the time (that's why he didn't answer his mobile)*. The auxiliary verbs need not be there in a verb string, but the lexical verb must. All verb strings that are not elliptical contain exactly one lexical verb (and possibly some auxiliaries, but not more than one lexical verb). This lexical verb is always the last verb form in any verb string. Hence in the following sentences, the verb string is in italics and the lexical verb is the one that is underlined:

John and Yoko *staged* their week-long 'bed-in.' (N#258:12)

Everybody *should do* it. (N#258:13)

They *have been eaten* by owls. (N#279:9)

The show *might meander*. (N#279:9)

As we saw in Section 4.7, lexical verbs vary a lot as to what elements they need in order to form a grammatical sentence: *meander* isn't followed by anything, whereas the earlier sentence with *do* would have been ungrammatical without *it*. We therefore divide the lexical verbs into categories depending on how many and what kind of elements they require. In order to do this, we revisit the terminology introduced in Chapter 4: subject, object (direct and indirect) and predicative complement (subject complement, object complement). We also explore in more detail the categories of verbs: INTRANSITIVE, MONO-TRANSITIVE, DI-TRANSITIVE, COMPLEX INTRANSITIVE and COMPLEX TRANSITIVE. We will return to verbs that take whole clauses as complements in Chapter 8.

Intransitive verbs

Intransitive verbs do not require any objects or complements; in fact, they don't permit any to be present:

The Empire State Building still _stands_. (N#279:9)

They _canoodled_ under the white sheets. (N#258:9) [this is John and Yoko again]

I _laughed_ nervously for some reason. (N#258:9)

In the last two of these sentences, the lexical verbs _canoodle_ and _laugh_ are indeed followed by something, namely _under the white_ sheets and _nervously for some reason_. However, these are not necessary parts of the sentence; _They canoodled_ and _I laughed_ are complete sentence in themselves. _Under the white sheets, nervously_ and _for some reason_ are typical optional adverbials; to be more precise, they have the function ADJUNCTS, which we introduced in Chapter 4. As typical adjuncts they are optional and they answer questions like _How?_ and _Why?_ When we sub-categorise lexical verbs, we only count the obligatory parts, and hence adjuncts are ignored for these purposes.

We can say that verbs require a certain number of objects or complements because the activity or state they describe requires that number of participants. Hence, an intransitive verb like _laugh_ is a verb describing something that only involves the subject. However, there are some intransitive verbs that don't even seem to need one participant, like _rain_. Still, the rules of English are such that we always need a subject, and hence *Rains is not a grammatical sentence, whereas _It rains_ is. The subject of verbs like _rain_ is usually referred to as a NON-THEMATIC SUBJECT because it does not actually have a semantic (thematic) role to fill in the event described by the verb. _It_ is also called an EXPLETIVE when it occurs in this type of construction.

We saw in Chapter 4 that some intransitive verbs can take something called a COGNATE OBJECT, i.e. an object very closely related in meaning to the verb itself. This is a noun phrase that is lexically related to the verb.

She was _laughing a sort of triumphant laugh_. (AUS#59:25)

[??She was laughing a laugh]

Some dogs _live a long life_. (AUS#56:10)

[??Some dogs live a life.]

These cognate objects are typically used for expressive purposes and must be accompanied by modifiers, otherwise the sentence becomes unacceptable; hence the oddity of the bracketed versions. Since it is such a limited phenomenon, this is not really enough to call verbs like *laugh* or *live* mono-transitive.

Consider the following sentences:

A press notice had <u>come</u> in. (N258:12)

Lennon and Ono <u>sat</u> up.

The lexical verb has been underlined here and it is followed by something that looks like a preposition, but which is sometimes referred to as a PAR-TICLE. These particles are very closely connected to the verb; in fact, one might really want to consider them part of the verb. Indeed, we will con-sider *come in* and *sit up* as units, and we will refer to such verb – particle combinations as INTRANSITIVE PHRASAL verbs. In a moment we shall see that phrasal verbs can also be transitive.

Mono-transitive verbs

Mono-transitive verbs take one object, which will always be a direct object. In the following examples, the mono-transitive verbs are underlined and their objects are in italics:

The Simpsons <u>revolutionized</u> *cartoons*. (N#279:8)

The Simpsons have <u>delivered</u> *hip irreverence and clever satire* for more than 10 years now. (N#279:8)

The last sentence contains adjuncts as well as the obligatory subject and object. But, as we have said, optional adverbials are not taken into account when it comes to determining the type of a lexical verb. The italic phrases here are all clear cases of objects, since we can create the corresponding passive sentences in which they have become subjects. (Note that some-times passive sentences may sound a bit odd out of context, but they are grammatical.)

Cartoons have been revolutionized by 'The Simpsons.'

Hip irreverence and clever satire have been delivered by 'The Simpsons' for more than 10 years now.

In all the sentences we have looked at so far in this section, the object is a noun phrase, and this is the most typical category of a direct object. However, there are other verbs which seem to be followed by a preposition phrase:

Ono generally <u>*looked*</u> *at Lennon* lovingly. (N258:12)

In the second part of her biography, 'Survivor,' she <u>*talks*</u> *about this period of her life*. (N#697:9)

These verbs are sometimes referred to as PREPOSITIONAL VERBS, but they are sufficiently similar to mono-transitive verbs for us to consider them as a sub-class of this category. Crucially, the element following the preposition can be made the subject of a corresponding passive sentence: *Lennon was looked at lovingly* and *This period of her life was talked about in the second part*. . . . With prepositional verbs, the prepositions are determined by the verbs, and they really do belong together (*look at* and *talk about*); this is confirmed by the passive sentences here. But prepositional verbs are also a little two-faced. For example, if you apply constituency tests like coordination, you will find that *at Lennon* works well as a constituent too (Ono *looked at Lennon* and *at Leon*); so even though *at* appears to belong to the verb *look* and 'look at' belong together, they don't seem to form a constituent in the same way.

There is another sub-type of mono-transitive verbs which look similar to prepositional verbs:

I picked up a strange young passenger the other day. (AUS#59:25)

An immaculate Osbourne tops up her own cup of tea. (N#697:9)

As with the prepositional verb, there are corresponding passive sentences: *A strange young passenger was picked up* and *Her own cup of tea was topped up*, which shows that they are transitive verbs. However, as we briefly discussed in Chapter 4, there is a crucial difference, and that is that the object can occur between the verb and the preposition (or particle as they are often called in this case); this is not possible with prepositional verbs:

I *picked* a strange young passenger *up* the other day.

Osbourne *tops* it *up*.

*Ono *looked* Lennon *at*.

*She *talks* this period of her life *about*.

This kind of mono-transitive verb where the object can occur between the verb and the particle is then called a PHRASAL VERB. In fact, if the object of a phrasal verb is a pronoun, it has to occur between the verb and the particle, *I picked it up* versus **I picked up it* and *She topped it up* versus **She topped up it*.

As we said in Section 4.4, there are verbs that need to be followed by a whole clause, and we will now look at how similar to objects these clauses are. Consider the following examples:

I <u>discovered</u> *that, when expected to speak foreign languages in front of each other, the Dutch can be strangely reticent.* (N#258:12)

I <u>wish</u> *I had gone that day.* (N#258:12)

We <u>wondered</u> *if we were in for some kind of bizarre sexual experience.* (N#258:12)

The YK3 bug <u>is threatening</u> *to bring down society.* (N#279:8)

The constituent in italics is a clause, we hope that for the time being this category makes some intuitive sense, but we will come back to it in more detail in Chapter 8. These clauses seem to resemble objects. The verb *discover*, for instance, can take a regular noun phrase object as in *I discovered the space ship*. And in all these sentences, the verb cannot occur on its own: **We wondered* (except elliptically). However, one thing that is different about clauses as complement is that they cannot always be the subject of a corresponding passive, as the following examples show (we have simplified the first example by removing the adverbial):

?That the Dutch can be strangely reticent was discovered (by me).

**I had gone that day* was discovered (by me).

**If we were in for some kind of bizarre sexual experience* was wondered (by us).

**?To bring down society* was being threatened (by the YK3 bug). (N#279:8)

It is clear then that these clauses cannot always occur as the subject in the passive sentences, even though we saw in Section 4.3 that clauses can occur as subjects in other contexts. There is then some argument in the literature as to whether these clauses should be considered objects or not, and hence whether the verb should be considered mono-transitive. We will call these verbs mono-transitive and refer to the italic clauses that follow them as object clauses.

One property clausal objects share with noun phrase objects is that they form the answer to *What?* questions: we can ask What *did The Simpsons revolutionise?* and the answer is the direct object *cartoons.* In the same way, we can ask What *did I discover?* and the answer is the whole italic object clause. We will come back to this kind of object in Chapter 8, since they are really clauses within clauses.

Now, so far we have said that mono-transitive verbs are those that take an obligatory object. We'll have to modify this a little. Consider the following sentence:

After all, I cannot eat *meat.* (AUS#104:16)

Given the standard passive test (*Meat cannot be eaten by me*), the italic phrase is a direct object, and hence *eat* is a mono-transitive verb. However, the object doesn't really seem to be obligatory since the following sentence is grammatical:

After all, I cannot eat.

Now what do we do? There seem to be two options. Either we say that an object can sometimes be optional, or we say that there are two verbs *eat*, one that is mono-transitive and one that is intransitive. Like any sensible linguist, we'll go for the first option here. The verb *eat* means exactly the same thing in the two sentences, and in the example without an object present in the sentence there is an understood object – you cannot eat without eating something. *Eat* is, then, a mono-transitive verb which can occur without its object. There are quite a few verbs like this in English, but it would seem that they all have to have quite a general meaning. A more specific '*eat*-verb,' like *devour,* doesn't allow the object to be deleted, so that *Oscar has devoured the fish* is fine, but **Oscar has devoured* is not.

A similar problem arises when the verb occurs in its passive form. Consider the following sentences:

Cartoons have been <u>revolutionized</u> (by The Simpsons).

Hip irreverence and clever satire have been <u>delivered</u> (by The Simpsons) for more than 10 years now.

Here we have the same verbs that we started this section with. We said then that they were clearly mono-transitive. Now, however, they lack an object and the question is: do we want to say that they are now intransitive? The answer to this has to be 'no.' Verbs that occur in passive sentences are still fundamentally transitive. The same point can be made for passive versions of di-transitive and complex transitive verbs too (these categories were introduced in Chapter 4 and we will return to them presently).

Sometimes when the object is left out, the verb may acquire a slightly different or more specific meaning. Consider the following pairs of sentences:

Bender, the neurotic and corrupt robot, <u>drinks</u>. (N#258:9)

Bender, the neurotic and corrupt robot, <u>drinks</u> *only mineral water.*

Fry <u>hides</u> in a head museum. (N#258:9)

Fry <u>hides</u> *the money* in a head museum.

He <u>broke</u> his artificial leg. (AUS#73:14)

His artificial leg <u>broke</u>.

Under normal interpretation, *He drinks* would be taken to mean that he drinks more alcoholic beverages than is good for him, and hence the understood object is more specific here than with, say, *eat.* If the object of *hide* is left out, the understood object refers to the same thing as the subject, so that the previous example means *Fry hides himself.* In the intransitive version of the sentence containing *break,* the subject corresponds to the object of the mono-transitive one. Still, the involvement of *the artificial leg* in both sentences is the same; the leg ends up broken in both sentences and one can assume that something must have broken it. Using terminology to which we will return in Chapter 9, we can say that the THEMATIC (or SEMANTIC) ROLE of *the artificial leg* is the same in both sentences. In some ways, the difference between the two sentences is similar to that between the mono-transitive sentence and its passive counterpart *His artificial leg was broken.*

Di-transitive verbs

A di-transitive verb takes two objects, a direct object and an indirect one. The indirect object always precedes the direct one.

Baker <u>gives</u> *the novel a real sense of chaos.* (N#279:48)

'The Big Issue' <u>offered</u> *me all the encouragement and assistance.* (AUS#51:10)

The indirect objects here are *the novel* and *me.* The rest of the italic string is the direct object. We can show that the indirect object really is an object by creating the corresponding passive sentences. (Of course, the case of the pronoun then changes from object case *me* to subject case *I.*)

The novel is given a real sense of chaos by Baker.

I was offered all the encouragement and assistance by 'The Big Issue.'

As we said in Chapter 4, indirect objects can normally be replaced by a preposition phrase (PP) involving prepositions such as *to* or *for*, but then they move to the other side of the direct object:

Baker gives a real sense of chaos *to the novel.*

'The Big Issue' offered all the encouragement and assistance *to me.*

It is difficult to decide whether or not the PP should still be considered a complement of the verb, or whether it now has the status of an adjunct. It is not a straightforward matter and we will not deal with it here; you may want to use the tests we have introduced in this book and see what conclusion you draw.

Turning now to the status of the direct object, we see that normally it can only become the subject of a corresponding passive if the indirect object occurs in its PP form:

A real sense of chaos is given to the novel by Baker. versus ?*A real sense of chaos* is given the novel by Baker.

All the encouragement and assistance was offered to me by 'The Big Issue.' versus ?*All the encouragement and assistance* was offered me by 'The Big Issue.'

We saw in Chapter 4 that in order to be able to undergo passivisation, an object must be adjacent to the verb, and the indirect object occurring as a PP allows the direct object to immediately follow the verb.

As with mono-transitive verbs, the objects are usually NPs. The direct object can also be clausal, as the following examples show:

I <u>ask</u> *him if he believes everybody should be middle class.* (N#274:11)

He <u>told</u> *me that everyone should be working class.*

Here *him* and *me* are indirect objects and the *if* and *that* clauses are the direct objects. As always with clausal objects, it is not easy to make them the subject of a corresponding passive. However, given the similarity between these two sentences and two sentences in which *ask* and *tell* take a noun phrase object we will still want to consider these di-transitive: *I ask him the question* and *He told me the answer.*

We noticed earlier that there are mono-transitive verbs where the object is optional. This is also true of many di-transitive verbs:

'The Big Issue' offered *all the encouragement and assistance.*

I ask *if he believes everybody should be middle class.*

We will still call these verbs di-transitive, given that the meaning doesn't change. If you compare these sentences with the original, you will notice that the object we have deleted is the indirect one. This is, in fact, a strong tendency: if a di-transitive verb allows you to delete one object it is the indirect one, leaving the direct object in. However, as we saw in Section 4.4, some verbs like *teach* and *tell* allow either object to be deleted. For example:

171

She taught young students Linguistics.

She taught young students.

She taught Linguistics.

There are also di-transitive verbs where neither object can be deleted:

*Baker gives *the novel*.

*Baker gives *a real sense of chaos*.

Complex intransitive verbs

COMPLEX INTRANSITIVE VERBS take one predicative complement and are sometimes also referred to as COPULAR VERBS or INTENSIVE VERBS. Some examples are:

My Iconic Air Sanitizer is not *the only oinkment in my swine flu kit*. (AUS#329:13)

You can get *complacent*. (N#235:10)

The predicative complement of a complex intransitive verb is a subject complement. As we said in Section 4.5, the main characteristic of a predicative complement is that it refers to the same entity as something else in the sentence, or describes some other element in the sentence, in this case the subject. The predicative complement is normally either a noun phrase, like *the only oinkment in my swine flu kit*, or an adjective phrase, like *complacent*. They can, however, also be clausal or consist of a PP as we saw in Chapter 4:

The fact is *that it's the numbers with nine on the end that are really spooky*. (AUS#302:14)

I was *in a deep purple haze*. (N#258:12)

It's *in a majestic location*. (AUS#61:6)

Complex transitive verbs

Verbs which require one object and one predicative complement are called COMPLEX TRANSITIVE VERBS. The object is a direct object and the predicative complement is an object complement, i.e. it refers to the same thing as the object. Some examples are:

Don't call *comedian Alex Boardman a bit of a lad*. (N#273:30)

We keep *our Facebook garden nicely tended*. (AUS#305:13).

In these examples, *Alex Boardman* and *a bit of a lad* refer to the same person; similarly, *our Facebook garden* and *nicely tended* refer to the same entity. This is what we described as co-reference in Section 4.5. As we have said before, complements are usually either NPs, like *a bit of a lad*; or APs, like *nicely tended*. Just as with the subject complement of some verbs, we will claim that the object complement can also be a PP:

Thatcherism <u>drove</u> many radical young English people *into exile*. (AUS#55:6)

There are also examples of what look like clausal object complements:

I found myself asking many of the questions. (N#258:12)

There are, however, other ways of looking at such sentences which we will discuss briefly in Chapter 8, but the issues involved are really too advanced for what we are doing here.

We'll conclude this chapter with a story showing that grammar can have surprising, and important, applications – a legal case where the court's decision came down to a question of transitivity.

Judge throws the (grammar) book at bank

In May 2018 the second largest bank in Australia was up on charges for manipulating interest rates. The whole case hinged on the grammar of the F-word.

One of the bank's traders, Colin Roden, was recorded saying the following words: 'I know it was completely wrong, but I thought f*** it, I might as well f*** it.' Putting aside the complicated financial details of the case (and the judge's long but at times fairly wild linguistic analysis of swearing in the workplace), there were two grammatical options discussed in the courtroom:

> Was the use of the verb here transitive (in other words, doing something to a following object, in this case a key benchmark interest rate) – a grammar ruling that would entail a fine for the bank of up to $1.1 million for unconscionable conduct. Alternatively was this simply an exclamation that reflected treasury boss' I-don't-care thinking at the time – a ruling that would supply the bank's 'get out of jail free' card (the *it* in this construction would be the dummy object, such as you find in expressions like *cark it* and *leg it*).

> Unfortunately for the bank, Justice Beach concluded the more sinister meaning that 'the f – word was being used here with its classic active transitivity'; in other words, the judge found Mr Roden had planned a 'doable activity.'

6.7 Trees

We have already provided arguments for why the constituent structure of verb strings is as indicated by the brackets in the following sentence:

The Y3K bug [*is* [*threatening* to bring down society]].

What we need to sort out now is how we make sure within our tree structure that the right features get assigned. We can use the following features to describe the different verb forms: FIN (finite), INF (*to* infinitive), BARE (bare infinitive), PPART (past or passive participle) and ING (-*ing* participle). The auxiliaries we have dealt with here can then be said to put the following restrictions on their VP complements:

Modals	*will, may*, etc. + V[BARE]
Auxiliary of the perfect:	*have* + V[PPART]
Auxiliary of progressive:	*be* + V[ING]
Auxiliary of passive:	*be* + V[PPART]

We said in Section 3.6 that the relationship between a lexical head and its complement is a close one, so that a lexical head can put restrictions on its complement as to how many there can be, what category they may belong to, etc. The step is not far to saying that a lexical head can also impose certain restrictions as to the feature of its sister. We can then capture this in trees as follows (in order to focus on the things we are discussing here, we only draw the VP immediately above the first auxiliary).

In this tree, we have a head V which is a modal auxiliary, i.e. it has the feature [AUX_MOD]. Since this head is also finite it has the feature [FIN] as well. Its complement VP has to have the feature [BARE] and this feature trickles down to the V which heads the complement, to make sure that we get *meander* rather than, say, *meanders* or *meandered*.

(4)

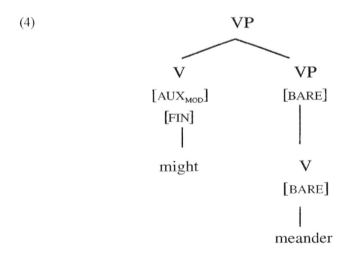

Now to a more complex tree:

(5)

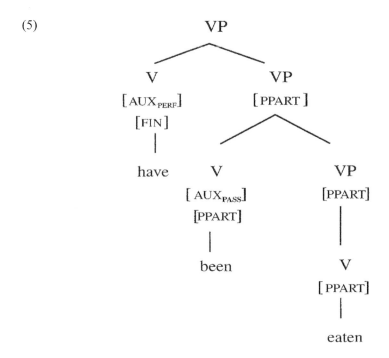

In this tree, we have the auxiliary of the perfect, *have*, in its finite form taking a VP complement, which of course has to have the feature [PPART]. The VP complement of the perfect auxiliary is headed by the auxiliary of the passive, *be*, and since it heads the complement of the auxiliary of the perfect it must occur in its PPART form *been*. This means that in this VP, *been* is the auxiliary of the passive and it occurs in its PPART form because it is the complement of the auxiliary of the perfect. So, it is important here to make the distinction between the verb itself and the form it happens to occur in. Finally, in this tree, the auxiliary of the passive takes a VP complement in its turn, and this VP complement must occur in its PPART form because that is the form the auxiliary of the passive requires; hence we get *eaten* rather than, say, *eating*.

How to draw the lexical verbs and their complements should not cause us any new problems here. The trees will have the same structure as those in Section 4.7, but they will have category labels rather than functional labels. We'll give a couple of examples here to remind you of what they look like.

The noun phrase *cartoons* is the object of *revolutionized* and hence it must be the sister of that verb in the tree:

(6)

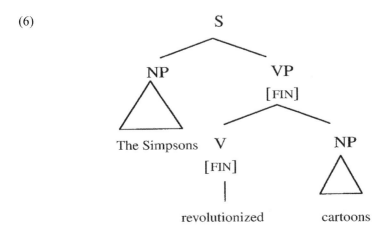

Here the verb takes two complements: a direct object NP and a predicative complement in the form of a PP.

(7)

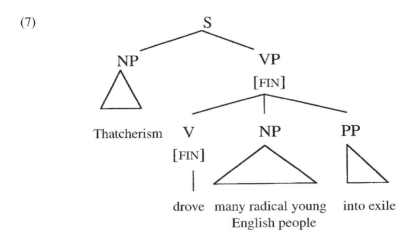

Remember that only complements occur as sisters of the verb. Optional elements like adverbials occur above this level, since they do not have the right kind of relationships with the head verb to be its sister. The adverbials are optional; they occur recursively and the verb has no influence on their form. This is something we discussed in Section 4.6. For a sentence like *The Simpsons have delivered hip irreverence and clever satire for more than 10 years*

now, we then get the following tree. This is about as complex as our trees will get.

(8)

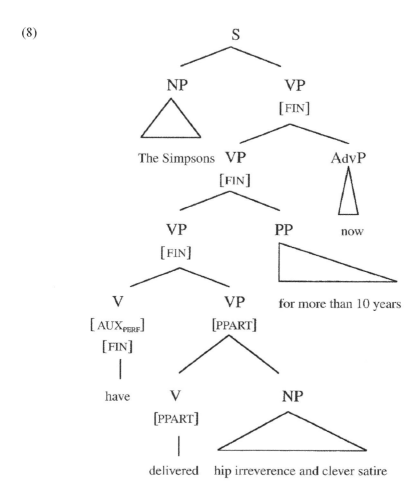

Let's go through this one from the top. There is no disjunct or conjunct; so the root node S has two daughters, NP and VP. The NP is quite straightforward, but the finite VP node gets more complex. The VP contains two adverbials, *now* and *for more than 10 years*, each of which attaches to the VP and forms a new VP. The feature [FIN] travels down along the VP until it comes to a head V, in this case the auxiliary of the perfect *have*. The auxiliary of the perfect as usual takes a VP complement which must have the feature [PPART]. The head of this VP is *delivered*, which takes an NP complement which functions as an object. If you take it easy and do the trees step by step, they aren't as horrible as all that.

We saw in Section 6.1 that little adverbs can also occur in the middle of the verb string, so that we get adverbs occurring between an auxiliary verb and its complement. This gives us trees like the following:

(9)

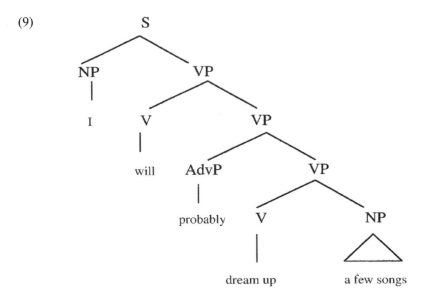

One verb form we haven't discussed yet in any detail is the one containing the infinitival marker *to*. What do we do with this? Sometimes it is considered part of the verb, but this is clearly not true since it is very common in English *to boldly go* and split the infinitive, and we wouldn't expect an adverb like *boldly* to occur in the middle of a verb form. Since it has the same shape as the preposition *to* in *to the dogs*, we might think that it is a preposition. However, if it was, it would be the only preposition that can combine with a verb in English. Also, it would form a PP with the verb, and a phrase like *to go to the dogs* doesn't have the distribution of a PP at all. In fact, its distribution is much like that of a VP. So, if it isn't part of the verb form, and it isn't a preposition, then what is it? Now, you had better sit down for this one. We will claim that it is in fact most closely related to an auxiliary verb. How's that, *to* is an auxiliary verb? Well, we are actually in quite good company when we say this. The major theories of syntax analyse the infinitival *to* in the same way they would an auxiliary verb. We will not go into all the arguments here, but for us, the most convincing evidence is related to ellipsis, the leaving out of a VP. In English, you can leave out a VP if the information can be understood from the immediate linguistic context. However, this is normally only allowed if you leave behind an auxiliary verb. Look at the following examples:

She said that they may have been seeing things,

and they may.
and they may have.
and they may have been.
*and they may have been seeing.

As long as the string ends in an auxiliary verb, we can delete the rest. If the string ends in the lexical verb as in the last version, then it is ungrammatical. As usual, when we need an auxiliary and there is no other one handy we can use dummy *do*:

She said that they saw some weird things,

> and they did.

Now look at the following examples:

She said that they may have been wanting to see some weird things,

> and they may.
> and they may have.
> and they may have been.
> *and they may have been wanting.
> and they may have been wanting to.

So, it seems that this kind of VP ellipsis is acceptable as long as the sentence before the missing VP ends in an auxiliary verb or *to*. We have said throughout this book that if some elements share some crucial properties, then they should be considered to be of the same category. Hence we can take this as evidence that the infinitival marker *to* is an auxiliary verb. It is an unusual auxiliary verb, granted, but this still seems the best analysis. As an auxiliary verb it has the feature [INF] so that it occurs as the complement of verbs which require a VP[INF] complement. The infinitival *to* itself requires a complement that has the feature [BARE]. We will return to constructions containing infinitival *to* in Chapter 8, but to make this section of trees for VPs complete, we include here a tree for *want to see things*:

(10)

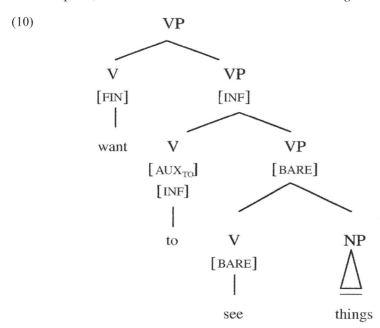

This seems a good place to stop drawing trees for a while.

6.8 Points to remember

❑ Auxiliary verbs are verbs with functional rather than lexical content. They take a VP complement and each auxiliary verb requires that complement to have a particular form. Auxiliary verbs can function as operators in the formation of *yes–no* interrogatives (by inverting with the subject) and sentence negation.

❑ Modal verbs combine with BARE infinitive VPs and have quite complex semantics.

❑ There are two aspects in English: perfect and progressive. The auxiliary of the perfect *have* requires its VP complement to occur in its PPART form and the auxiliary of the progressive *be* combines with a VP in its *-ing* form.

❑ The passive auxiliary *be* takes a PPART VP complement and indicates passive voice.

❑ When an operator is required and no other auxiliary is available, the dummy auxiliary *do* is used. It combines with a VP in its BARE form.

❑ Many auxiliary verbs have abbreviated forms which can attach to certain subjects. They also have special negative forms, with *n't* attached. In some cases the auxiliary with the contracted negation has a different interpretation from the one with the independent negation.

❑ It is important to keep time and tense separate. Time is something in the real world that we think of as having a past, a present and a future. Tense, on the other hand, is a verb form. In English, there are two tenses, present (or non-past) and past. Present tense can refer to both past and future time. In fact, the use of the simple present tense to refer to present time is relatively rare in English. Past tense can also be used to refer to the future. There is no future tense in English but many different ways of referring to future time.

❑ Lexical verbs can be subdivided according to the complements they require: intransitive, mono-transitive, di-transitive, complex intransitive and complex transitive. Cutting across these categories is the notion of phrasal verbs – verbs that occur with a particle to form a unit.

❑ Apart from the auxiliary verbs *have, be* and *do*, there are also three lexical verbs *have, be* and *do*. Lexical *have*, and even more so the lexical *be*, retain auxiliary-like properties even when functioning as lexical verbs.

Exercises

1. Tense versus time

Use the following sentences to support a distinction between tense and time:

(a) If you went to town tomorrow, I could meet you at Marks and Spencers.

(b) He has created some famous cartoon characters.

(c) I could help you with your homework tomorrow.

2. Marginal modals

In the text, we discussed the extent to which *need* is a modal verb. Now do the same with *dare* and *ought to*. Use your own native speaker judgements or that of others to decide how these verbs react with respect to subject–operator inversion, negation, tag questions, co-occurrence with other auxiliary verbs, etc. If you can get judgements from speakers of different ages you might get different results. Given that the world-wide web is also an amazing source of language, you could google for constructions involving these verbs.

3. Lexical versus auxiliary verbs

Indicate whether the verbs in the following sentences are main verbs or auxiliary verbs. (From Bill Flanagan's interview with Bob Dylan in *The Big Issue in the North* 801:12)

(a) Bob Dylan has at various times revolutionized folk, rock, country and gospel music.

(b) From the very first, this was an artist who made us look at the familiar with new eyes and ears.

(c) Isn't there enough irreverence in the world?

(d) The songs don't require much acting.

(e) The inflections would maybe differ if we changed the key and sometimes that might affect the emotional resonance.

(f) Did you have a favourite cowboy singer as a kid?

(g) Nothing back there would play any part in where I was going.

4. Categories of lexical verbs

For the italicised lexical verbs in the following sentences, state their sub-category. Discuss any difficulties. Remember that optional adverbials do not count for the purpose of sub-categorisation. All these examples are from the story about the Stockport ostrich farmer from *The Big Issue* (N#301:15).

(a) That didn't <u>stop</u> one of the sons of this unremarkable Cheshire town.

(b) A chance remark <u>gave</u> Warrington the idea of ostrich dealing over the Internet.

(c) I told him to check the Internet.

(d) Ostriches on line was born.

(e) I <u>marketed</u> everything to do with ostriches.

(f) The demand for leather and feathers is especially high.

(g) The ostrich industry is on the up.

(h) It might become the first ostrich theme park.

(i) I <u>treat</u> my ostriches very well.

181

(j) I don't <u>agree</u> with battery farming.

(k) I <u>met</u> my girlfriend through a website chatroom.

5. Passive voice

Part 1: Do the following have a passive counterpart? If yes, what is it? If no, explain why you can't form a passive.

(a) We sold them most of the furniture.

(b) The prosecutor clearly demonstrated that they had an excellent motive.

(c) They called five times.

(d) Her husband spent whatever she gave him.

(e) Her husband grumbled, whatever she gave him.

(f) The police arrested Roscoe at the rally to 'Save the Fitzroy Pool.'

Part 2: What are the passive forms for the (g) and (h) sentences? Why do you think the passive version of (g) is more acceptable than the (h) passive? (This one is a little tricky, and might require you to do some sleuthing!)

(g) Goldilocks has slept in my bed.

(h) Goldilocks has slept beside the river.

The noun phrase

7.1 How to spot a noun phrase

In this chapter, we look a bit more closely at the noun phrase. The first thing we need to know about noun phrases is how to spot them. Of course we already know that they are built around a noun, and we know how to spot a noun (don't we? Go back to Section 3.4 if you have forgotten). However, this is not all we need to know. Very often noun phrases consist of much more than the obligatory bits like a noun and possibly a determiner, so that it can be hard to decide where the noun phrase begins and ends without applying some tests. Fortunately there is an easy way of deciding exactly how much of a string belongs to the noun phrase. As we have said before, pronouns replace noun phrases, not nouns – and should more accurately be called pro-NPs. Hence to decide exactly what in a text is a noun phrase, we replace some string with a pronoun like *she*, *they*, *us* or *that*. All the material we need to remove to keep the sentence grammatical (though it may not make as much sense as it did with the full noun phrases) must then belong to the noun phrase. Consider the following text from an article in *The Big Issue* (N#151:8–10) about the possibility that all the Apollo moon landings were in fact fake and filmed in Hollywood rather than on the moon. Most of the examples in this chapter are taken from this article.

> In the early hours of May 16 1990, after a week spent watching old video footage of a man on the moon, a thought was turning into an obsession in the mind of Ralph Rene.
> 'How can the flag be fluttering,' the 47-year-old American kept asking himself, 'when there is no wind on the atmosphere-free moon?'

Now, something like *week* you should recognise as a noun and therefore something that will form a noun phrase, but how big is the noun phrase to which it belongs? The pronoun *it* or *that* would seem reasonable replacements for a noun phrase built around *week*. In order to use a pronoun, we must replace a whole noun phrase. If we replace just *week* by *that*, we get **after a that spent watching old video footage, a thought was turning into . . .* which is ungrammatical and hence the noun phrase must be bigger. Let's try to replace a longer string to see if that gives a grammatical sentence: *after that, a thought was turning into . . .* which is fine and we have found the full noun phrase: *a week spent watching old video footage of a man on the moon*. Now, as we shall soon see, the modifiers inside an NP can contain NPs, so that we get NPs inside NPs. Indeed, in the noun phrase we have just spotted, we could introduce pronouns: *a week spent watching it* and therefore *old video footage of a man on the moon* is a noun phrase too; *a week spent watching old video footage of him* is fine and hence *a man on the moon* is also an NP.

We can then use this test to spot all the noun phrases of the text. We have underlined all the NPs in the following examples, and in a second version we have replaced them all by pronouns. It does make the text sound rather silly since it removes so much of the meaning, but it is structurally correct.

> In <u>the early hours of May 16 1990</u>, <u>after a week spent watching old video footage of a man on the moon</u>, <u>a thought</u> was turning into <u>an obsession in <u>the mind of Ralph Rene</u>.</u>
> 'How can <u>the flag</u> be fluttering,' <u>the 47-year-old American</u> kept asking <u>himself</u>, 'when there is <u>no wind on the atmosphere-free moon</u>?'

> In it, after that, it was turning into that in him.
> 'How can it be fluttering,' he kept asking himself, 'when there is it?'

Note that *himself* is already a pronoun, so there is no need to try to replace it with anything.

The crucial thing when spotting noun phrases is that they are usually longer than you think; so try to replace a bit more of the string with a pronoun and if it turns out to be grammatical, then you have indeed found the whole noun phrase.

7.2 Who's the boss?

A noun phrase must have a noun as its head (otherwise it wouldn't be a noun phrase, would it?), though of course it may consist of just a pronoun. If a noun phrase contains just one noun, then that must be the head. However, given that a noun phrase may contain other nominal elements as (part of) noun phrase internal modifiers, a noun phrase can contain more than one noun. How do we decide which of the nouns is the real head? Let's look at the subject of the following sentence:

<u>The giant leap for mankind</u> was a fake.

The underlined string is clearly a noun phrase since we could say *It was a fake*. It contains three nouns: *giant, leap* and *mankind*. We can use the morphological properties in Section 3.4 to show that they are indeed nouns. Two of them have plural forms: *giants* and *leaps* and can form a noun phrase with *a: a giant* and *a leap*; all of them can occur on their own with a possessive *'s: giant's, leap's* and *mankind's*. (Remember that the possessive *'s* with nouns which are not living can sound a bit odd out of context, but is still grammatical: *this leap's importance only became clear a few decades later*.) So, we have one noun phrase and three nouns – which one is the head around which the noun phrase is built? For once, it is actually quite OK to be intuitive. Ask yourself the question *What kinds of things are we talking about?* There are only a handful of noun phrases for which this does not work (see exercise 4). *A giant leap for mankind* is clearly a kind of *leap*, rather than a kind of *giant* or a kind of *mankind*. Hence *leap* is the head of this noun phrase. As always, there is also a more formal way of checking that we are right. For a subject, it is the number (as in singular or plural) of the head noun which decides the agreement on the verb (but it has to be a present tense verb or *be*): if the head noun is singular, the verb occurs in its third person singular present tense -*s* form. If the head noun is plural, the verb occurs in the form lacking -*s*. So, make the noun phrase you are looking at the subject of a present tense sentence and change the number of the noun you suspect of being the head. If this means you have to change the verb form, then you were right. In the previous example, the NP is already the subject of an appropriate sentence; so all we need to do is to change the number of *leap* and see whether the verb form needs to change:

The giant leap for mankind was a fake.

The giant leaps for mankind were a fake.

Hey presto, we have shown beyond all reasonable doubt that *leap* is the head of *the giant leap for mankind*.

Now that we know how to spot the noun phrase and how to decide which noun heads it we are ready to look at the other parts of the noun phrase.

7.3 Determiners

The head noun is an obligatory part of a noun phrase (except when it consists of just a pronoun), but at least for some noun phrases there are also other obligatory parts. Consider the following underlined noun phrase:

Rene has now put all his findings into <u>a book entitled *Nasa Mooned America*</u>.

The head noun is clearly *book*, but what else is obligatory? We can certainly delete what follows *book* and still have a grammatical sentence:

Rene has now put all his findings into <u>a book</u>.

How about *a* – can that be deleted?

*Rene has now put all his findings into <u>book entitled *Nasa Mooned America*</u>.

No, it would appear that *a* is obligatory too. Little function words like *a* which allow nouns that couldn't function as full noun phrases on their own to do so are called DETERMINERS. As with other function words, there is a limited number of them and we will soon go through them. First we'll look at the obligatory parts of some other noun phrases:

<u>The photographs</u> and <u>the film footage</u> are the only proof that the Eagle ever landed.

We have underlined two of the noun phrases in this sentence (the two are coordinated to form one NP), and it turns out that in both cases we can strip the noun phrase down to just the noun and still end up with a grammatical sentence:

<u>Photographs</u> and <u>footage</u> are the only proof that the Eagle ever landed.

Why is this possible with *photographs* and *footage* but not with *book*? The answer is that a determiner is only obligatory with singular count nouns. Plural count nouns like *photographs* and non-count nouns like *footage* do not need determiners. However, they can all be used with determiners if they are needed to convey the meaning the speaker or writer wants to convey.

This is, then, the first step towards defining determiner: those little function words that allow a singular count noun to function as a full noun phrase. Returning to *the giant leap for mankind*, we see that it is not just *the* which can do this job:

$$\left.\begin{cases} \text{A} \\ \text{That} \\ \text{His} \\ \text{Which} \\ \text{No} \end{cases}\right\} \text{leap was a fake}$$

Another characteristic of determiners is that we can only have one of them. If you try to combine the elements you get ungrammaticality. Still, there is no reason why *that his leap* or *his no leap* shouldn't be possible – after all, there are noun phrases like *that leap of his* and *none of his leaps*. This turns out to be an important characteristic, since there are some determiners that can only occur with plural or non-count nouns, and since these can be full noun phrases anyway we wouldn't be able to tell them apart from things that aren't determiners. However, we know that things like *the*, *those* and *his* are determiners, and they can occur with plural nouns as well. Given that determiners (like other function words) are unique to their phrase, if an element can co-occur with one of the clear determiners, then it cannot itself be a determiner. A further property of determiners is that they really do not like to be modified. You cannot stick a *very* or a *so* in front of them.

Let's look now at one of the noun phrases occurring in the text and a slightly modified one:

NASA won't respond to <u>any claims</u>.

NASA won't respond to <u>many claims</u>.

How could we know whether *any* and *many* are determiners, since *claims*, being a plural noun, could occur on its own anyway? Well, we know that *the*, *those* and *his* are determiners and we have said that each head noun can only occur with one determiner; so we just need to check whether *any* or *many* can co-occur with them. We find that *many* can occur with all of them: *the many claims*, *those many claims* and *his many claims*. We can conclude, then, that *many* isn't a determiner. It is trickier with *any*: **any those claims*, **the any claims* and **any his claims*. It is not a question of meaning, since we have *any of those claims* and *any of his claims*. Why not have **any those claims* like we have *all of those claims* as well as *all those claims*? The reason is that *any* is a determiner and therefore cannot combine directly with another determiner; *all* is not a determiner and hence it can combine with a determiner. As expected, *many* – which is not a determiner – can be modified: *very many* or *so many*. *Any*, on the other hand – which is a determiner – cannot be modified: **very any* and **so any*.

It should be pointed out here that some introductory textbooks are much less strict on what counts as a determiner. In many of them *many* will be considered a determiner. It seems clear to us that *many* is in fact quite a typical adjective. Apart from accepting *very* as a modifier, it even has the comparative and superlative forms which we said in Chapter 3 were characteristic of adjectives: *many–more–most*. As we have said so many times throughout this book, if there is a set of words which behave in a similar way as far as form and distribution are concerned, then clearly the grammar of that language 'thinks' of those words as belonging to one category. Just because words are similar in meaning, i.e. in semantics, it doesn't mean that the grammar thinks of them as the same kind of animal.

Given our strict definition, what are the determiners? Well, just to give a clearer picture, they are commonly divided into five groups according to their meaning (but as far as the syntax is concerned they are all determiners): ARTICLES, DEMONSTRATIVES, *WH*-DETERMINERS, QUANTIFICATIONAL DETERMINERS and POSSESSIVES. The articles are the plain determiners in that they just make a three-way distinction between basic uses of noun phrases, DEFINITE, INDEFINITE and GENERIC. You use a definite noun phrase when you expect the hearer to know what it is you are referring to. So if we use a definite noun phrase like *the man* as in *the man wrote a book about the Apollo moon landings* and we haven't mentioned the man before, and it is not obvious from our shared knowledge of the world who we mean, then you are entitled to ask something like *Who are you on about?* The use of *the* with *Apollo moon landings*, on the other hand, is acceptable, since we can probably count on our hearer having knowledge of Apollo moon landings existing. If we use an indefinite noun phrase, on the other hand, there is no such assumption that the hearer knows the thing we're referring to. If we say *a man wrote a book about the Apollo moon landings*, we indicate that either we expect you not to know the man, or we don't mind much if you do or not. A common way of introducing something is with a *There is/are . . .* and this is then an environment where we normally only get indefinite noun phrases.

Often something unknown is introduced into the discourse with an indefinite noun phrase, and then once it is established, it can be referred to with a definite noun phrase. An example is found in the following slightly modified part of the article:

> But Rene has now put all his findings into a startling book entitled *NASA Mooned America*. Published by himself <u>the</u> book is being sold by mail order.

The author is not assuming that we have heard of the book and hence refers to it as *a . . . book . . .*, but when it is mentioned again we are familiar with its existence and hence the definite form *the book* is used.

Generic noun phrases, finally, are used when speakers want to refer to all instances of the kind they are is referring to:

<u>High pressure oxygen</u> is exceedingly explosive.

This means that all *high pressure oxygen* is explosive – it's just in its nature. Which particular determiner is used to achieve which meaning depends on which kind of noun it is used with (all examples here are invented):

Definite:	singular count noun:	<u>the</u> book that we bought yesterday
	plural count noun:	<u>the</u> books that we bought yesterday
	non-count noun:	<u>the</u> oxygen that we bought yesterday
Indefinite:	singular count noun:	there is <u>a</u> book on the table
	plural count noun:	there are Ø books/<u>some</u> books on the table
	non-count noun:	there is Ø oxygen/<u>some</u> oxygen in the tank
Generic:	singular count noun:	he knows a lot about the history of <u>the</u> book and printing in general <u>a</u> book makes a good Christmas present
	plural count noun:	Ø books make good Christmas presents
	non-count noun:	Ø oxygen can be dangerous

We have underlined the article in these sentences. The *some* which is used as an indefinite determiner is unstressed *some* (contrast this with stressed *some* as in *I only ate* some *cake, not all of it!*). For indefinite and generic plural and non-count nouns we have inserted a zero symbol, Ø. To our mind zeroes and gaps are used far too much in syntactic analyses these days, but this is one place where we actually think it may be defensible, because the fact that there is nothing there actually means something – the fact that the speaker doesn't use *the* means that the noun phrase is not definite. It is different from, say, not using an adjective – the fact that a speaker doesn't use *small* in a noun phrase doesn't mean that he thinks the thing referred to by the noun in question is big. He may just not have anything to say about the size. If you don't like this argument, then just think of it as an absence of an article, rather than the presence of a zero article. We will, however, use the zero article from now on. One of our former colleagues in Manchester, Alan Cruse, has the following example of 'meaningful nothingness.' You have agreed with a friend that unless she phones you before six o'clock you'll meet up in the Hog's Head for a drink at eight. Now, if your phone does not ring before six, that is a meaningful nothingness, i.e. we would be prepared to let a zero element into our system. If, on the other hand, you have made no such arrangement, then the fact that your phone does not ring has no such specific meaning and we would not want to represent that nothingness as a meaningful element.

Demonstratives are determiners that refer to something that is known and specific. They also indicate whether something is close to the speaker (*this* and *these*) or further away (*that* and *those*). The use of a demonstrative may be accompanied by some extralinguistic activity, like pointing. In some dialects *them* is taking over as a demonstrative with plural nouns, as in *I don't like **them new United kits***. *Wh*-determiners indicate that the noun phrase is being the focus of a question, as in ***Which United kit** don't you like?* Or that it is part of a relative clause as in *the team **whose strip** changes every year* (see Chapter 8). Quantificational determiners are words like *any, no, some* (and this time it is the stressed *some* we want) and *enough*, all indicating amount in some way. The possessives, finally, are the possessive pronouns that can function as determiners. A tricky problem is that full noun phrases with the possessive marker *'s* also seem to be able to function as determiners: <u>*man's*</u> *greatest achievement* and <u>*the flag's*</u> *shadow*. The problem with these phrases as determiners is that they are then the only determiners that don't just consist of one word. It would seem that as long as you attach *'s* to a noun phrase, that noun phrase can function as a determiner, no matter how complex the noun phrase is. This has in fact led people to assume that it is the *'s* which acts as a determiner. We will include it here as a type of phrase that **functions** as a determiner, but that it is still of the **category** NP and not a D.

We can sum up the determiners in English:

Articles	*the, a, some* [səm], (Ø)
Demonstratives	*this, that, these, those, (them)*
Wh-determiners	*which, whose, what*
Quantificational determiners	*any, some* [sʌm], *no, enough, every, each, neither . . .*
Possessives	*my, his, our, their, NP's . . .*

7.4 Pre-modifiers

Now we know how to spot a noun phrase, how to find the head noun and how to find the determiner. It is time to turn to the optional modifiers within the noun phrase. These are usually divided up into those that precede the head noun, pre-modifiers, and those that follow it, post-modifiers. We'll start with the pre-modifiers. Consider the following noun phrases.

<u>the</u> early <u>hours</u>	<u>no</u> direct <u>link-up</u>
<u>the</u> great moon <u>hoax</u>	<u>an</u> incredible space <u>odyssey</u>
two blurred white <u>ghosts</u>	powerful <u>spotlights</u>

In all these we can recognise the head nouns – they have been underlined in each case – as have the determiners. In the last two noun phrases, we have the zero article, which is allowed since it is the indefinite use of noun phrases headed by plural nouns. All the things between the determiners and the nouns must be pre-modifiers – but what category do they belong to? *Early, direct, great, incredible, blurred, white* and *powerful* are all adjectives. You can check yourself that they have the characteristics of adjectives: they have comparative and superlative forms (or the equivalent with *more* or *most*), they can be modified by *very*, and they have some of the characteristic endings. Not all of them have all of these properties, but each word has enough of the properties to clearly belong to the category of adjective. Now how about the other words: *moon* and *space* that modify *hoax* and *odyssey*, respectively? Well, they clearly aren't adjectives. In fact, they look like nouns too: they can form a noun phrase on their own with

189

the or *a*: *the/a moon, the/a space*; they can have the plural *s*: *moons, spaces*; and they can have the possessive *'s*: *moon's* and *space's*. (We discussed similar issues at the end of Section 3.4 when we look at tests for determining category membership.)

We have so far discovered two kinds of pre-modifiers: adjectives and nouns. The question now is – are these just adjectives and nouns, or are they potentially whole APs or NPs? Let's try to modify the adjectives within these NPs, first to see if they are in fact APs that happen to consist of one word only:

the <u>very early</u> hours   no <u>absolutely direct</u> link-up

the <u>unbelievably great</u> moon hoax   a <u>really incredible</u> space odyssey

two <u>completely blurred blindingly white</u> ghosts   <u>terribly powerful</u> spotlights

In all of these noun phrases, we have expanded the adjective phrase with an adverb modifying the adjective and in each case the result is fine. It seems quite clear, then, that the adjectival pre-modifiers are indeed full APs that just happened to consist of one adjective in our initial examples. How about the nominal modifiers – can they be expanded in a similar way? To make these examples clearer, we have removed the adjective phrases.

*the <u>Saturn's moon</u> hoax   *an <u>our space</u> odyssey

Here we have tried to make the pre-modifying noun into a full NP by adding a determiner, and it clearly does not work (unless you consider *Saturn's moon hoax* a name of a famous hoax). If we want to talk about a hoax to do with Saturn's moon or an odyssey in our space, we have to choose a different way to talk about it. So the nominal pre-modifier is clearly not a full NP. There are, however, some limited possibilities of modifying the nominal:

an outer space odyssey

Here the obvious interpretation would be that *outer* (which is an adjective) modifies *space* and not *odyssey* – it is an odyssey into outer space. Note, however, that the adjective and the noun must form a close unit in this position. Not any old adjective could go in this position and be interpreted as modifying *space*. So, the nominal pre-modifier is clearly smaller than a full NP, but may be bigger than a noun. In noun phrases with a nominal pre-modifier, there is a feeling of a compound, and in close relatives of English, like Dutch or German, these combinations would often be written as one word. Even in English, these nominal modifiers have to stay close to the noun. An adjective phrase cannot occur between a nominal modifier and the head noun: *the moon great hoax* or *a space long odyssey*. In fact, we feel there are arguments for assuming these combinations are in fact compound-like. We will return to the exact formal analysis of this when we talk about tree in Section 7.8.

Consider now the following noun phrases:

the self-taught engineer   pressurised gloves

Self-taught and *pressurised* do look a lot like verbs, in particular like the participle form of the verb. We can find sentences with similar meaning where the participle clearly has verb status: *the engineer taught himself* and *the gloves have been pressurised (by this process)*. We need to find out whether they still behave as verbs in this environment so that we should have a separate category of participle pre-modifiers. It turns out that it is usually very difficult to decide; often these words have some properties of adjectives and some properties of verbs. *Pressurised* for instance doesn't sound too good with an adjective modifier like *very* but much better with an adverb which could modify a verb, like *slowly* or *highly*. On the other hand, *pressurised* sounds quite good with *more* and *most*, which typically go with adjectives but not with verbs. Since it is such a difficult distinction to draw, we feel at this level it isn't really necessary to make the distinction. We'll just consider these pre-modifiers adjectives. But you should be aware of the fact that they have developed from the participle forms of verbs and that they still have some verbal properties. There are many interesting issues involved here, but we don't need to deal with them at this stage.

Finally, how about *only* in the following noun phrase?

The only casualty

It doesn't seem to have the characteristics of a typical adjective – it doesn't allow any modification, it doesn't have any of the typical inflections, etc. Yet it clearly isn't a determiner – you cannot have noun phrases like *only book*. In the literature these words are often referred to as restrictive adjectives. Some other examples are found in the following invented noun phrases:

a certain flair   the very wallpaper (I was looking for)

Even though they don't look much like adjectives, they don't share enough syntactic properties for us to be able to assign them to any smaller category, though some books put them in a category of 'quantifiers' or 'quantifying adjectives' which may include typical adjectives like *many*. We don't really see an argument for this. Usually these restrictions are the fallout of language change; for example, when it entered English from French, *very* meaning 'true, real' was a well-behaved adjective – examples like *the very wallpaper* are rather like fossils.

Another tricky category is numerals, as in:

two completely blurred blindingly white ghosts

One thing we can say is that they are not determiners, since we can say *the two ghosts*. Similarly with *second; the second ghost*. Numerals like *two* are called CARDINALS and those that indicate order, like *second*, are called ORDINALS. They don't show many of the hallmarks of adjectives, though *first* can be modified by *very; the very first man on the moon*, though the other ordinals can't: *the very seventh goal*. In terms of meaning we can say that they

191

are similar to words like *many* which do behave like adjectives. We refer you to the major grammars of English mentioned under the 'References and further reading' section at the end of this book for a proper description of the properties of numerals. We shall treat them as adjectives here, but mainly because we do not want to have a separate category for them and they are better off with adjectives than with determiners.

Our conclusion about pre-modifiers is, then, that for our purposes we need only distinguish two types of pre-modifiers: adjective phrases and nominals smaller than NPs. But you should be aware of the difficulties involved with some of the pre-modifiers.

As we saw in Section 3.4, speakers are sometimes quite adventurous with the pre-modifiers they use. For instance, a publisher tried to convince us that what she was selling was *a must have educational CD*. Also, what do you think of the following examples?

That being blond and riding on a white horse along the beach feeling (AUS#73:38)

the whole shiny bald chest solarium tan thing (AUS#92:39)

7.5 Pre-determiners

The pre-modifiers we have discussed so far appear between the determiner and head noun, but there are also elements that can precede the determiners. There are not many of them. The principal ones are *all*, *both* and *half*. Less commonly, *many* can also occur before the determiner, as in *many a mile I have travelled*. Words like *twice* and *double* can also occur in this position as in *twice the age* or *double that distance*, as can *such* and *what* in expressions like *such a dangerous thing* or *what a cover-up*. It's quite clear in most cases that the 'pre-determiner' modifies the whole noun phrase and not just the determiner, so that the rest of the phrase forms a constituent without it. The categorial status of the elements, however, varies from element to element and is often less than clear. *Half* seems to be quite a straightforward noun: *the half*, *many halves*, etc. It does not function as a determiner: **half biscuit* is not a good noun phrase, it has to be *half a biscuit* or *half the biscuit*. (Though do you remember the British pop group with the memorable name Half-Man Half-Biscuit and their cracking album *Back in the DHSS*?) *Many* we have already classified as an adjective, but in the old-fashioned combination *many a*, it seems most likely that we are dealing with a combination that now forms a unit *many-a*, in much the same way that *an+other* has become *another*. For *what*, the case can be made for determiner status: *what colour do you prefer*? Noun phrases like *what a shame* are, then, very unusual in that they would appear to have two determiners, but note that their distribution is quite limited. They can only occur in exclamatives: *What a shame that you cannot come!* And not in ordinary declaratives or interrogatives: **I thought that was what a shame* or **What a book did you buy?*

The main choice for the other elements seems to be between a separate class 'pre-determiner,' a sort of odd determiner, or an unusual adjective. It is difficult to make a case for calling them determiners since many of them cannot occur with singular count nouns. Note, however, that even for the ones that can, we can't say *twice man he is*, but need a determiner: *twice the man he is*. Similarly, you can't combine *such* with a singular count noun and get a complete noun phrase: *such disaster* has to be *such a disaster*. On the other hand, the case for calling the elements we are now left with adjectives is also very weak. Having a separate category for just a handful of elements may seem a bit overdone, but these elements really are a bit odd. We will then follow the major grammars of English and refer to them as PRE-DETERMINERS.

Doge – Wow! Very grammar!

The Internet is sprouting all kinds of (probably short-lived) playful linguistic curiosities. A well-known one currently is Doge (usually found in the texts accompanying pictures of a Shiba Inu dog). In addition to its appearance (always a brightly coloured comic sans font), the most striking aspect of Doge is the mismatch between modifiers/determiners and word class. Take the following examples:

much wiki, much donation

many science; many fast

very linguist, very adjectives

so mystery; so amaze

such fascinate; such linguistics

For example, *much* typically precedes non-count nouns (*much food*), and *many* precedes count nouns (*many apples*). If you reverse this, you will create an appropriate sentence in Doge (with the added twist that *many* seems to be able to modify adjectives as well). Intensifying expressions like *so* and *very* normally modify adjectives (*so good* and *very nice*), but in Doge they appear with nouns and verbs. We've just described *such* as one of the rare pre-determiners that modifies the whole noun phrase (*such a dangerous thing*), but in Doge there seems to be no restrictions on what it can modify (as long as it doesn't form a grammatical noun phrase!).

Doge is likely a short-lived Internet fad, perhaps even well out of date by the time this book appears. But if you're interested, you'll find other examples of its idiosyncratic rules in the numerous discussions of Doge grammar on the net. And while you're at it you can check out the curious double-inflected-auxiliary construction (e.g. *can haz*) of LOLcat.

7.6 Post-modifiers

We turn now to modification that follows the noun.

A man <u>on the moon</u>	the thickness <u>of heavy-duty aluminium foil</u>
the pressure <u>inside a space suit</u>	the beginning <u>of an incredible space odyssey</u>

In each of these examples, the post-modification begins with a preposition, one of those little words indicating position or relation and that can't be inflected, e.g. *on*, *of* and *inside*. This means that the post-modifying phrase as a whole is a preposition phrase, a PP. A preposition phrase normally consists of a preposition and a noun phrase, and hence each example contains a second noun phrase that is part of the post-modification: *the moon, heavy-duty aluminium foil, a space suit* and *an incredible space odyssey*. This is something we will return to when we draw trees to represent the structure of noun phrases in Section 7.8.

A different kind of post-modifier is found in the following examples:

the conspiracy theory <u>to *end* all conspiracy theories</u>

their capsule, <u>*pumped* full of high pressure pure oxygen</u>

standard astronauts <u>*orbiting* earth in near space</u>

Here the heads of the post-modifiers (in italics) are verbs. And this time they really are verbs – they take objects as verbs normally do and they can have any verbal modifier. In the first case it is the TO-INFINITIVAL form of *end*, in the second it is the PPART form of *pump*, and the last one is the -ING form of *orbit*. These phrases are full VPs since they can contain all the things that a VP can contain. We won't consider them full clauses since they don't have subjects. We should warn those of you who will carry on with grammar beyond this level that some theoretical analyses assume that there is a zero subject in these post-modifiers. We will return to the issue of different types of verbal phrases in Chapter 8.

The status of the following post-modifiers is a different matter:

conditions <u>that should have made it useless</u>

an event <u>that actually happened</u>

'whistle blowers,' <u>who were keen for the truth to one day get out</u>,

a physicist <u>who worked for NASA</u>

These phrases look more like complete clauses. They begin with a *wh-*word or *that*, and in fact, *that* can always be replaced by *which* or *who*: *conditions which should have made it useless* and *an event which actually happened*. These clauses are all RELATIVE CLAUSES. They are like sentences, except that they have a *that* or *wh*-constituent added. Since they are like clauses with a little bit extra, they are referred to not just as S (for sentence) but as S' (pronounced S-bar). We will have more to say about them in Chapter 8. Meanwhile, we just need to note that even though it looks as if these phrases too lack a subject, exactly like the VPs we just talked about, these phrases are different in that the role of the subject seems to be played by the *wh*-word.

In Section 7.4, we saw that APs pre-modify nouns. However, under certain circumstances they can also function as post-modifiers. Consider the following noun phrases adapted from the text, which all contain a participial – but remember we've decided not to distinguish these from adjectives since this is too difficult to do:

the <u>enthralled</u> group – *the <u>enthralled by the film</u> group – the group <u>enthralled by the film</u>

a <u>manned</u> mission – *a <u>manned by rats</u> mission – a mission <u>manned by rats</u>

The first noun phrase in each case is grammatical, as we would expect. However, when we add some post-modification to the adjective, i.e. when we change from *enthralled* and *manned* to *enthralled by the film* and *manned by rats*, it would appear that the AP has to follow rather than precede the noun. So, APs follow the noun when the AP itself contains post-modification; though remember the supermarket's *easy to open packs* in Section 3.4. When we looked at the behaviour of adjectives in Chapter 3, we also noted that there is a handful that follow the noun even when there is no post-modification. We have no examples of this from the text since they are rather rare:

time <u>immemorial</u>   heir <u>apparent</u>   prime minister <u>designate</u>

Phrases with post-nominal simple adjectives often have an official ring to them. They would frequently have been borrowed from French, where most adjectives follow the noun, so that English has kept the French order for these expressions. Sometimes this order can be used for a more poetic (or archaic) effect (think of *years past, dreams forgotten, matters financial*). Here's what Hugh Hefner had to say about paying US$75,000 to be buried in the crypt next to Marilyn Monroe:

I'm a believer in **things symbolic**. Spending eternity next to Marilyn is too sweet to pass up. (AUS#547:9)

7.7 Complements

At first blush, the following post-nominal element looks just like the relative clause we discussed earlier:

the only proof <u>that the Eagle landed</u>

The underlined clause here is an S' constituent, just like the relative clauses. However, there are a number of crucial differences. We cannot replace *that* by a *wh*-word here: *the only proof which the Eagle landed*. Whereas in the relative clauses there was an element missing in the clause which seemed to be taken over by the *wh*-word, if we remove *that* in this clause we have a complete sentence: *the Eagle landed*. There is also a close relationship between the noun and the clause. It is indeed similar to that between a verb and its object: *He proved that the Eagle landed.* This type of clause is, then, more appropriately described as a complement clause than as a modifier. The distinction is parallel to that between an object and an adjunct in the verb phrase.

A similar distinction between types of PPs can also be found. We can compare the following examples, based on the text, with those discussed earlier:

the incineration <u>of the three astronauts</u>

the removal <u>of men who weren't made of 'right stuff'</u>

Again, these phrases are more closely related to the noun than the PPs we dealt with in the previous section and there is a parallel verb – object combination: *incinerate the three astronauts* and *remove men who weren't made of 'right stuff.'* These are, then, PP complements of the noun. As we shall see in the next section, this difference between complements and modifiers can be represented in a tree.

7.8 Trees

We have said here that a noun phrase must consist of a head noun, and if we assume a zero article, then the determiner is also obligatory. To our mind, one of the characteristics of determiners (except possessive NPs) is that they cannot be modified. Hence the determiner should occur underneath a Det node and not a DetP node. But again we should warn those of you who will move on to syntactic theory that many theories assume all categories must have a whole phrase above them and therefore consider something like *the* a DP. There are also arguments in favour of considering the determiner, rather than the noun, the head, so that many theoretical approaches assume that *the* is in fact the head of a noun phrase like *the astronaut* and the whole phrase is a DP, rather than an NP. These are all issues that need not concern us at the moment.

The view we take for the purposes of this book gives us the basic tree for a full noun phrase:

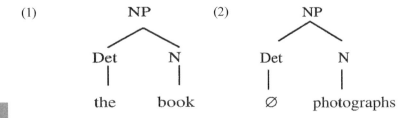

If we turn now to NPs like *those two white blurred ghosts*, then we need to consider first of all the constituent structure. We have a determiner and we have a head noun and we know where they go, but what do we do with *two white blurred* – do they form one constituent, or are they three distinct ones? Well, remember that one characteristic of a constituent is that it can be replaced by one word. Obviously, within an NP, a pronoun won't do much good since pronouns replace whole NPs. There is, however, one word in English that replaces parts of NPs: *one*. We can make the following grammatical responses:

Which ghosts?   Those two white blurred <u>ones</u>   replacing *ghosts*
Which blurred ghosts?   Those two white <u>ones</u>   replacing *blurred ghosts*
Which white blurred ghosts?   Those two <u>ones</u>   replacing *white blurred ghosts*
Which two white blurred ghosts?   Those <u>ones</u>   replacing *two white blurred ghosts*

This shows that all these sub-phrases of the whole noun phrase are constituents and we get the following tree:

(3)

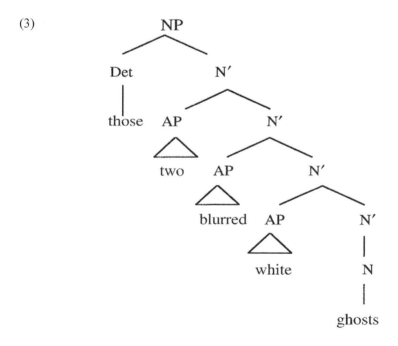

We said in Section 3.6 that the 'inbetween nominals' are called N' (pronounced N-bar). Note that in this tree *ghosts* then is both an N and an N'. This is because even though *ghosts* is clearly a noun, in this NP it can also be replaced by *one* and is therefore also an N'. If we didn't have that extra N' node in the tree, then the last AP would be the sister of an N node and that would make the wrong predictions. As we have seen before, the sister of a lexical category in a tree is reserved for complements, and the adjectives are clearly not complements in the way that objects are complements of the verb. The first two trees we drew in this section should then more appropriately look like this:

(4) (5)

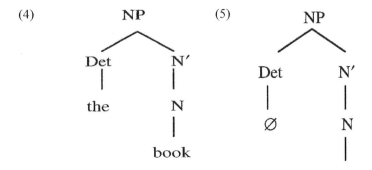

Post-modifiers work in very much the same way as pre-modifiers; they attach at the level of N':

(6)

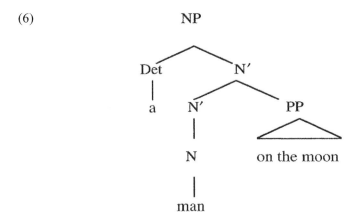

Of course, many NPs contain both pre- and post-modification and then very difficult questions of constituency arise. How about something like *the first man on the moon*; is *first man* a constituent combining with *on the moon* or is *man on the moon* a constituent combining with *first*? (In either case, the whole *first man on the moon* combines with *the* to form the whole NP.) Well, if we assume that the meaning of a phrase combines gradually in the same way that the syntactic bits do, then the meaning of the phrase may help. Here, the meaning is clear – of all the entities referred to by *man on the moon* we want to pick out the *first* one. It is not the case that of all the things referred to by *first man* we are talking about the one who is on the moon. Hence, when it comes to building up meaning, *man on the moon* must be a constituent without *first* and we get the tree:

(7)

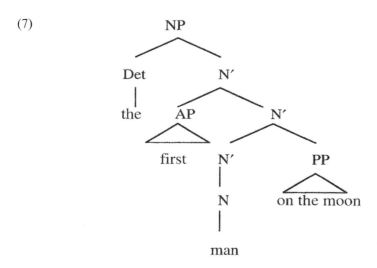

However, it is quite rare that the meaning is this helpful. If we embellish one of the early NPs to *powerful spotlights with black holders*, then it seems impossible to decide whether these are *powerful spotlights* which happen to have *black holders*, or whether they are *spotlights with black holders* which happen to be *powerful*. We can't decide and can therefore not decide which of these two trees is the better one; for this reason, we assume they are both fine. If you can think of strong arguments, then please let us know.

(8)

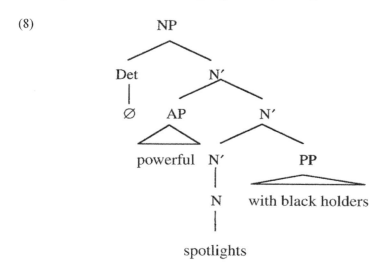

(9)

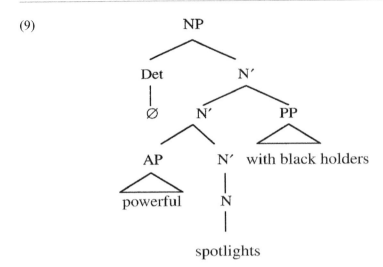

In Section 7.7, we discovered that the distinction between modifiers, or adjuncts, and complements can be made also within the NP. The usual properties of complements, as opposed to modifiers, hold here too. Let's add a post-modifier to one of the NPs with a complement we used there: *the incineration of the three astronauts in that first attempt*. Now compare the two types of PPs. The first PP, *of the three astronauts*, is selected by the noun, just as the verb *incinerate* could select an object like *the three astronauts*. The first obvious thing is that the complement PP normally is closer to the noun. (Though if it is very long it can be put at the end of the phrase. This is what English often does with long phrases – clausal subjects are for instance often shifted to the end of the sentence, as we shall see in Chapters 8 and 9.) The second difference between complement PPs and adjunct PPs is that there can only be as many complements as the head specifies. For nouns, that is never more than one (though verbs can have two). So even if some rats were incinerated at the same time, we cannot express this as *the incineration of the three astronauts of some rats*. Instead we have to make a coordinate noun phrase, *of the three astronauts and of some rats*. With the modifiers we can add as many as we want: *the incineration of the three astronauts in the space shuttle in that first attempt*. So, our tree needs to show that the first PP, *of the astronauts*, belongs closer to the head noun and that it cannot be repeated the way optional adjuncts can. As we saw more generally in Section 3.6, this is done by making the complement the sister of N, and the adjunct the sister of N'. The mother of the N and the PP complement must be an N' (it cannot be N, since it is more than just a noun). We couldn't add another complement PP, since there is no N left for it to be sister to, and the lowest noun cannot have more than one sister. The mother of the N' and the adjunct, on the other hand, is also an N' and we can therefore add another adjunct PP to that N', or indeed any other modifier we come across.

(10)

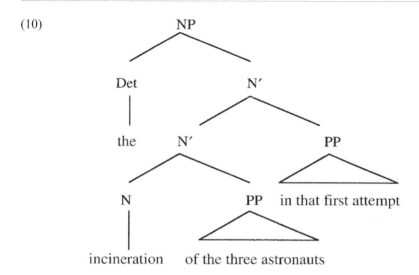

The final issue is now how to fit in the nominal pre-modifiers that we saw examples of in Section 7.4. Some examples that we gave there were *the great moon hoax* and *an incredible space odyssey*. Remember these nominal modifiers cannot be full NPs, but they can have some limited pre-modification, as in *outer space odyssey*, which is clearly an *odyssey* in *outer space*, rather than a *space odyssey* of the *outer* kind. This is one of these difficult issues where you can find yourself a bit torn between what you really see and your theoretical assumptions. The kind of linguist who draws syntactic trees will often assume that there can be no sub-tree that ends with anything below XP, so that an N′ would always have to have an NP above it. (As mentioned before, such people would of course also have objections to the fact that we have only Det, rather than DetP, above the determiner.) For normal NPs or APs, for instance, this makes sense, because there could always be a full phrase. So, in *a great moon hoax*, *great* could have had more modification: *the unbelievably great moon hoax*, for instance. However, with these nominal pre-modifiers, we cannot have a determiner, so that for a grammarian who just looks at the things we can actually see – the surface structure – it would seem wrong to have a whole NP dominating *moon* or *space* here. One way out of this would be to say that we have a form of compounding, so that lexical categories combine to form new lexical categories, so that *space journey* or *moon hoax* are nouns, just as *blackbird* is. An argument in favour of this is that these combinations have stress on the first element rather than on the second one. This is typical of compounds, so that if you say *blackbird* with the stress on the first part, then you are talking about a particular kind of bird, whereas if you put more stress on the second part, then it is interpreted as any old bird that happens to be black. According to this view, we would draw the following tree for *the great moon hoax*.

(11)

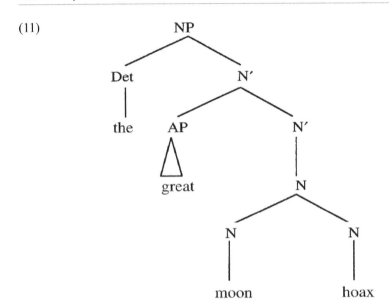

Now, what do we do when the modifying noun actually has some modification of its own, as in *the outer space odyssey*? Well, the pre-modification also seems to be limited to one word, and it has to have quite a close relationship with the noun. For instance, *outer space* works, but if we try to have, say, *cold* in the position of *outer*, to give *cold space odyssey*, then we end up with an interpretation of *cold* as modifying *space odyssey* rather than just *space*. So, if we went on an odyssey in cold space, but had a nice cosy fire going inside our rocket, then we wouldn't talk about a cold space odyssey. We could then say that the adjective–noun combination also has some compound like qualities so that the A+N forms a new N, much as it does in *blackbird*.

(12)

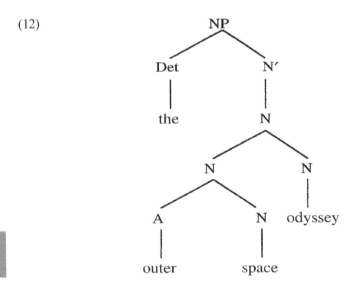

We find this the most appropriate solution given the facts, but many analyses would have both these elements represented as full phrases – but then of course they do have to explain why the AP can only ever consist of one word and why the pre-modifying NP can never take a determiner.

Now for the million-dollar question – what do we do with NPs where the determiner seems to consist of a full NP with the possessive 's? There is much literature on this issue, but there isn't any solution that we feel really is as satisfying as a plate of black pudding. Some linguists think that since only possessive NPs can function as determiners, the 's is really a determiner which heads a determiner phrase. Others would say that the possessive NP is still just an NP which has some feature [+POSS(ESSIVE)] allowing it to occur in this position and fill the same function as a determiner. Then there are some solutions that are radically different from the type of analyses we have used here, but this doesn't seem to be the place to discuss them. We have emphasised throughout this book that the category of an element and its function must be kept apart, and therefore, the fact that the possessive NP does the same job as an element of the category determiner doesn't mean that it is or contains a determiner. So, in Section 7.3, when we listed NPs under determiners this wasn't entirely accurate; NPs can do the job of a determiner, but they aren't themselves determiners. We would, then, prefer an analysis in which these NPs are just that: NPs. What distinguishes them from other NPs is the fact that they have a feature [+POSS] which allows them to occur in this position and have this function. This gives us the following analysis of *the flag's shadow*:

(13)

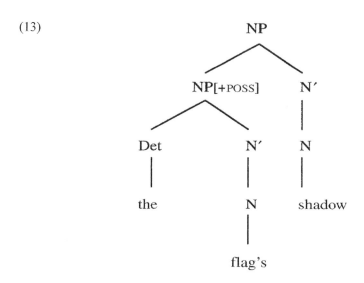

Two things to note about this tree: first, when an NP is marked by the feature [+POSS] we get an 's at the right edge of the NP. In this tree the right edge of the NP happens to be the head of that NP, namely *flag*. This is, however, a coincidence, albeit a frequent one. If we replace *the flag* by *the man on the moon*, where the head *man* is not on the right edge of the NP, then we see that *'s* does not occur on the head: *the man in the moon's shadow*. In fact, the *'s* does not even have to attach to a noun: *the man who left's shadow*. (Also, remember the example we gave on p. 52: *this guy who I used to know at school and who went to Cambridge and got a First in Engineering's brother*.) The second point to make here is that the determiner *the* belongs to the NP[+POSS] and not to the highest NP. This is easy to see in NPs like *these men's first attempt*, where *these* is plural and must therefore belong to the plural *men* and not the singular *attempt*.

7.9 Points to remember

- ❏ Noun phrases consist of minimally a noun and a determiner, though the determiner can be the zero article.
- ❏ Noun phrases may also contain a large number of optional elements which can be either pre- or post-modifiers or pre-determiners. Since pronouns replace whole NPs, we can replace strings by pronouns to find out exactly where NPs begin and end.
- ❏ Determiners have special status within the NP. Apart from being obligatory, they are also unique and cannot be modified. There are five types: articles, demonstratives, quantifying determiners, *wh*-determiners and possessives.
- ❏ The possible pre-modifiers are adjective phrases and nominal elements. The adjectives which head the APs sometimes derive from verbs, but it is quite difficult to make a clear-cut distinction between these verbal participles and pure adjectives. When nominal elements pre-modify the head nouns of an NP, these nominal elements themselves have very limited modification possibilities and we have analysed them as compound-like.
- ❏ The possible post-modifiers are PPs, clauses (VPs and S') and certain types of APs. As with verbs, the post-nominal elements can have two different structural relationships with the head noun: complement or adjunct.

Exercises

1. Identifying noun phrases

Identify all the NPs in the following text (from the same *Big Issue* as the examples in this chapter). Remember they can be much longer than you think. Also remember that NPs can contain NPs.

> Their film stock was unaffected by the intense heat and powerful cosmic radiation on the moon, conditions that should have made it useless.
> The shadows could only have been created with multiple light sources and, in particular, powerful spotlights. But the only light source on the moon was the sun.

Not one still picture matches the film footage, yet NASA claims both were shot at the same time.

2. Which is the head?

For each NP you identified in exercise 1, decide which noun is the head noun and what is the determiner. Then state the category for all pre- and post-modifiers if there are any.

3. Analysing noun phrases

Here is a selection of NPs. For each of them find the head noun and the determiner and decide the category of each pre- and post-modifier. If you feel so inclined (or if your tutor has told you to) you could draw a tree for each noun phrase.

(a) the self-styled apostle of the New Labour philosophy (N#274:11)

(b) an all-singing, all-dancing, devastatingly handsome cash machine (N#269:9)

(c) one of several Latinos springing up from the Spanish-American diaspora that is gaining ground (and financial muscle) on the mainstream music industry in Nashville, Los Angeles and New York (N#269:9)

(d) the little boy at the birthday party who nobody ever wants to talk to (N#274:10)

(e) this nascent Miami-based power house (N#269:9)

(f) an absurdly pointless dexterity with my hands (N269:22)

(g) a new, younger audience, all eager to buy merchandise (N269:26)

(h) the first legal nude beach in Australia (AUS#61:6)

(i) the denial of the validity of material things (N#258:12) (back to John Lennon)

(j) the undisputed king of the on-line ostrich dealers (N#301:15)

4. Find the head noun

We said in Section 7.2 that there is one type of NP for which you cannot find the head noun by asking 'What kind of thing is this?', but where you have to use the formal agreement criterion. A few such NPs are:

(a) what kind of thing

(b) this brand of whisky

(c) that sort of crisps

Use the agreement test to decide what is the head of these NPs and analyse the other components of the NP too.

5. *Space odyssey* versus *spiritual odyssey*

Early in this chapter we said that words like *moon* and *space* that modify hoax (in *moon hoax*) and *odyssey* (in *space odyssey*) are clearly not adjectives. Traditional grammar, however, does label these 'adjectives,' the argument being they describe, or give us further details, about a noun. Revisit Chapter 3, where we described the properties of adjectives and (in Section 3.4) gave some tests for category membership, and outline the pros and cons of both approaches. (As part of your answer you could contrast *moon hoax* and *space odyssey* with something like *great hoax* and *spiritual odyssey*.)

8

Clauses within clauses

8.1 Clauses

Until now, we have said that a sentence is the unit formed around a lexical verb, containing all the bits that the verb requires as well as any optional bits the speaker has chosen to include. Strictly speaking, this is not really true – this is the definition of a CLAUSE, not a sentence. When a clause is not part of any larger clause, that clause forms a sentence and can also be called a MAIN CLAUSE. For this reason it has not mattered that we have used the definition for sentence rather than clause. The clauses we have looked at have almost all formed sentences; that is, they have been main clauses. This is not always the case, however. A sentence often consists of more than one clause. Let's look now at different ways of having more than one clause in a sentence. In each case, the two clauses have been set in italics.

We can listen to records and *I'll probably dream up a few songs.* (N#258:13)

It's very nice to get married but *I don't want to make a habit of it.* (N#258:12)

In both these sentences we have two separate clauses which are completely independent of each other. *Listen* occurs as part of a verb string *can listen* – the string is preceded by a subject *we* and followed by *to records*, and hence *listen* has all the elements it needs in that clause. Following *and* we have another complete clause, *I'll probably dream up a few songs.* Similarly, in the second sentence we have an independently complete clause on each side of *but*. In both these examples we have two clauses which are conjoined with the elements *and* and *but*, respectively.

We turn now to a different way in which a sentence can consist of more than one clause:

I swear that I didn't dream it.

Here, the lexical verb that the sentence is built around is *swear*. This verb takes a subject, *I* in this case, and an object, *that I didn't dream it*. The main clause is then the whole sentence, not just *I swear*. The string which we have referred to as the object here is in itself a clause, built around the verb *dream*, which also takes a subject, *I*, and an object, which in this case is *it*. Since there is negation, an auxiliary verb is required and the lexical verb is part of a verb string: *didn't dream*. There are a number of ways in which clauses in this function do not behave exactly like noun phrase objects, but that need not concern us here. This sentence differs from the two we looked at earlier in that one of the clauses forms part of the other clause – it is not independent the way the previous clauses were.

In the very first two sentences, we have COORDINATION of clauses. *But* and *and* coordinate two constituents of equal categorial status, in this case two clauses, to form a new constituent of the same categorial status. These elements are referred to as COORDINATORS or COORDINATING CONJUNCTIONS. In the sentence *I swear that I didn't dream it*, where one clause is part of the other, we have SUBORDINATION. The higher clause, i.e. the whole sentence, is the main clause and the lower clause is referred to as a subordinate clause or a sub-clause (the two terms mean the same). In this case, there is an element which actually marks explicitly the beginning of the subordinate clause, namely *that*. As we saw in Chapter 3, such elements are referred to as COMPLEMENTISERS or, in more traditional descriptions, SUBORDINATORS or SUBORDINATING CONJUNCTIONS. The coordination of clauses is relatively straightforward at this level and we will focus on subordination in this chapter.

We have shown in Chapter 5 that there are four major types of sentences: declarative, interrogative, imperative and exclamative. In this chapter, we'll look more closely at clauses that don't function as sentences, but which form part of some other clause, i.e. we will concentrate on subordinate clauses (or sub-clauses for short). As always, there are two aspects to consider: form and function. We'll look in turn at the major forms of clauses and for each discuss the functions that this particular type of clause can fill.

When it comes to form, there is one major sub-division of sub-clauses according to the form of the first verb of the verb string, namely, finite versus non-finite sub-clauses. Sentences are always finite, but clauses that form parts of sentences may be finite or non-finite. If you need to remind yourself which verb forms are finite and which are non-finite, have a quick look at the following table before you continue (you could also revisit Section 6.1).

Verb forms – finite versus non-finite

Base form	3rd sing. present	Past tense	Past participle	*-ing* form
want	*wants*	*wanted*	*wanted*	*wanting*
eat	*eats*	*ate*	*eaten*	*eating*
hit	*hits*	*hit*	*hit*	*hitting*
make	*makes*	*made*	*made*	*making*
drink	*drinks*	*drank*	*drunk*	*drinking*

Finite clauses can be divided into sub-classes depending on their form. We'll consider three main types:

❑ declarative clauses
❑ interrogative clauses
❑ relative clauses.

When we consider the non-finite clauses, we'll divide them into sub-categories depending on which particular non-finite form of the verb is involved.

Before we get moving on this, we need to discuss the notion of clauses and what their categorial status is. Each lexical verb builds a clause and hence a sentence contains as many clauses as it contains lexical verbs. We have said that a clause contains at least all the bits that the lexical verb requires. So far, we've looked only at clauses that also function as sentences and the bits required by the verb have been the subject and any complements. Altogether these elements have formed a constituent of the category S, for sentence. We'll soon see that subordinate clauses may have some properties which make them different from main clauses, particularly the non-finite sub-clauses, and this will be a reason to assign sub-clauses to different categories.

The first striking difference we have already seen exemplified, namely that subordinate clauses may be introduced by complementisers such as *that* in *I swear that I didn't dream it.* In this sense, then, subordinate clauses can be like 'sentences with a complementiser on top.' When we looked at interrogatives in Section 5.3, and when we briefly looked at relative clauses in Section 7.6, we said these could be assigned to the category of S′ (S-bar). We'll use the same terminology here, and hence *I swear that I didn't dream it* is an S and *that I didn't dream it* is an S′ constituent. There are also subordinate clauses that can't have a complementiser, and they are S constituents, just like ordinary sentences. This may sound a bit complex at the moment, but it should become clearer soon. For the time being, we can represent it with simple trees:

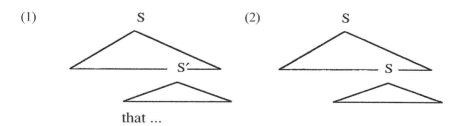

(1) S   (2) S

S′   S

that ...

Another difference is that non-finite verbs may allow the subject not to be there overtly, though we can always understand what the meaning of the subject is. This means that we get non-finite sub-clauses that lack subjects:

We intend *to grow our hair even longer for the cause.* (N#258:12)

We have said that there is a clause built up around every lexical verb. In this sentence we have two lexical verbs, *intend* and *grow*, and hence we have two clauses. The clause built around *intend* is the whole sentence, and the clause built around *grow* is italicised in the example. There is one odd thing about the italicised clause and that is the fact that there is no subject. In English this is only allowed with non-finite verbs (apart from what we referred to a 'diary/postcard English' in Section 1.4). In this sentence, we can still interpret the meaning of the subject; we can say that the sentence means 'We intend that we shall grow our hair long for the cause.' We'll return to discuss such sub-clauses in Section 8.3. At this point we need only decide what the category of such constituents is. We shall follow our habit here of considering only what we see. Hence a clause that lacks an overt subject must be of a smaller category than a clause which has a subject. Remember that an ordinary clause, i.e. one without a complementiser, is of the category S, and has two daughters, the subject NP and the predicate VP. So, if you have an S clause and take away the subject NP, you are left with a VP. It seems quite reasonable, then, to call a clause that lacks a subject a VP.

This means that sub-clauses come in three different sizes: a full clause with a complementiser; a full clause without a complementiser; and a clause with no complementiser and no subject. The biggest of these is an S', the one lacking a complementiser is an S and the one lacking a subject is a VP. They are all clauses since they are built up around a main verb. Approaches to grammar which are keener on empty categories than we are will often use S', or an equivalent category, for all these clause types and assume a zero complementiser and empty subjects. There are, however, also theoretical approaches to grammar which follow the distinction we have made here.

8.2 Finite sub-clauses

We can subdivide finite clauses into declarative and interrogative clauses. Remember that the distinction between declarative sentences and interrogative sentences lies in the position of the operator (the finite auxiliary) – interrogative sentences have undergone subject–operator inversion, but declarative ones haven't. This criterion cannot be used for subordinate clauses, however, because there is no subject–operator inversion in subordinate clauses. Instead we recognise interrogative clauses either by the fact that they contain the complementisers *if* or *whether* or by the fact that they begin with a *wh*-phrase. These are parallel to *yes–no* interrogatives and *wh*-interrogatives, respectively, but being sub-clauses, they lack the subject–operator inversion of their main clause colleagues. Declarative sub-clauses, on the other hand, can be divided into two kinds: *that*-clauses, which occur as subjects or complements, and adverbial sub-clauses. As we shall see, the latter may occur with a wide variety of complementisers.

Declarative sub-clauses

Finite declarative sub-clauses look exactly like declarative sentences in terms of structure, with the one exception that they can always have a complementiser. If we look at *that*-clauses first, we see in the following examples that the sub-clause, which has been italicised, looks like an ordinary sentence with *that* added to it:

He's proud *that I'm not on stage as a dying leech anymore.* (AUS#558:22)

We know *that skinny jeans have long since eclipsed bum-cleavage jeans.* (AUS#305:13)

I'm not on stage as a dying leech anymore and *skinny jeans have long since eclipsed bum-cleavage jeans* could both occur as independent sentences. As far as form goes, *that*-clauses are clearly of the category S'. In terms of function, *that*-clauses can have many of the functions that we have already seen noun phrases fill: subject, direct object, subject complement. We have just seen examples of *that*-clauses functioning as the object of *imagine* and *know*. On the basis of the same two sentences we can create sentences in which the clause is a subject or a subject complement:

That I'm not on stage as a dying leech anymore is a good thing.

The issue is *that skinny jeans have long since eclipsed bum-cleavage jeans.*

Apart from these functions, as the first example shows (and as we saw in Section 7.6), *that*-clauses can also occur within other phrases, as complements of nouns (like *observation*) and adjectives (like *proud* and *aware*):

the observation *that it was easy to stay so long in bed* (N#258:13)

We are aware *that most members of the local parrot community like our balcony.* (AUS#339:12)

Since clauses are quite complex and 'heavy' constituents, and English prefers not to have heavy constituents in subject position, clausal subjects often get moved to the end of the clause – they get EXTRAPOSED. So, in the next example, instead of *That people can print complete lies totally amazes me* with the clausal subject, we find:

It totally amazes me *that people can print complete lies.* (AUS#65:21)

Here the clause is found at the end of the sentence and in the subject position we find the expletive *it* which we talked about in Section 4.3. As we said there, this is an element that English inserts in subject position when there is no other subject, or as here, when the subject has left the typical subject position. We can refer to *it* here as the FORMAL SUBJECT and the clause as the EXTRAPOSED SUBJECT. In Chapter 9 we return to extraposition when we go beyond sentences to look at the structure of texts.

Now consider the sub-clauses in the following sentences:

I wish *I had gone that day.* (N#258:12)

I swear *I didn't dream it.* (N#258:12)

These lack a *that* at the beginning, but otherwise they are identical to *that*-clauses in terms of both form and function. It turns out that they are in fact *that*-clauses, but *that*-clauses in which *that* has been deleted. It can be inserted in these sentences:

211

I wish *that I had gone that day*.

I swear *that I didn't dream it*.

In fact, returning to the sentences at the beginning of this section, we find that we can delete *that* in these:

He's proud *I'm not on stage as a dying leech anymore*.

We know *skinny jeans have long since eclipsed bum-cleavage jeans*.

We are aware *most members of the local parrot community like our balcony*.

In all these clauses, *that* is optional, but this doesn't hold for some of the other clauses we have looked at:

*the observation *it was easy to stay so long in bed*

People can print complete lies totally amazes me.

?It totally amazes me *people can print complete lies*.

It turns out that *that* is optional in *that*-clauses except when the clause functions as the subject or when it is the complement of a noun. In fact, sentences where *that* is absent is the norm for informal language (and they are by far more common in our *Big Issue* magazines). When the *that*-clause functions as an extraposed subject, as in the last example, then some speakers accept it and some don't. Given that we assigned *that*-clauses to the category of S' because they contained a complementiser, we now need to think about what category to assign to *that*-clauses in which *that* has been deleted. The question is whether we want to say that *that*-clauses without *that* belong to a different category, namely S. Our view is that we should call all *that*-clauses S', regardless of whether or not the complementiser is there. The reason is that the complementiser can always be inserted, and apart from the lack of complementiser, the two have the nearly same properties in terms of form and distribution, the exception being that *that* is obligatory in the environments we mentioned earlier.

Before we leave *that*-clauses behind, there is one final comment we want to make. Consider the following two sentences:

I was afraid *that such a condition might be contagious*. (AUS#339:12)

It's odd *that there's no sick dog*. (AUS#69:29)

Initially, these two would appear to have very similar structure. However, in the first of the two, the sub-clause functions as a modifier of the adjective *afraid* and in the second it is an extraposed subject. We can represent the structure with brackets as follows:

I was [afraid *that such a condition might be contagious*].

It's odd [*that there's no sick dog*].

If we look at the sentences more carefully, the difference is in fact easy to spot. Where the clause is an extraposed subject, we have the expletive *it* in the subject position; otherwise there is a personal pronoun or a full noun phrase in that position. And, finally, even though it may sound a bit awkward, the extraposed subject can of course go back to the subject position, whereas the clause that modifies an adjective cannot occur in the subject position:

That such a condition might be contagious was afraid.

That there is no sick dog is odd.

There are also sub-clauses that fill the function of adverbials. Such clauses occur with a large number of different complementisers. Traditional grammars often attempt to provide a complete list of such complementisers, but there are a few too many of them for us to do that here. Some examples of adverbial clauses are:

Before he recently joined Lennon in the great jam session in the sky, my old editor confessed to me. (N#258:12)

As I come from Montrose, I laughed nervously for some reason. (N#258:12)

Although one of the figures wore a beard and National Health specs and the other was female and Japanese, they looked remarkably similar. (N#258:12)

I train *because I have the time management skills of a golden retriever.* (AUS#503:29)

You may remember that two things which characterise the adverbial function are that it is optional and that the element filling it answers questions like *why*, *when*, *how often* or *where* and not *what* or *who*. The italicised clauses here are, then, typical adverbials in both ways: the rest of the sentence could function as a sentence without the adverbial and they do indeed answer the right type of questions. Which complementiser is used depends on the exact function of the adverbial clause; for example, whether it is an adverbial of time, of manner or of place. Note that we can replace each of these clauses with typical adverbials, compare the following sentences with those used earlier:

Previously my old editor confessed to me.

Therefore I laughed nervously for some reason.

Nonetheless they looked remarkably similar.

Consequently I train.

Interrogative sub-clauses

We said in Section 5.3 that there are two kinds of interrogative clauses: those that give rise to *yes–no* questions and those that make *wh*-questions. Similarly, there are two kinds of interrogative subordinate clauses and both types can occur as finite and non-finite clauses. We'll deal with the finite ones here and return to the non-finite ones in Section 8.3. As already pointed out, the most striking property of main clause interrogative structures, subject–operator inversion, does not occur in subordinate clauses (except in a rather unusual form such as *I wonder what shall I do*, where the subject *I* follows the operator *shall*). Instead, the subordinate clause parallel to a *yes–no* question is marked by one of two complementisers: *if* or *whether*. The two complementisers do not have exactly the same distribution, but they are pretty similar. Look at the following sentences with *if* interrogative subordinate clauses and think about whether you could use *whether* instead.

We wondered *if we were in for some bizarre sexual experience*. (N#258:12)

Who knew *if this was going to pan out*. (N#279:9)

Someone asked *if Jeff and Akbar were brothers or a gay couple*. (N#279:9)

(The last was a question that the creator of *The Simpsons*, Matt Groening, got about his first cartoon strip and the answer was 'Whatever offends you most.') Probably you will find that *whether* works just as well in all the clauses.

Finite subordinate *yes–no* interrogative clauses can occur in the same positions as *that*-clauses. Some examples with *if*- or *whether*-clauses as the complement of an adjective or a noun can be constructed:

I was not certain *if this was going to pan out*.

Someone asked the question *whether Jeff and Akbar were brothers or a gay couple*.

Of course, this type of clause can also be the direct object of a verb, but not with the same set of verbs as the non-interrogative clauses. So whereas *wonder* can be followed by an interrogative subordinate clause, it cannot be followed by a *that*-clause. However, there are verbs, like *know*, which can take either type of subordinate clause, though for an interrogative subordinate clause to work, *know* needs to be negated: *I know that City will win* as well as *I don't know whether United will come second*.

In some of the positions, you can only have a *whether*-clause and not an *if*-clause. For instance, in a subject clause that is not extraposed only *whether* will do (and here we have just changed the sentences we have already used):

*If Jeff and Akbar were brothers or a gay couple was not clear.

Whether Jeff and Akbar were brothers or a gay couple was not clear.

If the subject is extraposed, on the other hand, either *whether* or *if* can do the job:

It was not clear *if/whether Jeff and Akbar were brothers or a gay couple*.

As we shall see in Section 8.3, *whether* can also occur in *to*-infinitive clauses, whereas *if* cannot.

The other type of finite interrogative clause, the *wh*-clause, has the same form as a main clause *wh*-interrogative with the usual subordinate difference that there is no subject–operator inversion. Just like the corresponding main clauses, subordinate *wh*-clauses have a 'gap' somewhere corresponding to the *wh*-constituent. For example, the sub-clause in the sentence

I wonder *why he was gawping at me like that.*

has a corresponding main clause version which is identical except that subject–operator inversion forces the presence of dummy *do*:

Why was he gawping at me like that? (AUS#306:12)

Wh-sub-clauses can occur in the same positions as the other clauses; so when they are subjects they are normally extraposed to the end of the sentence:

It remains unclear *how and why Van Houten drastically transformed from an exceptionally smart, driven young woman, class secretary and homecoming princess, to a member of one of the most notorious cults in history.* (AUS#517:9)

[compare *How and why Van Houten drastically transformed from an exceptionally smart, driven young woman, class secretary and homecoming princess, to a member of one of the most notorious cults in history* remains unclear.]

We have already seen an example of a *wh*-sub-clause as an object of the verb *wonder*, and we can construct sentences parallel to those for *yes–no* interrogative sub-clauses in which the *wh*-sub-clause is the complement of an adjective or a noun:

I was not certain *why he was gawping at me like that.*

I asked the question *why he was gawping at me like that.*

Furthermore, *wh*-subordinate clauses can function as adverbials, as the following example shows:

When I got back home, I tried a little experiment. (AUS#306:12)

Relative clauses

Clauses sharing some properties with *wh*-clauses are RELATIVE CLAUSES. Like *wh*-clauses, they have a constituent missing inside the clause and that is represented by a *wh*-constituent. One difference is that whereas *wh*-clauses often appear in functions in which NPs could also appear, e.g. subject or direct object, relative clauses actually occur within NPs. Consider the following example where the relative clause is set in italics:

a picture *which appeared within the sleeve of a Lennon LP* (N#258:12)

Here we have an NP which is headed by *picture*. However, to help the hearer get some idea of which picture he is referring to, the speaker adds the information that is roughly *the picture appeared within the sleeve of a Lennon LP*. We could then say that the idea behind this NP is something like:

'a picture *the picture appeared within the sleeve of a Lennon LP*'

To make this into an NP, we need to turn the italic part into a real relative clause. This is done by removing the NP that is shared between the NP itself and the relative clause, namely *the picture*, and replacing it with a suitable *wh*-word. Since *the picture* is the subject of the italic clause, it is already in initial position, but otherwise we would have had to move it to the front. We then get *a picture which appeared within the sleeve of a Lennon LP*, in which *which* is the RELATIVE PRONOUN, and *picture* is referred to as the ANTECEDENT.

The job of a relative clause of this kind is to restrict the number of possible referents for the NP and thereby help the hearer pick the correct one. *A picture* could refer to a tremendously large number of things – many more than *a picture which appeared within the sleeve of a Lennon LP*. Because this type of relative clause helps the speaker by restricting the number of potential referents, it is called a RESTRICTIVE RELATIVE CLAUSE.

Now look at the following NP adapted from the article on *Futurama*:

Fry, *who gets frozen in a cryogenic chamber*,

This NP consists of a proper noun, *Fry*, followed by a relative clause. In this case, there are commas around the relative clause, whereas there weren't in the last one. When spoken, there would usually be a slight pause where the commas are. There is also a bigger, more important difference. A proper noun like *Fry* has a very restricted reference already – it just refers to this one person called Fry. Hence, the relative clause is not here to restrict the reference of the noun phrase, but to add incidental information. So the meaning of this clause is something like *oh, and by the way, he gets frozen in a cryogenic chamber*. Clauses such as these are called NON-RESTRICTIVE RELATIVE CLAUSES because the clause is not there to restrict the reference of the noun itself. According to traditional English punctuation rules, non-restrictive relative clauses should have commas around them, but if you read a newspaper, you'll often find things like *Hillary Clinton who started her campaign in New York*. If we say this without any pause after *Clinton*, it does sound a bit as though we thought there were more than one Hillary Clinton and we needed to help the hearer decide which one we were referring to. The example one of us was given when learning English as a foreign language was:

my wife *who lives in New York* versus my wife, *who lives in New York*,

In one of these NPs, it sounds as if the speaker had more than one wife. Do you get this difference too if you read the two aloud with a brief pause representing the commas?

So far, we have encountered two *wh*-elements that can introduce a relative clause, namely *who* and *which*. Both of these can occur in restrictive and non-restrictive relative clauses. There is a third relative pronoun which some people use when the shared noun which the relative pronoun replaces is an object, namely *whom*. Take a look at the following sentence, which was how Bill Borrows' (editor of *Loaded*, apparently) mother described Mick Hucknall of *Simply Red*:

the little boy at the birthday party *who nobody ever wants to talk to* (N#274:10)

Here we have a restrictive relative clause modifying a nominal that already contains a PP post-modifier, *little boy at the birthday party*. However, what we are interested in at the moment is the relative clause itself and in particular, where in the clause *who* originates. If we try to put it back inside the clause, we find that it is the object of the preposition *to*: *nobody ever wants to talk to who*. Normally, the pronominal object of a preposition occurs in a special object form if there is one for that pronoun. There is indeed such a form of the relative pronoun, *whom*, and many prescriptive grammarians would say that this relative clause is incorrect and that it should be:

the little boy at the birthday party *whom nobody ever wants to talk to*

However, certainly in speech and increasingly in writing (as this example shows), people do not use the object form in this case. Of course, as real linguists, we don't interpret this as 'people don't speak English properly anymore.' The way we express this is that many English speakers are losing the distinction between subject form and object form in this environment.

Whom can be useful

The history of English has seen the ongoing erosion of little grammatical endings (or inflections) – in Chapter 3 we discussed the few that are still around. One of the endings hanging in there is this little *-m* on *whom* (versus *who*). But how many of you were happy with 'the little boy at the birthday party *whom nobody ever wants to talk to*'? And what about something like: *Whom did you see?* For some of you these sentences might sound rather pompous – in fact such are the changes to English structure that they might now even sound wrong. Certainly, the prediction for some time has been that *whom* is not long for this world. However there are signs of a possible new role being fashioned for *whom* and this could well be breathing new life into this little pronoun.

If you're pursuing a romantic interest online *whom* might come in handy. In a piece on Language Log entitled *Whom loves ya*, Geoff Pullum reports on a large-scale study that had looked at the language of online dating ads [http://languagelog.ldc.upenn.edu/nll/?p=10398]. One set of results showed that men who use *whom* get 31% more contacts from opposite-sex respondents (regardless of whether or not the use was Standard English). Pullum recommends to his male readers interested in dating females – 'write an ad saying you are looking for "someone whom will love you".'

From the point of view of prescriptive grammarians, there is another problem with a relative clause like the one we have just been looking at – it has the preposition *to* left at the end of the clause. We mentioned this when discussing *wh*-interrogatives in Chapter 5. What we said there holds here too. People like us who are interested in studying the English that is really used just take note of the fact that prepositions are often stranded at the end of clauses. The solution for the prescriptivist is the same here: you can always front the preposition with the relative pronoun:

the little boy at the birthday party *to whom nobody ever wants to talk*

This phenomenon is sometimes referred to as PIED PIPING because the preposition follows the noun just like the rats followed the Pied Piper of Hamelin. When the preposition accompanies the relative pronoun to the front, we suspect that most speakers would use the object form, or could you say:

?*the little boy at the birthday party *to who nobody ever wants to talk*

We should add here in fairness that there are sentences where the preposition has to move to the front or where it sounds a lot better if it does, at least in certain styles. Earlier on we used the following relative clause: '. . . *in which* which *is the* RELATIVE PRONOUN.' Wouldn't you agree that here the sentence sounds strange with the preposition left at the end? (We replace the second instance of *which* with *this* to make it a slightly more natural-sounding sentence.)

a clause *in which this is the* RELATIVE PRONOUN versus a clause *?which this is the* RELATIVE PRONOUN *in*

In the same article on the Simply Red star, we can read that *Hucknall's mother left him when he was just three* (N#274:10). Now if we want to make that into a relative clause, modifying Mick Hucknall, what do we have to do? Well, it would have to be a non-restrictive relative clause, since *Mick Hucknall* is a proper noun with very specific reference already. Since *Hucknall* is the shared noun, this has to be replaced in the relative clause, but in the relative clause there is a possessive *'s* on *Hucknall* and so the relative pronoun needs to have some indication of this too. We need to use *whose*, which we classified in Chapter 7 as a *wh*-determiner:

Hucknall, *whose mother left him when he was three,*

In this relative clause, *whose mother* is the subject and so it is already at the front of the clause. The question now is whether *whose* can be fronted on its own, without the noun *mother*, just as *who* could be fronted without the preposition. In order to find out, we need to construct a clause in which *whose mother* is not the subject. Such an example would be *I never knew Hucknall's mother*, from which we could get the relative clause:

Hucknall, *whose mother I never knew,*

Here we find that that the whole noun phrase *whose mother* has to be fronted; **Hucknall, whose I never knew mother,* is ungrammatical.

Some speakers are unhappy using *whose* if it refers to something inanimate and find sentences like the following awkward.

It is a day *whose arrival few could have predicted.* (AUS#69:6)

The alternative for Standard English speakers is the really rather formal *the arrival of which*. Alternatively, you can replace it by a different construction type. Speakers of non-standard varieties have a number of options like *thats arrival* or *that its arrival* (or maybe that should be *that's*; since it is not generally written, it is hard to tell).

We can, then, sum up the use of relative pronouns in relative clauses as follows: with people (and pets), we get *who*, and in some cases *whom*; with non-human antecedents, we get *which*. If the relative pronoun functions as a possessive determiner of a noun, the correct form is *whose* (though with the reservation we discussed before for inanimates). When *whose* is used, the whole NP of which it is a part must be fronted. When the relative pronoun is the object of a preposition, either the relative pronoun can be fronted on its own or the whole PP can be fronted. If you are reading the chapters of this book in order, then this should sound very familiar from the section on *wh*-questions, since their *wh*-constituents are formed in much the same way.

For non-restrictive relative clauses this is all we need to say, but there is one more aspect of restrictive relative clauses that we need to comment on. If we return to the first example of this section – *a picture which appeared within the sleeve of a Lennon LP* – we said that it was adapted from the original text. In fact, in the original it looks like this:

a picture *that appeared within the sleeve of a Lennon LP* (N#258:12)

Instead of *which* we have *that*; it doesn't seem to matter much which one we use. We should add here, however, that many prescriptivists (including the grammar check on our computer!) feel that *that* is the appropriate one to use in writing. In fact, in all restrictive relative clauses in which the relative pronoun occurs on its own at the front we can replace it by *that* – the choice of *that* instead of a relative pronoun seems to be largely a matter of individual style and the relative informality of the situation:

any celebrity *who is big enough* versus any celebrity *that is big enough*

the little boy at the birthday party *who nobody ever wants to talk to* versus the little boy at the birthday party *that nobody ever wants to talk to*

However, *that* cannot replace the relative pronoun in non-restrictive relative clauses:

Fry, *who gets frozen in a cryogenic chamber*, versus *Fry, *that gets frozen in a cryogenic chamber*,

Or indeed when the relative pronoun has not been fronted on its own:

the little boy at the birthday party to *whom nobody ever wants to talk* versus *the little boy at the birthday party *to that nobody ever wants to talk*

Hucknall, *whose mother* I never knew, versus *Hucknall, *thats mother* I never knew,

As we have already said, the version with *thats* is used in some (non-standard) varieties, though generally as long as the antecedent is not human.

Not only can the relative pronoun be replaced by *that*, in almost all the relative clauses in which it can be replaced by *that*, it can also be deleted. (In the following we have left the PP of the original relative clause out, since when the PP is there it sounds much better with *who* or *that* present.):

The little boy __ *nobody wants to talk to.*

We say that this is almost always possible, since it is not possible when the *wh*-word fills the subject position in the relative clause. It is quite easy to see why this should not be possible. Let's look at one of our previous examples:

any celebrity *who/that is big enough*

What would happen if we deleted *who* and *that* here? Well, there would be nothing left to distinguish it from a clause:

any celebrity __ *is big enough*

and therefore it would make a sentence sound very strange:

Any celebrity *who/that is big enough* is welcome.

*Any celebrity __ *is big enough* is welcome.

So we can assume that there is some constraint of information preservation at work to stop this. We should point out, however, that some non-standard varieties can leave a subject *wh*-constituent out in some environments, as in the following:

There's a man on the phone ___ *wants to talk to you.*

That-clauses versus relative clauses with *that*

If you have been paying attention, you may have noticed that we have talked about *that*-clauses and relative clauses with *that*, and you may have wondered whether they are the same thing or not. They are not. And as we shall see, there are actually quite straightforward ways of telling them apart. The fact that both types of clauses begin with the same element is no accident – they have developed from the same source, a type of development that is quite common cross-linguistically.

There are two clear differences between *that*-clauses and relative clauses with *that*. First, in relative clauses, *that* can always be replaced by *who* or *which* – this is not possible in *that*-clauses. Second, in relative clauses there is always some element missing in the clause – this is the constituent represented by the relative pronoun. The following example illustrates the differences. We have chosen one that involves a *that*-clause within an NP since this is where relative clauses occur and therefore the potential for confusion is biggest.

that-clause   And what about the rumours *that you slept with your male co-star*? (AUS#33:39)

relative clause: And what about the rumours *that you spread with your male co-star*?

In the *that*-clause, *which* is ungrammatical and there are no gaps; it is complete in itself:

that-clause   *And what about the rumours *which you slept with your male co-star*?

                    You slept with your male co-star

In the relative clause we can have *which* instead of *that* and we see that the object that we would expect to find immediately to the right of *spread* isn't there; there is a gap:

relative clause: And what about the rumours *which you spread with your male co-star*?

                    you spread _____ with your male co-star

So, even though the standard labels for these two types of clauses are a little confusing, the difference between them is clear.

A further difference to note here is that whereas the relative clause functions as a modifier of the noun, the *that*-clause functions as the complement of the noun (or of a verb or an adjective, of course). Where we have the *that*-clause, the rumour is that he slept with his male co-star; the *that*-clause defines the noun. In the case of the relative clause, it just narrows down the potential reference of the noun. We still don't know exactly what the rumours were, just that he and his male co-star were responsible for spreading them. Some additional differences are due to this distinction. As we have said before (in Section 3.6), complements need to be close to their heads, whereas modifiers can be separated from their heads. Furthermore, complements are unique, whereas modifiers can occur recursively. Have a look at the following:

the rumour *that you slept with your male co-star that you categorically deny*

complement   modifier
that-clause   relative clause

?*the rumour *that you categorically deny that you slept with your male co-star*

modifier   complement
relative clause   *that*-clause

*the rumour *that you slept with your male co-star that you slept with your leading lady*

complement   complement
that-clause   *that*-clause

221

the rumour *that I read about in 'The Big Issue' that you categorically deny*

modifier   modifier
relative clause   relative clause

8.3 Non-finite clauses

In the section on finite clauses, we subdivided them according to structural criteria, between declarative, *yes–no* interrogative and *wh*-interrogative. All these clause types exist also in non-finite forms; so we could in principle have the same titles for the following three subsections as for the ones in Section 8.2. However, we have chosen to subdivide this section according to the different verb forms around which non-finite clauses can be built. There are so many differences between each of these types, for instance with respect to the kind of verb string that can occur and what type of clauses they can form, that we feel it is clearer if we deal with each non-finite verb form separately. If you need to remind yourself of the different verb forms available in English, revisit the table at the start of this chapter, or for more a detailed account Section 6.1.

Just as there are finite subordinate clauses with or without a complementiser, so there are non-finite clauses with complementisers and non-finite clauses without complementisers. A difference between finite and non-finite clauses is that in the latter, a complementiser is never optional – either it has to be there or it can't be there. Another major difference is that non-finite clauses need not have a subject and hence they may look like simple VPs of the type we discussed in Chapter 6. We will return to these differences several times in what follows.

Bare infinitive

Non-finite subordinate clauses can be built up around the bare infinitive form of the verb (this is the basic form of the verb that you would find, say, in a dictionary entry). Since the bare infinitive form is identical to the finite third person plural present tense form, there is a potential for confusion between finite and non-finite clauses here. Let's illustrate the difference:

We can make *the characters **act** the way real kids act.* (AUS#51:2)

We can think *the characters **act** the way real kids act.*

In both sentences we have a subordinate clause built around the verb *act*, but we can't actually tell whether this is the finite or the non-finite form. At least, we can't in these sentences, but if we change them slightly, the differences will show up. What do we know about finite forms in English? Well, there are two important things: finite forms can be either present or past tense and finite forms in the present tense have a special *s* form for third person singular subjects. So, let's try to make these changes in both sentences and see how it works. In the first of each pair we have changed the subject to a third person singular one and in the second of each pair we have introduced past tense on both verbs:

We can make *the characters act the way real kids act.*

> *We can make the character **acts** the way real kids act.
> *We made the characters **acted** the way real kids act.

We can think the *characters act the way real kids act.*

> We can think the character **acts** the way real kids act.
> We thought the characters **acted** the way real kids act.

We can conclude that the complement of *make* is a non-finite sub-clause built around a bare infinitive and that the complement of *think* is a finite clause. In fact, it is just our old friend the *that*-clause with *that* deleted. It could have been *We can think that the characters act the way real kids act.*

Bare infinitive clauses cannot have complementisers and the verb string can only consist of one verb; we don't get clauses with the bare infinitive of auxiliaries. They can have subjects, though sometimes these sound a bit forced. Here's one we've invented:

Rather than *him leave his wife*, I think they should sell the dog.

One odd thing about the subjects of non-finite clauses is that they do not occur in their subject form; we get *him* and not *he*. In fact, it seems an NP in English is only nominative when there is a good reason to be, i.e. when it is the subject of a finite verb. When it isn't, it occurs in its object form. For instance, the answer to *Who wants a beer?* is **me**, not *I*, and the emphatic construction is **Me, I'm thirsty**, not **I, I'm thirsty* (which is actually what it would be in a close relative to English like Swedish or Dutch).

There are also many examples of bare infinitive complements where it is quite difficult to decide whether they have a subject or not. Take the next slightly adapted example:

Someone saw <u>Barry</u> *boot Kennett out of the taxi.* (AUS#33:16)

Here we clearly have a clause built around the bare infinitive form of the verb *boot* and that clause functions as the complement of *saw*. However, it is not obvious how big this clause is: just the italic material, or does it also include the underlined material? Non-finite clauses can occur with or without subject, as we have seen. Now, if *Barry* is not the subject of *boot*, what is it then? Well, the thing is here that it could be the object of *saw*. How could we possibly tell? There are some things pointing in favour of it being an object. For instance, in this sentence, it is true that *Someone saw Barry*, as we would expect if the NP was an object. Since the subject of a non-finite form always occurs in the object form, the fact that Barry would be replaced by the object pronoun *him* here does not help us. As far as the meaning goes, *Barry* seems to function as the object of *see*, and we conclude that the sub-clause in *Someone saw Barry boot Kennett out of the taxi* is only *boot Kennett out of the taxi*. We can contrast this with the earlier sentence

We can make the characters act the way real kids act. Here it does not follow that *We can make the characters* and hence we will not assume that *the characters* is the object of *make*. In Section 8.4, we will return to the question of the meaning of subjectless clauses.

As far as the functions of bare infinitival clauses go, we have seen that they can function as objects of verbs like *make* or as adverbial clauses in *rather than him leave his wife*. Apart from this, the distribution of bare infinitival clauses is restricted and you don't in fact come across them very often except in a particular kind of clause called PSEUDO-CLEFT clauses. We discuss these in Chapter 9, but here's one example until then. From *The Big Issue* (AUS#33:36) sentence *British milkman Wilf Sneddon burnt down the houses of customers who failed to order enough Gold Top*, we can create the following pseudo-cleft (it is a way of emphasising what appears in the infinitival clause):

What British milkman Wilf Sneddon did was *burn down the houses of customers who failed to order enough Gold Top*.

To-infinitive

We turn now to subordinate clauses built around the *to*-infinitive form of the verb. There is a bit more going on here than with the bare infinitives, with respect to both the structure of the clauses themselves and the functions they can fulfil within the clause. Just look at the following italicised sub-clauses, where the *to*-infinitival clause functions as the object of a verb (*intend* and *chose*, respectively):

We intend *to grow our hair even longer for the cause.* (N#258:12)

My friendship group chose *to do an educational skit on how to kill leeches.* (AUS#558:22)

The next example shows an example where both the subject and the subject complement are *to*-infinitivals.

To subscribe to The New Yorker is *to enter a fabulous hell.* (AUS#564: 13)

As with earlier examples, you will probably find the extraposed versions of the next two sentences more natural-sounding than the bracketed versions where the *to*-infinitivals appear in the normal subject position.

It's certainly permissible *to let your Facebook page grow weeds.* (AUS#305:13)

(compare *To let your Facebook page grow weeds* is certainly permissible.)

It's evidently quite uncool *to sport a fulsome, springy bed of chest hair.* (AUS#92:38)

(compare *To sport a fulsome, springy bed of chest hair* is evidently quite uncool.)

Just as with *that*-clauses, there are clauses which look similar to those with extraposed subjects, but in which the clause at the end actually modifies the adjective. Consider the following two sentences:

I was too tired to create another catch phrase.

It was fun to create catch phrases. (N#279:9)

These do look to have very similar structures, but in the first of the two, the sub-clause functions as a modifier of the adjective *tired*. The second example has an expletive *it* in the subject position and the subject sub-clause has moved to the end (compare *To create catch phrases* was fun). The same ways of distinguishing between the two functions can be used for these as for the finite ones; in the second example, where the clause is extraposed the sentence with the clause back in subject position is grammatical, but where the clause is a complement of the adjective, it is not possible:

*To create another catch phrase was too tired.

To create catch phrases was fun.

To-infinitival clauses can function as adverbial clauses. In the following examples it is an adverbial of purpose – it could have started with *in order to*.

I'll have to get a little man in *to change them over.* (N#258:13)

I do need a glass of alcohol in one hand and a smoke in the other *to prevent myself from biting a stranger's fingernails.* (AUS#73:38)

Finally, in the following examples, the clause functions as a modifier internal to an NP (modifying *lot* and *guts*, respectively).

Rupert Murdoch has a lot *to thank Bart Simpson for.* (N#279:8)

'Neighbours' is with us forever because no-one will ever have the guts *to take it off the air.* (AUS#75:39)

Not only are these clauses varied in the functions they can fill, they also vary in structure. For one thing, even though in all the clauses we have seen here the *to*-infinitive consists of one lexical verb only, it is possible to have an auxiliary verb in a *to*-infinitive clause, though we cannot of course have modals, since they are always finite:

It's all right *to be mildly appalled by the outsized blankness of Big Brother.* (AUS#305:13)

We intend *to have grown our hair longer by the end of the year.*

a lot *to be thanking Bart Simpson for*

Here we have the auxiliary of the passive *be*, perfect *have* and the auxiliary of the progressive *be*, in their *to*-infinitival forms.

Most of the clauses we have seen here lack overt subjects. However, we can easily adapt a number of these *to*-infinitivals to have subjects:

It's certainly permissible *for you to let your Facebook page grow weeds.*

We intend *for all our friends to grow their hair even longer for the cause.*

For Matt to create catch phrases was fun.

The catch phrases were fun *for Matt to create.*

So, in the clauses that didn't have a subject, we could quite easily insert one. Hence *to*-infinitivals can occur with or without subjects. One striking thing about all these clauses is that when we inserted the subject, we also had to insert the element *for*. This element fills the function of complementiser here. It can only do so in *to*-infinitival clauses, and in Standard English, it can only occur when that clause has a subject:

*We intend *for to grow our hair even longer for the cause.*

**For to create catch phrases* was fun.

In older forms of English, however, *for to* without an intervening subject was the norm. There are also dialects of English which allow *for* even when there is no subject. People of our age remember Bob Dylan's 'Mr Tambourine Man' being 'ready for to fade.'

Just as with bare infinitival clauses, we get some cases where it may at first seem to be difficult to decide whether or not an NP which precedes a *to*-infinitival is the subject of that non-finite clause or the object of the matrix verb. Consider the following sentences:

I told <u>the pretty blonde</u> *to find herself her own husband instead of other people's.* (AUS#65:17)

He warns <u>laser-toting mischief-makers</u> *to take heed.* (AUS#66:5)

Again, the argument is in favour of assuming that *the pretty blonde* and *laser-toting mischief-makers* are the objects of *told* and *warns*, respectively, and that the non-finite clauses lack subjects. The evidence is the fact that it is actually true that I told the pretty blonde and that he warns laser-toting mischief-makers. Compare this to the following example:

changes in legislation, requiring <u>people</u> *to provide two forms* of ID, (N#279:4)

Here it is not true that the changes in legislation *required people*, they *required [people to do something]*. You could argue that it is true that *the pretty blonde* and *laser-toting mischief-makers* are also in a sense the subject of the clauses *to find herself her own husband instead of other people's* and *to take heed*, but as we shall see in Section 8.4, non-finite clauses without overt subjects always have understood subjects. There are very similar sentences in which the understood subject is not the NP:

He promises <u>laser-toting mischief-makers</u> *to take heed.*

Here we would argue again that *laser-toting mischief-makers* is the object of the higher verb, since it is true that *He promises laser-toting mischief-makers* something. Of course there is an understood subject of the non-finite clause, but this time it is not *laser-toting mischief-makers* – the referent of *he* promised *laser-toting mischief-makers* that he would take heed.

Before we move on to other non-finite forms, we just need to note that we can get interrogatives with *to*-infinitivals. Here are two from Dylan lyrics. Note that only *whether*, not *if*, can occur in *to*-infinitivals (compare with finite clauses on p. 214).

I didn't know *whether to duck or run.*/*I didn't know *if to duck or run.*

It's a wonder you still know *how to breathe.*

-ing participle

The next kind of non-finite verb form involves *-ing* participles, and there are non-finite clauses constructed around them. Let's look at a few examples:

Asking for identification from the vulnerable is totally wrong. (N#279:4)

Lusting after hairy-chested men might be unfashionable. (AUS#92:38)

Here we have two clauses built around the *-ing* forms of *ask* and *lust* which fill the subject position of the predicate *is totally wrong* and *might be unfashionable*. As you may expect by now, the subject clause can be extraposed, with the expletive it replacing it in subject position:

It is totally wrong *asking for identification from the vulnerable*.

It might be unfashionable *lusting after hairy-chested men*.

In the following sentence the *-ing* clause is the object of the verb *imagine*:

I imagine *popping in my coin*. (AUS#73:17)

The *-ing* clause can also be the complement of a noun:

homeless people *looking for hostel accommodation* (N#279:4)

The sentence in which this noun phrase occurs makes clear that the *-ing* clause functions as the modifier of the noun. It is not a case of an *-ing* clause with a subject: *New laws which would have forced homeless people looking for hostel accommodation to stay on the street have been overturned.*

   This type of example resemble restrictive relative clauses in the way they add meaning to the noun phrase, and are similar (maybe even identical) in meaning to relative clauses like *homeless people who are looking for hostel accommodation*. As far as the structure of the clause goes, however, the *-ing* modifiers are very different from relative clauses. The relative clause has a complementiser which in a sense functions as the subject and the *-ing* clause clearly lacks both a subject and a complementiser.

   Non-finite clauses built around the *-ing* participle often function as adverbials:

Stubbing out my cigarette, I got on my bike. (N#258:12)

Shrouding himself in a cloak of exclusivity, Tim gave his loyal followers a window of opportunity. (AUS#73:17)

When they function as adverbial clauses, *-ing* clauses are often introduced by a preposition, as in the following example:

In Moscow, a performer with the state circus expired *after attempting to swallow an eight-pound bowling ball*. (N#258:44)

You may wonder why we don't call the verb forms we are discussing here the progressive participle instead of the *-ing* participle. The reason is that even though their form is identical, their distribution does not seem to be the same. Compare the grammatical *-ing* form in *I resent having been asked to provide a permanent address* with the ungrammatical progressive **Regularly, I was having been asked to provide a permanent address*. *Having* is the auxiliary of the perfect in both cases; we can tell because it is followed by *be* in its past participle form. The fact that the second sentence is ungrammatical is because in order to get this form of *have*, we have put the auxiliary of the progressive before it to give *was having*. However, as we saw in Section 6.4, the auxiliary of the perfect always precedes the auxiliary of the progressive, so that we can only get *had been asking*, not *was having been asked*. The two occurrences of *having* in the examples must then be different.

Another reason to distinguish between the *-ing* form and the progressive is that (as we saw in Section 4.6), there are certain verbs that don't occur in the progressive because the activity that is expressed by the verb cannot easily be seen as something that is 'in progress.' For example, **I am knowing that* and **He is having a large nose*. Even though these verbs cannot occur in the progressive, they are perfectly acceptable in non-finite *-ing* clauses:

Knowing what I know now about homeless people, I am much more sympathetic.

Having a large nose, Ringo was often teased as a child.

There are good reasons, then, to separate two uses of the *-ing* participle: it can follow the auxiliary of the progressive *be* in progressive constructions and it can occur in non-finite clauses.

Non-finite clauses headed by *-ing* participles never have complementisers. However, as you can see in something like *I resent having been asked to provide a permanent address*, it is possible to have complex verb strings in these clauses. It is also possible to have *-ing* clauses with a subject, and such subjects can occur either in the usual object form, or in the possessive form:

His mother doesn't like *him sleeping rough*.

His mother doesn't like *his sleeping rough*.

As with the other non-finite complementation, it can sometimes be difficult to decide when we have an *-ing* clause preceded by a noun phrase whether that noun phrase is the subject of the non-finite clause or the object of the higher verb. This problem doesn't arise with the possessive subjects, since verbs in English never have possessive objects. However, in a sentence like:

I think I saw *someone smoking while they were handling food*. (AUS#75:22)

someone could in principle be either the object of *see* or the subject of *smoking*. The most plausible choice is to say that it is the object of *see*, and this is for the same reasons we gave for the similar sentence with a bare infinitive and for *to*-infinitives in the previous sections; if this sentence is true, it is also true that *I think I saw someone*.

Passive participle

Passive participles can form non-finite subordinate clauses, and when they do, the passive meaning is clearly present. They can occur in a variety of positions, for instance as objects of verbs:

We should have had *the kids checked for Y2K compliance*. (AUS#73:9)

In this case, the NP *the kids* is clearly the subject of the lower clause and not the object of the higher verb, since it is not true to say that *we should have had the kids*. Hence we have a non-finite clause with a subject. In the same clause, we could include a *by*-phrase, typical of passive clauses:

We should have had *the kids checked for Y2K compliance by experts*.

The active equivalent of this non-finite clause is a bare infinitival clause: *We should have had experts check the kids for Y2K compliance*.

In the following example, the non-finite clause functions as an adverbial:

I discovered that, *when expected to speak a foreign language*, the Dutch can be strangely reticent. (N#258:12)

Passive participle clauses can modify nouns, as in the following example:

the book, *edited by professor Hartley Dean from Luton University*, (N#279:4)

Just like the *-ing* clauses modifying nouns, these resemble in meaning relative clauses, in this particular case a non-restrictive one: *the book, which is edited by professor Hartley Dean from Luton University*. Of course here too, the structural differences between the clauses are still there: in this example, the passive participle clause lacks both subject and complementiser.

Non-finite clauses built round a passive participle can never have a complementiser. They can occur with a subject as in the first example in this section, or without, as in the rest of the previous examples. Just as with the other non-finite clauses, we get cases where it may be difficult to decide whether the clause has a subject or not. Consider the following example:

The librarian found *the book stolen*.

Here it does seem that the underlined NP must be the subject of the (rather small) clause built around the passive participle *stolen*. After all, the whole problem in this scenario is that it isn't true that the librarian found the book.

8.4 Subjectless clauses

We have seen in Section 8.3 that all types of non-finite clauses can occur without subjects. The question now is how this affects the meaning; normally almost all verbs need subjects because the semantics of verbs is such that they involve the participant represented by the subject. If the subject is not there, how do we know who is doing what the verb expresses? Look at three of the examples used here again and see if you know what the understood subjects of the verbs *burn*, *grow* and *ask* are.

What British milkman Wilf Sneddon did was *burn down the houses of customers who failed to order enough Gold Top.*

We intend *to grow our hair even longer for the cause.* (N#258:12)

Asking for identification from the vulnerable is totally wrong. (N#279:4)

We suspect that you find no problem in understanding who or what is meant to be the subject: it was *Wilf* who burnt the houses, it is *we* who are going to grow our hair, it is wrong for *anybody* to ask for identification from the vulnerable. So, even though there is no syntactic subject in these clauses, there is an understood subject. In some cases, the meaning for that subject is picked out from somewhere else in the sentence, as in the first two of these sentences, or it is assumed to be general, to mean *for anybody* as in the last sentence.

When the meaning of the missing subject is the same as that of some other element in the sentence the terms CONTROL and CONTROLLED SUBJECT are often used. When the meaning of the subject can't be found inside the sentence so that the interpretation becomes general, *for anybody*, we talk about ARBITRARY REFERENCE.

In control constructions, there are only certain noun phrases that are potential CONTROLLERS. When the subjectless non-finite clause functions as an adverbial, it is the subject of the sentence that supplies the reference. So, in a sentence like *Being aggrieved at being woken up, the playful worker bit Orozco*, the understood subject of *being aggrieved* can only be *the playful worker* and not *Orozco*.

Sometimes this can go wrong. The following are what prescriptive grammars would refer to as 'dangling participles': *Lying under the table the secretary found a large pile of important papers* or *Made in Australia with the finest ingredients, Kraft introduces an exciting range of fresh dips.* Formally, if only the subject of the clause can control the meaning of the missing subject, then these two sentences would imply that the secretary was lying under the table and that Kraft was made in Australia with the finest ingredients. However, people do use these sentences and generally other people seem to understand them correctly.

Unfortunate wording in the Monash University advertising and community services bulletin

On Wednesday, we will participate in an International Day of Student Action. At 1pm, a banner will be dropped from the building, followed by three prominent speakers.

When the subjectless clause is the complement of a verb, the interpretation we get for that subject slot depends on the verb. Compare the following two examples:

He warns laser-toting mischief-makers to take heed. (AUS#66:5)

He promises laser-toting mischief-makers to take heed.

In both these cases we said that the NP *laser-toting mischief-makers* is the object of the higher verb, so that the non-finite subjectless clause *to take heed* lacks a subject. With *warns*, the missing subject gets interpreted as referring to the same entity as the object, *laser-toting mischief-makers*, whereas with *promise* we get the same reference as the subject *he*. This is referred to as OBJECT CONTROL and SUBJECT CONTROL, respectively; *warn* is an object control verb and *promise* is a subject control verb.

In many syntactic analyses of sentences such as these, it is assumed that there is in fact a subject present in these control sentences, namely an invisible pronoun that like other pronouns borrows its reference from somewhere else. However, we feel that the interpretation we get in controlled clauses is not a matter of syntactic structure, but rather is related to the semantics of the sentence, and hence we treat these subjectless clauses as VPs, rather than Ss with a zero subject.

8.5 Trees

When it comes to drawing trees representing the structure of sentences containing sub-clauses, there are two things that make it tricky. First of all, we have to draw a tree in which the position of the sub-clause within the sentence as a whole is correctly represented and, second, we have to represent the internal structure and the category status of the sub-clause itself appropriately. In terms of syntactic category, every sub-clause belongs to one of three categories: S', S or VP. It belongs to S' if it has a complementiser, or could have had a complementiser; it belongs to S if it cannot have a complementiser but has a subject; and it belongs to VP if it has neither a complementiser nor a subject. As for position within the sentence as a whole, there are the same options as for the corresponding non-clausal functions (and these were given in Chapter 4). Schematically, we can give these as follows:

Subject:

(3)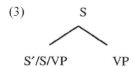

                To create catch phrases was fun

Extraposed subject:

(4)

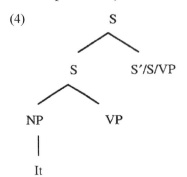

It was fun <u>to create catch phrases</u>

Object/subject complement:

(5)

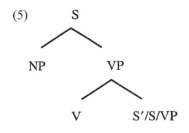

The question was <u>if/whether Jeff and Akbar were brothers or a gay couple</u>

I swear <u>that didn't dream it.</u>

Adverbial:

(6)   or   (7)

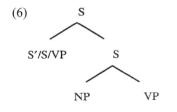

<u>To be quite honest,</u> I like *The Simpons.*   The Dutch can be strangely reticent <u>when they are expected to speak a foreign language</u>

Complement of N:

(8)

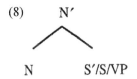

Someone asked the question <u>whether Jeff and Akbar were brothers or a gay couple</u>

Modifier of N or A:

(9)

a picture <u>which appeared within the sleeve of an LP</u>

These trees are the ones we get if we make minimal assumptions about things being there which we cannot see. Those who carry on to do syntactic theory will find that some theories include in the syntax many phenomena which we have assumed to belong to another dimension, and therefore there will be many more empty nodes in such trees.

To illustrate how the internal structure of sub-clauses is represented, we will now draw trees for a few of the sentences we have dealt with above:

(10)

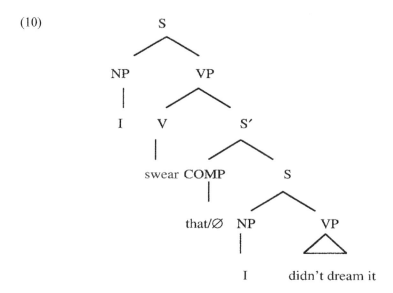

Here the finite clause functions as the object of *swear*. It has a complementiser (though this is optional) and being a finite clause it also has a subject. Of course, the lowest VP also has internal structure, but this is something which we went into in some detail in Chapter 6, so we will just use the triangle notation here.

Now for a finite clause with a *wh*-complementiser which forms the complement of a noun:

233

(11)

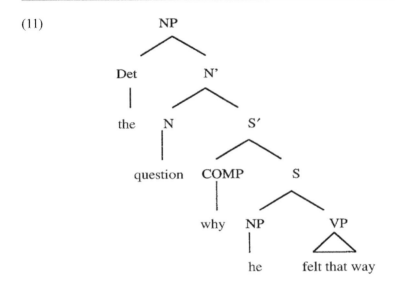

Note that the clause is a sister of N here since it is a complement; the question is why he felt that way. When the clause is only a modifier, as in the case of a relative clause, then it attaches at N′ level, like all modifiers (we dealt with this difference in Chapter 7). We use a simplified version of the noun phrase here, but the whole NP is included in exercise 3 in Chapter 7, so you may well already have looked at the general structure of the NP:

(12)

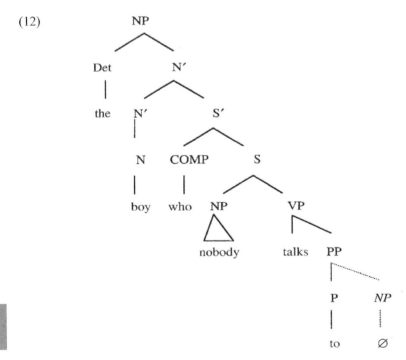

As in all *wh*-clauses, some part of the clause has been substituted by a *wh*-constituent and this constituent has been fronted (if it wasn't already at the front by virtue of being the subject). This means that there is a gap somewhere in the clause; in this case it is the complement of the preposition *to* which is missing. As we said when we dealt with *wh*-interrogatives on p. 135, some people prefer to mark this position with a zero in order to make clear where the *wh*-constituent came from. This is indicated by the NP under the dotted line in this tree.

A number of points we made about *wh*-interrogatives in Chapter 5 hold here too. Even though in this case the *wh*-constituent consists of only one word, it can also be a whole constituent, so that the COMP position can hold either a lexical category, like *that*, or a whole phrase, like *which picture*. As we said in Chapter 5, in syntactic theory this is dealt with through a more extended system of phrase structure, something that need not concern us at this stage. Furthermore, we argued in Chapter 5 that the reason there is no subject–operator inversion when the *wh*-constituent fills the function of subject is that the subject is no longer there in the S (but is found under COMP). There is no inversion in subordinate clauses, so we cannot show the same argument here. But we shall assume that the same holds true for relative clauses, so that we get the following tree for a noun phrase like *a picture which appeared within the sleeve of a Lennon LP*:

(13)

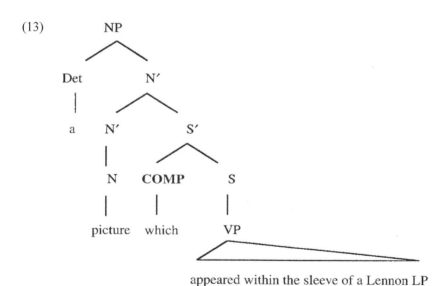

appeared within the sleeve of a Lennon LP

We turn now to non-finite clauses, first one *which* has a complementizer, and *which* occurs in the position of subject. Again, we refer to Chapter 6 for the detailed analyses of the VP (although we have given the feature of the VP here).

(14)

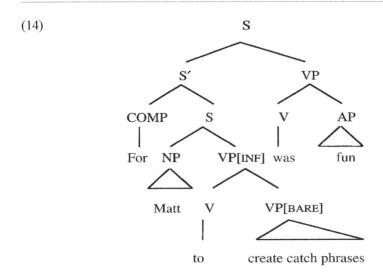

Remember that in Chapter 6, we argued that the infinitival marker *to* actually shares certain properties with auxiliary verbs and for that reason we put it under a V node in the tree. We compare this structure now with a sentence in which an infinitival clause lacking a subject is the extraposed subject:

(15)

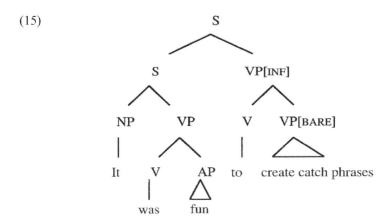

We can now compare this with a sentence in which there is a full referential subject and the non-finite clause modifies the adjective:

(16)

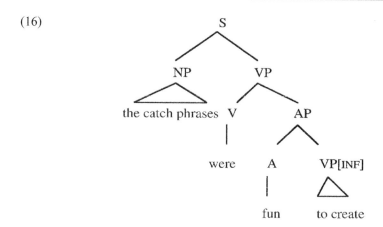

Since bare infinitival clauses, -*ing* clauses and passive participle clauses never occur with a complementiser, they can never be of category S'. Instead they are S or VP, depending on whether or not they have a subject. A few examples of how they would fit into trees for sentences are given here:

(17)

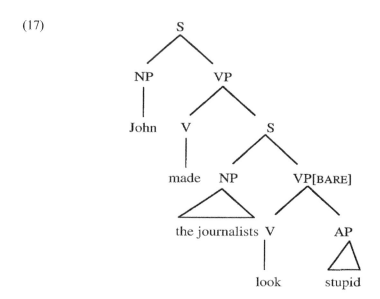

(18)

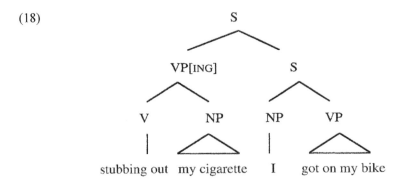

(19)

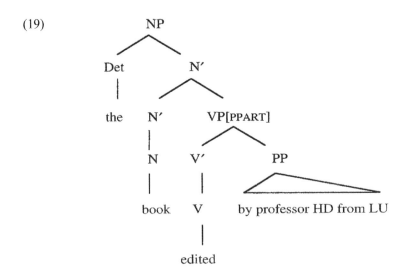

8.6 Points to remember

- ❑ If there is more than one lexical verb in a sentence, then there is more than one clause. There is a clause built around each lexical verb. The clause that also forms the sentence is the main clause and if one clause forms a part of another clause, then it is a subordinate clause.
- ❑ Coordination involves the linking of two clauses of equal status via coordinators like *but* and *and*.
- ❑ Subordination involves a clause forming part of another clause. Elements that mark the beginning of subordinate clauses are complementisers (or, more traditionally, subordinators).
- ❑ Main clauses are always finite, i.e. the first verb of their verb string is finite, whereas subordinate clauses may be either finite or non-finite.
- ❑ Subordinate clauses come in three sizes: (1) S' (S-bar) is a clause with a complementiser added (though in some cases that complementiser may

be optional). All finite clauses are of this category. Non-finite clauses can also be of category S,' but when they do have a complementiser it is obligatory. (2) Category S obligatorily lacks a complementiser. (3) Category VP lacks a complementiser and a subject.

❏ Subordinate clauses can be either declarative or interrogative, but when they are interrogative they differ from main clause interrogatives in that there is no subject–operator inversion.

❏ We looked at three kinds of finite clauses here: *that*-clauses, interrogative clauses and relative clauses. There are two types of interrogative clauses, *if/whether* or *wh*-clauses. Relative clauses and *wh*-interrogative clauses share the property of having a 'missing' element that is represented by the initial *wh*-constituent. This property they also share with main clause *wh*-questions.

❏ The non-finite clauses we divided according to the form of the first verb in the verb string. Each kind of non-finite verb can build a clause and hence we get bare infinitive clauses, *to*-infinitive clauses, past participle clauses and *-ing* clauses.

❏ Non-finite clauses can occur without subjects. If the meaning for the subject cannot be found inside the sentence it is known as arbitrary reference. The terms control and controlled subject are used when the interpretation of the subject depends on some other element in the sentence.

Exercises

1. Analysing sentences

Identify how many clauses there are in the following sentences and (using brackets) show exactly where each clause begins and ends. Remember that every lexical verb gives rise to a clause. Say whether the sub-clauses are finite or non-finite:

(a) I thought I'd dealt with my chest fetish. (AUS#92:38)

(b) It is possible to do something about the extreme poverty. (N#279:4)

(c) Since leaving ER, George Clooney is finally learning how to relax. (N#301:8)

(d) When you get older, you've been through a few of those films where they tell you how great you are. (N#301:8)

(e) I thought it was a black comedy like *M*A*S*H* and *Catch 22*. (N#301:8)

(f) Did they intend to become parents during their stay? (N#258:13)

(g) The great thing about those moral and political issues is that we raise them but we don't answer them. (N#301:8)

(h) There were times where you just had to pump your way through it. (N#301:8)

(i) I think they expect me to be some Texan cowboy rather than a quiet Englishman. (N#301:15)

(j) Impressed by what he saw, he commissioned them to make a Christmas video-card he could send to his friends. (AUS#51:23)

2. Function of clauses

For each of the subordinate clauses in 1, identify its function within the higher clause (often this will be the sentence, but there may be a clause in between).

3. Control

Examine all sub-clauses in exercise 1 and identify those without subjects. Say if they are controlled and identify the controller.

4. Clauses within NPs

Each of the following NPs contain post-modifying clauses. Identify each clause and state its type: finite or non-finite. If finite, is it declarative or interrogative; if non-finite, what kind of non-finite verb is it?

(a) changes requiring people to provide two forms of identity (N#279:4)

(b) evidence that social policy is failing (N#279:4)

(c) a new book which brings together leading poverty commentators (N#279:4)

(d) Sneddon, who blew up another customer's lorry (AUS#33:36)

(e) an afternoon talking to putzes like yourself (AUS#33:39)

(f) the small children whose parents have decided (AUS 51:39)

(g) a hard habit to break (AUS#92:38)

5. Identifying post-nominal clauses

At a first blush, the following pair of clauses post-modifying nouns seem very similar:

It's a fantasy that our readers have (AUS#66:21)
It's a fantasy that our readers have a bit on the side

Describe the differences, with respect to both the position of the clause within the NP and the structure of the clause. Illustrate your answer with appropriate trees.

6. Trees

Draw trees for the following sentences. (From 'The Chesty Bond' AUS#92:38.)

(a) I concede that chest hair is no longer *de rigueur*.

(b) Lusting after hairy-chested men might be unfashionable.

(c) I thought I'd put my chest lust to bed in the 80s.

(d) A thick-hairy rug on the back and shoulders makes me vomit.

(e) I just want the waxing to stop.

(f) It can be a hard habit to break.

(g) Sydney boys are the worst because they have chronic wax syndrome.

(h) I hope this article starts a wave of revolution that empowers the hairy.

9

Beyond the sentence

9.1 Introduction

So far we have been exploring some of the structural features of individual English sentences. We've seen, for example, that there is a subject and a predicate in basic clauses and that the subject precedes the predicate – that is, unless there is a special grammatical reason for putting it somewhere else, as in the case of special clause types like interrogatives and exclamatives. But sentences rarely occur in isolation in this way and to get the full picture we really need to go beyond the sentence to something called COMMUNICATIVE STRUCTURE. This involves the ways in which we distribute our bits of information in a text, in order to provide the right sort of cues to help our audience follow and interpret a piece of discourse appropriately; in short, how we as speakers (or writers) go about packaging our messages. You see, our discourses are really much like stories. Any shifts in focus, changes of players, beginnings and endings of scenes all need to be signalled. The ways in which we do these things are collectively known as DISCOURSE STRATEGIES. Potentially they involve all linguistic levels; for example, syntax (e.g. word order, special constructions), morphology (e.g. specific markers), lexicon (e.g. expressions like *as for*, *well*) and phonology (e.g. intonation, pausing). Even elements of body language (e.g. gesture, eye contact) may be used to drive home the points made through discourse strategies. But we will of course only deal with grammar here.

At first blush our language appears to be full of redundancy in its grammar. We've already come across a number of different constructions that seem to convey precisely the same information. Consider the following four sentences (adapted from *The Big Issue* AUS#564: 13); initially they appear to be different ways of saying basically the same thing:

(1) *The New Yorker* sent Fiona a magazine tote bag.

(2) *The New Yorker* sent a magazine tote bag to Fiona.

(3) Fiona was sent a magazine tote bag by *The New Yorker*.

(4) A magazine tote bag was sent to Fiona by *The New Yorker*.

These four sentences don't contrast in basic (or propositional) meaning, but they would be used in different contexts of use. Which construction we choose depends on what part of our message we want to highlight, what we think is most important, what is new and exciting information and what we assume our audience already knows. If it was assumed that *The New Yorker* gave something to Fiona and the magazine tote bag was new information, this context would favour (1). On the other hand, if sending tote bags to subscribers was already established, this context would favour (2). In this case, Fiona would be the point where we expect people to pay special attention. However, another situation might have *The New Yorker* as the new arrival in this story, and perhaps a surprising bit of information; in this context versions (3) and (4) would be appropriate. You perhaps also feel the stylistic effects of these two are different – they are passive constructions and might come across as more formal than the two active versions (1 and 2).

Speakers and writers are constantly drawing on the grammatical resources of their language in this way for different expressive or communicational ends, in much the same way as they select from their stores of different vocabulary items. It's a matter of choice. So what might seem like grammatical overkill is there for a reason. It's not so very different from what happens in marketing. The content might not change, but effective packaging can make the world of difference – whether it's a matter of promoting products or getting messages across.

9.2 Information packaging

In the following, we will look at three basic principles for organising or packaging information in a sentence and some of the grammatical strategies available for varying the information structure according to these principles. In particular, we will concentrate on those that involve variations from basic clause structure for achieving these special communicational needs; many of these grammatical strategies will already be familiar to you. All examples are drawn from the short story 'Moth Sea Fog' (by Gregory Day) about one father's fears of losing a son in the fog (AUS#519: 45–57).

Given information comes before new

In spoken and written language there are two basic kinds of information: GIVEN (or OLD) versus NEW. Given information is familiar. It either refers to something that has already been mentioned, or it is given in the sense that it is common knowledge, perhaps privately or culturally shared. New information is what drives the discourse forward. It's where we expect our audience to pay special attention. This flow of information (the 'given before new' order) appears to have a value in language processing – it's easier for production and comprehension to have early mention of things that are already established (and therefore more accessible and easier to talk about) before new or unpredictable information is introduced. Texts that follow the given–new preference appear more cohesive, because the given information at the beginning links the sentence to the previous discourse, while the new information is usually taken up in the continuing discourse.

Consider the opening paragraph of 'Moth Sea Fog':

> I talk **to the moth caught in the car**. . . . I tell **him** about *the fog of the day before*. *It* was not just any fog, but a time-fluxing sea fog outrolling the waves, creeping over neap-tide ledges, tickling the glossy anemones with its smoky edges. It made silhouettes of the gods.

The beginning of the sentence is reserved for the old and unsurprising material or given information (in other words, information that has a lower communicative value), and the end for whatever is novel and unexpected – in this case, the moth that has been caught in the car. (You might be wondering why the writer uses 'the' here to introduce the moth, given that this is its first mention – this is an expressive practice often found in narratives; compare the start of a story such as 'Like, I met this guy. . .'.) The moth once introduced is then established information and can be replaced by a pronoun form (here *him*). With given information, we clearly don't need to include the same sort of detail that we do if we are identifying something for the first time. One way we can give it less than full mention is via PROFORMS, little words such as pronouns, which occur in the place of longer constituents. (Substitution by a single word was one of the constituency tests given in Chapter 2.) To keep repeating the moth would be unnecessary – in fact it would sound odd (though this technique is sometimes done for special effect).

Another way of giving old information less than full mention is by omitting it altogether. Remember, this is something called ELLIPSIS. It just means we leave out that part of a sentence that is totally reconstructable from previous utterances or that can simply be inferred from the context. For example, if someone asked if you had read 'Moth Sea Fog,' you might reply, 'No, I haven't' (or 'No, I haven't read it'). But you are unlikely to reply in full: 'No, I haven't read "Moth Sea Fog"' – this would sound unnatural. Like proforms, ellipsis leads to economy of expression. It means we're being efficient. And conversational dialogues, as we'll see in Chapter 10, are full of it.

As the narration unfolds, the next bit of new information is the fog. What was new then becomes old and is taken up again at the beginning of the next sentence (with the pronoun *it*). We are then provided with a lot of new information about this fog (here italicised). Once again the length and complexity of the material are tied in with the informational aspects of sentence meaning. Because it requires more detail, new information will typically be longer than old information, and constituents are more likely to be complex or 'heavy' (e.g. weighed down by modifiers); so all this heavy stuff is better placed late in a sentence (or the sentence runs the risk of coming across as unwieldy). This is known as the PRINCIPLE OF END-WEIGHT.

The following table sets out the sentences from the introductory paragraph of the 'Moth Sea Fog' and shows more clearly how information packaging works here.

Notes	Given (less informative) material Background/ presupposition	New (informative) material Focus
Introduction of the moth	I talk	to the moth caught in the car
Introduction of the fog	I tell him	about the fog of the day before
New information about the fog	It was not <u>just any fog</u>	but a time-fluxing sea fog outrolling the waves, creeping over neap-tide ledges, tickling the glossy anemones with its smoky edges
Introduction of the silhouettes	It made	silhouettes of the gods

What is introduced as new information then becomes old and is taken up again at the beginning of the next sentence. The result is a kind of chaining effect of old (or 'givenness') followed by new (or 'aboutness') and this arrangement is what gives the passage its coherence. Often authors will begin sentences with some sort of adverbial element (such as *so, sometimes, furthermore* and so on); their initial position also helps the information flow, either by setting the scene or by linking the sentences and creating cohesion. The narrator continues:

And **so** I tell him more . . .

You can see here how the given–new and end-weight principles work hand in hand. New information requires more detail than old information; the unmarked word order is for longer, more complicated and heavier structures to appear towards the end of the sentence. Let's see how the narrator puts this into practice when he finally tells the moth the full story:

Once upon a time . . . a sea fog rolled in . . .

Here he uses the classic fairy story opening (cp. *Once upon a time in a land far away there lived a king . . .*). The reason for this is simple – this is a handy device for ensuring that the end of the sentence is kept for the newest and most relevant information. And an effective trick to build up suspense is to deliberately delay mention of this information until the last moment. This is the technique the narrator used here to introduce the story of the fog – here is the opening in full:

> *Once upon a time, on an otherwise ordinary day, insofar as a too-hot day can be ordinary these days*, **a sea fog** rolled in from the endlessness of ocean and gently covered the reefs, the coves, the cliffs and downsloped shoulders and valleys of our town.

245

In this example, the narrator has stacked up adverbial expressions (here italicised) and this builds up the suspense. He's delaying mention of the fog – this heightens our expectations and gives the fog extra prominence. So it's the endings of sentences that really push the discourse forward – and if full use isn't made of this slot, a sentence can fail miserably (in a moment we'll see examples of this).

We said at the outset that when we speak or write we have at our disposal a range of grammatical structures tailored for different communicational nuances. We saw in Chapter 4 that indirect objects have the option of appearing immediately after the verb or in a prepositional phrase headed by *to* or *for*. Earlier sentences (1) and (2) were examples; here are two others from 'Moth Sea Fog.'

(a) I told the moth the story

(b) I told the story to the moth

Both sentences have the same basic meaning, but the narrator used (a) here, for the reason you'd expect. The moth is well-established information; introduced right at the start, it has already been mentioned on many occasions. The story, on the other hand, is where readers are now expected to pay special attention. It reveals the whole point of the narrative – the father's fears of losing his son, swimming in the fog.

Topic comes before comment

Another useful distinction to draw here is TOPIC versus COMMENT. Even though it interacts very closely with the given–new distinction just discussed, there are, as you'll soon see, occasions when they part company. We therefore need to keep them distinct.

The topic (or THEME, as it is sometimes called) is the part of the sentence which indicates what is being written or talked about. It is basically a discourse-oriented notion, as opposed to the subject, which is part of the internal structure of the sentence. And because it characterises what the discourse (or the sentence) is about, it is therefore typically given.

There are, however, occasions when the topic doesn't coincide with old information – for example, where the topic switches to a new one or in discourse initial structures where a topic is presented for the very first time (recall how the fog was introduced in the very first example). In a moment we'll look at some of the special strategies that the language has for coping with new topics.

The rest of the sentence makes some sort of statement about the topic and this is called the comment (or RHEME). In the natural order of things, the comment (providing the new information) follows on from its topic – if the topic is what we are talking or writing about, the comment is what we are saying or writing about it.

The earlier table laid out topic–comment arrangement of the opening sentences of 'Moth Sea Fog.' Each sentence said something about some entity and fell into two parts. The first part related the sentence to what had gone on earlier in the discourse. The second part was longer and more newsworthy – it contained the new information about already established participants in the discourse. The result was a kind of chaining effect of old followed by new and this arrangement is what gave the passage its coherence – a common thread to follow.

Now, topic and comment are terms that refer to the informational aspects of sentence meaning. Subject and predicate refer to grammatical functions. More often than not, subjects and topics coincide and so do predicates and comments. This has been the case in the examples we've seen in this chapter so far, but it isn't necessarily the case. For example, English has an array of expressions for specially highlighting a topic, often picking up a topic from earlier in the discourse. These include phrases like *considering, as for, with regard to, speaking of,* and so on, which are used to announce the arrival of a topic, the linguistic equivalent if you like of a trumpet blast or fanfare. Here we've adapted a sentence from 'Moth Sea Fog' to show how these can work. (The narrator doesn't actually use this device here, probably for the reason that his style is to use strings of verbless sentence fragments to put the spotlight on entities):

As for the younger boy, the father broke clear of the grip of little hands . . .

In a little while we will look at other ways speakers play around with topic–comment structure for creative effect.

Initial position can provide extra focus

We should warn you at this stage that discourse organisation is subject to a number of constraints which are sometimes in conflict. We have just said that that ends of sentences are important for communication, because they contain what is of special significance – in the unmarked order, new important information occurs at the end of the sentence. The previous sentence (beginning *As for the younger boy*) illustrated that the beginnings of sentences can be positions of special focus too; in fact there are several ways in which information can be put at the front in order to signal its importance. This is a phenomenon we will refer to as FRONT FOCUS, and there are a number of grammatical strategies available to achieve this.

How to distinguish between information which has been put in a special position because it is new and important and information that has been put in a special position because it has been focused is a notoriously hairy one. Maybe it is helpful to think of focused information as emphasised information, and the sentences that contain a structural focus position are quite different from the sentences in which we have a simple old-precedes-new order.

The situation is made more complicated by the fact that the information which speakers or writers want to put in focus is often the new information. This means that they may use a number of strategies to manoeuvre new information into an end-of-sentence position; at the same time, they may use a number of different strategies in order to get new information into an initial position, if it is so important that they want to draw attention to it. And an effective way of doing this is to take it out of its customary position. For instance, by bringing forward material which would usually be placed last, the effect is to give it much greater prominence. It's another way of grabbing the audience's attention. Normally it's the subject that appears in initial position (ignoring conjunctions and short adverb phrases that often precede the subject). This is the basic (or thematically neutral) word order for English. Arrangements that place something other than the subject in this position are therefore less usual and are more marked.

Consider the following extract from 'Moth Sea Fog' (we provide more detail here to better show the information status of the constituents but focus on the italicised elements):

> It's like someone you meet who you know loves travelling. You talk destinations. Or someone who loves to cook. You talk food, or kitchenware. *To a friend of the stars* you talk astronomy, myth, astrology. *To a friend of the river* you talk birds who've roosted in the river-trees.

Consider the last two sentences. The new information here appears in its usual end position. But the focus falls on the information (here italicised) that appears in front position; it's not old information but it amplifies what has come earlier and it does provide the cohesive link here. You could think of the package in this way: (Focus)–Topic–Rest of Comment.

In short, both the ends and beginnings of sentences are discourse spotlights, but different things activate them. This may seem like doublespeak, but hopefully all will become clear after the Section 9.3 when you see some of the grammatical strategies at work.

9.3 Special discourse strategies

It is usual to describe these different kinds of discourse strategies in terms of movement. We assume that there is a basic English clause structure from which we may deviate for the sorts of discourse reasons we have been exploring in this chapter. In other words, speakers may 'move' items out of their usual spots to other positions in the sentence. In Chapter 2 we used a number of these non-canonical orders to test for constituency; remember, only constituents (not bits of constituents) can move this way. Here we examine these structures more closely and explore why in terms of information structure we might want to use them.

Given–new strategies

Some languages (like Russian) have flexible word order and achieving organisational principles such as given–new is not such a big deal. Earlier on in the history of English, it wasn't such a big deal either. Old English word order was flexible; in fact all logically possible arrangements of subject, verb and object appeared during that time. Though the grammar didn't force a particular word order the way it does for modern English, this doesn't mean that word order was free – this was a time of expressive word order, where the placement of elements was controlled by information structure and other contextual considerations (e.g. given versus new information, what the speaker considers important, what s/he assumes the audience already knows and so on). In the modern language, however, word order is used to signal what is essentially grammatical information; for example, clause types and the grammatical relations expressed within them. In something like *The narrator loves the boy* versus *The boy loves the narrator*, it is the order of constituents that tells us who loves and who is being loved. In earlier English, inflections on nouns and modifiers provided this information; so the narrator and boy could have appeared in any order.

As you can probably see, the rise of basic SVX (X = everything else) order in English has brought with it a potential conflict between grammar and discourse. Prosodic effects aside – how can we continue to accentuate and emphasise the crucial parts of our message, how can we get attention and create expectation within the confines of such rigid ordering conventions? In short, English grammar requires fixed word order, while discourse requires word order rearrangements for communicative and expressive ends. Who wins?

We have resolved this conflict by making greater use of special devices that can somehow satisfy both conditions – for example, subject-forming strategies that actually create new subjects and move what would normally be non-subject noun phrases leftwards into initial position. We have also evolved a set of new purpose-built devices such as empty (or dummy) subjects like *it* and *there*. These are meaningless little words which simply function as subject placeholders. These developments allow movement of material without violating the requirement that every sentence has a subject, and this subject appears sentence-initially and before the verb.

Passives – creating new subjects

Look at the following sentence. It shows the neutral SVX pattern with an actor/agent subject and a patient object (see Chapter 4). This is the ACTIVE version.

The fog	abducted	him
Subject	Verb	Object
(Agent)		(Patient)

In Chapter 6, we saw that the PASSIVE version of this sentence reverses the functions, so that the original patient becomes the grammatical subject and the original agent gets moved into a prepositional phrase headed by *by*. The following passive is the original version used in this story.

He	was abducted	by the fog
Subject	Verb	Adverbial
(Patient)		(Agent)

The basic meaning remains more or less the same, but the emphasis has changed. In the original, the pronoun *he* is the given topic (the boy) and is the less informative part of the sentence. So it's not surprising the passive sounds more natural here with the pronoun (old information) early in the sentence. What we should be focusing our attention on is the fog – hence the passive construction allows this constituent to appear in the end position, appropriate to its new information status. Whether the active or passive is used here is not a matter of 'grammar' but rather depends on the discourse context and considerations like new versus old information, focus and emphasis.

The passive lets us place in initial position the patient or what is the direct object in the active version. It also allows us to shift the agent or subject out of its usual position to the end. More often than not, though, the agent gets left out. This can be because it is irrelevant information, or because it is already obvious or even because it's undesirable to mention it. (See the discussions in Section 10.4 on Sports-Talk and Bureaucratese.) Have a look at the following example, the continuation of the story being told to the moth. The verb forms that follow are passive (in italics) but all are without agent by-phrases.

> Once upon a time . . . a sea fog rolled in from the endlessness of ocean . . . Every pond *was lightly brushed*. Every road sign [was] *shrouded*.

In each instance we can take for granted that it's the fog which is brushing the pond and shrouding the road signs. Here the passive enables the narrator to omit uninformative (highly topical) elements that would otherwise have to be stated in the active version (i.e. the fog), and the reader's attention is on the pond and the road that are now in initial position.

Passives – a thorn in the flesh of many editors

For some time now passives have been attracting bad press – many style guides, usage books and online writing tips even recommend people write in the active voice. Such recommendations are the reason for your helpful grammar checker's green squiggly lines.

But as we've just seen, the passive has all sorts of advantages. For one, it allows us to omit certain information, which comes in handy when the information is not particularly relevant (*No animals were harmed in the writing of this book*). Consider the following extract from a foodie piece that appeared in *Vogue Entertaining*.

> At Armstrong's Tables of Toowong fat oysters had been lifted from their shells, and then returned onto a gently spiced cushion of noodles, touched with an olive oil, lemon and saltwater vinaigrette, and topped with a dollop of oscietra caviar. Linguini had been tossed in truffle oil, studded with shards of crisp asparagus, topped with a soft-poached egg and a generous slice of fresh, black truffle.

Sounds gorgeous – it's beautifully written too. And yet every clause is a passive (though the auxiliaries have been omitted). We can take for granted that it's the chefs who are doing all this lifting, returning, touching, topping, tossing and studding. Here the passive allows the writer to omit such unexciting information that would otherwise have to be stated in the active version – 'Linguini had been tossed in truffle oil' is snappier than 'The chefs had tossed the linguini in truffle oil.'

OK, of course there's always scope for misuse. Doing away with agents is a way of concealing information – and perhaps creating psychological distance between perpetrators and their actions. It'd be honest for us to fess up to something like – *We've eaten all the hobnobs*. More likely we'd resort to the agentless passive to downplay our involvement – *The hobnobs have all been eaten*. Its impersonal style can also lend a kind of sham authority to the wording, setting up the impression of a consensus (where there might well be none): *It was decided to close the school down* versus *I decided to close the school down*.

It's the inappropriate use of the passive that has given the construction such a bad name. But the problems have been overstated and the behaviour of our computer grammar checkers is quite harebrained – most of the time those green squiggly lines are unwarranted.

Different semantic types as subjects

As earlier described, the conflict between strict SVX word order and discourse considerations has also partly been resolved by the fact that we now allow more types of noun phrases to be subjects than before, and as subjects they can occupy sentence-initial position. It's not surprising that we had trouble coming up with a neat semantic roles to characterise English subjects in Chapter 4. Look at the range in the semantic roles of the following subjects – none are prototypical agents or actors; the first isn't even an NP. The first three come from the short story, and then we've added a few:

Around the point is the way to the beach	[= location]
The loom wove your wings	[= instrument]
The wattle faded	[= theme]
The tent sleeps four people	[= location]
The wine drinks well <u>but</u> *the soup* eats salty	[= patient]
This edition has added a fifth exercise to each chapter.	[= recipient]
Tomorrow promises a much sunnier day.	[= time]

English shows considerably more diversity than even its close Germanic relatives as to what can appear as a subject.

'Tough' movement

The semantic diversity of our subjects is also illustrated by something known as 'tough'-movement (so called because textbooks typically use examples with *tough* – *It's really tough to find good books about English grammar*). This is another strategy for creating new subjects, and the process works with a range of adjectives beyond *tough* (including *amusing, annoying, bad, boring, comfortable, confusing, dangerous, depressing, easy, educational, embarrassing, fine, fun, good, great, hard, horrible, ideal, illegal, loathsome, necessary, nice, odd, painful, pleasant, rare, risky, safe, strange, tedious, tricky, unpleasant, useful, weird*).

In the following we adapt a sentence from the story to show how this works:

(a) It was fun to visit the cove.

(b) The cove was fun to visit. ('tough' version)

Sentence (a) is the neutral version. In (b) the object *the cove* in the second clause has been moved leftwards and turned into the subject of the main verb (semantically it has the same relation to *visit*). We interpret (b) exactly like (a); i.e. what is fun is *to visit the cove*. The difference between them is one of emphasis. Sentence (a) is the neutral version and the 'tough' version is more marked – (b) is specifically a comment on *the cove*.

Existentials

Sometimes the subject is completely new information that we want to reserve for the end of the sentence. We can do this by creating a dummy subject using the pronoun *there*, which then appears in the position normally occupied by the subject NP. This then allows the logical (or understood) subject with all its new and exciting information to appear later, giving it much greater prominence. *There* has no meaning, though it is the subject of the clause (and recall in Chapter 4 we applied the tests of subjecthood to show this was the case). Its purpose is purely structural – to hold the place of the understood subject.

The following example is taken from 'Moth Sea Fog' (we have included the basic version in brackets).

There was something in those dried stalks, those clefts and crannies of the car.

[Something was in those dried stalks, those clefts and crannies of the car]

The reason we call this an EXISTENTIAL SENTENCE is because it expresses the existence or the presence of something at a particular time or in a particular place. The construction is often employed to introduce new topics – we've already seen how it is used as the stock-standard fairy-tale opener 'Once upon a time there was a king.'

As new participants these NPs are typically indefinite – they're new on the scene. Definite NPs, you'll find, don't generally participate in this construction. In fact, the structure *there is/there are* is often used to test whether or not an NP is definite (as in Section 7.3).

There are occasions where existential *there* is compulsory, namely, when the clause contains only the subject and verb and no adverbial constituent. Have a look at the following example, a tense moment in the story when the narrator's son has disappeared. The basic version without existential *there* is not grammatical (and neither is the sentence we began this paragraph with).

There was only absence.

[*Only absence was.]

The examples so far have involved copular *be*. It is possible to use other intransitive verbs (generally presentational verbs of movement or location such as *emerge, come, arise, appear* and so on). They tend to make for a more dramatic effect and have a slightly literary flavour, as you can see from the following examples (the original versions are in the brackets; we've adapted them to create the existential clauses).

There comes a secret message travelling through the air between us.
[A secret message comes travelling through the air between us.]

Once upon a time, there rolled a sea fog in from the endlessness of the ocean.
[Once upon a time, a sea fog rolled in from the endlessness of the ocean]

Extraposition

As we saw in Chapter 8, it is possible for the subject of a sentence to be an entire clause, finite or non-finite. What extraposition does is change the whole sentence around so that this subject clause appears in the end position. Because it appears outside its usual spot, this is labelled EXTRAPOSITION. In its place is the pronoun *it* – this is another dummy pronoun subject, a kind of structural placeholder. We'll shorten one of 'Moth Sea Fog' sentences to show more clearly how this works:

(a) *To be inside the cabin of my ute* seemed like a dream. [basic version]

(b) *It* seemed like a dream *to be inside the cabin of my ute*. [extraposed version]

Here extraposition is optional. But there are some constructions that have no non-extraposed versions; with certain verbs (e.g. *seem*, *appear* and *happen*) extraposition is mandatory:

(a) *That the fog had lifted seemed.

(b) It seemed that the fog had lifted.

There is another option here that turns *the fog* into the subject of *seem*; compare *The fog seemed to have lifted* with the extraposed version *It seemed that the fog had lifted*.

As far as information packing goes, extraposition (like the existential construction) makes good sense – it's the subject clause that usually has all the new information in it. So what lies behind extraposition are the principles of end-weight and of given–new – we don't want heavy newsworthy subjects up front, and the heavier and the more newsworthy the subject clause, the more likely extraposition will occur. To illustrate we'll leave the story for a moment and give you two examples from J.R.R. Tolkien's *The Hobbit* (Tolkien is a writer who makes much use of 'heavy' clausal subjects). Look how awkward the sentence (in brackets) becomes when the understood subject is not extraposed, but is followed by its short and not terribly newsworthy predicate.

> 'It is true *that we were wrongfully waylaid by the Elvenking and imprisoned without cause as we journeyed back to our own land*,' answered Thorin. (p. 189)
> [?'*That we were wrongfully waylaid by the Elvenking and imprisoned without cause as we journeyed back to our own land* is true,' answered Thorin.]

> It is not unlikely *that they invented some of the machines that have since troubled the world, especially the ingenious devices for killing large numbers of people at once*. (p. 189)
> [?*That they invented some of the machines that have since troubled the world, especially the ingenious devices for killing large numbers of people at once*, is not unlikely.]

There are times though when writers can get away with not extraposing even heavy clausal subjects. This is true of the fuller version of our first sentence given at the start of this section. The following is the original without extraposition:

(a) *To be inside the cabin of my ute, its plastic and steel*, could have also seemed like a dream to the moth. [original non-extraposed version]

(b) *It* could have also seemed like a dream to the moth *to be inside the cabin of my ute, its plastic and steel*. [adapted extraposed version]

Both (a) and (b) versions are acceptable. The content of the italicised clause follows straight on from a detailed description of the inside the cabin of the utility truck (nothing terribly newsworthy). So sentence (a) shows no violation of the given–new principle here.

Focus strategies

Processes like those we've just seen are all part and parcel of the organisational principle that ensures that given information appears early and new information at the end. We will now look at strategies that ensure that emphasised information appears in special focus positions. We looked at these sorts of strategies briefly in Chapter 2 when we used movement as a test for constituency. As we discussed at the time, some occur only infrequently in the written language – with more rigid (SVX) word order, we simply don't have this sort of creative potential with our wording. However, they are commonly found in spoken language and we explore this difference in the next chapter when we compare spoken and written varieties of English. For the moment, let's look at some of the most important strategies.

Cleft constructions

CLEFTING was one of the important constituency tests we introduced in Chapter 2. As we mentioned at the time, there are two basic kinds of clefts: *it*-clefts and *wh*-clefts. Both have the effect of 'cleaving' an original sentence into two clauses as a way to shift the focus of interest. So clefts not only shift things around in the sentence, they also build new structure. In this way, they are like the earlier processes we've seen (passives added special verb morphology and the old object became the subject; existentials and extraposition created dummy subject pronouns).

Take the sample sentence *The grey fog painted the ocean cliffs* (with constituents in the basic unmarked word order). But let's say the narrator wanted to really highlight the grey fog. An *it*-cleft has the effect of splitting off this constituent and giving it prominence. Two clauses are formed, the first introduced by an empty subject *it* and a form of *be*, followed by the focused constituent. The rest of the sentence is recast as a relative clause beginning with *that*.

(a) *The grey fog painted the ocean cliffs.* Original

(b) *It was <u>the grey fog</u> that painted the ocean cliffs.* **it**-cleft foregrounding *the grey fog*

(c) *It was <u>the ocean cliffs</u> that the grey fog painted.* **it**-cleft foregrounding *the ocean cliffs*

The advantage of using *it*-clefts is that they allow speakers/writers to show what is foregrounded and what is backgrounded. The backgrounded information is generally assumed to be known or presupposed. But don't be surprised if these sometimes sound a little contrived – clefts require surrounding discourse to make sense.

They might also sound odd because clefts are normally reduced. Old information requires minimal mention and one way of doing this is omitting it altogether. So if we were to ask, *What painted the ocean cliffs?*, the expected reply cleft would be: *It was the grey fog.* The information in the relative clause (*that painted the ocean cliffs*) is already given and doesn't need to be mentioned.

The formula for forming an *it*-cleft is quite straightforward: *It is/was X that . . .* As with existentials and extraposition, the emphasis is thrown onto whatever follows the dummy subject and its verb, i.e. X in the formula. As you can see, *it* anticipates the new information after *be* (underlined in this example). It's a way of getting our attention by delaying mention of what is of special significance.

Note, some constituents resist clefting, notably VPs, complements and indirect objects. (This is not true for all dialects though – Irish English, for example, is distinctive in showing a much wider range of clefting possibilities, including VPs and complements; e.g. *Is it tricking me you are* and *It's a teetotaler he is*).

Wh-clefting (or PSEUDO-CLEFTING, as it is sometimes called) also cleaves basic sentences into two – an introductory *wh*-clause (a fused relative construction) and a complement of (some form of) the verb *to be*. In this case what is in focus follows the verb and is then given extra prominence by virtue of being shifted into end position. For example, different *wh*-cleft versions of the previous example sentence would read:

What painted the ocean cliffs was *the grey fog*.

What the grey fog painted was *the ocean cliffs*.

What the grey fog did was *paint the ocean cliffs*.

Both types of cleft construction assume a certain amount of background detail, otherwise they'd sound out of place. In this case narrator has already in graphic detail established 'those honeyed cliffs which the fog greyscales into.' Neither of the clefted versions would make a lot of sense here, unless the narrator could assume that the reader had this information.

Fronting

FRONTING simply places constituents that are normally positioned late in the clause up at the front. By moving them out of their usual position, they acquire extra prominence. Have a look at the following sentences from 'Moth Sea Fog,' and see if you can determine the sort of constituent (category and function) that has been fronted in each instance. (See also question 5 in the exercises at the end of this chapter.)

Another thing I tell the moth [cp. I tell the moth another thing]

The sunlight was a recent memory, I tell him [cp. I tell him *the sunlight was a recent memory*]

Every late October I wait for the moths [cp. I wait for the moths every late October]

One day a boy swam into the sea fog [cp. A boy swam into the sea *fog one day*]

The feeling we have that the world hides and reveals [cp. We have the feeling that the world hides and reveals]

In this deep and secret shroud the truth of seek is made real [cp. The truth of seek is made real in this deep and secret shroud]

Star War fans will recognise this as the characteristic feature of Yodish. However, Standard English doesn't have quite the same creative potential as Yoda's fronting:

Found someone you have.

Then a Jedi will you be.

Tired I am, *rest* I must.

Consume you it will.

Anger, fear, aggression; *the dark side of the Force* are they.

Fronting can also trigger something called INVERTED SUBJECT–VERB ORDER, as some of Yoda's examples illustrate (though some Star Wars enthusiasts have suggested Yoda has made an error in his sentence production here). By moving the subject out of its natural environment, it involves a shift of emphasis and represents another aspect to this focus device. Compare the following three (adapted) sentences with the bracketed version without inverted word order:

In rolled the sea fog. [cp. The sea fog rolled in]

Into the sea fog swam a boy [cp. A boy swam into the sea fog]

Under the skin of the water slipped the boy [cp. The boy slipped under the skin of the water]

As this examples illustrate, these constructions always involve fronted phrases (such as directional and positional adverbials), and the verbs are intransitive (typically verbs of movement or location, here *crept, swam* and *slipped*).

In Old English this inverted order had considerable dramatic force; it was typical of lively narrative sequences and it still retains something of this effect. Think of the lines in Tennyson's *The Charge of the Light Brigade*: 'Into the valley of death rode the six hundred . . . Into the mouth of hell rode the six hundred.' Here's another example from the *Vogue Entertaining* food magazine cited earlier (of course the principle of end-weight is also at work here):

> Out will come beef dusted with Japanese pepper, fingers of salmon with dill sauce and all that rocket in olive oil.

Left-dislocation

Have a look at another sentence from 'Moth Sea Fog' that involves fronting:

Those bonnets of steel, they come from the same marketplace.

This example illustrates a different kind of focus strategy that involves something more than simple fronting. It is known as LEFT-DISLOCATION. Again the movement metaphor is useful here. You simply move a constituent (here *those bonnets of steel*) to the extreme left of the sentence, leaving behind some sort of proform copy (here the pronoun *they*) in the gap left by the fronted constituent. Typically, an intonation break separates the fronted item from the rest of the sentence. In a sense it is left 'hanging' outside the sentence structure, and this has the effect of making it stand out even more. In this example the focused constituent is the subject (whose basic position is initial anyway), so this is a way of emphasising this is something of interest (Yoda's last example also illustrates this nicely). The following example shows a fronted object with a pronoun left in object position.

(a) The moth doesn't speak French.   Original
(b) *French*, the moth doesn't speak *it*.   Left-dislocation of object

The grammatical relations have not changed: 'the moth' and 'French' are still the subject and object, respectively, but the object has become detached from the rest of the sentence, separated by a distinct pause (indicated here by the comma). So it's different from, say, passives, which must change a constituent into a new subject in order to be able to front it. In writing, left-dislocation is rather rare, and it is heavily marked. Speech, however, is built much more along discourse lines and, as we will see in Chapter 10, left-dislocation structures like these are very common.

Right-dislocation

RIGHT-DISLOCATION involves the same process as left-dislocation but with the movement rightwards of material; in other words, it involves the movement of a constituent to the end of the sentence rather than the beginning, and once again a proform is left in its place. If the position of the constituent would more usually be early, then this has the effect of giving it extra focus by postponing its mention. It can be also used for clarification, as a kind of afterthought (*I saw it, the accident*).

And so *we* went, *the moth and I*.

Notice how the right-dislocated element (the subject here bolded) is separated off from the rest of the clause by a distinct pause, indicated here by a comma. To better illustrate the process, take the following where we have two versions: (a) the original sentence and (b) the right-dislocated version where the object has been separated off from the rest of the sentence.

(a) Every late October I wait for the moths.   Original
(b) Every late October I wait for *them, the moths*. Right-dislocation of object

Like clefting, extraposition and *there*-insertion, right- and left-dislocation introduce a pronoun. However, in dislocated constructions the pronouns are referential and point to what is coming up in the discourse; they aren't just empty placeholders. It can be a good way of building up expectations. We'll illustrate this with a final example – here the complex clausal object has been replaced by *that* and has been moved to the right of the basic clause, separated off prosodically (as indicated by the colon).

I told him *that*, as we drove over a bridge: *how he reminded me of the fog, how they seem connected.*

9.4 Points to remember

❏ Communicative function involves the way sentences are packaged as messages within larger structures or discourses. In order to achieve the best packaging of information a number of strategies are at a speaker's disposal. Sometimes these strategies compete with each other and have different effects.

❏ Elements of an English clause have a neutral or basic position where they appear unless there are special reasons for putting them somewhere else. Elements can deviate from this basic position for expressive or communicational ends.

❏ New information is salient; it is the information which is meant to gain the audience's attention and move the discourse forward. Given information is familiar in the sense that it refers to something which has already appeared earlier in the text, or which is common knowledge.

❏ The unmarked word order is for new important information to occur at the end of the clause. This is THE PRINCIPLE OF END-FOCUS.

❏ The unmarked ordering of phrases and clauses by size within a sentence is to move from small to large. This is THE PRINCIPLE OF END-WEIGHT.

❏ The distinction between topic and comment typically runs parallel to that between given and new, but there are occasions where it doesn't (as in the case of new topics). Topical material typically occurs early in the sentence, often to provide a cohesive link with what has preceded.

❏ The unmarked word order is for the topic (what is being talked/written about) followed by the comment (what is being said/written about the topic). This is THE PRINCIPLE OF TOPIC-COMMENT.

❏ There are a number of grammatical changes (like passive, 'tough' movement, existentials, extraposition) which can be made to a sentence to maintain this neutral old–new order.

❏ Sentence-initial is a focal position for emphasised information. Moving material to this position gives it much greater prominence.

❏ Ellipsis is the omission of items in a sentence because they either appear elsewhere or can be reconstructed from the context.

❏ The normal order of old–new information can be overridden by focus strategies like clefting, left/right-dislocation and fronting (with or without subject–verb inversion). These are aimed at adding extra emphasis to some constituent, usually new information.

Exercises

1. Focus strategies (fronting, clefting)

The following are examples of fronting. Give the corresponding basic versions (without fronting) and identify the function and category of the focused phrases. (Note, all of these examples come from J.R.R. Tolkien's *The Hobbit* – a masterful example of effective discourse structure.)

(a) *With the women and the children, the old and the unfit*, the Master remained behind. (p. 241).

(b) *That* you MUST NOT do, for any reason. (p. 132)

(c) *Very puffed* he was, when he got to Bywater. (p. 38)

(d) *Tidings* they had gathered in secret ways. (p. 264)

(e) '*Very comforting* you are to be sure,' growled Thorin. (p. 137)

(f) *Lake* it was, wide and deep and deadly cold. (p. 77)

(g) *Goblin* he thought good, when he could get it. (p. 77)

(h) *Up, up*, the dwarves went, and they met no sign of any living thing. (p. 228)

(i) *At that* they gazed and wondered. (p. 232)

(j) *Swiftly along this* they ran. (p. 229)

For each sentence in the following (all from *The Hobbit*, pp. 77–78), give the corresponding *it*-cleft sentence, focusing on the italicised item. Make note of where the corresponding cleft is ungrammatical. On the basis of these, decide what type of constituents can't be focused in this way. (Take note of its category and function.)

(a) Gollum was *really hungry*.

(b) He was *a Gollum* – as dark as darkness.

(c) He had *a little boat*, and he rowed about quite quietly on the lake.

(d) Actually Gollum lived *on a slimy island of rock in the middle of the lake*.

(e) *Bilbo* could not see him.

For each of the following sentences write the corresponding non-cleft version.

(a) It was just then that Gandalf came back. (p. 46)

(b) It was the wizard's voice that had kept the trolls bickering and quarrelling. (p. 50)

(c) It was he that made the dwarves begin the dangerous search on the western slopes for the secret door. (p. 197)

(d) It is always poor me that has to get them out of their difficulties. (p. 201)

(e) It was at this point that Bilbo stopped. (p. 205)

2. Given–new strategies (existentials, extraposition)

Rephrase each sentence as an existential sentence (as it was in Tolkien's original).

(a) A good deal of food was jumbled carelessly on shelves. (p. 50)

(b) Black squirrels were in the wood. (p. 138)

(c) Now a glimmer of light came before them. (p. 67)

(d) Strange things are living in pools and lakes in the hearts of mountains. (p. 76)

(e) No safe paths are in this part of the world. (p. 136)

Decide whether the following sentences illustrate existential *there* or adverbial *there*. Explain the difference between these two *theres*.

(a) And there in rows stood great jars and vessels filled with a wealth that could not be guessed. (p. 206)

(b) There was a hill some way off with trees on it, pretty thick in parts. (p. 41)

(c) And far away, its dark head in a torn cloud, there loomed the Mountain! (p. 183)

(d) And there he lay, a vast red-golden dragon, fast asleep. (p. 205)

(e) In the middle there was lying a great oak-trunk with many lopped branches beside it. (p. 118)

Write a paraphrase of the following using extraposition. Out of context which version do you think sounds better? Why do you think Tolkien chose not to use extraposition here?

(a) That it was Thror's grandson not Thror himself that had come back did not bother them at all. (p. 190)

(b) To hunt the whole mountain till he had caught the thief and had torn and trampled him was his one thought. (p. 208)

3. Given–new strategies (Passives)

Identify all the passive verb forms in the following extract (adapted from *The Hobbit*, p. 32). Note that some of these are reduced passives.

[Thorin is speaking here]
Long ago in my grandfather Thror's time our family was driven out of the far North, and came back with all their wealth and their tools to this Mountain on the map. It had been discovered by my far ancestor. I believe they found a good deal of gold and a great many jewels too. Anyway they grew immensely rich and famous, and my Grandfather was King under the Mountain again, and treated with great reverence by the

mortal men, who lived to the South, and were gradually spreading up the Running River as far as the valley overshadowed by the Mountain. They built the merry town of Dale there in those days. Kings used to send for our smiths, and reward even the least skilful most richly. Fathers would beg us to take their sons as apprentices, and pay us handsomely. So my grandfather's halls became full of armour and jewels. Undoubtedly that was what brought the dragon. Dragons steal gold and jewels; and they guard their plunder as long as they live (which is practically for ever, unless they are killed), and never enjoy a brass ring of it. There were lots of dragons in the North in those days, and gold was probably getting scarce up there, with the dwarves flying south or getting killed.

Now switch all the passive forms into the active and where possible make all the active forms into passive (you may also have to alter other aspects of the structure occasionally, especially where the passives have been reduced). In terms of information structure (given versus new, for example), what does this do to the passage? Why does the original version read better?

One of the passives in Thorin's speech has used the 'get' passive construction, where *get* instead of *be* is the auxiliary. Suggest a reason why the 'get' passive has been used here. Try to replace all the 'be' passives by 'get' passives in the speech. Do you notice any differences between the two versions – perhaps in meaning, or stylistic nuance? Try to reconstruct possible contexts to illustrate how each might be used.

4. Discourse strategies (varied)

For each of the following sentences, identify the special discourse strategies that Tolkien has used and give the basic version. Although these are out of context, can you say why Tolkien might have employed these techniques? (Some illustrate more than one strategy.)

(a) This was made by Thror, your grandfather, Thorin. (p. 29)

(b) Each of these could be reached by paths that ran down from the main mass of the Mountain in the centre.

(c) Already behind him among the goblin dead lay many men and many dwarves, and many a fair elf that should have lived yet long ages merrily in the wood. (p. 267)

(d) Gandalf it was who spoke, for Bilbo was fallen quiet and drowsy. (p. 278)

(e) It took him ages to get the beastly stuff out of his eyes and eyebrows. (p. 157)

(f) Then in crept the hobbit. (p. 172)

(g) On this western side there were fewer signs of the dragon's marauding feet. (p. 198)

(h) Right in the middle of the fight up came Balin. (p. 45)

(i) 'It was a good story, that of yours,' said Beorn.

(j) 'Water is not easy to find there, nor food.' (p. 131)

(k) As for 'little fellow bobbing on the mat' it almost made him *really* fierce. (p. 28)

5. Agentless passives

Suggest why Tolkien used the agentless passive (i.e. no by-phrase) in each of the following extracts. Note, these passive constructions are of course contextually motivated but we have tried to provide enough context for each example.

(a) 'Moon-letters are rune-letters, but you cannot see them,' said Elrond, 'not when you look straight at them. They can only be seen when the moon shines behind them. The dwarves invented them and wrote them with silver pens. These must have been written on a midsummer's eve in a crescent moon, a long while ago.' (p. 60)

(b) Later Smaug used to crawl out of the great gate and come by night to Dale, and carry away people, especially maidens, to eat, until Dale was ruined, and all the people dead or gone. (p. 33)

(c) At the southern end the doubled waters poured out again over high waterfalls. In the still evening air the noise of the falls could be heard like a distant roar. (p. 185)

(d) Out jumped the goblins, big goblins, great ugly-looking goblins, lots of goblins, before you could say rocks and blocks. There were six to each dwarf, at least, and two even for Bilbo; and they were all grabbed and carried through the crack, before you could say tinder and flint. (p. 67)

(e) It is not unlikely that they invented some of the machines that have since troubled the world, especially the ingenious devices for killing large numbers of people at once, for wheels and engines and explosions always delighted them, and not working with their own hands more than they could help; but in those days and those wild parts they had not advanced (as it is called) so far. (p. 69)

Grammar at work

10.1 Introduction

In Chapter 1 we introduced the notion of dialects; in other words, varieties of English associated with groups of users. These involve regional and social variation. This chapter now introduces the notion of REGISTERS; in other words, varieties associated with particular contexts or purposes. No one behaves linguistically the same way all the time. One of us has a good friend who generally uses phrases such as *it commences prior to* or *it is operational* in preference to *it begins before* or *it is working* even in situations you would not expect to hear them. Normally the former expressions would belong to a formal register that people would only use for particular situations, like a business environment, or sometimes to impress people or exclude those who do not know the more formal words. However, our friend could by no stretch of the imagination be described as pretentious or as wanting to make people feel ill at ease. Also, he is not actually a one-register man since he has also been known to say things like: *my desktop computer is not operational and my laptop is out of juice*. This can be described as mixing registers. So speakers will differ in what they consider to be appropriate language for a specific context.

Our linguistic behaviour varies constantly in response to a complex set of different situational factors and if any one factor is changed, our language changes accordingly. These factors include things like: the relationship between speakers and their audience, and even anyone else who might be within earshot – are we chatting to a chum or our local priest? The setting – are we in a formal meeting at work or at the races? The subject matter – are we debating who will win the Melbourne Cup, the FA Cup Final or is the topic the existence of God? Whether a spoken or written medium is used – are we chatting on the phone, chatting online or sending a piece of snail mail?

Register is the general umbrella term to cover all aspects of variation in use and can be distinguished at various levels of generality. At one extreme we can identify very general registers to do with physical mode – as earlier mentioned, language can be perceived and transmitted as speech or as writing. At the other extreme we can identify highly specialised registers such as Computer Program Talk, Sports-Talk, Auto Mechanic Talk, Journalese, and so on; in other words, registers involving occupational varieties or 'jargons' that are peculiar to the activities of a trade, a profession or some other group sharing a special interest. Though 'jargon' tends to have negative connotations and some registers annoy people not familiar with them, there is a need for language to vary with context. At the same time, people or groups of people sometimes adopt a particular style of language in a particular environment, not because it makes it easier to do what needs to be done, but as we said earlier, in order to confirm their own status as a member of a group or to exclude those who have not mastered that particular register. Let's look at some examples, starting by identifying the grammatical features of the two general registers, speech and writing.

10.2 Speech versus writing

Consider the following example of spontaneous conversation between two close friends. Speakers are indicated with an initial followed by a colon. Each line represents one intonation unit. Continuing intonation units are marked with a comma and final intonation units with a full stop or question mark. In conversation, overlapping is very common, and simultaneous speech is here indicated by two sets of square brackets vertically aligned. Pauses are marked by three dots. Laughter is indicated by the 'at' sign [@]. We will explain the significance of the bold items later.

1. C: think they only went for one night.
2. C: It cost her a hundred 'n,
3. C: . . . a hundred 'n fif-,
4. C: . . . a hundred 'n,
5. C: fifty dollars I think it was.
6. C: Not a hundred 'n.
7. C: no.
8. C: A hundred 'n five dollar,
9. C: it was.
10. C: Must've been for a night.
11. C: **And** she said the dinner was,
12. C: The woman cooks,
13. C: does all the cooking herself.
14. C: **But** she said you got heaps of,
15. C: ya know,
16. C: courses 'n,
17. C: really,
18. C: really lovely food. [. . .]
19. [speakers move on to discuss new venue]
20. C: **But** she said it was fun.
21. C: She said they had a nice night so.
22. C: **But** she said Sarah was very nice.

23. C: That's where um,

24. C: Nathalie had hers.

25. C: Amelia said the food was,

26. C: it was alright.

27. L: Lucy enjoyed it,

28. L: [the] food.

29. C: [Yeah].

30. C: **An' I,**

31. C: I said to Mrs Kenny,

32. C: something,

33. C: she said about the pla-

34. C: she said they were big plates an' a small meal.

35. C: **An' I** said yeah,

36. C: Amelia said the meal was small.

37. C: **Coz,**

38. C: forty-five dollars or whatever it was,

39. L: Yeah.

40. C: I think the,

41. C: some of the kids thought it was a bit expensive.

42. C: I said,

43. C: you pay for the venue,

44. C: that's what you're paying [for].

45. L: [Hmm].

46. C: **And** uh,

47. C: **but** uh,

48. C: Amelia said they were,

49. C: ginormous plates,

50. C: **An'** ya didn't get,

51. L: yeah.

52. C: M-,

53. C: **And** uh,

54. C: Alice Kenny said,

55. C: yes.

56. C: She said some of the men when they came to the tables were, (C. pulls a face)

57. L: [@@@@@@@@@]

58. C: [She said oh well,

59. C: ya know.

60. C: This is,
61. C: It's all part of the atmosphere].
62. L: @@@
63. C: [Apparently the men sort've
64. C: really preferred their steak and veggies]
65. L: [@@@@@@@]
66. C: Ah.
67. C: They went to have a good time.
68. L: We went to a restaurant night,
69. L: Sis came out,
70. L: **but** with another couple.
71. L: **And** that was a place like that.
72. C: Hmm.
73. L: Stylish and grand piano,
74. C: Hmm.
75. L: pianist there playing and everything.
76. L: **An' then** she got the big plates an',
77. C: Hmm.
78. L: [where's] the food?
79. C: [@@@@]
80. C: A couple of snow peas arranged,
81. C: in a nice,
82. L: @@@@
83. C: pattern.
84. C: Yeah.
85. C: This,
86. C: I said well it's a night.
87. C: **An'** at least you can say you've been there.
88. L: Hmm.
89. C: **But** Alice said it would've been nice to be there in the day,
90. C: because she said the gardens looked like they'd be beautiful,
91. C: [down there].
92. L: [Hmm].
93. C: It would be great.
94. C: She said you couldn't really see them,
95. C: at night.
96. C: **So** she said,
97. C: she would've liked it to have been

98. [in the] afternoon,
99. L: [Yeah].
100. C: **which** I think
101. C: Nathalie's was a lunch.
102. C: I think.
103. C: **But** um,
104. C: yeah.
105. C: It was nice.
106. C: Oh,
107. C: it was an experience for them,
108. C: [isn't] it
109. L: [Mhm].
110. C: . . . Something's,
111. C: we never did anything like that.
112. L: No.
113. L: neither did I.
114. C: We left school 'n that was it.
115. C: [An'] yet I mean it was a real,
116. L: [Yeah].

[We are grateful to Julie Reid for this example.]

Try to convert this passage into a piece of acceptable writing and you will quickly discover that speech and writing are very different forms of communication. There are many utterances here that simply do not correspond to the well-formed sentences of English that we have been examining in previous chapters. Until quite recently, even the activities of linguists have overwhelmingly concentrated on the structures of planned and highly standardised speech – relatively little was known about the unplanned and more spontaneous discourse varieties. Of course, this is hardly surprising, given that recording is a modern phenomenon. We simply did not have proper access to live unsolicited speech. Unfortunately, the legacy of this is that people have come to equate 'normal' language with the written form. This, together with the increasing importance of writing over speech, has meant that common spoken features like discourse markers, ellipsis and contractions are stigmatised (though the increasing informalisation of language has meant that many people are more relaxed about these features).

But speech is not 'spoken writing' any more than writing is 'speech written down' – each medium has its own distinctive capabilities of expression, its own sets of 'rules.' So let's now turn our attention to speech and discover what is so distinctive about it. We concentrate here on structural differences and ignore the very obvious formal differences; for example, the fact that speech is produced orally and received by the ear and uses non-verbal features like gesture and facial expression to aid communication. Clearly, though, it's these formal features that are the trigger for many of the structural features we'll be discussing.

'Non-fluency' features

When you first encounter a speech event like the earlier dialogue between C and L, it's tempting to ask – where are the sentence boundaries? In place of the well-defined structures we're used to seeing, there are false starts, interruptions, self-corrections, repetitions, hesitations and what appear to be empty fillers like *umm* and *err*. Now, generally these are lumped together under the rather pejorative label 'non-fluency features.' But remember; don't judge speech through the spectacles of writing. The spontaneity and speed of speech exchanges like this one mean instant feedback and little or no time for planning. Consider for a moment just what's going on. For one thing, speakers like these are having to monitor what they're saying to make sure it's coming out as they intended and that their audience has understood it this way too. They are also having to plan what to say next. Is it any wonder that some repairs and repetitions have to be made on the go and there are hesitations, false starts and the occasional filler? It's true, these look glaring on paper, but the speakers seem unaware of them – there is nothing particularly tongue-tied about C and L in this impromptu conversation!

Breathing of course accounts for some of the pauses when we speak, and typically you find these at grammatical boundaries. Combined with different prosody, they function much like punctuation marks in writing, except what is grammatically significant in speech is rather different from what is significant in writing, as we'll see later. Most of the pauses, however, involve hesitations – drawn-out words or else pauses filled with noises like *umm* and *err*. Certainly *umms* and *errs* can be used in order to prevent someone else from taking the floor (they do make it harder to interrupt), but generally they're for planning purposes. And they help hearers too – after all, they don't have the luxury of pausing and going back to something they didn't follow. Researchers appear divided as to exactly where these hesitation pauses occur, although all agree it is somewhere within the clause. This suggests that we are already planning our next clause while we are in the middle of our current one.

Discourse markers

Conversations like the one earlier are dotted with what are called discourse markers. These are little words and expressions (sometimes called particles) that fulfil a range of different functions to do with the management and flow of interaction. They are many and varied and include expressions such as *you know*, *yeah-no*, *I mean*, *well*, *anyway*, *sort of*, and so on. Often these features are mistaken for the aspects of language just mentioned, hesitation noises that speakers use to fill in time while they plan what they're going to say next. But in fact, they have rich and complex meanings that have to do with creating cohesive discourse and expressing a speaker's feelings and attitudes.

Words like *well* and *anyway* have important discourse functions to do for instance with focus and change of topic. Others have important conversational functions to do with turn-taking. When speakers start their turn they often do this by acknowledging the turn of the previous speaker. *Yeah-no* can have this function. Others play a significant role in expressing social relationships, personal attitudes and opinions, conveying sometimes quite subtle nuances of meaning. Consider the complexity of a phrase like *sort of*. This can of course express approximation or imprecision (e.g. *it's a sort of blue colour*), but it's also a typical hedging expression which is used in informal contexts to reduce the force of an utterance. Often its use is simply to minimise the distance between the speaker and the audience and it does this by tempering the authoritative tone and creating friendliness. Speaker C uses it only once in the earlier dialogue (line 63), but in an earlier chat with L, a rather awkward conversation about the serious illness of a mutual friend, her discourse is splattered with *sort of*s. Spoken interaction is much more personal than writing and speakers continually involve themselves and their audience via expressions such as these. Speaker C also uses the phrase *ya know* a lot of the time (here lines 15 and 59). This could be signalling sensitivity towards L, actively inviting participation and emphasising common ground between them. But C might also be using *ya know* to check that L has understood, to ask for her reaction to what has been said, or to seek empathy from L. Such phrases typically have an array of different functions and have quite a complex effect on the utterances in which they occur.

Ellipsis

Conversational dialogues like the one between C and L are full of examples of ellipsis. Try fitting their utterances into the basic clause patterns we discussed in Chapter 5 and you will find that crucial elements are often simply not there. In the following example (line 10) the subject pronoun is missing:

C: Must've been for a night.

Even though sentences like these are incomplete from a strictly grammatical point of view, this is not the case from a discourse point of view. Oral communication of this kind is face-to-face and can exploit the context of the interaction much more than writing can. Speakers supply extralinguistic cues like gestures, facial expressions and of course nuances of intonation, loudness, tempo and rhythm. For example, when L is describing the huge plates with the tiny morsels of food, there are important visuals accompanying her description of the meal. Clearly, speakers don't need to supply everything – and it would be irritating if they did! Most of us quickly grow bored with what we see as long-windedness. So subjects and verbs frequently get left out: *Wanna leave now? You tired?* Of course they can always be 'recovered' from the context, and if the meaning should ever become unclear, the breakdown can easily be repaired. Writing, without the same immediate context, doesn't have this luxury and doesn't tolerate omissions to the same extent.

Syntactic complexity

In the dialogue between C and L we can more or less separate off the clauses. Identifying sentences, however, is more of a problem. Even if we remove the false starts and repetitions, the structures are still very different from those discussed in earlier chapters – the concept of 'sentence' just doesn't seem appropriate. Long, loosely connected structures appear to be the norm and there is very little in the way of subordination. But of course presentation of information involves quite different skills in this medium. As just discussed, speakers have available to them a vast repertoire of expressive devices like intonation, stress, pitch, speed, silence, laughter and voice quality, as well as a range of non-linguistic factors all of which can be used to signal logical relations between clauses. Speech (especially spontaneous conversation like this) has what is called a PARATACTIC style; in other words, clauses are often strung together either without any linking item at all or linked by some sort of coordinating element, typically *and*.

Speech also has types of constructions that rarely occur in writing. For example, in C's speech you might have noticed an instance of an unusual tag, one that you perhaps associate with non-native speakers of English (line 107):

C: it was an experience for them C: [isn't] it

Both C and L are native speakers of English, even though both make use of this simplified tag in place of standard tags like *wasn't it*.

Towards the end of the previous conversation (lines 100–101) there is also a rather curious-looking relative clause, one which seems to defy all the rules of relative clause formation we discussed in Chapter 8.

C: which I think
C: Nathalie's was a lunch.

This sort of relative clause (sometimes dubbed the LINKING RELATIVE) is very typical of spoken English. It differs from the relative clauses you know and love in the following ways:

❏ no antecedents – linking relatives elaborate on a stretch of discourse, often reiterating earlier information;
❏ no missing arguments in the linking relative clause – *which* has no grammatical function in the relative clause;
❏ replaceable by a coordinating conjunction like *and*.

In this example, the 'linking relative' is actually picking up on, indeed reiterating, information that was mentioned much earlier in the discourse. C began her story by pointing out that Nathalie also had her function in the same restaurant – *That's where um, Nathalie had hers*. Here *which* has a linking function, loosely connecting the material in the clause with this earlier information.

Speaker C also uses *coz* (from *because*) very differently (lines 35–41).

C: An' I said yeah,
C: Amelia said the meal was small.

C: Coz,

C: forty-five dollars or whatever it was,

L: Yeah.

C: I think the,

C: some of the kids thought it was a bit expensive.

Rather than simply introduce an adverbial clause of reason, *coz* here is used to present a new piece of information, loosely connecting it with what has previously gone on the discourse (here there is a vague causal link). It's another linguistic trumpet blast or fanfare to announce the arrival of something significant and relevant to what was said before.

In the extract of dialogue between C and L we've marked in bold all of the linking elements. As you can see, each new intonation unit is typically marked either with a coordinating conjunction *and* and *but* or one of these linkers *coz* and *which*. While they clearly have a grammatical function to link pieces of information together, they also share a discourse function by providing the speaker with an opportunity to pause, at the same time clearly indicating to the hearer that there is more to come. *Coz* in the previous extract signals that C intends to continue the turn with something of new relevance to the topic. C as you can see is quite successful at retaining the floor! Here's another extract from the same dialogue, where we have italicised the linkers:

1. C: **And** breakfast was all done,

2. C: in a bain marie,

3. C: **so** you served yourself.

4. L: Mm [hm]

5. C: **An'** she said it was beautiful.

6. C: **And** she had a spa,

7. C: **An'** you,

8. C: book the spa.

9. C: **An'** I think it was twenty-five dollars for,

Presentation of information

Speakers can also manipulate word order to a much greater extent than writers; they can exploit different sequences of noun phrases to highlight or to contrast more salient information. In short, speech has EXPRESSIVE WORD ORDER. Exchanges like this one are typically full of the kinds of highly topic-oriented structures we looked at in Chapter 9. Here are examples of both left- and right-dislocation from the first extract (lines 25–28).

C: Amelia said the food was,

C: it was alright.

L: Lucy enjoyed it,

L: [the] food.

'Wicked which' – an exploration of the linking relative

Linguist Izzy Burke has been studying the Australian English version of 'this black sheep of the relative clause family,' as she describes it, and she identifies two main discourse functions. The first is that of a 'resumptive topic marker' (returning to a topic earlier in the conversation), and we've just seen an example of this. The second is that of 'focus' (highlighting up-coming text as especially important). As the following exchange between M and K illustrates, *which* is rather like *coz* in this function:

M. I think I've got the Smith genes (laughs)

K. I've got. I've got dad's genes **which his three sisters are all big fat, they're like**

M. Are they?

K. Oh yeah they're like size 22

M. Really?

The next example shows how this 'focus' *which* can also introduce a clause that provides relevant background information (in this case, that dying of septicaemia is now rare, making the death here all the more surprising and horrible):

PB: Yeah he started to get sick and then he sorta made a bit of a comeback, and then he really started to get sick. And he was buggered, he was on his – he was on the ropes then. And then he died, and on his death certificate he actually died of septicaemia, which is blood-poisoning. **Which no one dies of blood-poisoning these days.**

Speakers are even using *which* to introduce emotion, such as laughter, interjections or, in the case of the following extract, retching noises:

K. but it's basically just like a combination of art and biology **both of which I'm like, (retching noise)**, so. Yeah good luck transcribing that, (laughs), (retching noise).

This is an expressive use that takes *which* a long way from its usual job within the relative clause system of Standard English.

The picture we have painted here is that speech and writing form a straightforward dichotomy. However, this is not the case. Some examples of spoken language, such as you might find in a well-planned lecture or seminar for example, have many of the organisational features of written language. On the other hand, some examples of writing, a scribbled note to a friend for instance, or much online communication as we will soon see, are much closer to the speech end of things. Some linguists (sensibly in our minds) abandoned the general labels 'speech' versus 'writing,' preferring instead PLANNED versus

UNPLANNED discourse. These labels better capture the fact that different types of speech and writing show different features depending on their degree of planning and formality. Either way, these labels imply two polar extremes. The reality of course is that there are many intermediate varieties that exhibit features of both types of discourse to a greater or lesser extent.

10.3 A third option – or somewhere between speech and writing

The electronic revolution is both a technological revolution and a social revolution. At the same time it is also a language revolution. Emails, tweets, online forums, blogs, message boards, text messages and other social media are now routine aspects of most people's lives. They involve, of course, written language, but clearly also share many of the features not just of spoken language, but of actual conversation. Internet language has been famously described as a 'language centaur – part speech, part writing' (Baron's description; 2000: 248) – though we feel perhaps a more accurate description might be a language ammit (part lion, hippopotamus and crocodile), since there is a third part to this hybrid beast – the various electronically mediated features that characterise different online texts. As David Crystal (2006) describes, '(e)lectronic texts, of whatever kind, are simply not the same as other kinds of texts . . . they display fluidity, simultaneity . . . have permeable boundaries . . . one text may be integrated within others or display links to others' (pp. 51–52).

There are many different forms of e-communication and these will feature different linguistic properties depending on a number of situational factors. For example, is the discourse socially interactive and to what degree? Does the interaction take place between strangers or participants who know each other well, and is it public or private? Does it occur in real or postponed time? In real-time online communication (e.g. chat rooms, online conferencing), people exchange messages in much the same way as they would chatting face-to-face – synchronous chat is pretty close to casual speech. By comparison asynchronous modes (e.g. emails, discussion boards) involve a time lag and are closer to writing, although there will be a lot of variation here because writers will vary as to how much they bother with careful revising and rewriting – in other words, the sorts of drafting processes and layers editorial intervention that otherwise go to reinforce the written standard and to support distinction between speech and writing.

The following example, Figure 10.1, comes from Severin's (2018) study of online normative language debates on the discussion forum website Reddit (specifically the subreddit R/badlinguistics, dedicated to the sharing of 'all the worst linguistics-related content on Reddit and the Internet'). This extract shows a multi-participant discussion (on whether or not the gender-neutral use of *they* is 'proper'); replies to comments are displayed below those to which they reply and are indented slightly to the right. Even though the communication is asynchronous (so users are sending messages and getting

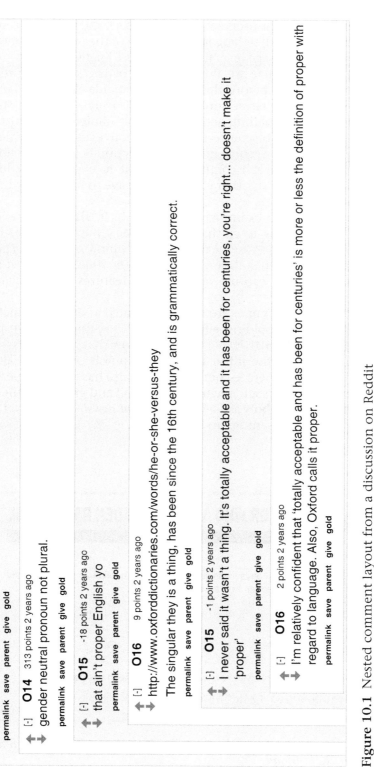

Figure 10.1 Nested comment layout from a discussion on Reddit

Source: Severin (2018)

replies at any time), these users are responding back and forth in the manner of a conversation, and their language has many of the features that we associate with spoken language (e.g. 'that ain't proper English yo'):

In electronic discourse we find examples of the sort of far-reaching variation that existed before there was any standard written language. Regional, social and even personal variation is usual, with non-standard spellings of words signalling accent or dialect/idiolect (e.g. *fing* 'thing'; *wid* 'with'). Language of course is all about conveying information, but never lose sight of its second important function – to express identity. If people in virtual speech communities want to express their identity, personal and shared with other groups, they have to break away from the written standard.

Consider the next example, Figure 10.2. It shows some of the responses provoked by a 'crash blossom' (see Chapter 3) that headed a feature article on the American news and opinion website *The Daily Beast* (the ambiguous headline was *Doctor Who Aided Bin Laden Raid In Jail*). These responses capture many of the features we associate with spoken language.

We see here examples of expressive devices such as unusual punctuation (capitalisation, italics, bolding, ellipsis points <. . .>, the tilde <~>), and creative spellings (<OHHHHHHH>); these can show that a word has a special sense, or can express the intonation and emphasis of speech. Although there are no examples here, e-communication also has its own repertoire of special graphic devices such as emoticons, emoji and grawlixes (the strings of non-alphabetic symbols as in *?#*! Have I got news!!!!!!*) that can supply additional nuanced meanings and emotions.

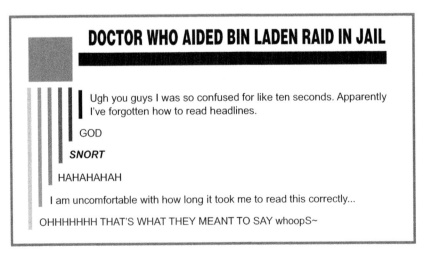

DOCTOR WHO AIDED BIN LADEN RAID IN JAIL

Ugh you guys I was so confused for like ten seconds. Apparently I've forgotten how to read headlines.

GOD

SNORT

HAHAHAHAH

I am uncomfortable with how long it took me to read this correctly...

OHHHHHHH THAT'S WHAT THEY MEANT TO SAY whoopS~

Figure 10.2 Responses to ambiguous headine *Doctor Who Aided Bin Laden Raid In Jail*

Punctuation with attitude

There are fascinating developments currently on the punctuation front – beyond the world of emojis/emoticons. E-communication formats have been busy resuscitating the careers of many moribund characters, bestowing upon them new tasks and new responsibilities. For a start, there's the interrobang <‽>; dating from the 1960s, this 'cool little punctuation mark' (Urban Dictionary) is now making regular appearances online.

No longer aligned to grammar or rhythm (two functions that have always been murkily intertwined for English punctuation), a number of other symbols have broken free of the standard and are taking on a whole heap of new significances. When people choose to use a full stop now, there's more to it than simply ending a sentence. These writers are showing emphasis – maybe even displeasure or frustration. A simple *Thanks.* in a text message becomes 'thanks for nothing.'

Ellipsis points are being used more creatively now. No longer simply indicating missing text, <. . .> invites the reader to infer the meanings hidden in that succession of full stops. On Wired.com Sam Greenspan offers this example:

Yeah, Kickboxer 4 could work . . . I've also heard good things about that Katherine Heigl movie Falling in Love Is Neat* . . . either way, meet you there at 8?*

Reading between the lines, Greenspan translates this:

I'd rather die than see a movie about the underground world of kickboxing, and you're an idiot for suggesting that we go see it. I'd rather see a romantic comedy. And now, because this has gotten a little awkward, I think we should meet at the theater so I have an escape plan.

And then there's the oblique stroke / known as the slash. Traditionally this symbol has been used as a way of capturing alternatives such as we did earlier (emojis/emoticons). But it's the actual word *slash* (not the punctuation mark) that is now taking off. Geoffrey K. Pullum on Language Log was the first to point to unusual uses of *slash* in sentences such as *There is also a study slash guest bedroom*, concluding that the word is a rare example of a new coordinator (the last addition was *but*, which evolved out of the preposition *butan* 'outside' in medieval English).

As Anne Curzan describes in her blog *Slash: Not Just a Punctuation Mark Anymore*, this use of *slash* (as a conjunction/conjunctive adverb) is also taking on more expressive meanings – *so what've you been up to? slash should we be skyping?* Akin to a discourse marker (such as *like*), *slash* seems to be signalling an afterthought here or even a change of topic.

The spontaneity and speed of electronic exchanges also mean a looser construction with comment clauses and asides, discourse markers, interjections, filled pauses, repetition, false starts, and even digressions. There are also the expressive opportunities in word order that we typically associate with spoken language, and there is plenty of lexical and grammatical informality as well (*Ugh you guys I was so confused for like ten seconds*) – all things normally frowned upon in writing.

Non-standard 'linking *which*' occasionally makes appearances too, as in the following example (here bolded) taken from a blog post written by young adult author Maggie Stiefvater (and thanks to Izzy Burke for this example):

> Noah's supernatural tantrumming continues back in Monmouth Manufacturing. He gets upset again – this time over his soul decaying (**which, fair, I was just doing that last week**) – and begins to creepily freak out. Blue pulls the plug on her energy and he diminishes immediately.
>
> (Maggie Stiefvater, 'Recap of Blue Lily, Lily Blue,' post on Recaptains.co.uk)

There is also reduction, and plenty of it. Whether it's to save keystrokes, or to type something closer to casual spoken language, this kind of writing is full of the omissions, contractions and non-standard spellings that represent the short cuts and assimilations we associate with ordinary speech (*wanna* 'want to'; *wassup* 'what's up'; *dno* 'don't know'). The language can also appear rather fragmented with function words (like articles, pronouns) often elided

Because fashion

This reduction can influence grammar in interesting ways. Take the changes currently underway involving *because*. As described in Chapter 8 *because* is a causal conjunction used to link clauses. An example of this use might be: *We love grammar because it's always surprising.* It also forms part of a compound preposition, so one that occurs in a sequence with another preposition, as in *because of grammar*. But *because* is spreading its wings, and the Internet now abounds with examples where it appears as a preposition without *of*, as in *I missed my grammar lecture because Game of Thrones*. This illustrates the kind of reduction we've come to expect of casual E-speak, but in fact it's more interesting than this. *Because* not only appears before NPs (as a standard preposition would), it also precedes APs (*I missed my grammar lecture because tired*), VPs (*I missed my grammar lecture because fell asleep*); there's even an expressive *because* where it introduces interjections (*I felt terrible because eek!*). You will find plenty of examples in Urban Dictionary – and while they might appear rather faddish creations, it's precisely these sorts of jokey constructions that often provide the basis for real change in the language. In this case, prepositional *because* appears to have already escaped the net and, if examples like the following are anything to go by, it has already taken off:

She squished her feet regardless into pointy shoes because, as women always do, fashion. (AUS#558:11)

as they are in informal spoken language. The result is that the language is often lacking the canonical grammatical clause (with a subject and finite predicate) that we have spent a good part of this textbook describing.

10.4 Occupational varieties

Now that we've identified these different communicative modes, we move on to explore some occupational varieties of English. Too often these are characterised solely in terms of their vocabulary. Certainly specialist terms are important to occupational varieties, but they are more than simply esoteric vocabularies. They draw from inventories of style features at all levels of the language – phonology, discourse, grammar. Here we concentrate on the grammatical features. We show that what makes a variety distinctive are important grammatical choices to do with (among other things) complexity of sentences and organisation of content. Of course, many of the linguistic features we look at occur in ordinary language too, but as with all stylistic varieties, it is the relative frequency and the special combination of these features that make a variety different from others. Texts of instruction like recipes and knitting patterns show an abundance of imperatives (*Zest the lemon; knit 8 rows plain knitting*); scientific writing shows large numbers of impersonal passive constructions (*The data were collected during 1998*); legal documents are characterised by full noun phrases in place of pronouns (*Where an offeree receives a copy of a notice, the offeree may, by notice in writing given to the offeror within one month after receipt of the first-mentioned notice and accompanied by any consideration that has been received by the offeree . . .*); diary writing is distinguished by missing subject pronouns (*Felt sick. Spent day in bed*), advertising language plays with word classes (*Monash University – where brilliant begins*) and so on.

In this chapter we offer brief case studies of two different registers: 'Sports-Talk' (here the language of basketball), and 'Legalese'/'Bureaucratese,' two very closely related varieties. We must emphasise that although we use labels like Legalese, Bureaucratese and Sports-Talk as if they were discrete entities, these varieties are by no means fixed. They vary continuously in response to a complex of different situational factors, including the relationship between the speaker/writer and audience, the setting, and of course whether a spoken or written medium is used. We speak, then, of individual registers as having different styles. Take the example of Legalese. A very rigid style of Legalese occurs in written documents like wills, but can also be spoken in the case of a witness's pledge to *tell the truth, the whole truth, and nothing but the truth*. A less rigid although still formal style occurs in written briefs; it can be spoken too, as in the arguments of counsel or the examination of witnesses. A very informal style occurs in the casual conversations between lawyers. These represent different varieties of Legalese. All show some features of Legalese, but differ in the relative frequency of these features.

And finally, a brief note about the sort of grammatical features we will be looking at. Often they start life with a clear function, but over time take on

279

a more decorative role. In the case of Legalese, for example, anaphoric pronouns are avoided to ensure clear, unambiguous identification: *The Lessor hereby leases to the Lessee and the Lessee hereby agrees to take from the Lessor the property described as the Premises in paragraph 3*. Nonetheless, there are many occasions where identification is perfectly clear and the use of a pronoun would be quite unambiguous. Over time a feature like lexical repetition can become a matter of stylistic choice, a conventionalised earmark of the variety – in this case it becomes almost part and parcel of the ritual magic of the legal process.

Sports-Talk – language of basketball

As we mentioned at the start of this chapter, linguistic labels like 'Sports-Talk' are fictional conveniences. There is no one Sports-Talk. The name encompasses a medley of different varieties across a range of written/spoken and formal/informal styles. Varieties include broadcasted commentary (TV versus radio; scripted versus unscripted), coaching talk, sports reporting, and all of course involving a gamut of very different sports from individual-oriented games like darts to team sports like rugby. Nonetheless we can identify a bundle of common organisational and functional features that characterises the Sports-Talk register generally. In addition to the common pool, each variety will have its own individual repertoires of distinctive features.

Here we have selected the language of basketball commentary. The following examples are all extracts from a TV broadcast of the last quarter of a game – The Titans (Melbourne) versus The Hawks (Wollongong), recorded on 7 November 1998. There are three commentators involved. Two (C and P) are in the commentary box; a third (AJ) is on court-side.

Background remarks are often made during the quarter breaks and periods of time-out. This between-action commentary shows all the grammatical features characteristic of spoken language. The following example is typical:

You don't, you don't wanna have sort of around 13 turnovers at, uh, three-quarter time, but it's saying that, uh, both teams have had . . . are being very active in their defence.

Since we have already discussed these general features, we concentrate here on the commentary itself; in other words, the impromptu speech of the broadcasters as they describe and comment upon events as they are actually unfolding. We should add here that this commentary is surprisingly free of the sort of non-fluency features (false starts, fillers, and so on) that you find in background remarks like the previous extract, which is more conversational in nature. This sort of fluency of delivery is characteristic of sporting commentary generally and suggests that, far from being spontaneous, commentating requires considerable training and practice. Commentators also draw from a range of rather formulaic phrases that also add to their overall fluency.

Parataxis

The colourful description 'shredded English' is how Crystal and Davy (1969: 185) characterise the language of the tabloid press. It's a very apt description of sporting commentary too. Outbursts of short, snappy, loosely connected clauses are typical.

Shot clock down to 14
Game clock at 1.05
McDonald against Bruten
Skip pass for Kelly
Pulls the trigger on the three
It would have ended it had it gone
It doesn't
Minute to go
Hawks down by 6
Need a score here, preferably a three but a two will do
Ritter to Campbell
Wide open three
He makes it
3 point game
Unbelievable

Telegraphic speech – ellipsis

Structures such as those in the extract just given do not fit the usual canonical subject–predicate arrangement we have identified for English clauses. Items we think of as crucial are simply not there. But the subject–predicate pattern is not a particularly useful one here. Sporting commentary generally is organised more according to discourse considerations (like topic–comment).

Good ball movement the Hawks

As with some other economy registers, not only are dispensable function words like pronouns, articles and auxiliaries omitted, but also full verbs. The material is always recoverable from the context of situation, but the result is a kind of telegraphic language that in no way resembles fully grammatical written English. (The description 'telegraphic' stems from the time when people sent telegrams and cables – because they paid for each word, nonessential words were simply left out.) In the following extracts, we have done our best to reconstruct something more akin to normal writing (restoring grammatical words and even objects and full verbs).

Hawks running four on two
Bruten to Saddle
Bruten goes alley-oop
Oh, risky play
Cook pulls it in

Drimik knocks it away
Ritter with the follow

[The Hawks are running with four players on two. Bruten passes the ball to Saddle. Bruten goes for the alley-oop [= a pass caught above the height of the rim and converted into a slam dunk in one move]. Oh, this is risky play. Cook pulls it in. Drimik knocks it away. Ritter shoots the ball with the follow.]

Flexibility of word order

Unscripted commentary shows the flexibility and expressiveness of word order that is typical of spontaneous speech. Certainly commentators exploit unusual sequences to highlight or to contrast more salient information. In addition, the fact that they are speaking off-the-cuff and having to describe events as they unfold results in widespread infringements of the norms of English syntax.

Fighting hard is Jason Smith

Subjects and verbs are often inverted. In the case of a basketball commentary, this is probably less a focus strategy and more a survival technique – a means of delaying mention of a player's name until the identity is known for sure.

Spears the pass into Pepper does Kelly

Sporting commentary exploits other strategies too like left- and right-dislocation. Typically examples occur as side comments on the events taking place or in the between-action commentary. The intention seems to be to make referential assignment clearer, or to lend focus to referents by setting them apart from the rest of the sentence.

Ronaldson, Drimik, Pepper and McDonald, those five [sic] will go the rest of the way
Really gotta try and get a couple of cheap baskets here, The Hawks

Passive

Passives are surprisingly frequent in this sort of discourse, perhaps because they offer another handy delaying technique – if the commentator hasn't yet identified the player, the passive provides some breathing space.

He's held from behind by David Smith

If the patient is the highly obvious and not particularly interesting 'basketball' then it's usually missing (as part of the more general strategy to omit 'very given' information).

Knocked away by McDonald

Occasionally the agent (in the *by*-phrase) gets omitted too and the focus shifts to the patient or recipient of the action. Usually this is because the agent is irrelevant information, or because it is already obvious. In the following this is the umpire:

Campbell being called for the foul

Heavy noun phrase modification

From the previous extracts you can see that basketball commentary is full of noun phrases that are heavy with modifiers, particularly post-modifiers like prepositional phrases, relative clauses, appositional noun phrases (which restate the noun), and even postposed adjectives. The frequency of modified proper nouns (*The never-say-die Wollongong Hawks*) also distinguishes it from other varieties. This extensive modification is the by-product of the widespread ellipsis, especially of verbs. These overloaded NPs are an economical way of packing information into the event-reporting clause.

Overloaded NPs are not confined to the unscripted commentary of events. Examples like the following are also typical of the commentators' background discussions. You even find them in sports sections of newspapers.

So there's Brian Gorgen the coach of the Victorian Titans the team winning by 21 with 8.48 remaining

Present tense

Sports commentary is unusual in its use of the present tense. You might be wondering why this is remarkable – after all, basketball commentary reports events happening at the time. But if you recall the discussion of tense in Section 6.2, present tense is rarely used now to report strictly present time. In ordinary language, it reports habitual actions as in *I play basketball*. The use of present tense in basketball casting makes for particularly lively narrative sequences and gives considerable dramatic force to a commentary. It also appears to distinguish it from football commentary (at least of the two we are familiar with – Soccer and Australian Rules), which is more prone to use the progressive.

Saval gets it in

Campbell quick release shot

He makes it

2 point basket, back to the 16 point split

Hawks extend the D here, McDonald crosses halfway

They turn it over and Bruten comes up with it

Bureaucratese

At some stage in your lives you will no doubt have encountered the sort of incomprehensible language now commonly dubbed *gobbledygook*. We encounter gobbledygook in many different domains: the law, education, and linguistics, to name just a few of them. More usually, though, it's a label used to describe the language of government; in other words, Bureaucratese. Gobbledygook can of course be both spoken and written, but we will concentrate here on writing.

One overwhelming feature of written Bureaucratese is its grammatical complexity. Indeed, both Bureaucratese and its relative Legalese are what can be described as highly syntacticised registers, the apex of our developing writing tradition. It's this complexity in combination with obscure vocabulary that makes these varieties at times so befuddling and so offensive to their readers. Not surprisingly there has been quite a backlash against this sort of writing. Currently there are many social and political movements pushing for clear and simple English, particularly in laws, legal documents like contracts and government documents of all kinds. There are now 'Plain English' movements in Britain, America, Australia and New Zealand. (But this is by no means confined to the English-speaking world. In Sweden there has long been a push for comprehensible Swedish officialese in place of *byråkratsvenska* – in fact, parallel cries can be heard all over Europe, and there is an International Plain Language Working Group which meets regularly.) Plain English campaigns have had great success in eradicating many of the grammatical horrors. Nonetheless, we still receive letters from people frustrated at some piece of virtually unintelligible official language that they have received. Doublespeak awards are still bestowed annually in America. Clearly, not all the problems of gobbledygook have been eradicated.

Let's look now at some of the grammatical features that have become the target of the cleaning up activities of the various Plain English movements around the world. Consider the following example: two passages 2 (a) (i) and 2 (b) taken from clause 28 of the Melbourne Metropolitan Planning Scheme. As you read these passages, you might like to imagine you are about to convert an inner-city warehouse into five flats and you need to figure out how many car parking spaces you will have to provide for these flats. [We are very grateful to Pia Herbert for providing this example – and for her insightful comments!]

(2) (a) (i) Provision for accommodation of stationary vehicles (not being brought or kept on the land for sale, hire, repair, service or refuelling) shall be made upon any land used or developed or intended to be used or developed for any purpose specified in Column 1 of Table 1 of this Clause not less than in the ratio or of the percentage of site area specified in Column 2 and quantified in Column 3 of such Table, but so that the number of car spaces to be provided shall be not less than the nearest whole number to the number arrived at when the ratio or percentage is applied, and the use or occupation of the development of any such land for the purpose specified in the said Column shall not be commenced until the requisite accommodation for stationary vehicles has been provided.

(b) Notwithstanding the provisions of paragraph (a) hereof the responsible authority may grant permission for a reduction in the number of car spaces to be provided or required to be provided upon any land for the accommodation of stationary vehicles if to its satisfaction and subject to such conditions as it may impose provision is made upon other land in the vicinity for the accommodation of such vehicles and the number of car spaces so provided is not less than that by which the number provided or required to be provided is to be reduced. For the purpose of this paragraph 'reduction' includes the wavering of the requirement and 'reduced' has a corresponding meaning.

Grammatical complexity

Sub-clause 2 (a) (i) consists entirely of one sentence, comprising 141 words; sub-clause 2 (b) consists of two sentences, comprising 94 and 19 words, respectively. In addition to their extreme length, these sentences are complex in structure. We've already seen plenty of examples of parataxis and we now move to the other end of the spectrum – HYPOTAXIS; in other words, clauses linked by means of overt subordinating markers. Hypotaxis is the earmark of this sort of prose. Examine the previous two passages and try to identify and classify all the subordinate clauses. As you do so, note the characteristic dearth of punctuation, particularly in sub-clause 2 (b).

What makes language like this so befuddling is not only the complexity but also the consistent violation of what has been dubbed Behagel's First Law, namely, 'that which belongs together cognitively is arranged close together' (our translation). For example, notice the huge gap between the subject and its verb at the beginning of sub-clause 2 (a) (i): *Provision for accommodation of stationary vehicles (not being brought or kept on the land for sale, hire, repair, service or refuelling) shall be made* . . . The interruption of the significant proposition in the main clause makes it difficult for readers to extract the information.

In the exercises at the end of this chapter we give you a taste of more examples of this kind of writing. Take a look at the sentence in exercise 3 (Subsection 27 (12) from the Companies (Acquisition of Shares) (Victoria) Code). It begins with a conditional clause 'Where . . .,' which contains no less than four relative clauses. It's not until halfway down the passage that we first encounter the main clause. The image that often comes to mind is one of Chinese boxes (or Russian dolls, if you prefer) – a complex of constantly embedded clauses.

Word order

We have seen how specialised registers writers or speakers will deviate significantly from basic ordering and this can actually enhance comprehension – in the case of sports commentary the ordering reflects events as they unfold. In the case of the language of law and bureaucracy, however, unusual word orders often cause problems. Note the fronting of the long adverbial string *to its satisfaction and subject to such conditions as it may impose* in the conditional *if* clause of sub-clause 2 (b). This has the effect of significantly delaying the appearance of the conditional clause subject (*provision*) and its predicate, which in effect withholds the context the reader needs in order to properly understand the information in this fronted adverbial string. In Chapter 9 we saw how the chaining effect of old followed by new information gives a piece of discourse its coherence. In passages like this one there is no clear topic–comment arrangement and no common thread to follow. The constant shifting of topic blurs the focus of the discourse – the point of the passage becomes lost.

Lack of anaphora

As mentioned earlier, '-eses' like Bureaucratese and Legalese are characterised by a dearth of anaphoric expressions. In place of some sort of pro-expression, full NPs like *the accommodation of stationary vehicles* are repeated. The repetition of full NPs removes any doubt as to the intended referent and was originally motivated by the degree of precision demanded by the legal profession. But if precision were the only issue, why do writers often vary the full NP? For example, the writer of sub-clause 2 (b) alternates between *off-street accommodation of stationary vehicles* and *car spaces* – should we understand that these things are somehow different? Indeed, as we said at the start, even in Legalese there are many occasions where the use of a pronoun would be quite unambiguous and the lack of anaphora seems more a matter of stylistic choice. Features like lexical repetition can turn into self-perpetuating idiosyncrasies of registers. They become a grammatical routine.

Nominalisation

English has many derivational affixes (see Section 3.1) which can turn verbs into nouns. The phrases that function as subject(s) and object(s) then get a new syntactic role. For example, *We provide car spaces* can be turned into *The provision of car spaces* or *The provision for accommodation of stationary vehicles*. Both these more nominal versions appear in Clause 28. (Note, the agent has now disappeared.)

You can see how such a heavily nominal style introduces more abstractness. Compare the complex nominalisation in (a) with its verbal counterpart in (b).

(a) in the event of default in the payment

(b) if you don't pay what you owe

As the (a) version illustrates, a nominal style gives speakers the opportunity of being non-committal as to who is doing what to whom – a sneaky device, you might be thinking, and one eminently suited to the language of government offices, where it might be desirable to conceal precisely this sort of information! Turning verbs into nouns allows us to do away with subjects and objects – *we executed the prisoner* can become *the execution of the prisoner by us* or simply *the execution*.

Nominal strings

Another earmark, and one that distinguishes bureaucratic writing from 'ordinary' usage, is the propensity for compounding. Unfortunately our extracts from the Melbourne Metropolitan Planning Scheme don't happen to offer good examples this time, but ones from elsewhere are easy to find. Coagulated clusters of nominals like *occupational choice–vocational interest congruency; backlog reduction object; prototype crisis shelter development plans;* and *young driver risk-taking research* surely stretch the limits of what are considered acceptable compounds. Like nominalisations, these compounds are economical but difficult to process. They introduce more density and more abstractness into a piece of writing that is already lexically dense and abstract.

Synonym strings also contribute to the density. Take the infamous doublets and triplets of Legalese where two or three (near) synonyms are strung together: *act and deed; cease and desist; rest, residue and remainder; will and testament.*

Passives

Both sub-clauses contain a high frequency of passives, especially agentless passives; for example, *Provision . . . shall be made; land used or developed or intended to be used or developed; the number of car spaces to be provided; the ratio or percentage is applied; the development . . . shall not be commenced; the requisite accommodation for stationary vehicles has been provided.*

The passive is a striking feature of this prose and the *bête noire* of many Plain English translators, who see it as a source of confusion for readers. But the problem of passives has been overstated. Here the agentless passive enables the writer to omit elements that would otherwise have to be stated in the active version. As we saw in Chapter 9 and earlier in this chapter, agents get left out often because they are irrelevant, uninteresting, or because they are already obvious.

This doesn't mean of course that writers don't occasionally misuse the passive. For example, agentless passives can provide another sneaky strategy. Perhaps you want to downplay your involvement in a particular unpopular event. A sentence like the following that uses both nominalisation and passive allows you to omit any reference to yourself. *The decision has been made* [but by whom?] *to continue this line of action.* Compare *I have decided to continue this line of action.* Agentless passives are also characteristic of the impersonal (some would argue pretentious) style found in a lot of academic writing, particularly from science. And because it is reminiscent of more prestigious registers, it can have the effect of making even the most simple and mundane things sound complex and profound. Pia Herbert has given us a wonderful anecdote that is relevant here. Amidst all the excitement and media hype surrounding the release of the brand-new Plain English version of the Melbourne Metropolitan Planning Scheme the following carefully drafted departmental memo appeared out of the offices of the former City of Fitzroy in Melbourne; it concerned council rubbish collection:

287

Refuse and rubbish shall not be collected from the site or receptacles thereon before the hour of 8.00 am or after the hour of 6.00 pm of any day.

Some linguistic habits die hard!

Negatives

Another earmark of Bureaucratese is a type of understatement called LITO-TES, namely, the expression of an affirmative in terms of the negative of the contrary, e.g. *a not insignificant amount; not unnaturally*. If you think this needlessly complicates things, you're right – it is well established that multiple negatives pose difficulties for cognitive processes.

Another feature is the general stacking of negatives and we see plenty of examples of this in the Melbourne Metropolitan Planning Scheme: *the number of car spaces so provided is not less than . . .; provided any existing accommodation for stationary vehicles is not diminished and the purpose . . . does not differ . . .; Notwithstanding the provisions of paragraphs (a) and (b) hereof.* The difficulty stems from not only overtly negative markers like *not, never* and *un-*, but also semantically negative words like *default, diminish* and negative connectors like *unless, except, provided that* and *however*.

I couldn't exactly not say . . .

Litotes is beautifully parodied in the following exchange between Prince Charming and Pinocchio from *Shrek the Third*:

Prince Charming: You're telling me you don't know where Shrek is?

Pinocchio: It wouldn't be inaccurate to assume that I couldn't exactly not say that it is or isn't almost partially incorrect.

Prince Charming: So you do know where he is!

Pinocchio: On the contrary. I'm possibly more or less not definitely rejecting the idea that in no way with any amount of uncertainty that I undeniably

Prince Charming: Stop it!

In a footnote in his famous essay *Politics and the English Language* (1946), George Orwell offered some therapeutic advice for the treatment of the *not un-X* construction:

One can cure oneself of the *not un-* formation by memorizing this sentence: *A not unblack dog was chasing a not unsmall rabbit across a not ungreen field.*

10.5 Points to remember

❏ Different situations call for different varieties. Register is the name generally given to varieties associated with particular contexts or purposes.

❏ Registers can be distinguished at various levels of generality. At one extreme are general registers to do with physical mode – speech or writing. At the other extreme are highly specialised registers such as journalese or computer-speak – registers involving occupational varieties peculiar to trades, professions or any other group sharing a special interest.

❏ Speech and writing are very different forms of communication, each with their own expressive capabilities. Speech has its own repertoire of devices like intonation, stress, pitch, speed, silence, laughter and voice quality; it shows a complexity in structure that is quite different from that of writing.

❏ E-speak is a very different medium of communication that comprises properties of both speech and writing, as well as the properties exhibited by electronic texts.

❏ In addition to lexical and phonological features, registers have distinctive grammatical and discourse structures.

❏ Features of basketball commentary, and sports commentary in general, include greater flexibility of word order, passives, heavy noun phrase modification, present tense and ellipsis.

❏ Features of Bureaucratese include lexical density, grammatical complexity (hypotaxis), agentless passives, and a rich exuberance of negatives.

❏ Register distinctions derive from the relative distribution of linguistic features. For each register we can identify a bundle of frequently occurring grammatical and lexical characteristics that makes that register distinctive.

Exercises

1. What makes a register distinctive?

Provide a sample (about a paragraph of text will do) of a special register/occupational variety. It can involve any medium (you could choose one of the registers discussed in the chapter, but it would be better to select a different one). In around 800 words describe the grammatical features (or combination of features) that earmark this variety as being distinctive.

Note, that this should be in essay format (i.e. **not point form**) and you should back up your account with illustrative examples taken from your sample (these don't count in the word length).

2. Journalese

A distinction is often made between broadsheets (newspapers for the serious reader) and tabloids (more popular newspapers). Take a report of the same event from two such newspapers. Describe and analyse the grammatical features that make each journalistic style distinctive. Do you find significant differences in language between these two newspaper types, or do you think the distinction between broadsheets and tabloids is blurring? Crystal and Davy have described the language of the tabloid press as 'an echo of the rhythms of colloquial speech' (1969: 185) – is this still a distinctive feature of the tabloid style?

3. Legalese

The following is a piece of Legalese. Identify the combination of features that is the source of confusion for readers here. Why is it so difficult to extract the information?

Now try your hand at writing a Plain English translation of this piece. What has your rewritten version done to redress the problems?

Subsection 27 (12) from the Companies (Acquisition of Shares) (Victoria) Code:

> Where an offeree who has accepted a take-over offer that is subject to a prescribed condition receives a copy of a notice under sub-section (10) in relation to a variation of offers under the relevant take-over scheme, being a variation the effect of which is to postpone for a period exceeding one month the time when the offeror's obligations under the take-over scheme are to be satisfied, the offeree may, by notice in writing given to the offeror within one month after receipt of the first-mentioned notice and accompanied by any consideration that has been received by the offeree (together with any necessary documents of transfer), withdraw his acceptance of the offer and, where such a notice is given by the offeree to the offeror and is accompanied by any such consideration and any necessary documents of transfer, the offeror shall return to the offeree within 14 days after receipt of the notice, any documents that were sent by the offeree to the offeror with the acceptance of the offer.

4. Spoken language

Here is a piece of spontaneous conversation. Describe the features that distinguish it from writing. (Review the conventions for writing spoken English outlined in the chapter. Also note that a question mark here indicates rising intonation.)

M: And,
M: as when C developed glandular fever,
M: and she caught glandular fever in hospital with [J]?
C: [Ooh].

M: And she thought she had post-natal depression.
M: . . . And that's all they treated her for.
M: And so that was 16th of October J was born.
C: I expect the symptoms would be very similar.
M: Hmm.
C: Absolutely.
C: [Hav]ing had glandular fever.
M: [And] –
M: wasn't diagnosed,
M: until the long weekend in January,
M: which she had actually glandular fever at the time.
M: . . . She was nearly beside herself be[cause] they would give her,
C: [Yes]
M: Amoxil,
M: which is a penicillin [thing].
C: [Yeees].
M: Well see it has no effect at all.
M: And umm,
M: all you need is rest.

[Many thanks to Julie Reid for this example.]

5. Grammatical features of E-speak

Consider the list of grammatical features of spoken (versus written) language from this chapter and, using a passage of electronic communication of your choice, describe how the passage you have selected relates to spoken and/or written features of language. To what extent are the two systems mixed in your example? Are there particular features of speech that participants work especially hard to render in their writing? What purpose do these features serve? (You should give examples to support your analysis.)

English worldwide

11.1 Introduction

Our world is now well and truly global in orientation – never before have we seen so many people from different language backgrounds wanting to chat to each other. The need for international intelligibility coupled with a series of geographical, cultural, economic and political episodes has secured – at least for the moment – the position of English as a global *lingua franca* or common language. So when Homer Simpson says *English? Who needs that? I'm never going to England!* he is way off the mark and not just because English is the standard language in the United States. Worldwide opportunities involving trade, international travel, satellite broadcasting, the information superhighway, world press, world stock markets and multinational corporations have changed the concept of the English speech community beyond recognition. No longer are we simply looking at a group of people bound together because they live close by and speak the same language. The world's population is approaching eight billion and a staggering proportion of this eight billion are already regular users of English – approximately one person out of every five speaks English to some level of competence.

Recall what we said at the beginning of this book. When varieties come to dominate in this way, it has nothing to do with any inherent linguistic superiority, but rather economic, political and social context. During the 19th century it was British political imperialism that sent the language around the globe and the legacy of this is still felt today. Even when the pink bits on the map (signalling the Empire) started to disappear, many of the newly independent nations (especially in Africa and the Pacific) ended up choosing English as an official or semi-official language – its global success made it a handy language, especially as a *lingua franca* for multilingual nations. The 20th century saw America takeover from Britain as the leading nation, giving English another winning card – the fact that North America was English speaking.

While the 'success' of English might be good news for English speakers, bear in mind that one of the effects of the worldwide movement of English and its use as an international language is widespread linguistic destruction. Around the world, languages are dying and at distressing rates – American Indian, Celtic, Australian Aboriginal, Austronesian and Papuan languages, to name just a few (UNESCO provides an atlas of endangered languages on their website). Even in those places where local languages appear healthy, the high status of bulldozer languages like English (and Mandarin Chinese, Hindi and Indonesian) suggests their survival is precarious.

The spread of English around the globe has triggered a burgeoning of diversity in the form of new dialects, second language varieties, pidgins, creoles and mixed languages, all influenced by the many different cultures and languages it has come in contact with. A singular designation of English is no longer adequate to describe a language that now involves almost every linguistic area in the world. As David Crystal once put it: 'No one nation can any longer be said to "own" English.' Non-native speakers are now outnumbering native speakers three to one. It's not even clear whether such labels as 'native speaker' and 'non-native speaker' remain appropriate – the sociolinguistic situation is far more complex than simple labels suggest.

In this short chapter, there is no way we can do justice to the remarkable range of morpho-syntactic features found in the Englishes worldwide. We therefore restrict ourselves to a small number. We begin by looking at Indian English, one of the so-called New Englishes; for people who speak this variety, it is usually not their first language and hence this kind of English is often referred to as L2 (second language) or ESL (English as a Second Language), even though such labels are misleading. According to the 2001 Census the number of English speakers in India was more than 125 million, and many of those consider English their primary language.

We then move on to consider some of the typical features of the new contact varieties of English known as pidgins and creoles (the so-called Other Englishes). Here we have selected three Pacific creoles that had their roots in earlier Melanesian Pidgin; namely, Bislama (Vanuatu), Pijin (Solomon Islands) and Tok Pisin (Papua New Guinea). And lest you think that exotic-looking morpho-syntax can only be found in the new varieties of English, we conclude by briefly considering some striking non-standard features that appear in some of the Native Englishes around the world (L1 or ENL – English as a Native Language). We will have to ignore here the huge number of consumers of English who frequently use it as their international language, both in work and in play (sometimes dubbed EFL speakers or English as a Foreign Language). The estimated number of these users of English is around a billion, but it is hard to estimate because numbers are growing so remarkably quickly and we are also potentially dealing with such a wide range of abilities – from fully competent speakers to those millions with just a smattering of English.

It is difficult in such short summaries to convey the rich diversity that exists in these varieties. As we discussed in Chapter 1, the reality is that speakers from different regions, from different social classes, of different ages, of different occupations, of different gender identification, of different sexual orientation will all talk differently. People talk differently in different contexts, too – an informal chat, an interview, a lecture and so on. Labels like 'Indian English' or 'Australian English' are simply convenient cover terms for what are really clumps or clusters of mutually intelligible speech varieties. In the case of the New and Other Englishes, the variation is particularly striking. There are two main linguistic factors involved here: (1) the influence of local vernacular languages (which may or may not be the first language of speakers) and (2) contact with English (particularly for urban groups, a growing force of influence). Typically, these languages range along a continuum of varying features and abilities, from varieties close to Standard English in everything but accent (the 'acrolects') through to varieties that are not mutually intelligible with the standard (the 'basilects'). Situated between these two polar extremes, there exists a range of varieties (or 'mesolects'). Speakers have command of a number of these linguistic types and use depends on the situation and the audience. In the grammatical sketches we provide here, we will be drawing features from the mesolectal and basilectal varieties, since these are where the morphological and syntactic innovations are the most interesting.

11.2 New Englishes: Indian English

English is now the official or co-official language in more than 75 countries; they include places with colonial associations with Britain or America, as well as those without these traditional links. In many cases, the varieties in these regions have such distinct grammar, vocabulary, pronunciation and conventions of use that they are labelled 'New Englishes.' Examples include Singapore English, Malaysian English, Hong Kong English and Indian English. The rise of these new varieties has been a major motivation for the status of English as a global language. In some of these places we even are seeing English shifting from L2 and stabilising as L1. In Singapore, for example, the majority of children are now growing up speaking English as an L1 – so English as a second first language.

The variety we focus on here is Indian English. English came into India as early as 1600 with the establishment of the East India Company. Here it encountered a range of Indic, Dravidian, Munda and Tibeto-Burman languages, and this did much to shape the linguistic varieties that emerged. By the time India had gained its independence from Britain in 1947, English was firmly entrenched. Today it enjoys associate official status and continues to play an important role in government, the courts, higher education, the media and other public domains. Standard Indian English differs little in its core grammar from the mainstream standards. In the vernacular variety, however, differences are more striking and it's these we focus on here. Our descriptions are based on accounts provided in Sedlatschek (2009) and Bhat (2008). On occasion, we also consider features from Indian South African English, which (as described by Mesthrie 2008) differs from its antecedent in India due to influence from other second language varieties of English in South Africa and the substrate languages, in particular Tamil and Bhojpuri. (You will find these publications, and more, listed in the 'References and further reading' section at the end of this book.)

Verbs and verb phrases

Indian English differs from Standard English in a number of salient features to do with tense and aspect. One is the extended use of the progressive beyond the standard contexts of use (as we described them in Chapter 7):

❑ In place of the perfect with adverbial phrases of time:

I'm staying this house seven year.

❑ With stative verbs:

You must be knowing him.
I am understanding you.

This variety also shares with many others the generalisation of the present perfect to simple past contexts of use. For example, the present perfect may occur with past time adverbials, where Standard English can only have simple past:

They've done that three years ago.

I have read this book yesterday.

A further difference is that in construction with *since*, Indian English uses the present where Standard English is more likely to use the perfect:

I am here since 1972.

There is also a more widespread use of the past perfect in contexts where standard usage would demand other tense forms. As the following extract from a student essay illustrates, one function of the past perfect is to signal distant pastness:

> *Today if we look back around hundred years ago we will find that there <u>had been</u> a lot of change in our Indian society. Or in other words we can say that there <u>had been</u> a lot of developments in our Indian society with the adoption of western culture. As the <u>time had passed</u> western culture had given us lot of knowledge and ways to develop our culture.*
>
> (Sedlatschek 2009: 266–267)

Another often cited 'Indianism' is variation within auxiliaries. For example, *would* and *could* appear as polite and tentative forms in place of *will* and *can*:

I would be going to New York this weekend.

Compare the standard use of these modals in interrogatives like *Would you shut the window* versus *Will you shut the window*. The modal may also appears in place of *should* as an expression of polite obligation:

These mistakes may please be corrected. (These mistakes should be corrected.)

Nouns and noun phrases

A common feature of New Englishes generally is article variability. For some time, it was assumed that the apparent whimsical dropping or inserting of the articles in Indian English was simply the result of second language learning difficulties with Standard English articles and substrate influences from Hindi or Tamil:

Let's go to city.

He is not aware of hardship of life.

Women can prove to be a great help to the humanity.

More recent studies, however, have uncovered a more systematic use of articles that has grown out of the standard system (for full details, see Sedlatschek 2009: Ch. 5).

We have already seen that English dialects do not necessarily see eye to eye as to whether nouns are individuated entities or groups of unindividuated entities. In short, what is a count noun in one variety may be a mass noun in another and vice versa. Indian English has examples of non-count nouns used as count nouns, as in *furnitures, apparels, deadwoods, equipments*. However, a count noun like *biscuit* used as a non-count noun is less usual.

Simple sentences

We have seen that colloquial spoken versions of Standard English sometimes allow the subject pronoun to be omitted in those contexts where the reference is recoverable, like diary writing. Pro-drop (the dropping of pronouns in certain contexts) is much more widespread in Indian English. In vernacular Indian English, it is common in both subject and object position:

(Question: *You got the tickets?) No, sold already.*

(Question: *Doesn't his wife work now somewhere?) Yes, teaches at school here locally.*

This variety also does not require dummy subjects *it* or *there*:

Is clear that he will not come.

Rained yesterday only.

Word order varies from the standard in a number of ways. Adverbials appear late in the clause:

They're late always.

Adverbials can also intervene between the verb and its complement, especially when there is some focus on the complement:

He will buy over there tickets only.

Although the basic ordering of constituents in Indian English is Subject-Verb-Everything Else (= SVX), a number of varieties show unusual word order patterns for an SVX language; these are the result of influence from the substrate languages. South African Indian English, for example, shows some use of postpositions (*side, time, part, way*):

I'm going Fountain Head-side tomorrow. (I'm going towards Fountain Head tomorrow.)

Afternoon-part gets too hot. (It gets too hot in the afternoon.)

This variety also has coordinated structures that are very different from those we discussed in Chapter 8. Note the lack of ellipsis in the following example, and the *too* in clause-final position:

I made rice too, I made roti too.

In *wh*-interrogatives, the *wh*-phrase moves to the front of the clause, but there is no inversion of subject and operator. You might compare examples like the following with the colloquial (but perfectly standard) '*how come* construction,' which also lacks inversion (*How come you're arriving so late?*).

What he has eaten? (What has he eaten?)

When you are coming home? (When are you coming home?)

One surprising feature of vernacular Indian English is that it allows multiple *wh*-words in initial position (and note the order of the *wh*-phrases is object – subject):

What who has eaten? (Who has eaten what?)

This variety also shows the invariant tags that we described in Chapter 5 as occurring in varieties all round the English-speaking world:

You are going home soon, isn't it?

Note that negative responses to *yes–no* interrogatives are answered positively:

(Question: *Didn't I see you yesterday in college?*) *Yes, you didn't see me yesterday in college.*

(Question: *You didn't come on the bus?*) *Yes, I didn't.*

Complex sentences

Indian English shows considerable variation with respect to the possibilities of subordinate clauses that are built around the *to*-infinitive form of the verb. The following is but one example:

We are involved to collect poems.

297

There are also striking differences with respect to the formation of interrogative sub-clauses. Unlike Standard Indian English, vernacular varieties show subject–operator inversion:

I wonder where does he work? (I wonder where he works?)

Do you know where is he going? (Do you know where he is going?)

Recall that in vernacular Indian English, regular *wh*-interrogatives show no inversion; so the general pattern of interrogative formation here is the mirror image of the standard pattern we outlined in Section 5.3.

Indian English has a wide variety of strategies for forming relative clauses. For example, in South African Indian English constructions range from those that are just like the standard (*People who come an' visit without phoning first make her cross*) to some very unEnglish substrate-influenced structures as in *People who got working here for them sons . . .*, which is equivalent to *People who've got sons who are working here . . .* The following is a selection of these clauses (from Mesthrie 2008: 508–509).

Almost standard relative clauses:

That's the maid which one was here. (That's the maid who was here.)

(non-standard relative pronoun)

We talking about my friend lives down here. (We're talking about my friend who lives down here.)

(missing subject relative pronoun)

Substrate-influenced relative clauses:

Which-car they supposed to give us, someone else got it. (Someone else got the car which they were supposed to give us.)

(the *wh*-relative has an anaphoric counterpart (here *it*) in the main clause; the full NP appears in the preceding sub-clause (here *which-car*))

That's all we had trouble. (That's all the trouble we had.)

(pre-nominal relative clause; no relative pronoun)

Discourse organisation

Topicalisation structures are a characteristic of this variety, the most frequently focused constituent being the object noun phrase; adverbials (of time and place) are also common:

These people I telephoned yesterday only.

Alone you came.

Change I haven't got.

Near to Margate that is.

This word order is by no means a feature unique to Indian English but is widespread in colloquial varieties of even Standard English worldwide. We also saw examples like these in earlier chapters and Star Wars fans will immediately recognise Yoda's syntax here (think examples of Yodish like *Tired I am, rest I must*). What distinguishes examples like these from those that occur in the standard language, however, is that the fronting is not always triggered by discourse considerations. Mesthrie (2008: 517) gives the example: *Your tablet you took?* It occurs at the beginning of a stretch of discourse, with no sense of givenness or contrast (in other words, there had been no previous discussion of illness or medication). Another distinctly Indian feature is that these topicalised structures also occur in sub-clauses:

His friends know that her parents, he doesn't like at all; Indians, I donno why they like that!

11.3 Other Englishes

Because of their unique development, pidgin/creole varieties are often labelled as 'Other Englishes.' Generally speaking, pidgins are a type of make-shift language that springs up when speakers of different linguistic backgrounds come into contact and need to talk. In the formation of a pidgin, there are always two (or more) languages that are involved, although the pidgin takes one language, usually the socially dominant one, as its point of origin for the lexicon. This language contributes most of the vocabulary, though significant features of the grammar are likely to derive from other sources. Traditionally, people thought of these languages as simply debased forms of English and they used derogatory labels such as 'broken English' and 'gibberish.' This 'me Tarzan – you Jane' image for pidgins is totally inaccurate. Pidgins quite clearly have their own grammars; they are not simply 'broken' Englishes. However, they do differ from other varieties in a number of respects: they aren't anybody's first language but are used when speakers venture outside their usual speech community; because they are used in limited contexts, pidgins lack the range of stylistic variation characteristic of a normal language; they also make do with reduced vocabularies and require far less complex and flexible structures (English-based pidgins are syntactically and morphologically much simpler than the variety of English on which they are based.)

Typically, a pidgin is short-lived. Speakers abandon it in favour of the source language, or if the contact ceases, the pidgin will simply die. However, if the situation stabilises, and the contact continues, change is typically rapid, especially in vocabulary and grammar, as the makeshift pidgin metamorphoses into a fully fledged and dynamic language, able to serve its speakers in all kinds of settings and circumstances. In theory, it is straightforward to say when a pidgin ends and a creole begins. As soon as children in a community are brought up speaking the pidgin as their first language, it becomes a creole. Accordingly, a creole is simply a nativised pidgin. The linguistic reality, however, is another matter; linguistically it is impossible to say where the boundary lies. Even before a pidgin becomes somebody's first language, it can develop a highly elaborated structure (close to that of a creole), if it is used for a number of different purposes. For this reason, some linguists avoid the labels 'pidgin' and 'creole' and refer to these varieties straightforwardly as 'contact languages.'

Because of their common origin, Bislama, Pijin and Tok Pisin share a number of characteristics and, unless we specify a creole, you can assume that the feature is common to all three (our descriptions here are based on Crowley 2008; Jourdan 2008; Smith 2008; Dutton 1985; see the 'References and further reading' section). As you might predict, however, these creoles are now growing further apart and differences are emerging, especially because of contact with native vernaculars in the region. Many speakers also know a local variety of Standard English and switch regularly between this and their creole. The label 'variety of English' might seem problematic when dealing with these creoles, especially at the basilectal end of the continuum. The very 'unEnglish-looking' structures that characterise creoles, as well as their unique development (as contact languages resulting from pidgins), set them apart. There is also the question of the lack of mutual comprehension – creoles have their own distinctive grammars, and when spoken by fluent speakers are not mutually intelligible with Standard English. The speakers themselves would never call their language a kind of English. Nonetheless, these contact languages share vocabulary and grammatical features that align them with the English of the international community. All can be said to have some sort of historical connection to the group of continental Germanic dialects that ended up in the British Isles sometime in the fifth century AD, and for this reason we have included them here.

Verbs and verb phrases

Contact situations are generally calamitous for inflectional morphology – when languages come into contact with one another, it can have a kind of grammatical stripping effect. We need only look at English to see how contact with French and Norse speakers sped up the changes that led to the demise of its inflectional system. Not surprisingly then, these contact varieties all display limited morphology for both nouns and verbs. However, as the creoles stabilise they start creating new verbal morphology via the normal processes of language change. Often these developments involve the reanalysis of what were originally English lexical and grammatical forms. For example, these creoles all add some kind of suffix -Vm (where V = vowel) to the end of (most) transitive verbs. This represents the reanalysis of the third person singular masculine object pronoun *him*. Here are some examples from Tok Pisin:

dring (to be drinking)	*dringim* (to drink (something))
marit (be married)	*maritim* (to marry (someone))
gaiman (to be lying)	*giamanim* (to deceive (someone))
	(early slang – *gammon* 'humbug, rubbish')

This has become an extremely productive suffix in these languages and any new verbs entering the language (from, say, English) will appear with -*Vm*; for example, Bislama *imel-im* 'email (someone).' However, there is a group of typically common usage transitive verbs, such as, *save* 'know' and *luk* 'see,' which regularly appear without any suffix. (This sort of unusual behaviour suggests that something interesting is going on with this group of verbs.)

Verbs are typically unmarked for tense. Depending on the context, Bislama *Mi kam* can mean 'I am coming,' 'I came' or 'I will come.' If necessary, speakers can add extra sentence modifiers such as *bin* or *bae* to indicate either past or future time: *Mi bin kam* 'I came' and *Bae mi kam* 'I will come.' Increasingly, it is becoming normal to include this sort of information, even when it is clear from context. For example, Tok Pisin has now quite a range of temporal, aspectual and modality particles (usually preverbal). Some of these are listed next; see if you can make out the English words that have given rise to these grammatical forms.

bai/baimbai (future)
laik (proximal future)
bin (past)
klosap (inceptive)
pinis (perfect)
save (habitual)
stap (continuous)
inap (ability)
ken (permission)
mas (necessity)

In the creoles of this area, reduplication is widespread as a productive feature of verb morphology and one that is markedly different from other varieties of English. It is usually partial reduplication, involving the repetition of the first syllable or first two syllables of the verb root (or material from these syllables). The pattern is generally used to indicate intensity, duration or repetition of an action; for example Pijin *kra/karae* 'cry' versus *kakarae* 'cry continuously.' It can also express reciprocal action, as in Bislama *save* 'know' versus *savsave* 'know each other.'

These languages have a range of negators that generally appear in front of the verb and any tense markers (without *do*-support). For example,

Bislama has *no* which can combine with the emphatic marker *nating* or *wanpis* after the verb:

You no save kam. (You cannot come.)

Mi no bin toktok nating. (I didn't talk at all.)

Nouns and noun phrases

Before we launch into the structure of noun phrases, first a note about pronouns. The pronominal paradigms of these creoles are at the same time simpler and more complex than what we find in the standard language. While forms are not distinguished for case or for gender (for example, Bislama third person *hem* is gender neutral), the systems generally allow for a much more elaborate set of distinctions involving dual and sometimes also trial number. Hence, the two-way number system of English has been expanded into a four-way system: singular (= one), dual (= two), trial (= three) and plural (= more than three). First person non-singular forms also distinguish between something called 'inclusive' and 'exclusive.' This is a handy feature. Say, someone said to you *We should go now*, you cannot be sure whether you are included in this *we* or not. Bislama forms like the following make the meaning explicit:

yumitu(fala) (first dual, including you)

yumitrifala (first trial, including you)

yumi (first plural, including you)

mitufala (first dual, excluding you)

mitrifala (first trial, excluding you)

mifala (first plural, excluding you)

These categorial distinctions have arisen via influence from the substrate languages and they overcome the ambiguity of the first person plural pronoun in Standard English.

Number on nouns tends to be implicit in the context and if it is indicated at all, it is generally not on the noun but via some kind of free-standing quantifier, such as *olketa/olgeta ~ ol* 'all.' In these languages, the shortened form *ol* is well on its way to becoming a plural marker (e.g. Bislama *olgata man* 'all the people/men' versus *ol man* 'people, men'). Pressure of Standard English is also seeing a handful of nouns being marked both morphologically and analytically (i.e. via a free-standing form); e.g. Pijin *olketa gels* 'the girls.'

Possessive constructions in these contact varieties generally show the possessor following the possessed, connected by a free-standing marker (a preposition) such as *blong/blo/bl-* (from English *belong*). For example, Pijin *Mam blong mi* 'my mother.' This preposition also signals a number of other relationships between two noun phrases. The following examples come from Bislama:

Bae mi katem bred blo yu (I will cut the bread for you = benefactive)

Man blo smok (smoker = characteristic association)

Linguistic fall-out from the mutiny on the *Bounty*

Norfolk Island is a small Australian territory that sits in the South Pacific Ocean somewhere between Australia and New Zealand. This subtropical 'hellhole' or 'paradise' (which label it receives depends on the period of its history) is home to a remarkable contact variety described variously as Norfolk Island-Pitcairn English, Norfolkese, Norfuk-Pitkern or simply Norf'k (the label we'll use here).

The language represents the linguistic outcome of contact between the British English of the *Bounty* mutineers and Tahitian. Some of you might know of the gripping tale of the mutiny on the *Bounty* that took place in the South Pacific on 28 April 1789 – it's a story that has been told and retold in books, comics and movies (going back to 1916). A bunch of disgruntled crewmen, led by Acting Lieutenant Fletcher Christian, seized control of the Royal Navy ship from their captain, Lieutenant William Bligh. After setting Bligh and 18 loyalists adrift, the mutineers settled either on Tahiti or Pitcairn Island; the settlement on Norfolk Island came later in 1856. The language is a remarkable example of a contact variety since we know precisely the number of speakers who originally settled on Pitcairn in 1790, their birthplace and even their names.

There is much that is of linguistic interest here. Like the other English-based creoles we looked at, Norf'k has a more elaborate set of pronouns involving singular, dual and plural number. It also has the clusivity distinction earlier described – first person non-singular forms distinguish between 'inclusive' and 'exclusive' (e.g. first person dual inclusive *hemi* 'you and me'). Most strikingly though, Norf'k also has special first person 'insider' pronouns: *aklan* (probably from 'our clan') and *auwa* (probably St Kitts Creole *awe* 'all we') – both translate as 'we' but can refer only to those descendants of the *Bounty* mutineers and the early settlers of Pitcairn Island. As Peter Mühlhäusler (2004) points out, these two pronouns are strong markers of islander solidarity.

Orl **aklan** noe **auwas** kamfram

'We all (ie. Norfolk Islanders of Pitcairn ancestry) know our forebears'

Finally Norf'k has a di-transitive construction (with direct and indirect object) that shows a highly unusual placement of the indirect object pronoun. In the following example you'll see it appears to break up the direct object NP (i.e. in between 'one' and 'cup'); note also the form of the indirect object *ai* (under certain conditions, the subject form can appear as an object and vice versa; see pronoun exchange discussed later).

Giv	*wan*	*ai*	*cup*	*ar*	*tea*
give	one	I	cup	of	tea

'Give me a cup of tea'

Standard English noun phrases are either definite or indefinite (*the cat* versus *a cat*). This is not the case for the creoles, however. For example, Pijin *kokorako* can mean 'a/the chicken.' However, if speakers want to include this information, they can draw from elsewhere, such as numerals and demonstratives. This is an area of rapid change in these languages and many of these forms are well on their way to developing into determiners. In Pijin, for example, the quantifier *wanfala* 'one' is currently being rean-alysed as an indefinite singular article and the demonstrative pronoun *ia* (from English *here*) as a definite article, as in *Man ia mi lukim long sip* 'I saw the/this man in the ship.'

In these languages, the class of true adjectives is small. Indeed, given the overall paucity of inflectional morphology and the fact that adjectives often reduplicate according to the same patterns as verbs, it is sometimes difficult to make a clear distinction between these two word classes. (Note, reduplication in adjectives usually has some kind of intensifying quality, as in Bislama *fas* 'stuck' versus *fasfas* 'well and truly stuck.') Generally adjectives will appear before the noun and often with a derivational suffix such as Tok Pisin *-pela* (or *-pla*) and Pijin *-fala* (from English *fellow*). For example:

Dispela tupela naispela liklik pik. (These two nice little pigs.)

A handful of (often intensifying) adjectives follow, as in:

tok nogut (bad language)

man nating (just an ordinary man)

tok Inglis (English language)

Simple sentences

The various offspring of Melanesian Pidgin have in common what can be thought of as some kind of verb phrase marker *i* (sometimes called a 'pred-icate marker'). It cannot be translated in English, although clearly it has its origin in the third person English pronoun *he*, originally as part of some sort left-dislocation structure (e.g. *That fellow, he's a fool*). The following examples come from Tok Pisin:

Kakiri i wokabaut long rot. Em i lukim wantok. (Kakiri is walking along the road. She sees a friend.)

Elements of the earlier topicalisation construction are still apparent. For one, *i* is systematically excluded after first and second person subjects, as evident in examples like Tok Pisin *mi kam, yu kam* 'I come, you come' ver-sus *em i kam* 's/he comes.' However, the development has already taken it a long way from its original focus construction and it is a hotly debated grammatical feature of these languages.

The constituent order of these creoles is basically SVX. Pronominal objects (especially those with inanimate reference) are often omitted, as in Bislama:

Mi laikem. (I like (it).)

Similarly, third person singular subjects can be unexpressed, the only signal being the predicate marker *i*. Hence:

Em i laik-em ~ i laik-em. ((S/he) likes (it).)

Creoles typically lack a copula corresponding to English *be*. Equational sentences are therefore non-verbal constructions involving the simple juxtaposition of the topic and comment noun phrase or adjective phrase, as in the following Pijin example:

Mami blong mi siki. (My mother (is) sick.)

However, these sorts of sentences are more usually expressed as a topicalisation construction, where the topic constituent is followed by a pronoun and then the predicate marker, as in Bislama:

Tija blo skul hem i no man blo smok. (The teacher of the school (s)he is not a smoker.)

These languages all use rising intonation to form a *yes–no* interrogative. There is also a variety of invariant tags, such as *no, e* or *o(wat)*. For example, (Bislama):

Bae you kam, no? (Will you come?)

Open interrogatives also lack inverted word order. Moreover, the forms that correspond to the English '*wh*-words' (for example Melanesian Pidgin *wanem* 'what') do not necessarily move to the front of the sentence, but remain in the structural position of the corresponding declarative. The following example (from Bislama) has the same structure as the Standard English echo question that speakers use when they find a piece of news astonishing (as we mentioned in Chapter 5, this structure is also used by quiz masters and police interrogators):

Yu wokem wanem? (What did you do?; literally, You did what?)

In Bislama, the *wh*-word can be fronted to form a more strongly expressed interrogative, but note there is no subject–verb inversion:

Wanem yu wokem? (What did you do?; literally, What you did?)

Complex predicates and sentences

These contact varieties share a characteristically paratactic structure; in other words, clauses are strung together, either without any linking item at all or linked by some sort of coordinating element, such as Bislama *mo* 'and' or *be* 'but' (see the discussion of paratactic style in Section 10.2). A striking characteristic is also something called the serial verb construction. Typically this involves a series of verbs with no marker conjoining them. There is a single subject preceding both verbs and potentially a single object following both verbs. Moreover, where there is a predicate marker *i*, it only appears once and has scope over the entire verb series. The following is an example from Tok Pisin:

Em i brumim rausim ol pipia. (S/he swept (lit. 'brush discard') away the rubbish.)

There are other construction types where the verb sequences are less tight, as in this next Bislama example:

Kali i send-em buk i kam. (Kali sent the book here.)

It is important to note that the Standard English *go see* and *come see* constructions come nowhere near the extensive patterns of verb serialisation that are found in these languages. These constructions represent a significant typological divergence from English and gain their motivation primarily from the languages they have come in contact with in their respective regions.

Subordinate clauses are indicated by a range of markers that have emerged (or grammaticalised) from prepositions, such as *for/fo, blong/blo* and *long/lo*. For example, in Bislama, *blo(ng)* is used to introduce a purpose clause (= 'in order to') and *lo(ng)* a *that*-clause:

Mi kam blo harim nius. (I came to hear the news.)

Mi inters lo pem trak. (I am interested in buying the car.)

An interesting development is the reanalysis of the Melanesian Pidgin form *se* (< *say*). This was originally used at the start of clauses introducing indirect speech (e.g. Bislama *Mi talem lo hem se bae mi kam* 'I told him/ her that I would come'), but is in the process of extending its contexts to include a range of complement clauses beyond locutions. The following example also comes from Bislama:

Mi hop se bai yu kam. (I hope that you will come.)

Like Standard English, these creoles have various ways of forming relative clauses. One is by simple embedding with no overt marking, as in the following Tok Pisin examples:

Mi lukim dok i ranim pik bilong me. (I saw the dog (that) chased my pig.)
Tupla brata mama i bin dai stap wantain papa. (The two brothers (whose) mother had died lived with their father.)

They have also developed a number of optional relatives markers (usually from pronouns), such as *husat* ('who') and, more commonly, *we* or *wea* ('where'), as in the following Tok Pisin examples:

Mi lukim bas we i bagarup. (I saw the bus that was broken down.)

Yu lukim ol manki husat i sutim muruk bilong mi? (Did you see the boys who shot my cassowary?)

Non-subject noun phrases often leave a pronoun copy that appears in place of the deleted co-referential noun phrase. Here is a final example from Tok Pisin. Note that *longen* here is the unstressed form of the prepositional phrase *long em* (literally, 'to it'):

Yu putim kago long dispela ples we diwai i sanap longen.

(Put the goods in the place where the tree is standing (in it).)

Discourse organisation

Speakers frequently manipulate word order, exploiting different sequences of noun phrases to highlight or to contrast more salient information. Speech exchanges are typically full of different kinds of highly topic-oriented structures, such as fronting (with or without special focus markers), left- and right-dislocation. While such expressiveness is typical of spontaneous spoken language generally, it is the relative frequency and the special combination of these features that make these Englishes different from more mainstream varieties. Not surprisingly, these languages typically do not have a passive construction. Instead, fronting is used as a device for focusing the object. For example, the English sentence *My car was stolen by the youth* would be rendered in Bislama as the following (here we've provided a glossed example so you can follow the syntax more easily):

Trak	blo	mi	boe	ya	i	stil-im
car	belong	me	youth	here	predicate marker	steal-transitive

Summary

It is not only between the creoles in Vanuatu, Solomon Islands and Papua New Guinea that linguistic similarities exist. English-based creoles in the Pacific and Australasian regions generally, indeed worldwide, share striking resemblances, most dramatically in their grammars. Examples of these shared features include the following:

❑ Little in the way of grammatical morphology: plural and possessive noun suffixes typically omitted; no agreement between subject and verb in the present tense; past tense expressed with the base form of the verb.
❑ Invariable tag questions like *isn't it, init, ini, ana* and *na*.
❑ Main and auxiliary verb *be* is often omitted.
❑ Particles often used to indicate plurality.
❑ Possession expressed by the juxtaposition of the possessor and possessed noun phrases, or by some particle.
❑ Particles used to signal tense and aspect; e.g. *been/bin* for past; *gon(na)* or *gotta* for future.
❑ Serial verb constructions common.
❑ No case distinctions for pronouns.
❑ *He/she* often used as a general third person singular.
❑ Elaborate pronoun system, distinguishing, for example, dual and plural and inclusive and exclusive first person.
❑ Prepositions are frequently omitted.
❑ Frequent use of repetition for rhetorical effect.

As you probably have observed, many of these grammatical features can also be found in non-standard varieties of English around the world and we return to this point later in the chapter.

307

Mixed languages

Extensive language contact can also see the birth of a type of contact language that is different from either pidgins or creoles. In this case speakers are typically fluent in one or both of the source languages, and they also take and adapt their lexical and grammatical subsystems from each source language (so they don't share grammatical features as creoles do). For example, in Australia, extensive language contact has seen new mixed languages created via bilingual speakers' switching between an English-based creole and an Australian traditional language; these have then conventionalised into new autonomous languages that are now acquired by children as one of their two first languages. Linguists Felicity Meakins and Carmel O'Shannessy describe two such new mixed varieties, Light Warlpiri and Gurindji Kriol (see the 'References and further reading' section for details). We'll focus on Light Warlpiri here.

This language systemically combines the lexical and morpho-syntactic systems from the Aboriginal language (Warlpiri), an Australian creole (Kriol) and Standard Australian English. It draws most verbs and verbal morphology from Kriol, nouns from Warlpiri and English, and nominal morphology from Warlpiri. The following example shows the linguistic mix (the Warlpiri-derived forms are italicised and Kriol/English forms are in plain font):

junga	*mayi*	*nyuntu*	yu-m		go	*karnta-kurl*
true	question	2 singular	2sg-nonfuture		go	woman-with

'Is it true that you went with the woman?'

This example shows an English/Kriol verb, *go* 'go,' an innovative auxiliary form, *yu-m* '2 singular-nonfuture', (derived from the English/Kriol pronoun) and elements other than the verb and auxiliary from Warlpiri.

These hybrid languages may well be stabilising, or else they could be in the process of a more dramatic shift towards Kriol.

11.4 Variation in the native Englishes

Trudgill and Chambers (2017) contains a treasure trove of articles that deal with grammatical variation in some of the more mainstream native English dialects, or what might be described as 'traditional dialects' (see also chapters in Kortmann et al. 2004). Because space is limited, we confine ourselves to only a handful of the most strikingly different features.

Some of these dialects have very different pronominal systems. The traditional dialects of the south-west of England (and their descendants in Newfoundland) must have one of the most perplexing features for speakers of Standard English – a construction dubbed 'pronoun exchange' (Ihalainen 1991). Here the subject pronouns appear in object function (or other functions needing the non-subject form); similarly, object pronouns can appear in subject function (although there are restrictions here):

Give it to he, not they – her don't need it.

Us don' think naught about things like that.

You remember he?

He never interfered with I.

Other dialects show what looks to be the genesis of a gender system in pronoun assignment (where 'gender' refers to morpho-syntactic classes of nouns). As described by Pawley (2004), in vernacular Australian English (most notably that spoken in Tasmania), the appearance of the pronominal forms *he* and *she* is triggered, not just by animate nouns (like *girl* and *boy*), but also by inanimate nouns (furniture, tools, body parts, plants and so on). For example, items of food and drink, and body parts (other than male genitals) are feminine; trees and other plants are masculine:

I put 'er [= the bottle of beer] *down that bloody quick that I blew the top off 'er. And* [he] *took 'er* [= leg of lamb] *in and put 'er on the plate.*

She [= a wisdom tooth] *was no use to me anyway, so I 'ad **her** out.*

The snottygobble [= parasitic creeper] *is into this one, but 'e's not goin to kill 'im.*

Some traditional dialects show remarkable differences with respect to the verbal system. A fine example is the so-called double modal construction. As we saw in Chapter 6, speakers of Standard English have a strict requirement that only one modal verb may appear in a sentence. In the American English of the South, Scots and some north-eastern dialects of English, sentences like the following are commonplace:

He might could do it.

He should can do it.

You might oughta do that.

If you are struggling to understand what these might mean, all you need to do is unpack the modal verbs. *He might could do it* suggests 'he probably could do it'; *He should can do it* something like 'He ought to be able to do it' and the *might* combined with *oughta* in the third example makes the obligation less forceful. If you think these are confusing, try the triple modal construction that is found in some varieties of Scots (and occasionally in southern American English):

He'll might could do it for you.

He'll should can come in the morn.

Again, unpack the meanings of the modals and the sentences become 'He might be able to do it for you some time in the future' and 'It's likely that he'll be able to come tomorrow.' Scots even allows something like *He might used to could do it*. Subtle nuances of meaning can be captured very neatly by these compound modal constructions – and with time you'll might could get used to it!

Without a doubt, the vast majority of native English speakers around the world differ most in terms of phonology – features of accent are what most obviously distinguish these varieties. Nonetheless, when we take into account the full gamut of variation, it is clear that some remarkable diversity also exists in English structure. We have only been able to give you a taste here.

11.5 Vernacular universals

Kortmann and Szmrecsanyi (2004) set out to identify the most frequent grammatical features in non-standard varieties of English around the world (see also Szmrecsanyi and Kortmann 2009). On the basis of the seven regions they examined (British Isles, America, Caribbean, Pacific, Australia, Africa, Asia), they identified, as they describe as true candidates for what have been described as 'vernacular universals' (p. 1142). In the next subsection are listed the 12 most frequent grammatical features (and in brackets are the number of varieties showing these).

Worldwide top 12 grammatical features (based on 46 varieties)

(1) Lack of inversion in main clause *yes/no* questions. (41 varieties)
(*You get the point?*)

(2) *Me* instead of *I* in coordinate subjects. (40 varieties)
(*Me and my brother were late./My brother and me were late.*)

(3) *Never* as a past tense negator. (40 varieties)
(*He never did it* [= he didn't do it].)

(4) Adverbs same form as adjectives. (39 varieties)
(*Come quick.*)

(5) Absence of plural marking after measure nouns. (37 varieties)
(*four pound, five year*)

(6) Lack of inversion/lack of auxiliaries in *wh*-questions. (36 varieties)
(*What you doing?*)

(7) Multiple negation/negative concord. (35 varieties)
(*He won't do no harm.*)

(8) Degree modifier adverbs lack -*ly*. (35 varieties)
(*That's real good.*)

(9) Special forms of phrases for the second person plural pronoun. (34 varieties)
(*youse, y'all, you 'uns, you guys, yufela* etc.)

(10) Levelling of difference between present perfect and simple past. (34 varieties)

(*Some of us have been years ago.*)

(11) Double comparatives and superlatives. (34 varieties)

(*That's so much more easier to follow.*)

(12) Irregular use of articles. (33 varieties) (*I had nice garden; I had the toothache.*)

(Based on Kortmann and Szmrecsanyi 2004: 1154–1155)

Many of these examples are also universals (or near universals) for New Englishes generally; to these might be added the following six. These are among the most salient features from Kortmann and Szmrecsanyi's top 19 features from the 11 L2 varieties (English as a second language) in their sample.

Some additional top L2 features (based on 11 varieties)

(1) Wider range of uses of the progressive. (10 varieties)

(*I'm liking this.*)

(2) Inverted word order in indirect questions. (10 varieties)

(*I'm wondering what are you gonna do.*)

(3) Resumptive/shadow pronouns. (10 varieties)

(*This is the house which I've painted it anyway.*)

(4) Zero past tense forms of regular verbs. (10 varieties)

(*I walk* [= I walked])

(5) Invariant non-concord tags. (nine varieties)

(*We've missed something here, isn't it?*)

(6) Invariant *don't* for all persons in the present tense. (eight varieties)

(*He don't like me.*)

(Based on Kortmann and Szmrecsanyi 2004: 1188–1189)

All of these features appear in educated speech somewhere in the English-speaking world. Many crop up in the spoken standards we are familiar with (British and Australian English) and you have probably iden-tified some as occurring in your own speech. Some like the following are well on their way to becoming standard:

(1) The adverb *never* (Worldwide feature 3) appears in 40 out of the 46 in Kortmann and Szmrecsanyi's list. The Standard English nega-tor *not/-n't* is ripe for renewal and *never* is a likely candidate to replace it.

(2) The more extensive use of the present perfect (Worldwide feature 10) is on the increase in native varieties of English around the world.

(3) Invariant non-concord tags (L2 feature 5 above) like *isn't it?*, *init* are taking the place of standard tags like *weren't they*, *didn't she* and so on in colloquial native Englishes globally. Others, such as *right?*, *eh?*, *ok?*, *you know?*, *huh?*, are already well established.

(4) The expansion of the progressive (L2 feature 1) is also underway in Standard English. As discussed in Section 6.2, the simple present tense is used for events that happen regularly. The progressive is stepping in to fill its shoes and extending beyond its original function of expressing ongoing action (a development well-attested in other languages).

11.6 The future of Standard English

No one nation can any longer be said to 'own' English, and no one nation's anxieties over local norms of usage will make much impact in a world where diverse regional standards are the norm, and where the Internet provides these varieties with new levels of public display. A new intellectual sociolinguistic climate is slowly but surely being formed.

(Crystal 2006: 412)

Developments in the 21st century are doing much to challenge the authority of Standard English. For one, standards are hard to maintain for a language that has established itself in almost every corner of the globe. In countries such as Britain, the United States and Australia, distinct regional standards have been around long enough for considerable regional variation and social variation to emerge. Globalisation is also fostering new socially defined ethnic variation in these countries. Massive flows of people, including tourists, refugees and migrants, have produced an intermixing of people and cultures that is unprecedented. Culture and language at the local level have been changed irrevocably by this 'inter-national' movement of people. And as each individual group seeks to assert its own identity, different ethnic varieties of English have become an important means of signalling the group boundaries.

However, it is in those regions where English has established a strong non-native presence that diversity is the richest. Countries such as Africa, the Pacific, South and South-East Asia have extensive regional variation, reflecting the expansion of English geographically in these areas. There is also widespread social and idiolectal variation, reflecting factors such as ethnicity and education. Of particular relevance here is the influence of local vernacular languages, which may or may not be the first language of speakers.

The other pressure on the standard comes from computer-mediated communication and the simple fact that the traditional written language is losing its clout. As we saw in the previous chapter, in E-speak we find features such as ellipsis and the sorts of highly topic-oriented structures that are characteristic of spoken language. Moreover, writers on the Internet don't usually experience the sort of drafting processes and layers of editorial intervention that reinforce the distinction between speech and writing. Here we find the sort of far-reaching variation that existed long before standardisation and long before there was any autonomous prose style – regional, social, even idiolectal variation is rampant on the net. The features of fast and furious speech have broken through the lines and now appear in writing, just as they did in the manuscripts of medieval English and earlier.

You can read the works of those writing in the 18th century, say, Jane Austen, or even Jonathan Swift (both writers in the Early Modern English period), but someone in their day would read only with great difficulty the writing of the medieval literary figure Geoffrey Chaucer, some 300 years earlier. With standardisation and the powerful authority of writing, the normal processes of linguistic change are retarded, perhaps even reversed. However, this influence is now waning. Everything points to greater variety, less standardisation, the increasing influence of the newer varieties of English and the diminishing authority of native speakers. Non-native speakers are now outnumbering native speakers three to one (cf. Crystal 2006; McArthur 2006). It is not even clear whether such labels as 'native speaker' and 'non-native speaker,' 'New English,' 'Other English' and so on remain appropriate for a linguistic ecosystem where English is commonly spoken as a second first language. The sociolinguistic situation is far more complex than these simple labels suggest. In short, globalisation, together with colloquialisation, liberalisation and the electronic revolution mean de-standardisation; informal, non-standard, unedited English is going public and the audiences have become more receptive.

Any language change represents a complex network of different influences, involving the interaction of typological, functional, phonological, socio-cultural, psychological and external contact factors. Predicting change is always tricky. We can take note of what we imagine to be changes underway, but we can never be sure they will run their full course. There is always the human wild-card factor, too. As Crystal (2006: 432) put it recently: 'Fashions count, in language, as anywhere else.' He goes on to suggest that, as the numbers of mother-tongue speakers further decline, so we may well see linguistic fashions being started by second language, foreign language and creole/pidgin speakers (already evident in rap lyrics). Consider features such as lack of number agreement (*the teacher/ teachers shout*), variation in the count/non-count distinction (*staffs, furnitures, equipments*), loss of auxiliary *be* (*She crying a lot*), habitual *be* (*he be sick*) and very unusual structures like nominal/adjectival reduplication (*different-different things*) and *say*-based complementisers (*Dat mean say* . . . 'That means that. . .'). All reflect natural processes of change and, though not yet candidates for vernacular universals, do not rule out the possibility of these becoming part of some local standard, first in speech and later in writing. And with increasing international contacts, it is also conceivable that any one of these will one day slip out of the national and into the international arena to become part of a Standard English spoken all around the world.

11.7 Points to remember

❏ Recent trends in globalisation indicate two distinct effects of the global village. While there is greater conformity appearing at the global level (World English), diversity continues to thrive at the local level.

❏ The worldwide spread of English illustrates the different effects of these homogenising/differentiating forces. Globalisation requires international intelligibility (a world standard). The preservation of national identity, however, fosters diversity (distinctive Englishes).

❏ Speakers who are traditionally associated with English (L1 speakers) are speakers of English as a Native Language (ENL). Native Englishes include British English, Scottish English, American English, New Zealand English and Australian English.

❏ Speakers of the New Englishes (L2 speakers) are regular users of English as a Second Language (ESL). Included here are Singapore English, Malaysian English, Indian English, Nigerian English and Hong Kong English.

❏ Speakers of English as a Foreign Language (EFL) include the growing number of people who speak English as a foreign language. They belong to an expanding circle of nations such as China, Egypt, Japan, Indonesia, Thailand, Saudi Arabia and Taiwan.

❏ The label 'Other Englishes' refers to English-based pidgin and creole varieties around the world. These varieties aren't degenerate forms of 'broken' English. They have their own distinctive linguistic features and styles and are the result of English in contact with other languages.

❏ Developments in the 21st century are doing much to challenge the authority of the Standard. Globalisation, colloquialisation, liberalisation and the electronic revolution point to greater variety, less standardisation, the increasing influence of the newer varieties of English and the diminishing authority of the Native Englishes.

Exercises

1. Singapore English

Here is a transcript of a police taped conversation between Teo (who later served 20 months in jail for soliciting sexual favours from two shoplifting suspects) and Yap (one of the alleged shoplifters). The transcript shows that Singlish (Singapore English) has a number of quite distinctive characteristics.

Teo (sigh) Something very big has . . . happened.
Yap What thing happen? I know at my client's place, know?
Teo . . . Uh, I'm now under investigation.
Yap Why you are now under investigation?
Teo Yeah by . . . CPIB.
Yap Why?

Teo	I just got the news.
Yap	What news?
Teo	I don't know what, I don't know what case. Just . . . just now around four o'clock, I was being called up.
Yap	Call up by who?
Teo	Okay. One of my, one of my CIO lah.
Yap	Who's your, who's your CIO?
Teo	Don't ask who lah! Why you ask ask ask?
Yap	You so fierce for what?
Teo	I'm not fierce okay. I'm very blur now okay! I'm very messy now!
Yap	Okay, okay, okay, okay.
Teo	So just now he asked me to rush back home first and clear all the stuff in my house lah, what . . . what . . . ever police thing that I got bring back home, the notes and so on lah. So he asked me to clear all this sort of thing lah . . .
Yap	But you don't know why they investigate you or whatever shit?
Teo	I don't know who the hell is the one who go and lodge the case with them or whatever lah.
Yap	You left your house already, now you are outside?
Teo	Yes! I have done all the thing, burn all the thing ready. Can we don't talk on the phone because I'm . . . I know how they work, you see? They might tap on the tape, the phone and so on. I don't know if they have tap the phone yet.

(Ooi 1999)

Rewrite this extract into Standard English and comment on any features of Singlish that strike you as being very different. Make note of any variation you find in this passage, such as where both Standard English and Singlish features appear side by side.

2. Singapore English

Here is an extract from a satirical piece on Singlish written by Chua Mui Hoong. Much of the humour comes from the fact that she crams as many Singlish features in her writing as she can. Rewrite this passage into Standard English and describe the features of Singlish that appear here.

I tell you, Singlish very good. English ah take so long. Singlish faster. Like I talk to my children like that.

The *ang moh* [= white person], their tongue can say all those long sentence. From birth they talk like that what. We all Singaporean tongue different, shorter *lah*. [. . .]

I dunno why they say Singlish so bad. Everybody in Singapore talk Singlish what. [. . .]

If you not in business, like me, not lawyer, not those big shot, speak so good English for what? Let people laugh at you only.

Like my son. He say his class got this boy talk perfect English, everybody make fun of him. I tell my son, you don't anyhow laugh. Next time you go to work you also have to speak like that. He make face, say eeee, dowan.

I tell him ah boy, listen to Pa-pa. You learn your English good good, don't become like me.(Ooi 1999)

3. Tok Pisin

The following conversation in Tok Pisin (as spoken in Papua New Guinea) illustrates some typical creole features. Read through this text and describe the non-standard grammatical features you find here.

Mi planim kon.	I'm planting corn
Sapoti i wok long gaden.	Sapoti is working in the garden.
Heni i kamap na em i tok.	Heni comes up to them and says:
H: *E, Sapoti, yu wokim wanem?*	Hey, Sapoti, what are you doing?
S: *Mi planim kon.*	I'm planting corn.
H: *Yu planim kaukau tu?*	Are you planting sweet potatoes too?
S: *Nogat. Bihain.*	No. Later.
H: *Orait inap mi halivim yu.*	All right. Can I help?
S: *Gutpela. Yumitupela wok wantaim!*	Great. Let's work together!

(Dutton 1985: 5)

4. Grammatical description

In the 'References and further reading' section at the end of this book, you will find references for grammatical descriptions of non-standard varieties of English spoken all round the world. Select one of these varieties and in 1000–1500 words give a brief account of the grammar of this language. Focus on those features that are most strikingly different from Standard English. As part of your account, you should also identify any of the features that occur in the colloquial versions of your own English (especially those that might be characterised as 'vernacular universals').

5. Research essay

Mufwene (http://fathom.lib.uchicago.edu/2/21701718/) writes: 'native Englishes, indigenised Englishes and English pidgins and creoles have all developed by the same kind of natural restructuring processes.' In other words, all varieties of English have been influenced to some degree by local languages and by other varieties of English. Research this claim and then write an essay saying whether or not you agree, and why.

References and further reading

Included here is a collection of additional readings to start you off on topics that might interest you further. Rather than give these chapter by chapter, we have organised them according to various topics. You will also find here references that have been given in the chapters.

General references on language and linguistics

Aitchison, J. 2011: *The articulate mammal*. New York: Routledge.

Bauer, L., Holmes, J. and Warren, P. 2006: *Language matters*. London: Palgrave Macmillan.

Blake, B. 2007: *Playing with words: humour in the English language*. London: Equinox.

Blake, B. 2008: *All about language*. Oxford: Oxford University Press.

Bolinger, D. 1975: *Aspects of language* (2nd edn). New York: Harcourt Brace Jovanovich.

Bolinger, D. 1980: *Language: the loaded weapon*. Harlow: Pearson Longman.

Burridge, K. and Stebbins, T. 2016: *For the love of language*. Melbourne: Cambridge University Press.

Crystal, D. 2010: *The Cambridge encyclopedia of language* (3rd edn). Cambridge: Cambridge University Press.

Hudson, R. 1984: *Invitation to linguistics*. Oxford: Wiley-Blackwell.

Parker, F. and Riley, K. 2005: *Linguistics for non-linguists: a primer with exercises* (4th edn). Boston: Pearson Longman.

Radford, A., Atkinson, M., Britain, D., Clahsen, H. and Spencer, A. 2009: *Linguistics: an introduction* (2nd edn). Cambridge: Cambridge University Press.

Rowe, B. and Levine, D. 2009: *A concise introduction to linguistics* (2nd edn). Boston: Pearson Longman.

Yule, G. 2006: *The study of language* (3rd edn). Cambridge: Cambridge University Press.

Major grammars of English

Biber, D., Johansson, S., Leech, G., Conrad, S. and Finegan, E. 1999: *Longman grammar of spoken and written English*. London: Pearson Longman.

Huddleston, R. and Pullum, G. K. 2002: *The Cambridge grammar of the English language.* Cambridge: Cambridge University Press.

Quirk, R., Greenbaum, S., Leech, G. and Svartvik, J. 1985: *A comprehensive grammar of the English language.* London: Pearson Longman.

General references on English

Bolton, W. F. and Crystal, D. (eds) 1987: *The English language.* Harmondsworth: Penguin.

Burridge, K. 2010: *Gift of the gob: morsels of English language history.* Sydney: ABC Books (Harper Collins Publishers).

Crystal, D. 2003: *The Cambridge encyclopedia of the English language* (2nd edn). Cambridge: Cambridge University Press.

Culpeper, J. (ed) 2009: *English language: description, variation and context.* London: Palgrave Macmillan (with P. Kerswill, R. Wodak, F. Katamba and T. McEnery).

McArthur, T. (ed) 1992: *The Oxford companion to the English language.* Oxford: Oxford University Press.

Introductions to syntax and morphology

Booij, G. 2007: *The grammar of words: an introduction to linguistic morphology.* Oxford: Oxford University Press.

Carstairs-McCarthy, A. 2018: *An introduction to English morphology: words and their structure* (2nd edn). Edinburgh: Edinburgh University Press.

Haspelmath, M. and Sims, A. D. 2010: *Understanding morphology* (2nd edn). Abingdon: Hodder Routledge.

Plag, I. 2003: *Word-formation in English.* Cambridge: Cambridge University Press.

Tallerman, M. 2015: *Understanding syntax* (4th edn). Abingdon: Hodder Routledge.

History of English and historical linguistics

Aitchison, J. 2012: *Language change: progress or decay* (4th edn). Cambridge: Cambridge University Press.

Algeo, J. and Butcher, C. A. 2014: *The origins and development of the English language* (7th edn). Boston: Wadsworth.

Barber, C., Beal, J. C. and Shaw, P. A. 2009: *The English language: a historical introduction* (2nd edn). Cambridge: Cambridge University Press.

Baugh, A. C. and Cable, T. 2002: *A history of the English language* (5th edn). London: Routledge.

Beal, J. 2004: *English in modern times.* London: Routledge.

Burridge, K. and Bergs, A. 2017: *Understanding language change.* London: Routledge.

The Cambridge history of the English language. Vols. 1–6. Cambridge: Cambridge University Press.

Denison, D. 1995: *Historical English syntax.* London: Pearson Longman.

Graddol, D. et al. 1996: *English: history, diversity and change.* London: Routledge.

Hogg, R. and Denison, D. (eds) 2006: *A history of the English language.* Cambridge: Cambridge University Press.

Hopper, P. and Closs Traugott, E. 2003: *Grammaticalization* (2nd edn). Cambridge: Cambridge University Press.

Mugglestone, L. (ed) 2012: *The Oxford history of English* (2nd edn). Oxford: Oxford University Press.

Nevalainen, T. and Traugott, E. 2016: *The Oxford handbook of the history of English.* Oxford: Oxford University Press.

Strang, B. M. H. 1970: *A history of English.* London: Methuen.

Prescription and the rise of Standard English

Bex, T. and Watts, R. J. (eds) 1999: *Standard English: the widening debate.* London: Routledge.

Burridge, K. 2007: 'Linguistic purism: the tug-of-love between standard and non-standard'. In K. Dunworth (ed) *English in South East Asia: challenges and changes* (pp. 12–37).

Cameron, D. 2012: *Verbal hygiene* (2nd edn). London: Routledge.

Freeborn, D. 2006: *From old to standard English* (3rd edn). London: Palgrave Macmillan.

Milroy, J. and Milroy, L. 2013: *Authority in language* (3rd edn). London: Routledge.

Shopen, T. and Williams, J. M. 1980: *Standards and dialects in English.* Cambridge, MA: Winthrop.

Trudgill, P. *Standard English: what is isn't* [Revised version (2011) of Trudgill, 1999: 'Standard English: what it isn't'. In Tony Bex and Richard J. Watts (eds), pp. 117–128]. (http://lagb-education.org/wp-content/uploads/2016/01/SEtrudgill2011.pdf).

English discourse and style

Baron, N. S. 2000: *Alphabet to email: how written English evolved and where it's heading.* London, New York: Routledge.

Biber, D. 1988: *Variation across speech and writing.* Cambridge: Cambridge University Press.

Biber, D. and Conrad, S. 2014: *Register, genre, and style.* New York: Cambridge University Press.

Crystal, D. 2006: *Language and the Internet* (2nd edn). Cambridge: Cambridge University Press.

Crystal, D. 2009: *Txtng: the gr8 db8*. Oxford: Oxford University Press.

Crystal, D. and Davy, D. 1969: *Investigating English style*. London: Pearson Longman.

Freeborn, D., French, P. and Langford, D. 1986: *Varieties of English: an introduction to the study of language* (2nd edn). London: Palgrave Macmillan.

Halliday, M. A. K. 1985: *Spoken and written language*. Waurn Ponds, VIC: Deakin University Press.

Herring, S. C. 2003: 'Computer-mediated discourse'. In Heidi Ehernberger Hamilton, Deborah Schiffrin and Deborah Tannen (eds) *The handbook of discourse analysis* (pp. 612–634). Oxford: Wiley-Blackwell.

Kuiper, K. 1996: *Smooth talkers: the linguistic performance of auctioneers and sportscasters*. Mahwah, NJ: Lawrence Erlbaum Associates.

Loftus, E. 1975: 'Leading questions and the eyewitness report'. *Cognitive Psychology* 7(4): 560–572.

Severin, A. A. 2018: *The nature of prescriptivism and descriptivism online: The case of Reddit and r/badlinguistics*. PhD thesis. Monash University.

Shopen, T. and Williams, J. 1981: *Style and variables in English*. Cambridge, MA: Winthrop.

Shuy, R. 2012: *The language of sexual misconduct cases*. Oxford Scholarship Online.

Social variation

Cheshire, Jenny 1981: 'Variation in the use of *ain't* in an urban British english dialect'. *Language in Society* 10(3): 365–381.

Coates, J. 2015: *Women, men and language* (3rd edn). London: Routledge.

Holmes, J. 1995: *Women, men and politeness*. London: Pearson Longman.

Holmes, J. and Wilson, N. 2017: *An introduction to sociolinguistics* (5th edn). London: Routledge.

Labov, W. 1972: *Sociolinguistic patterns*. Philadelphia: University of Pennsylvania Press.

Leith, D. 2003: *A social history of English* (2nd edn). London: Routledge.

Machan, T. W. and Scott, C. T. (eds) 1992: *English in its social contexts: essays in historical sociolinguistics*. New York: Oxford University Press.

Milroy, L. 1987: *Language and social networks* (2nd edn). Oxford: Basil Blackwell.

Trudgill, P. 2000: *Sociolinguistics: an introduction to language and society* (4th edn). Harmondsworth: Penguin.

Wardhaugh, R. and Fuller, J. M. 2014: *An introduction to sociolinguistics* (7th edn). Oxford: Wiley-Blackwell.

English around the world

Bhatt, R. M. 2008: 'Indian English: syntax'. In R. Mesthrie (ed) *Varieties of English: African, South and Southeast Asia* (pp. 546–562). Berlin: Mouton de Gruyter.

Brown, K. 1991: 'Double modals in Hawick Scots'. In Trudgill and Chambers. pp. 74–103.

Burke, I. 2017: 'Wicked which: the linking relative in Australian English'. *Australian Journal of Linguistics* 37(3): 356–386.

Christian, D. 2017: 'The personal dative in Appalachian speech'. In Trudgill and Chambers. pp. 104–119.

Crowley, T. 2008: 'Bislama: morphology and syntax'. In K. Burridge and B. Kortmann (eds) *Varieties of English: the Pacific and Australasia* (pp. 444–466). Berlin: Mouton de Gruyter.

Crystal, D. 2012: *English as a global language* (2nd edn). Cambridge: Cambridge University Press.

Dutton, T. 1985: *A new course in Tok Pisin*. Canberra: Pacific Linguistics.

Engel, D. and Ritz, M. E. 2000: 'The use of the present perfect in Australian English'. *Australian Journal of Linguistics* 20: 119–140.

Graddol, D. 2000: *The future of English?* London: The British Council. (www.teachingenglish.org.uk/sites/teacheng/files/pub_learning-elt-future.pdf).

Graddol, D. 2006: *English next*. London: The British Council. (http://vigdis.hi.is/sites/vigdis.hi.is/files/images/einangrun_enskumaelandi_folks.pdf).

Hickey, R. (ed) 2012: *Areal features of the anglophone world*. Berlin: Walter de Gruyter.

Hughes, A., Trudgill, P. and Watt, D. 2012: *English accents and dialects* (5th edn). London: Routledge.

Ihalainen, O. 1991: 'On grammatical diffusion in Somerset folk speech'. In Trudgill and Chambers. pp. 104–119.

Jenkins, J. 2009: *World Englishes*. London: Routledge.

Jourdan, C. 2008: 'Solomon Islands Pijin: morphology and syntax'. In K. Burridge and B. Kortmann (eds) *Varieties of English: the Pacific and Australasia* (pp. 446–487). Berlin: Mouton de Gruyter.

Kachru, B. B. 1986: *The alchemy of English: the spread, functions and models of non-native Englishes*. Oxford: Pergamon.

Kirkpatrick, A. 2007: *World Englishes: implications for international communication and English language teaching*. Cambridge: Cambridge University Press.

Kirkpatrick, A. 2010: *The Routledge handbook of world Englishes*. London: Routledge.

Kortmann, B. and Szmrecsanyi, B. 2004: 'Global synopsis: morphological and syntactic variation in English'. In Kortmann et al. pp. 1142–1202.

Kortmann, B., Burridge, K., Mesthrie, R., Schneider, E. and Upton, C. 2004: *A handbook of varieties of English* (Vol. 2 *Morphology and syntax*) with CD-ROM. Berlin: Mouton de Gruyter.

McArthur, Tom 2006: 'English world-wide in the twentieth century'. In L. Muggleston (ed). *The Oxford History of English* (pp. 394–414). Oxford: Oxford University Press.

Meakins, F. 2013: 'Gurindji Kriol'. In S. Michaelis, P. Maurer, M. Haspelmath and M. Huber (eds) *Atlas of Pidgin and Creole structures Vol. II: The language surveys*. Oxford: Oxford University Press.

Mesthrie, R. 2008: 'Indian South African English: morphology and syntax'. In R. Mesthrie (ed) *Varieties of English: African, South and Southeast Asia* (pp. 501–520). Berlin: Mouton de Gruyter.

Mesthrie, R. and Bhatt, R. M. 2008: *World Englishes: The study of new linguistic varieties.* Cambridge: Cambridge Univesity Press.

Moore, B. (ed) 2001: *Who's centric now? The present state of post-colonial Englishes.* Melbourne: Oxford University Press.

Mühlhäusler, P. 2004: 'Norfolk Island Pitcairn English (Pitkern Norfolk): Morphology and Syntax'. In W. W. Schneider, K. Burridge, B. Kortmann, R. Mestrie and C. Upton (eds) *A handbook of varieties of English, vol. 2 morphology and syntax* (pp. 789–804). Berlin: Mouton de Gruyter.

O'Shannessy, C. 2005: 'Light warlpiri: A new language'. *Australian Journal of Linguistics* 25(1): 31–57.

Ooi, V. 1999: 'Globalising Singaporean-Malaysian English in an inclusive learner's dictionary'. Paper presented to the conference 'Who's Centric Now' held at The Australian National University, October 27 to 29; proceedings Moore, 2001.

Paddock, H. 1991: 'The actuation problem for gender change in Wessex versus Newfoundland'. In Trudgill and Chambers. pp. 29–46.

Romaine, S. 1988: *Pidgin and creole languages.* London: Pearson Longman.

Sedlatschek, A. 2009: *Contemporary Indian English: variation and change.* Amsterdam: John Benjamins.

Severin, A. A. 2018: *The nature of prescriptivism and descriptivism online: The case of Reddit and r/badlinguistics.* PhD thesis. Monash University.

Smith, G. 2008: 'Tok Pisin: morphology and syntax'. In K. Burridge and B. Kortmann (eds) *Varieties of English: the Pacific and Australasia* (pp. 488–513). Berlin: Mouton de Gruyter.

Svartvik, J. and Leech, G. 2006: *English: one tongue, many voices.* Houndvilles: Palgrave Macmillan.

Szmrecsanyi, B. and Kortmann, B. 2009: 'Vernacular universals and anglo-versals in a typological perspective'. In M. Filppula, J. Klemola and H. Paulasto (eds) *Vernacular universals and language contacts: evidence from varieties of English and beyond.* New York: Routledge, pp. 33–56.

Todd, L. 1990: *Modern Englishes: pidgins and creoles* (2nd edn). New York: Routledge.

Trudgill, P. and Chambers, J. K. 2017: *Dialects of English: studies in grammatical variation.* New York: Routledge.

Trudgill, P. and Hannah, J. 2013: *International English: a guide to varieties of Standard English* (5th edn). New York: Routledge.

Glossary

ADJECTIVE
A category of words which includes words like *hungry, intelligent* and *wicked*. The ability to occur in comparative and superlative forms is characteristic of many adjectives (*hungrier–hungriest, more intelligent–most intelligent*). Adjectives can often be turned into ADVERBS by the addition of the derivational affix *-ly*.

ADVERB
A category which includes words like *hungrily* and *slowly*. Like ADJECTIVES, they are often gradable: *more hungrily–most hungrily*.

ADVERBIAL
The function which answers questions like *when, where, why* or *how* but not *what* or *who*. Adverbials tend to be optional: Fido chased the cat **for three hours/behind the fence/because it had teased him**.

AFFIXES
MORPHEMES that can be added to a STEM to form a more complex word. They are classified according to where they appear with regard to the stem: suffixes follow the stem (e.g. *-ed, -s, -ing* in *cooked, cooks, cooking*), prefixes precede the stem; e.g. *in-, non-, un-* in **in**toxicating, **non**alcoholic, **un**cooked. A third minor type, infixes, must occur inside the stem. In English the only viable infixes are non-standard intensifiers like *bloody* as in *fan-**bloody**-tastic*.

AGENTLESS PASSIVE
A PASSIVE without an agent or doer of the action (in other words, the subject in the active version); for instance, in the sentence, *Bronwyn Pike is considered one of the leading intellectuals among our politicians*, there is no agent noun indicating by whom she is considered to be a leading intellectual.

AGREEMENT
When a word shows morphological marking for a property associated with another word in the same sentence or phrase. English has a limited amount of agreement, but it does have verb agreement. Properties like PERSON and NUMBER are associated with noun phrases, but a verb can be marked for the person and number features of its SUBJECT: *The dog was chasing a duck – The dogs were chasing a duck*. Many languages related to English, such as German, Dutch or the Scandinavian languages, also have agreement inside the

noun phrase, where determiners and adjectives are marked morphologically for the features of the noun.

ANAPHORIC PRONOUNS

Expressions that refer back to something that has gone on before in the discourse (= the antecedent). The antecedent is necessary to provide the information for the expression's interpretation. For instance *John$_i$ said that he$_i$ liked marmite better than vegemite*, where the subscript *i* indicates that *he* refers to the same person as *John*.

ASPECT

This is quite a complex notion relating to how actions and events are described. Whereas tense locates the action or event described by a verb in time, aspect says something about the temporal structure of it; whether it is completed or ongoing, for instance. English does not have an extended aspectual system, but there are verb forms in English for two aspects: progressive, indicating that an event is in progress (*Oscar is eating*), and perfect, indicating that an event has been completed (*Oscar has eaten*).

AUXILIARY VERBS

Verbs with functional rather than lexical content. They have some syntactic properties that set them apart from other verbs, in particular that when they are finite, they can function as OPERATORS. Auxiliary verbs take a VP as their complement and they require the head of that VP to occur in a particular form.

BOUND MORPHEME

A morpheme that cannot occur on its own, but which needs to attach to another morpheme. The past tense morpheme *-ed* and the plural morpheme *-s* are both bound morphemes (contrasts with FREE MORPHEME).

CATEGORY

Words can be categorised on the basis of their morpho-syntactic behaviour, that is to say on the basis of what inflections they can take and where in a sentence they can occur. The major categories are nouns, verbs, adjectives, adverbs and prepositions (though this is more limited than the other major categories). Examples of minor categories are determiners and complementisers. Phrases belong to phrasal categories and they are named after the head word of the phrase, for instance noun phrase and verb phrase. Contrast with FUNCTION.

CLAUSE

A clause is a linguistic unit which is built around a lexical verb; it contains all the elements required by the verb, and often also some optional modifiers. A clause built around a FINITE verb is a finite clause and a non-finite clause is headed by a NON-FINITE VERB. The clause that makes up the sentence is called a MAIN CLAUSE and a clause that occurs within another one is a SUBORDINATE CLAUSE.

CLEFT CONSTRUCTION

Has the effect of splitting off a part of the sentence in order to give it prominence. Two clauses are formed, the first introduced by an empty subject *it* and a form of *be*, followed by the focused constituent. The rest of the sentence is recast as a relative clause (see RELATIVE CLAUSE) beginning with *that*; for example, if you want to focus *last year* in the sentence *I saw him last year* you can create the cleft *It was last year that I saw him.*

COGNATE OBJECT

A cognate object resembles an object, but occurs with an intransitive verb and is closely related to the verb: *he smiled a nice smile.* They seem to function in a way similar to adverbial modification: *he smiled nicely* and they don't sound good without modification: *?He smiled a smile.*

COMMENT

See TOPIC

COMPLEMENT

The general term for a phrase that is selected by a head. All major categories can take complements (head in bold): verbs as in **study** *chemistry*; nouns as in **student** *of chemistry*; adjectives as in **proud** *of his daughter*; and prepositions as is **behind** *the bike shed.* These are different from MODIFIERS, which are not selected by the head, but are there because the speaker wants to add information. Any head can only occur with a specific number of complements, but there can be any number of modifiers. The term 'complement' is sometimes used also for the function referred to in this book as PREDICATIVE COMPLEMENT.

COMPLEMENTISER

A set of elements that can introduce a SUBORDINATE CLAUSE, for instance *that* in *that Oscar likes peanuts* or *whether* in *whether Oscar likes peanuts.*

COMPLEX INTRANSITIVE VERBS

Take one PREDICATIVE COMPLEMENT; for example, *The dog seemed* **tired**. They are also known as COPULAR or INTENSIVE VERBS. (See also LEXICAL VERBS.)

COMPLEX TRANSITIVE VERBS

Take one object (a direct one) and one predicative complement (an object complement); for example, *We keep our Facebook garden nicely tended.* (See also LEXICAL VERBS.)

CONJUNCTION

Items that link elements. There are coordinators, which link units of a similar status – they include *and*, *but* and *or*. There are also subordinators, which link a clausal element with a superordinate clause – they include *that*, *if* and *because.*

CONSTITUENT

A string of words that form a structural unit within a phrase or a sentence.

COORDINATION
The combination of two or more elements – words, phrases or clauses – that are equal in function and status. The elements are linked by coordinators or coordinating conjunctions, such as *and* and *or* (these are the only ones able to conjoin more than two elements).

COPULAR VERBS
See COMPLEX INTRANSITIVE VERBS

COUNT NOUN
Nouns that can be interpreted as individuated entities. They can therefore be counted and can occur in singular or plural forms, for instance *book–books* and *mouse–mice*. Count nouns may also be preceded by the indefinite article *a/an*. Compare MASS NOUNS.

DECLARATIVE
See MEANING TYPE/SENTENCE TYPE

DEICTIC EXPRESSIONS
Words such as *here* and *these*. They represent a way of using language to 'point' to the temporal, situational and personal aspects of the event.

DERIVATION
Derivation is a way of creating new words, either by combining a stem and a derivational affix or by combining two free morphemes into a compound. Unlike inflection, derivation creates new meaning and it may also change the category of the word; *like–dislike*, *print–printer* and *blue+berry* → *blueberry*.

DETERMINER
Determiners combine with nouns to form noun phrases: *the dog*, *those mice* or *which discussion*. There are five categories: articles (*the, a*), demonstratives (*this, those*), wh-determiners (*which, whose*), quantificational determiners (*any, no*) and possessive determiners (*my, his*).

DIALECT
A variety that identifies the geographical origin of the speaker.

DIRECT OBJECT
See OBJECT

DISCOURSE
Sequences of language that are larger than a sentence.

DISCOURSE MARKERS (PARTICLES)
Features of talk. They include expressions such as *well, anyway, yeah-no, like, I mean, sort of, you know*. Individual expressions can have many different discourse functions to do with focus and change of topic and conversational functions to do with turn-taking. They may also play a significant

role in expressing social relationships, personal attitudes and opinions, conveying sometimes quite subtle nuances of meaning.

DI-TRANSITIVE VERBS
Take two objects, a direct and an indirect one; for example, *Mirrors give me the heebie-jeebies*. (See also LEXICAL VERBS.)

EFL (ENGLISH AS A FOREIGN LANGUAGE) SPEAKERS
The growing number of people being taught English as a foreign language. They belong to an expanding circle of nations such as China, Egypt, Japan, Indonesia, Thailand, Saudi Arabia and Taiwan. In these places, English has no special status.

ELLIPSIS
The deletion of items in a sentence because they either appear elsewhere or can be reconstructed from the context; for example (*Fred wants to go fishing, but*) *I don't* or *Wanna go for lunch?*

ENL (ENGLISH AS A NATIVE LANGUAGE) SPEAKERS
Include speakers who are traditionally associated with English; in other words, the language is acquired as a first language (or mother tongue) or as a second first language. Native Englishes include British English, Scottish English, American English, New Zealand English and Australian English.

ESL (ENGLISH AS A SECOND LANGUAGE) SPEAKERS
Speakers of so-called New Englishes that belong to the 'outer circle' of countries where English has a special status, often as one of the official languages, or as an official second language. Included here are Singapore English, Malaysian English, Indian English, Nigerian English and Hong Kong English.

EXCLAMATIVE
See MEANING TYPE/SENTENCE TYPE

EXISTENTIALS
A structure used specifically to posit the existence of an entity; information-structurally, it can be described as a given–new strategy emphasising the existence of something. A dummy subject *there* appears in the position normally occupied by the subject NP, allowing the logical (or understood) subject to appear later, giving it greater prominence; for example, *There are fairies at the bottom of my garden.* Since it is used to introduce a new entity, the logical subject will generally be indefinite.

EXTRAPOSITION
The moving of elements to the end of the sentence, often because they are heavy (= long and/or complex). For example, in English it is possible for subjects of sentences to be entire clauses, but since they are heavy, they are often extraposed. Since English requires a subject in the subject position

the expletive *it* is used; for example ***That we were wrongfully waylaid by the Elvenking** is true* → ***It is true that we were wrongfully waylaid by the Elvenking.***

FOCUS
The element(s) to which speakers and writers want special attention to be paid. Front-focus: sentence-initial is a focal position. Moving an expression to this position gives it much greater prominence. End-focus: given (old, established) information comes before new (unpredictable, surprising) information. It is usual to arrange the information in our message so that what is most important comes towards the end.

FREE MORPHEME
A morpheme which can occur as a word on its own, like *cat* or *infatuation* (contrast with BOUND MORPHEME).

FRONTING
Similar to left-dislocation, except that no copy is left behind and the fronted constituent is not set apart from the rest of the sentence in the same way. Items are simply moved to the front of the sentence; for example, *Ice cream I love*.

FUNCTION
Functions describe the part a phrase plays in a particular sentence, they are also referred to as grammatical relations. The main functions are SUBJECT, DIRECT OBJECT, INDIRECT OBJECT, PREDICATIVE COMPLEMENT and ADVERBIAL. Contrast with CATEGORY and with SEMANTIC ROLE.

FUNCTIONAL
Pertaining to grammar. Functional (or grammatical) morphemes express abstract information like tense, definiteness, number or possession. They contrast with LEXICAL morphemes that are more contentful, such as *dog, bucket* and *anticipation*.

GENDER
Natural gender (where items refer to the sex of real-world entities) includes masculine and feminine and neuter, but within grammar, gender is used more broadly to describe noun classes not based on natural gender, or not exclusively so. In the grammar of English, gender plays a relatively small role; only singular pronouns show gender and, on the whole, contrasts are natural: *The girl ran as fast as she could* – *The boy ran as fast as he could*.

GIVEN INFORMATION
See OLD INFORMATION

GRAMMATICAL RELATION
See FUNCTION

HEDGES

Mitigating devices that speakers use to lessen the impact of an utterance. Typically, they are adverbs (or particles); for example, *Could I **like** borrow your lecture notes*? (See also DISCOURSE MARKERS.)

IDIOMS

Complex expressions whose meaning cannot be directly derived from the meaning of their parts; for example, *kick the bucket* meaning 'die.'

IMPERATIVE
See MEANING TYPE/SENTENCE TYPE

IMPERSONAL CONSTRUCTION

As used for English, this term refers to constructions in which only a third person is possible, such as *One can't tell* and *It is possible that*. Such constructions are sometimes employed for hedging.

INDIRECT OBJECT
See OBJECT

INFIXES
See AFFIXES

INFLECTION

Involves combining a stem with an inflectional affix. These are bound morphemes which represent grammatical, rather than lexical, meaning. Examples of inflectional affixes are plural *-s* and past tense *-ed*. Contrasts with DERIVATION.

INTENSIVE VERBS
See COMPLEX INTRANSITIVE

INTERROGATIVE
See MEANING TYPE/SENTENCE TYPE

INTERROGATIVE TAG

A type of interrogative that 'tacks' the interrogative onto the end of a declarative clause and requests the hearer to express agreement or disagreement. The tag is formed by repeating the auxiliary (or adding the relevant form of the auxiliary *do* if there isn't an auxiliary) and then a pronoun version of the subject noun phrase; for example, *The hot chocolate is pretty hot, **isn't it**?*

INTRANSITIVE VERBS

Verbs that cannot take an object; for example *he died, she ran*. (See also LEXICAL VERBS.)

INVERTED SUBJECT–VERB ORDER (SUBJECT–VERB INVERSION)

Can be used for grammatical ends in the formation of questions; e.g. *Are you leaving now?* It can also be employed for expressive means. By shifting the subject out of its natural environment, it represents a way of shifting focus. In Old English this inverted order had considerable dramatic force and was typical of lively narrative sequences. It has still retained a kind of mock dramatic effect; for example: *Out **will come** beef dusted with Japanese pepper, fingers of salmon with dill sauce and all that rocket in olive oil.*

JARGON
Language shared by those who belong to a profession, trade or some other occupational group. It can distinguished by lexical, phonological, grammatical and discourse features (although it is often characterised by its distinctive vocabulary). Jargons are what some people call REGISTERS. A jargon has two distinct functions: (1) to serve as a technical or specialist language (for precise and economical communication); (2) to promote in-group solidarity (and perhaps to exclude as outsiders those who do not use the jargon). In ordinary usage, the label *jargon* is often used pejoratively. The derogatory sense derives from the second function – those outside the group, who do not use the jargon, find it unintelligible and alienating. (See also REGISTER.)

LEFT-DISLOCATION
A way of focusing a constituent, but without changing the grammatical functions. A movement metaphor is useful here. You simply move a constituent to the extreme left of the sentence, leaving behind some sort of copy in the gap left by the fronted constituent. An intonation break separates the fronted item from the rest of the sentence and this has the effect of making it stand out even more; for example, *Ice cream, I just love it.* (See also RIGHT-DISLOCATION.)

LEXICAL
Pertaining to words (vocabulary) or to contrast with FUNCTIONAL.

LEXICAL VERBS
These are verbs with content and contrast with AUXILIARY VERBS. They can be subdivided according to the complements they require:

intransitive	no complements (*Oscar laughed*)
mono-transitive	one object (*Oscar kicked the ball*)
di-transitive	two objects (*Oscar gave the dog a bone*)
complex intransitive	one predicative complement (*Oscar became a teacher*)
complex transitive	one object and one predicative complement (*They voted Oscar their favourite teacher*)

MAIN CLAUSE
See CLAUSE

MASS NOUN
Nouns that are interpreted as indivisible masses of material and where a distinction between the singular and plural is not possible. A mass noun cannot be preceded by *a/an*. Examples are *gold* and *beer*. Many mass nouns

can also be used as count nouns, but then with quite a specific meaning: *a beer* means 'a glass of beer' or 'a kind of beer.' Compare COUNT NOUN.

MEANING TYPE

Whereas SENTENCE TYPE is a way of categorising sentences according to their structure, meaning types describe the way in which the sentence is normally used. This is also referred to as illocutionary force. We recognise four main meaning types: statement, question, directive and exclamation. Each sentence type normally expresses a particular meaning type:

SENTENCE TYPE	MEANING TYPE
Declarative:	making a statement
Interrogative:	posing a question
Imperative:	issuing a directive
Exclamative:	making an exclamation

It is quite possible to use a sentence structure in an untypical way, for instance a declarative structure with rising intonation can be used to pose a question: *You really like black pudding?*

MODAL AUXILIARIES

A sub-type of AUXILIARY VERBS. They are exceptional for a verb in English in lacking any inflection (**he musts*). The difference between present and past tense frequently does not relate to time the way it does for lexical verbs: *I may do it today* versus *I might do it today*. They have quite complex semantics relating to the attitude of the speaker or notions such as probability, possibility, doubt, contingency, wishing and so on.

MODIFIERS

See COMPLEMENT

MONO-TRANSITIVE VERBS

Take one object, which will always be a direct object; for example, *The Simpsons revolutionised cartoons*. (See also LEXICAL VERBS.)

MORPHEME

The smallest meaningful unit in the grammar of a language; for example, the word *unfriendly* has three morphemes: *un-, friend, -ly; bargain* has only one. We cannot break up any of these morphemes any more without losing the meaning; e.g. *friend* does not further divide into *fri + end* and *bargain* is not made up of *bar + gain*.

MORPHOLOGY

The aspect of linguistics that deals with the structure of words.

NEW INFORMATION

See OLD INFORMATION

NOMINALISATION

The process that turns whole clauses into noun-like structures. For example, ***That the chefs use powdered eggs** is unexpected* becomes ***The chefs' use*** *of powdered eggs is unexpected*. Prose that is heavily nominal in this way is more abstract – doing away with verbs means that we can also do away with subjects and objects as in *The use is unexpected*. This means speakers and writers can be non-committal as to who is doing what to whom.

NOUN
A category which includes words like *dog, dream* and *discussion*. A characteristic of all nouns is that they can combine on their own with the possessive *'s*. All nouns except proper nouns can form a noun phrase with *the*.

NUMBER
Noun phrases and pronouns are marked for number in English; there are two categories, singular (*dog, mouse* or *I*) and plural (*dogs, mice* or *we*). Some Other Englishes have more categories than that, for instance dual, meaning exactly two (Bislama *mitufala* 'I and one other person').

OBJECT
The function licenced by MONO-TRANSITIVE VERBS that immediately follows the verb and can become the SUBJECT of the corresponding PASSIVE sentence. The object of the sentence *Oscar drank the beer* is *the beer*. It can become the subject in the passive sentence *The beer was drunk by Oscar*. When there is just one object, this is normally the DIRECT OBJECT. Some verbs can occur with two objects: *Oscar bought Sarah a beer*. In this case, the first of the two is the indirect object and the second one the direct object. An indirect object can usually also occur as a preposition phrase: *Oscar bought a beer for Sarah*.

OBJECT COMPLEMENT
See PREDICATIVE COMPLEMENT

OLD (GIVEN) INFORMATION (VERSUS NEW INFORMATION)
Two kinds of information. Old (or given) information is familiar in the sense that it refers to something that has already appeared earlier in the text, or which is common knowledge. The new, most salient information is what gains audience-attention.

OPERATOR
The function of a finite AUXILIARY VERB. There are a number of syntactic constructions that require the presence of an operator; an INTERROGATIVE structure requires an operator to precede the SUBJECT and sentence negation requires the presence of an operator.

OTHER ENGLISHES
English-based pidgins and creoles around the world. These contact varieties are not degenerate forms of 'broken' English. They have their own distinctive linguistic features and styles and are the result of English being in contact with other languages.

PASSIVE
The discourse strategy that promotes an object to a subject and simultaneously demotes the subject to a *by*-phrase (or the subject is left out all together; see AGENTLESS PASSIVE). A special verb is used; the auxiliary of the passive *be*, and the appropriate form of the following verb. *The politician made a mistake* versus *A mistake was made (by the politician).*

PERSON
A grammatical category used to distinguish between speaker, hearer and others; first person refers to the speaker, second person to the hearer and third person to those who are neither speaker nor hearer. English has different pronouns for different persons and these pronouns also tend to express NUMBER: *I* (first person singular) versus *we* (first person plural), *you* (second person singular or plural), *he/she/it* (third person singular) versus *they* (third person plural). Some OTHER ENGLISHES have separate pronouns for second person singular and plural and some have different terms for first person plural depending on whether the hearer is included.

PHONETICS
The area of linguistics that deals with the nature of language sounds, how they are made and how they are perceived.

PHONOLOGY
The area of linguistics that studies the systems of sounds in languages. It deals with questions such as which sounds are used to make distinctions in a language, which sounds can occur together and which ones cannot.

PRAGMATICS
The area of linguistics that studies the way in which meaning interacts with the context within which the linguistic elements are used.

PREDICATE
The part of the sentence that provides the information about the subject. It includes the verb and everything else (apart from the subject); for example, *He **is a teacher**; She **has washed the car every week**.*

PREDICATIVE COMPLEMENT
The function that is characterised by referring to, or describing, something else in the sentence. When it describes the subject, as in *Oscar seems happy* or *Oscar is a teacher*, it is called a subject complement, and when it refers to the object, it is an object complement: *They elected Oscar president.* (See also LEXICAL VERBS.)

PREFIXES
See AFFIXES

PREPOSITION
A category of words such as *on, behind* and *of*. The majority of prepositions express spatial relations, but they can also be used for more abstract relations as in *the leg **of** the table*; they do not allow any inflection.

PRONOUN
Words like *it, them, his* that are used in place of a noun phrase.

PROSODY
Used in phonetics and phonology to refer to the characteristics of pitch, rhythm, tempo, loudness (= prosodic features).

RECURSIVE
The repeated addition of a function or category; e.g. if you have a VP *eat peanuts* and you add *slowly* this is still a VP, and therefore you can add another adverbial.

REGISTER
Any socially defined variety of language; in other words, language that is appropriate in a specific situation, occupation or subject matter (for example, a register of scientific or religious English). In addition to phonological, grammatical and even paralinguistic differences like gesture, registers have distinctive discourse structures. (See also JARGON.)

RELATIVE CLAUSE
A subordinate clause that modifies a noun. It is introduced by a relative pronoun (e.g. *who, which*) or the relative word *that* – the choice here depends on the function of the 'replaced' noun phrase in the relative clause and, with some relative pronouns, on whether or not the reference is to a person. For example, *Here's the picture **that appeared within the sleeve of a Lennon LP**; Fry, **who gets frozen in a cryogenic chamber**, was a good friend.* Except when it functions as the subject of the relative clause, the relative pronoun or word can usually be omitted.

RIGHT-DISLOCATION
The opposite strategy to LEFT-DISLOCATION. It involves moving something to the end of the sentence and leaving behind a pronoun copy. If the usual position of an item is early, then this has the effect of giving it extra focus by postponing its mention. Like CLEFTING, EXTRAPOSITION and EXISTENTIALS, right-dislocation introduces a pronoun that announces what is coming up in the discourse. Unlike those other three constructions, however, the pronoun is referential (not just a placeholder). It can be an effective way of building up expectations; for example, *I love it, ice cream.*

ROOTS
Roots are unanalysable lexical morphemes, such as *dog* and *walk*. They can function as stems and combine with affixes as in *dogs* or *walker* or they can combine to make compounds as in *doghouse*. It is not uncommon for ROOT and STEM to be used in more or less the same way.

SEMANTIC ROLE

A term used to refer to the underlying relationships that participants have with the main verb in a clause. For example, in the real or imagined situation expressed in the two sentences *The dog bit Fred*, and *Fred was bitten by the dog*, the semantic role of *the dog* is the 'agent' and that of *Fred* is the 'patient,' regardless of which sentence is used to describe the situation.

SEMANTICS

The area of linguistics that studies the meaning of words and how those meanings combine when words are combined into phrases and sentences.

SENTENCE

It is quite difficult to define a sentence, except in written language, where it is the string between two major punctuation marks. A sentence can consist of more than one CLAUSE.

SENTENCE TYPE

Declaratives, imperatives, interrogatives and exclamatives. These four main types of sentence can be defined in structural terms:

Declarative: (e.g. *I like ice cream*)	subject	predicate		
Interrogative: (e.g. *Does he like ice cream?*)	auxiliary subject		rest of predicate	
Imperative: (e.g. *Eat your ice cream!*)	*(You)*	predicate		
Exclamative: (*What a lot of ice cream there is!*)	*what/how*		subject	predicate

For each sentence type there is a corresponding MEANING TYPE that is typically expressed by that sentence type.

STANDARD ENGLISH

An idealised variety that constitutes a notional set of norms generally adopted by educated speakers of English. It is often (erroneously) believed that speakers of Standard English cannot be identified geographically. There are many standard varieties of English, according to age and generation and especially according to national origins.

STEM

The unit to which an affix is added. It can be either a root – as when the plural -s is added to *dog* to give *dogs* – or it can be a combination of a root and another affix – as when the plural -s is added to *walk-er* to give *walkers*. It is not uncommon for ROOT and STEM to be used in more or less the same way.

SUBJECT

The FUNCTION that is required in English sentences. It immediately precedes the verb in a DECLARATIVE structure. There are instances in English where there is no semantic subject, but since there is a requirement for a functional subject, an expletive is inserted: *It rains.*

SUBJECT COMPLEMENT
See PREDICATIVE COMPLEMENT

SUBJECT–OPERATOR INVERSION
Inversion of the finite auxiliary (the OPERATOR) and SUBJECT in the formation of INTERROGATIVES.

SUBORDINATE CLAUSE (OR SUB-CLAUSE)
A subordinate clause is part of another clause. A clause that is not part of any other clause is a MAIN CLAUSE.

SUFFIXES
See AFFIXES

SYNTAX
The branch of linguistics that studies how words are combined into phrases, which are combined into sentences.

TAG
An element attached to the end of an utterance, such as *eh?*, *ok?* or an INTERROGATIVE TAG, such as *is it?* or *doesn't it?*

TENSE
Verb form that locates the event described by the verb in time. English has two tenses: present (*Oscar laughs*) and past (*Oscar laughed*), but it has no specific future tense. Tense interacts with ASPECT to create a subtler way of describing how an event is situated with respect to time. It is important to distinguish between tense and time; present tense is not always used to locate events in present time and there are ways of locating an event in the past other than past tense.

TOPIC (VERSUS COMMENT)
That part of the sentence that indicates what is being written or talked about. It is the perspective from which a sentence may be viewed. The rest of the sentence makes some sort of statement about the topic and this is called the comment. In the natural order of things, topical material occurs early in the sentence, often to provide a cohesive link with what has preceded it. The comment (providing the new information) follows on from its topic.

VARIETY
A subset of a language that is common to a group of people sharing regional origin (regional variety/dialect) or social characteristics (social variety/sociolect). It is sometimes also employed to describe situational uses of a language, such as legal or formal varieties, but it would be more appropriate to call these REGISTERS.

Verb

A category which includes words such as *tickle*, *see* and *seem*. Verbs are characterised by having five different inflectional forms: base (*tickle*, *see*), third person singular present tense form (*tickles*, *sees*), past tense form (*tickled*, *saw*), past participle form (*tickled*, *seen*) and the *-ing* form (*tickling*, *seeing*).

Voice

A grammatical category that distinguishes between ACTIVE and PASSIVE. Though there is a form of the verb specific to the passive voice, the differences between a passive and an active clause go beyond the verb form.

Index

Note: Page numbers in *italic* indicate a figure and page numbers in **bold** indicate a table on the corresponding page.